ANNA
WICKHAM

Anna Wickham. Artist unknown. (Courtesy The Library, University of Reading, Reading, England.)

Anna
Wickham

A POET'S DARING LIFE

Jennifer Vaughan Jones

MADISON BOOKS

Lanham • New York • Oxford

First Madison Books edition 2003

This hardcover Madison Books edition of *Anna Wickham* is an original
publication. It is published by arrangement with the author.

Published by Madison Books
An imprint of the Rowman & Littlefield Publishing Group, Inc.
4501 Forbes Boulevard, Suite 200
Lanham, Maryland 20706

PO Box 317
Oxford
OX2 9RU, UK

Distributed by National Book Network

Library of Congress Cataloging-in-Publication Data

Jones, Jennifer Vaughan, 1950–
    Anna Wickham : a poet's daring life / Jennifer Vaughan Jones.—
1st Madison Books ed.
      p. cm.
    Includes bibliographical references and index.
    ISBN 1-56833-253-X (alk. paper)
    1. Wickham, Anna, 1884–1947. 2. Poets, English—20th century—
Biography. I. Title.
PR6045.I25Z74 2003
821'.912—dc21   2003004656

Contents

Acknowledgments

First of all, my thanks to George Hepburn, Margaret Hepburn and the late James Hepburn, sons and daughter-in-law of Anna Wickham. They talked with me at length and over a period of many years, providing insights into her life and poetry that no one else could have given. James Hepburn's memoirs both about his life and his mother are tangible proof that Anna's talent for writing was passed down through her genes, just as her passion for the spoken word sprang up in her son George, who delivers his mother's poetry unforgettably.

When I began the research for this book, most of Anna Wickham's papers were still in the Hepburns' possession; they let me work in the family home, a rare privilege. Over the years Jim and Margaret and George and Louise Hepburn became my dear friends. I deeply appreciate their incredibly generous permission to quote from the published and unpublished writings of Anna Wickham. An abundance of quotations from Anna Wickham's work gives, I hope, a sense of immediacy and a specificity of tone to the biography. I here thank them for their invaluable commitment and contribution to this book.

My interest in Anna Wickham dates from the moment I read her startlingly fresh poem, "Meditation at Kew." I knew then that I must learn more about this poet. My University of Wisconsin-Madison doctoral dissertation, *The Poetry and Place of Anna Wickham, 1910–1930*, was under the direction of Professor (Emeritus) James G. Nelson, who encouraged me in my research from our very first conversation on the topic. Jim Nelson, who always knows the right questions to ask, is an indefatigable researcher and an elegant writer. He is for me a model and friend. I thank him for his guidance and good cheer.

Many people took time to talk with me about Anna Wickham. I would particularly like to acknowledge the following for interviews given: Biddy Crozier, the late Mrs. Hetta Empson, Kathleen Gibbons, Miriam Herzog, David Holbrook, Leslie Marr, Edward Mautner, Antonia Hepburn Price, Anna Shinnie, Mrs. Heddi Stadlen, George Wickes, Susan Watson, Valerie Wilson, and the Hepburn family.

With so many individuals responding to inquiries, volunteering information and sources and giving support and advice along the way, it is impossible to list them all here. I apologize if you were missed. Take me to task! However, my particular thanks to Walter Baltz, Esther Cameron, Carolyn Decker, Gordon Bowker, Mary Braun, Helen Carr, Anna Davin, Bette and Thomas Duff, Beth Fiore, Peter Fribley, Beau Friedlander, Richard Garnett, Martha Gibson, Dee Hannemann, Kate Hepburn, Phillip Herring, Dominic Hibberd, Shirley Hokin, James Jung, Robert Langenfeld, and the anonymous reader for ELT Press, Joan Maizels, Thomas McKean, Ann Meo, Andrea Musher, Margot Peters, Thomas Pfister, Sandra Price, Fran Rall, Sybil Robinson, Joan Schenkar, Laura Severin, Dennis Stampe, Anne Summers, Shirley and Blaine Sutton, Judy Swift, Harriet Ward, and Colin Ward. A Room of One's Own Bookstore, Madison, lent a cozy space for my talk on Anna Wickham. CheapatanyPrice poets were always willing to listen. My thanks to them.

To those who read chapters of the biography-in-progress I am indebted for their very useful comments, questions, and editorial advice: Maytee Aspuro, Lynne Hume Burgess, Berent Enç, Diane Huffman, Edward Jones, Nancy Karg, Louise Mares, James G. Nelson, Cyril Owen, Norma Sober, Patricia Stachelski, Marilyn Taylor, Phyllis Walsh, and Harriet Ward.

Grateful thanks go to those whose care and concern keep vital and vibrant the collections in the following libraries: The Department of Special Collections, Memorial Library, The University of Wisconsin-Madison, with its comprehensive "little magazine" trove and Barney-Lang manuscripts and photographs; Manuscripts/Lilly Library, Indiana University, Bloomington,

Indiana, holding Louis Untermeyer material; Fonds Littéraire Jacques Doucet, Bibliothèque Ste. Geneviève, Paris, for Natalie Barney material, including all of Anna Wickham's letters to her; The Library, University of Reading, Reading, England, which holds John Gawsworth's collection of Anna Wickham material—some of it transcribed by hand by him; The Harry Ransom Humanities Research Center, The University of Texas at Austin, Austin, Texas, a holder of John Gawsworth/Anna Wickham material; The British Library and Department of Manuscripts, London, England, for the Harold Monro/The Poetry Bookshop material and for the Anna Wickham manuscripts, scrapbooks, letters, and photographs; and Special Collections, The Joseph Regenstein Library, The University of Chicago for the Harriet Monroe/*Poetry* collection. The following libraries, too, were crucial in contributing to the story of Anna Wickham: The Poetry/Rare Books Collections of the University Libraries, SUNY at Buffalo; Special Collections of the University Research Library, University of California, Los Angeles; The British Library, Newspaper Library, Colindale, London; The Arts Council Poetry Library, London; Department of Manuscripts, The Huntington Library; The New York Public Library; St. Bride's Printing Library, London; The Fact Library, London; The Library and Museum of Freemasonry, London; The Library, Royal Astronomical Society, London; Tate Gallery Archive, London; Warburg Institute, London; The Wellcome Institute for the History of Medicine, London. Much London research took place at The Family Records Centre, and at Somerset House. The Kew Public Records Office, where I first saw Anna Wickham's name on a ship's passenger list, where I found proof of her stay in Brooke House asylum, has, like the Records Centre and Somerset House, a staff devoted to the spirit of the search. Hurray for that!

For Australian research I would particularly like to thank Lex Brasher, researcher on Australian education; Sister Patricia Sullivan, All Hallows' School archivist, Brisbane, Queensland; Shirley Hokin, Honorary Archivist, Sydney Girls' High School; and the very helpful staff at The Mitchell Library Reading Room, State Library of New South Wales, Sydney. Delyth Sunley, Dunedin Public Libraries, New Zealand, dug out information about Anna Wickham's mother. Still, the country of Alice Harper's death remains a missing link in my chain of research.

The late John Kershaw gathered memoirs and letters about Anna Wickham, intending to write an appreciation of her in the 1950s. Thanks go to the family of John Kershaw. When they heard of my project they immediately sent me the letters and memoirs which proved so useful in getting a fuller picture of Anna Wickham's later years.

Mrs. Freda McGregor graciously gave permission to quote from the papers of Harold Monro and Alida Klemantaski, two people whose interactions with Anna Wickham were most colorful.

François Chapon responded readily and generously to my inquiries about Natalie Barney and gave permission to use the letters which shed light on Natalie Barney and Anna Wickham.

Dedicated individuals have written about Anna Wickham's poetry and have seen to it that her work is published in anthologies. Many of these contributions, including Jane Dowson's recent assessment of Anna Wickham as an important literary modernist, are listed in the bibliography and/or endnotes to this volume. I draw particular attention, however, to the following: R. D. (Reggie) Smith edited a 1984 collection, *The Writings of Anna Wickham, Free Woman and Poet.* His introductory essay laid the foundation for Anna Wickham's biography and included an analysis of Anna Wickham's poetry. I am indebted to the late R. D. Smith, and to the Hepburn family, who worked so closely with him on that venture, and to the publishers, Virago Press Limited, who early on did so much for women's literature. Thanks are also due to the editors of *Women's Review* which in 1986 not only published poems by Anna Wickham and an essay by James Hepburn but also the never-before published autobiographical essay, "I & My Genius," in which Anna Wickham wrote about her time in the asylum and its effect on her art and life. Finally, thanks to Illona Linthwaite, who commissioned and performed *Anna on Anna,* Adrian Mitchell's play that brought Wickham's complexity and humor to life on the stage.

For photographs, I am grateful to those who supplied them: Dominic Hibberd, Margaret Hepburn, George Hepburn, the Fonds Littéraire Jacques Doucet, Javier Marías (John Gawsworth's executor), the Hackney (London) Borough Archives, The Department of Special Collections, Memorial Library, The University of Wisconsin-Madison, and The Hulton Picture Library, and to Doug Austin, Suzanne Nagy, and Kate Hepburn, who photographed and transmitted them.

New England Publishing Associates first saw the possibilities of this project. Sincere gratitude to you, Elizabeth Frost-Knappman. Elizabeth, Kristine Schiavi, Alyssa Theodore (then at Madison Books), Ross Plotkin, Michael Dorr, and Chris Joaquim of Madison Books, John Calderone,

Laura Gottlieb, and others behind the scenes whose names I do not know, brought this book into print. I gratefully acknowledge their combined expertise, commitment, and imagination.

During the research and writing of this book my husband, Berent Enç, was never too busy to listen and respond and to help me untangle computer and rhetorical snares with his customary ease and calm. His advice, generosity, and love are my treasure. The children in our lives, Corey McCorkle and Summer McCorkle and Defne Enç, have also contributed to this book, from notetaking to flights of imagination. For this and earlier Anna Wickham projects, Michael Fiore, my brother-in-law, bought me my first (ever) computer; my dear sister, Beth Fiore, taught me to use it and helped in countless other ways.

This book is dedicated to my family—those mentioned above and those others not singled out by name—who encouraged me throughout the more than ten years this book was in preparation.

Permissions

An earlier version of "An Intriguing Mystery: How Did Editor Harold Monro Come to Know Poet Anna Wickham?" appeared in *English Literature in Transition, 1880-1920*. Permission courtesy ELT Press.

Permission to quote from a letter from Anna Wickham to Louis Untermeyer courtesy Lilly Library, Indiana University, Bloomington IN.

Permission to quote from a letter from Audrey Beecham to Lawrence Durrell courtesy Manuscript/Special Collections, Morris Library, Southern Illinois University Carbondale, Carbondale IL.

Permission to quote from Harold Monro and Alida Klemantaski's letters and works courtesy Freda McGregor.

Permission to quote from the unpublished manuscript and diary of David Garnett courtesy of The Estate of the Late David Garnett.

Permission to quote from the writings of the late James Hepburn courtesy Margaret Hepburn.

Permission to quote from the published and unpublished works of Anna Wickham courtesy of Margaret and George Hepburn.

Permission to quote from D. H. Lawrence goes to Laurence Pollinger Limited and the Estate of Frieda Lawrence Ravagli.

Permission to quote from unpublished letters from Natalie Clifford Barney to Anna Wickham courtesy François Chapon.

Every effort has been made to contact copyright holders. I would be glad to hear from those whose whereabouts I could not determine. All omissions will be corrected in forthcoming editions.

Wimbledon, and Then the Sea (1883–1890)

She had an epileptic fit during her labour with me, and I was helped into the world with forceps while my father sat, crying with terror, on the stairs outside the bedroom door. My mother's condition was so parlous that the midwife had no time for me, and I was actually put by on the chest of drawers for dead. I yelled, and so set out on my difficult way.[1]

So Anna Wickham sees herself as entering life on May 7, 1883: threatening her mother, frightening her father, little noticed by all concerned but getting through nevertheless.

She was born in Wimbledon, England, as Edith Alice Mary Harper, only taking the pen name Anna Wickham years later. Her parents, Geoffrey and Alice, christened her after members of their warring families. The choice of names was either some vain attempt to meld those factions into one, or perhaps the first skirmish in Anna's parents' ceaseless bidding for her loyalty.

Her father's family, the Harpers, lived just outside of London in the often-painted and praised suburb and former spa town of Hampstead. Once home to poet John Keats, painted by John Constable and Ford Madox Brown, its good air and long vistas had inspired generations of poets, writers, and artists.[2] When the Harpers came there in the mid-1800s from their farming roots in Shropshire, they left behind their forebears' rigorous Methodist enthusiasm for personal conversion and took on secular aspirations to music and art.[3]

Anna's father, William Geoffrey Harper, born in 1859, was the eldest son of nine surviving Harper children. His rather dour mother Mary suffered greatly from arthritis and took little notice of dust and disorder, but ran the emotional life of the home with a severe general's demeanor. Geoffrey's father, Edwin, an organist and choir director with a penchant for reading and a talent for the music business, owned a shop at 75 Haverstock Hill, Hampstead, selling pianos, pianofortes, and sheet music. He played chess, was a superb shot (a Shropshire champion), and led a dance band. Though there was little extra money for formal study, Edwin encouraged all of the Harper children to find a place in the arts.[4]

Geoffrey did not have a desire to follow in Edwin's footsteps and excel in music. Although he wanted to go to medical school his application failed. Casting around for a means of support, he first began helping his father tune pianos. Then he worked in an instrument factory learning how to build organs. But painful boils and melancholy, which he attributed to nervous distress, caused him to give up the work. Instead of a trade, this "cat who walked alone" wanted intellectual discovery.[5] Geoffrey, six-feet-tall, dark, and so refined in his appearance and so fastidious in his white collar and well-brushed coat that his sisters called him "the Marquis," was just as fastidious in his devotion to the life of the mind.[6] He pored over the writings of Auguste Comte, Herbert Spencer, and Hegel with an almost religious zeal. Attending popular lectures of the day, constantly reading, his mind was filled with new ideas that he yearned to discuss. This ultra-intellectual bent, coupled with the fact that he was much older than many of his brothers and sisters, resulted in an emotional divide between him and his family. It did not then help family relations when he fell in love at age twenty with Alice Martha Whelan, a very attractive woman two-and-one-half years older than himself, with a style more flamboyant than any of his sisters could condone.[7]

Alice came from a family accustomed to making the best of often difficult circumstances. When her father, William Whelan, an Irish plumber, died young, her mother Martha Whelan, who had spent most of her childhood out of the country with some vaguely defined attachment to the Court of Belgium royalty, showed great enterprise in feeding, clothing, and educating the children.[8] She rented rooms to several artists and made friends with more, many met through George Cruikshank, the celebrated caricaturist. Martha and her three daughters posed for many mid-Victorian artists. Frank H. Potter, a poor but socially well-connected Hampstead painter who made Camden Town his home, is supposed to have used Alice as a model for his most important work, the "Music Lesson." This and "A Quiet Corner," a painting of Alice's sister, Ellen Alice, both now owned by the Tate Gallery in London, show the Whelans as elegant, graceful women.[9] The two eldest Whelan sisters also took after their mother in resourcefulness. When English legislation established the system of universal education and instituted what were called "Board Schools," Alice and her sister, who both had been educated at Church of England schools, took the additional training, passed the competitive examinations, and began teaching.

Alice had a real presence, a hot temper, and an ability to self-promote that needed a larger forum than a classroom. At about the same time that Geoffrey's closest sisters Mary, Gertrude, and Beatrice were applying themselves to musical studies and art school, Alice was making a name for herself as "the new Siddons" as an actress in the amateur theatre.[10] She had confidence and charm, the ability and desire to command an audience, and a striking wardrobe carefully chosen from the best of lady's maids' second-hand gowns.

Besides letting rooms in Camden Town and later in a house on Henrietta Street, Anna's grandmother Martha had done cleaning, needlework, and occasional housesitting for wealthy Hampstead families on vacation. These friends, in turn, alleviated the family's poverty by various kindnesses. The generous Cruikshank came immediately and paid for William Whelan's burial; later he gave Alice a beautifully illustrated *Ingoldsby Legends*. Edward Aveling, the atheist lecturer, took the family to dine at the richly decorated Holborn Restaurant. Other friends or employers sent gifts from time to time: a frosted cake, a pineapple, a silver sixpence. Alice, therefore, remembered her childhood as one of deprivation mixed with luxury, and she definitely preferred luxury. But she passed on to Anna not so much this taste for extravagance as the profound impact of giving on both recipient and gift-giver; Anna would often use this theme in her later work.

The Harpers, having kept the Methodist attitude toward the necessity for hard work, may have approved the Whelan effort. They were, however, jealous of the Whelans' connections with artists and disliked their confident airs. After all, Martha had had a child by an artist who left for New Zealand with no recognition of his paternity; daughter Alice was "on the stage," in those Victorian times still an indication of moral looseness. Distrustful, competitive feelings between the two families existed almost from the start because of their differing views on gentility, education, and accomplishments. In the beginning, this had a chilling, yet paradoxically invigorating effect on Alice and Geoffrey, who were concentrating less on family opinion and more on romance.

Though one Harper family legend says that Alice and Geoffrey met at a church dance, Geoffrey actually first saw Alice at a dance given by the dramatic society of which she was "leading lady."[11] He was immediately smitten, and then returned often to watch her on the stage at the Regent Street Royal Polytechnic Theatre declaiming verses to tableaux vivants of the life of Mary, Queen of Scots. Alice as a stage star, resplendent in brown velvet and gloves, with her brown eyes and "very blue whites," fired Geoffrey's imagination.[12] He made a concerted bid for her attentions.

The Whelan sisters found fault with Geoffrey's manners. He was too absorbed in ideas, they thought, and besides, while heedlessly pontificating he had eaten the strawberries that he had ostensibly brought for Alice to enjoy. Alice, however, defended Geoffrey from her sisters' scorn. In Alice's eyes, Geoffrey had good taste.

Alice became pregnant. She and Geoffrey quickly set a wedding date and were married on September 17, 1881, though Geoffrey was ill and had to be pushed to the Parish Church of St. Matthew, Oakley Square, in a bathchair. These circumstances were quite unacceptable to the Harpers, but loyal sister Beatrice Harper joined Harry Whelan as witnesses to the ceremony.

Alice gave up her work at the theatre. Her father-in-law Edwin helped them to open a music store in a gray brick building at Number 5, The Ridgway, in Wimbledon. On March 10, 1882 their first child, William, was born but lived only eighteen hours. After this Alice suffered "hysteria, epilepsy and black moods." Her spirit seems to have come somewhat unhinged for a time. One member of the Harper family remembers hearing that she was found wandering in the street, and in police custody became so violent that she was put in a straitjacket.[13] Alice, in the dead of night, would get up and go to the graveyard in only her nightclothes to mourn over the boy.[14] Her emotional grieving probably both puzzled and frightened the stiff-upper-lip Harpers and they defined her as being quarrelsome and mentally unstable. The loss of their first child and the stingy sympathy offered had a corrosive effect on the relationship between Alice and Geoffrey.

She didn't suffer in silence. Because of her tirades, Geoffrey often traveled to his parents' home "with a very white face, asking advice and help."[15] Alice gave up the charade of contentedness she'd styled for the benefit of her own family, and began complaining bitterly to her own mother and sister about the man she'd married.

Still, a physical relationship remained. On May 7, 1883, about a year and a half after their son's sad stillbirth, Anna was born: their first and only daughter, and, as it turned out, their last child.

It was characteristic of Anna Wickham's life that her entry into it was more dire and dramatic than normal. Anna's first months read like a recipe for disaster. Alice, in her harrowing labor, had an epileptic fit; the birth was a forceps delivery that bruised Anna's head. When Anna was three months old, Geoffrey, who was reading with his feet propped on the mantlepiece, was "struck by a passage in his book" and accidentally upset a boiling kettle of water over mother and child.[16] Anna, wrapped for a time in "oiled cotton wool," eventually healed, but Alice's hands were permanently scarred from the burns. Then when Anna was five months old, Alice contracted "brain fever." Anna was sent to live with Grandmother Whelan while the illness took its slow course.

When baby Anna returned to the Wimbledon shop, her mother seemed reinvigorated and had even made arrangements for a nursemaid and daily outings for Anna on the nearby Commons and Park. Though Alice's attacks of "hysterio-epilepsy" continued, she'd recovered from her illness. Decisively and secretly, she began engineering an escape from life at the music shop in Wimbledon. As Anna later wrote, "My mother loved the idea of the sea, she wanted to travel, she wanted to go to Australia, and she contrived to do what she wanted."[17]

Anna was about eighteen months old when Alice quietly and abruptly quit home and shop and found a furnished room in London for the two of them. Geoffrey came home to find a silence that was broken by no word of Alice's intentions or whereabouts.[18] Shortly after, sometime in late 1884 or early 1885, toddler Anna and triumphant mother Alice sailed for Australia, 12,000 miles away across the seas.

From its start as a penal colony, Australia had become for many an "escape from an intolerable situation" of poverty and hopelessness at home; others had rushed for the gold found there in the 1850s.[19] Though the years of greatest emigration to Australia were past, there were many who continued to go for a chance at a better life, more pay, and a higher degree of independence. The situation in Australia was quite thoroughly, if rosily, reported by the English newspapers. This publicity about opportunity, coupled with the artificial prosperity caused by government loans and big spending on, for example, Queensland public works in the 1880s, drew the hopeful and the desperate, the disillusioned and the starry-eyed.

In fact, in 1883, the year of Anna's birth, there had been "record levels" of new arrivals.[20]

Alice was probably one of the hopeful. "Assisted immigration," offering members of certain groups financial and other services through assisted, free, bounty, or remittance settlement plans, had helped many people to make the long and otherwise expensive journey.[21] Since women were needed in the colony, many qualified to come to Australia under these programs. Other women came as part of a family, as wives, daughters, or servants. There is no record, however, that Alice Harper was assisted, and it appears that she traveled independently with her child as an educated woman with a means to earn her own livelihood. In this she would have been unusual. She probably realized that her personal and career situation had tremendous potential. Many immigrants, even if badly educated, could read and write, and they were highly ambitious for themselves. Their desire to improve their education would eventually create a niche market for Alice's skills.[22]

Though it may not have been true earlier, by the time that Alice and Anna made their journey, "Life at sea was . . . a safe, healthy and tolerable experience."[23] The great wooden sailing ships of the past had almost all been replaced by the faster, iron-sided steamships that used the Suez Canal and cut the time to a mere fifty-eight days.[24] Some wooden sailing vessels remained in service, however; it was on one of these that Anna and her mother traveled, curving around Africa's Cape of Good Hope and seeing the stars themselves appear to change.

Most sailing ships avoided leaving England in the rough weather months of January, February, and March.[25] Alice and Anna probably left late in 1885 and arrived in Sydney about March 1886. The vessel was most likely a "short ship," one carrying mail and freight and only a small number of passengers.[26] Although larger immigrant ships up until the early 1890s offered supervisory "matron" positions to capable women and most ships would pay a passenger a small gratuity in return for teaching the children on board ship, a smaller ship would have had little employment to offer a woman. Alice Harper supposedly worked her passage (babes-in-arms were free) to Australia as a seamstress, though "how there came to be so much sewing on a sailing ship she never attempted to explain."[27]

Sailing ships, unlike coal-fired steamers, didn't put in at ports along the way except in emergencies, so there was an insular quality to the voyage. Free of the roar and fierce heat of the steam engines, the ship was also free of the gritty coal dust that blackened everything. Mast-toppling storms, dead calms, and glassy seas were potential threats, but mostly it was day after day of no company except that on board, broken, perhaps, by the infrequent meeting of a homebound ship that would pause to take mail for England.[28]

As impossible as it may seem, Anna later claims memories of the four-month journey. She says that on the first day of the voyage she attempted to reach a hot potato for her mother and in so doing burned her hand severely on the galley. Her other memories of hot sleepless nights in the bunk are typical of travelers to Australia, who reported "steam-bath" temperatures on board.[29] Anna also later remembers thinking that the moon seen from her porthole window was close enough to touch. She recalled the sailors' shanties on the deck. (She was also told, by her mother, that once in a storm they were both lashed to a mast on the deck. Though it was not unusual for boats to encounter forty-foot seas, the adult Anna disavowed her mother's account.) The voyage was not one of those that made sailors say, "any man that would go to sea for pleasure would go to hell for a pastime."[30] But it did end badly. Alice went on deck dressed only in an oilskin cape and opened it at the neck so that the heavy rains of the southeast trade winds could bathe her before reaching Sydney. This was a custom often resorted to by grimy travelers, especially by women whose modesty prevented them from on-deck bathing in those years before improved shipboard washing facilities.[31] Anna's mother, however, became so ill after the drenching that, following the Sydney resident health officer's customary shipboard inspection, she was immediately taken to a public hospital and treated for pneumonia. That left the problem of what to do with two-year-old Anna. Under contract terms shippers usually had to care for sick passengers for seven to ten days after arrival at the port.[32] Anna was put in "some charitable institution" while the authorities contacted her father.[33]

Back in England there was considerable Harper debate about what to do. The Harper family had convinced themselves that Alice was the mistress of the ship's captain, and the journey reinforced their earlier prejudices against her. Should Geoffrey, who had been shamed by his wife's departure and wronged by having his child taken from him, take Alice back? Almost from the beginning of their marriage Geoffrey had taken his complaints home to his sisters, so Alice had no store of Harper goodwill on which to draw. All the Harper women felt that Geoffrey should divorce Alice, though they were not quite sure if he had cause. Finally, as family lore tells it, Geoffrey, in despair over what to do, made a pilgrimage of sorts to his grandfather William, still living then in Shropshire. William's reply, consistent with his religious ideas about "the indissolubility of marriage," probably only confirmed in Geoffrey his own wish—to be reunited with his wife and child. William offered to pay for the return fares and Geoffrey wrote to Alice asking her to come home to England and to him.

Alice, though, refused the money. After her illness, she had found work in Sydney, which would prove to be typical of her eventually quite astonishing ability to make a living. She worked the passage home. She and Anna had been gone for a year, probably returning in 1886. Anna later wrote,

> I remember the return to Wimbledon, and the gloomy walk together
> up the hill from the station. My father had brought me a wicker
> doll's pram. He had better have brought flowers for my mother. Our
> absence had done nothing to improve my parents' relationship with
> one another.

Life at the shop continued much as before. Geoffrey's Pianoforte and Music Warehouse, next to a saddler, a florist, a dairy, and a draper, was a poorer version of his father's shop. It offered only instrument strings, a few time-payment pianos, sheet music, and piano tuning. Since the income was small they rented out the one good flat directly above the shop and kept for themselves the less attractive basement and attic rooms. The word of the day was economize. Whereas competitors bought boldface type listings or full-page advertisements in the commercial directories, Geoffrey's shop was merely listed under "Tradesmen and Others." This designation, given his sensitivities, probably did nothing for his ego. England was still very much a stratified society and those "in trade" were looked down on by many of the wealthy and aspiring. Geoffrey spent much of his working time tuning pianos, an occupation that also did not put him high on the social scale. But he had the exciting life of the mind. Like his father, he attracted people who were also trying to understand new ideas about the world. Thus on Sunday evenings the music shop took on a different personality, with whiskey, cards, and talk, replacing commerce. James Lecky, a scholar who was nephew to Lecky the Irish historian, involved Geoffrey in discussions of folklore. George Riddell, later Lord Riddell of newspaper fame, even asked Geoffrey to write his early speeches for him. Philologist Henry Sweet and barrister Henry FitzMaurice brought to the group their love of words and argumentation. These evenings, and the proceedings of the Positivist Society and later the Fabian Society, were lifeblood to him. If Alice did not share his passion for ideas, at least she did not obstruct.

Under her mother's tutelage Anna could recite whole passages from the *Ingoldsby Legends*, that collection of tales about knights and pages, queens and captains, smugglers, ghosts, and monks. And Alice, who would lavish her talents on any available audience, often gave a performance-for-one with Anna as the cheering crowd:

> My mother took a great deal of interest in arousing emotions in me that she might not have done had she been able to continue her career in the theatre. She sewed as I sat on a hassock at her feet, singing to me her favorite ballads about death, and I would cry. I can remember that something seemed to click with satisfaction in my mother when I cried.

Everything had theatre. Anna later reports fully entering into the spirit of her mother's histrionics, crying "Beat me, Mother, but love me," when Alice used a stick in punishment. And when Alice's physical symptoms interrupted their days, Anna stood

> . . . watching my mother in a fit from behind the green baize curtain that divided the basement. A slope of gleaming white tiles went up to a grille let into the pavement. Above the grille one could see the feet of passersby. While my mother was in the fit I turned my eyes towards the feet of the passers, feeling that perhaps there among them was escape.

For her father, she was, by age four, writing verses and delighting him with her precocious talent. When she was five her parents took separate bedrooms. She would rush to her father's room in the morning and croon songs to him, holding his head in her arms. Her father's love was a balm, an antidote to her mother's anger and constant criticisms.

She became a sensitive child, and one whose feelings easily bruised. When there was enough money, and the emotional and intellectual needs of her parents were being met, peace sometimes reigned. If at times this calm allowed them to "improve" Anna and focus on her "inadequacies" it also provided Anna with parental attention. But the cost was high. Looking back as an adult she says that she developed a sort of antennae system that caught the waves of unease and distress, both individual and social.

The idea of "class" occupied the minds of the English before, during, and after the Great Reforms of the nineteenth century, and it was discussed with fervor. Her parents had, at this time of their lives, a great disdain for "villa dwellers" (the middle classes with upper-class pretensions). Because of Geoffrey's modest livelihood, he often felt the sting of class discrimination. From her earliest days Anna was made aware of the social gulf that existed between her family and those who thought themselves "better." Geoffrey, taking a perverse pride in his knowledge of how these attitudes played themselves out, would recount to his family the practical, as opposed to the theoretical, evils of the system:

> . . . my father had met a major of Horse Artillery at the Mechanics Institute who talked politics with him and, thinking him intelligent, had taken him home to lunch. But when the major found that my father was a piano-tuner he had ordered him out of the house.

Financial affairs at the music shop worsened in the late 1880s. Geoffrey's intellectual preoccupations began to seem like pretensions to Alice. She resented the dingy shop and the lack of money. "She . . . tired of Herbert Spencer and wished the anthropoid apes in Hades." Alice needed change. Alice, who had been a Board School teacher, who'd grown up knowing artists and had even worked for the famous atheist lecturer Aveling, that Alice who'd reveled in success on the stage, who loved change and variety for their own sake, found nothing to challenge her in the tiny music shop except economizing. Life for her at home was dull, and Geoffrey, busy with making a living and preoccupied otherwise with big ideas, had no entrepreneurial plans that would lift them out of their strait-ened circumstances. Alice again took work as a board school teacher.

Although Anna accompanied her mother to the school, her status as a teacher's daughter set her apart. Shied away from by the other children, scolded by her mother, and all-too aware of the disdain many teachers felt for their charges, Wickham states in her autobiography, "I felt here, as I had felt at the Harpers, that somehow it was an offence to be a child." When Alice decided because of her work to take a furnished room in London during the week, Anna stayed in Wimbledon and, she later reported, with relief began to live "the normal life of a little girl and the fits and fights were fewer."

A "pious old woman," Carrie Griffin, was hired to live with the fam-ily to care for Anna. The woman was such a strong influence that during Geoffrey's Sunday evening get-togethers he hid the whiskey and cards that she named the "Devil's playthings." She took Anna to hymn-singing ser-vices in a nearby chapel.

Now Anna had certainly been exposed to religion. Her grandfather Edwin Harper's musical duties meant a lot of time spent in the Roman Catholic church. "One magic night" she was taken by her father to the church and felt so moved, "alone with the beauty of the shining candles." Alice, possessing a strong religious streak and a tendency toward rather confrontational prayers, attended church only intermittently. Her spiri-tual leanings would soon be evidenced in trances and a belief in ghosts. Geoffrey, who even two decades later would give a friend a book inscribed, "Beware of the man whose God is in the skies," came down firmly on the side of science to answer such catechistic questions as why are we here, what are we to do. Listening to him and his friends, Anna, by age six, knew a collection of agnostic arguments and could trot out the conflict in the idea of a perfect god coexisting with the presence of evil. She knew that Geoffrey rejected those "spiritually self-conscious" Harper forebears who "left books of self-revelation of spiritual experiences" and "were not content to live in the world and enjoy it—they must travail and grow hot." But at the chapel in Wimbledon Anna came to love the hymns that she and D. H. Lawrence would sing together as adults in her sitting room. And it was in the modest chapel that Anna had a religious conver-sion experience.

A missionary had come, and using black, white, and pink paper discs, he explained the bad, good, or uncertain states of the soul.

There was something in all this that went to my heart. I felt myself
to be a very black child indeed and I set up such a heart-broken howl
that the young missionary came down from the platform and took
me in his arms. I told him that I was a sinner. . . .

She went on to confess that her father was also a sinner, and after prayers
at the service's end she conducted the missionary across the lane. Her
father, who took the young man's visit "very well, . . . did not let the young
missionary see that he was laughing."

Alice's absence seems to have brought out in Anna Wickham not only
religious feeling, but quite passionate feelings of admiration for her mother.
She would stand in the little shop on a Saturday morning, impatient for the
arrival of her mother after the week's work. Without her mother, the intensity of life was missing. Alice's red silk dress from the elegant and new Liberty
department store, her beautiful scent, and her essence, which Wickham later
would describe as almost "a ray," faded into the background those "black
rages," "fits," and scorn, the other side of Alice that so taxed Anna.

It wasn't long before Geoffrey had a premonition in a dream that a
powerful competitor would move in near his business. A week later, a large
music shop moved in near the station and the already gloomy fortunes of
his music shop were sealed. The eighty pounds per year that Alice was
making as assistant teacher at the school was insufficient for their needs.
Alice, to whom neither home nor board school had offered sufficient scope
for her talents and aspirations "saw a way out." They would go to Australia.
She had always wanted to go back, "for she always remembered the exciting dramas of our first departure in the sailing ship."

Three of Geoffrey's siblings took up her idea so energetically that Alice
was resentful. Mary Harper needed to seek distance from a forbidden love;
Beatrice and Geoffrey's brother, Charlie, sought out more opportunity than
they had in London. They were first to leave. Probably in November of that
same year (1889 or 1890), Geoffrey himself sailed from Tilbury on a ship to
Maryborough, Australia, a small city north of Brisbane and south of the
Tropic of Cancer on Australia's east coast. The sale of the shop furnishings
and stock had not garnered sufficient money to finance the upcoming trip.
The old housekeeper, Carrie Griffin, gave him a loan of fifty pounds.

Alice and Anna saw him off at the ship, giving him a "leather-covered
inkpot, contrived not to spill in the roughest weather." He would be traveling steerage and thus usually barred from the upper, open and pleasant

decks of the ship, but this hardship was perhaps somewhat offset by the fact that George Riddell, who came to bid Geoffrey goodbye, gave him *On the Origin of the Species* to read on board. At last a man could study.

Geoffrey's departure was, however, the beginning of a dismal period for six-year-old Anna and her mother. Finances had been so tight when the shop was closed that Geoffrey had gone back to living with his parents at the Haverstock Hill shop while Anna and Alice crowded into the furnished room near Primrose Hill. Anna's cat, ancient but loved, was to have stayed at the Harper place but "went mad" when released from his basket and, biting and scratching anyone in the way, disappeared down the hill and was never heard from again.

Their furnished room was devoid of comfort. The bed that they shared sagged in the middle. Their income allowed for few luxuries, although Alice always bought Anna a delicious box of sardines on pay day. Martha, Alice's mother, had died in the last year, so there was no comfort from that quarter. Anna and Alice were to wait for word from Geoffrey.

On a cold and dark winter morning Wickham remembers her mother crying on the way to school. The school itself was "an ugly barracks." The teachers thought "a scholar was an enemy, a poor scholar was doubly an enemy," and they did not share Anna's pity for some of the poorer students. She sat in the classroom trying to write clever stories to send to her father but felt utterly dispirited and miserable. In the evening Alice directed an amateur acting society to supplement their income, but this meant that Anna was left alone in their room with no light except that of the street lamp. Fear immobilized her, terrified as she was of "Jack the Ripper," who only a year or two before had mutilated and killed six women in London's impoverished East End.

Finally Geoffrey sent good news. He had found employment on a decent salary that could keep them all, if not in comfort at least in necessities. He also sent beautiful butterflies that he'd gathered.

In London students brought in armfuls of lilac and laburnum and gave them to Alice on her and Queen Victoria's birthday; according to Anna, "they made a glory in our little room."[34] Buoyed by all these things, Alice began to look for a way to work her passage to Australia and found it in an advertisement in the *Morning Post*. She agreed to do domestic chores and sewing for a Southend family with three children also bound for Australia.

In preparation for the great day, Alice and Anna moved to Southend. Alice made the sewing machine whir. She expertly stitched and fitted the family's wardrobe and since Anna's Whelan aunts had given Alice, who had been expertly trained in sewing as part of her Board School education, yards and yards of good fabric. By the time the ship steamed away from England, Anna had twelve crisp new dresses in which to enjoy the journey. This abundance, unlike anything she had experienced before, made an indelible impression.

All was not easy, however. Anna was accused of having brought in head lice and of being dirty, though she vigorously defended herself on both charges. Alice and her mistress argued. The arrangement, probably impractical from the start given Alice's independent frame of mind, faltered and failed. Before the boat reached Sydney Alice broke the contract and paid the remainder of the fare. She and Anna arrived in Australia, "as passengers not as servants."

They took a small boat for the rest of the journey from Sydney to Brisbane, 500 miles hugging the coast. From Brisbane to the Mary River entrance at Maryborough was another 100 miles. When they arrived at the dock in Maryborough, Geoffrey was waiting to meet them. Previous disagreements put off, he was full of plans for a future together on the new continent.

TWO

"I had traveled in my youth past saturation point" (Queensland 1890–1896)[1]

The long sea journey over, Anna celebrated with her parents in a town only a few years older than they were, and in a rented house that had been providing a free lunch for a small army of termites. But the young Australian settlement offered possibilities. Even the primitive, improvisational, and irregular structures, so different from the solid gray Victorian brick buildings of her London childhood, delighted Anna, and she believed that they would be happy here.

Maryborough, Queensland, picturesquely situated twenty-five miles inland from Wide Bay on a bend in the Mary River, had been settled only forty-two years before. The surrounding cedar and pine forest was relentlessly cleared: pulled up, cut down, or "ringbarked" (which killed the trees but kept their leafless trunks standing).[2] By now the railway terminus town boasted sawmills, a library, a Mechanic's Institute for adult studies, several banks, and government offices. It was no London.

The house Geoffrey had rented for Anna and Alice's arrival was a crude affair in a neighborhood of Irish laborers, and typical of a settler's house both in its simplicity and its modifications to withstand the subtropical climate. A one-story house raised on wooden piles, during the wet season "blinding rain . . . beat . . . a hell's tattoo on the corrugated iron roof."[3] The house was augmented only by a bath addition with drilled floor holes to drain waste water from the tin shower tub. There was a dining room, but no dining table. But in contrast to the lowering atmosphere of nights in the Primrose Hill rooming house and days in the barracks-like arrangement of the Board School, Anna found the wild weather, the crude house, and even the lack of furniture and possessions liberating and interesting. She did not find their life "barbarous," but felt that she belonged "to a civilised family."[4] They had some remnants of the familiar, a "fine oak chest . . . made without nails or screws, all the parts of it dovetailing into one another" that Geoffrey brought to Australia as part of his legacy from the Shropshire Harpers.[5] The walls were decorated with a watercolor painted by Gertrude, one of Geoffrey's younger sisters still in England, and with a metal-framed photograph of Charles Darwin, Geoffrey's intellectual hero. And of course Geoffrey had traveled with books, some 200 of them. One of Geoffrey's volumes was the nature writing of Richard Jeffries, used when he had taken Anna on nature walks on Wimbledon Common. That part of their lives, with its familiar fauna and flora, sounds and smells, was over.[6]

At this time Geoffrey and Alice were both twenty-eight years old; Anna was not yet seven. All were in reasonably good health (Alice's fits seem to have disappeared) and both Geoffrey and Alice had the intelligence and skill to make a way for themselves. But first the business of everyday living had to be sorted out. They had a sense of the vast potential of the country but a corresponding anxiety concerning their own fortunes in it.

Geoffrey and Alice had neither adequately anticipated the physical hardships of Australian living nor foreseen how different from England some aspects of life would be. Their work in Australia kept the family always fed, clothed, and housed. Geoffrey, the manager for the Emil Anderson, Pollard and Co. music shop on Adelaide Street, one of three principal thoroughfares, sold and tuned pianos here and in the two branch locations for people eager for a bit of the home country and a bit of culture. But like many recent arrivals, Anna's parents fell into thinking as "lonely exiles," criticizing the trees, the food, and the neighbors. Homesick for their traditions, threatened by the difficulties of making their way in the new land, they developed an attitude where, as Anna later stated, "Away from England, my parents saw romance in everything English. In a Utopia of cheap meat . . . they wanted kippers; in a paradise of peaches and bananas, nothing would do for them but strawberries."[7]

Tensions between Geoffrey and Alice soon resurfaced. Alice blamed Geoffrey. The lumber be bought to build a proper pony shed lay unused as he struggled with the construction. Money, always a source of friction between the two, escalated the level of recrimination since Geoffrey's three pounds ten per week sufficed only for their needs. One day Anna tripped and went right through the dining room wall to the kitchen beyond because the termites, or "white ants," had not only reduced the margins of all her father's precious books to a white powder but had also chewed through the flimsy room divisions.[8] Geoffrey had been trying to save money in rent, but, as Alice quickly pointed out, this now demonstrated a false economy. Not only that, but the rough dwelling lacked the inner passage or hallway that slightly better houses had.

Anna's mother found them a place on the other side of town, one with a passageway, verandahs, washhouse, and a shed for the irritable pony.[9] Next door was a man with an actual lawn, a nicety that impressed Anna.

For Anna, the fogs of 1880s London, the long, long nights of London midwinter and the cold walks down Primrose Hill were blissfully supplanted by the warmth of Maryborough. Because of her youth, or maybe because of her personality, it was Anna, with an amazing openness, who first woke up to the possibilities of life in Australia. She thought the gum trees, "flinging wild arms to the sky," were lovely and couldn't understand her mother's nostalgia for the English oak and ash.[10] She became an astute observer of her parents' wavering equilibrium and their distress, and was quite unsympathetic. She saw her parents as people with stopped senses in an Eden.

One reason for Anna's disapproval of her parents' slowness to adjust might be that the adjustment often played itself out with Anna as the hapless victim. Alice, with extra time on her hands while Geoffrey was working or away on business, became Anna's chief critic. A dirtied ruffled pinafore or torn sash, and Alice might yell and box Anna's ears. When Anna once purchased a small doll with the change from the store, thinking that her mother had given approval, Alice grabbed the doll by its sawdust-stuffed legs and smashed the china head to bits against the mantle shelf. When, however, her parents were preoccupied with each other and with making a living, Anna reveled in her freedom. Her father's music business had one branch in the mining center of Gympie, south along the Mary River, and one in Bundaberg, a pretty village in the sugar and corn plantations to the north, nine miles inland on the Burnett River.[11] When on a weekend he and Alice trotted off in the sulky to visit the shop branches, Anna was

> left with a half-a-crown to keep myself . . . , and instructions to go and spend the night with the shop girl. I bought a dozen pineapples for two shillings, and sixpenn'orth of biscuits. I lived on the biscuits and the pineapples, at night I slept with the shop girl, and all day I had the freedom of the town.[12]

These solitary pleasures were interludes in the confinement of school days, back bent over book or sewing.

Geoffrey, in return for tuning pianos, had arranged for her to attend the local convent school free of charge. But as a newcomer, as a little girl who knew her father "was an enemy to religion," Anna was extremely self-conscious socially and remembered with shame simply dropping a fork during the fish course.[13] She had, however, signal victories within the convent walls. Her teachers discovered Anna's remarkable voice, and made her sing to them, unaccompanied.[14] And though she wasn't allowed to go, a musician even proposed taking her on tour in a juvenile opera company called the Lilliputians. She began to spend time in the hammock on her verandah, "swinging to and fro in an ecstasy of singing."[15] Being offered the chance of touring as a child singer probably first sparked the idea that she might make a career on a scale grander than her father's business or her Harper aunts' piano teaching. Then too, singing provided a sort of inner retreat, a way to escape reality by the magic of the notes and by the imagination of future accomplishments.

She read freely from the public library. Her first novel was, appropriately enough, *Story of an African Farm*, with its vivid detailing of the landscape of Olive Schreiner's childhood and its concentration on feminist themes. Perhaps taking Schreiner as her model, Anna noticed everything: traveling shows, gum trees, and pineapples, madmen, bushwhackers and people relying on her mother to hide their possessions from the credit agency. Their hard-working Irish neighbors mocked the Harpers as green-horns. Her parent's relationship with each other was constantly shifting. It was easy to see herself, as she had done in England, as just one more char-acter in a drama playing itself out in the world around her.

Except for the library and the local Mechanics Institute, Maryborough society did not have many entertainments. Joy Hooton's 1990 study of Australian autobiographies points out that for women who did not work outside the home, loneliness was an additional hardship. Men's work kept them more in touch with people; if a woman stayed at home her circle was smaller.[16] Alice, used to the demands of teaching, channeled her energy, relentlessly starched and ironed Anna's pinafores, bought a few things to decorate the shelves, kept up the housework and, in short order, became frustrated. Geoffrey, on the other hand, who had been starved for wide-ranging conversation before Alice arrived, had found a conversation part-ner in Miss Naylor, a teacher of botany in the grammar school, and had experienced "great pleasure in making her beautiful coloured diagrams for her classes."[17] Alice, supposing infidelity, tried to commit suicide. Anna, in the first of what would eventually add up to several rescues, came home from the convent school and found Alice "in the middle of the day, in a curious kind of sleep. She muttered, and she smelt odd."[18] Anna, dis-traught and fearful, rushed to Geoffrey at the shop and they saved Alice from her deliberate overdose of laudanum.

After recovering from this episode, Anna's mother took herself in hand, made a new lilac-colored dress with material the Whelan aunts sent from England, and began teaching elocution classes at the grammar school where she could "meet Miss Naylor on her own ground."[19] She seems not to have given any thought as to how her attempted suicide would affect her daughter. She gave a highly successful adult lecture at the Mechanic's Institute, a social event to which "everyone in the town" came, eager for diversion and education.[20]

Anna was thus once again witness to her mother's remarkable jack-in-the-box recovery from trauma. The first time had been in London when, during recovery from a serious illness, Alice had planned her escape from London to Australia. This time Alice had done an abra-cadabra over feelings of loneliness, jealousy, anger, and despair. With stage powers that had won praise from the critics in England, she intently planned and practiced her lectures until they came out sounding natural and spontaneous. Her introductory sentence Wickham remembers clearly:

"Mr. Chairman, ladies and gentlemen, elocution is the art of reading and speaking with accuracy and ease." In her lilac dress, with her confident, graceful air early developed from sitting as artists' model, Alice probably did inspire.[21]

Alice's elocution classes for children at the Mechanic's Institute grew popular, and soon the houses and backyards of Maryborough echoed with the sound of small voices practicing Tennyson's "The Charge of the Light Brigade," and "The Women of Mumbles Head." The institutes, forerunners of Technical Colleges and Schools, were features in England and Australia. Alice would often give introductory lectures there to attract business for her private consultations. She also organized a dramatic society, performed the "learning by looking" Tableau Vivantes as she had done in London, and played the lead, opposite the local chemist, in "The Happy Pair." Geoffrey was given a small part, but his voice did not carry.

More at ease in the community and with herself, Alice let up on the critical and sometimes physically abusive treatment of Anna. There was in Alice a resurgence of that indomitable spirit that would inspire, frighten, and challenge her daughter even in adulthood. And the money that Alice brought in helped the family economy at a time when larger forces began to work against their success.

The gold boom that had shored up the Australian economy had long ago declined. The late 1880s were years of poor crops and lower overseas prices.[22] The 1890s saw an economic collapse. By 1893 there were abrupt closures of almost every private bank and finance company.[23] The Australian journalist and poet Henry Lawson wrote to his Aunt Emma Brooks from the bush near Hungerford, Queensland, "You can have no idea of the horrors of the country out here. Men tramp and beg and live like dogs."[24] When Geoffrey's branches in both Gympie and Bundaberg folded due to flooding and hard times, the family's financial condition became precarious.

Anna saw her mother step in and take charge. With teaching references from England that found her "quite satisfactory as to teaching ability and character," and with six years' teaching experience to recommend her, Alice was accepted on July 4, 1892, for a position as Assistant Teacher in the town of Hughenden.[25] Geographically distant, its pastoral economic base was a world apart even from such a modest urban coastal settlement as Maryborough. Only a year earlier Hughenden was the location of one of the first big shearers' strikes; its school system, too, was beset by trouble.

Due to the influx of families working either for the railway or as carrier drivers for the horse and bullock teams, the school was full to bursting. The eight-year-old building was being expanded again only after all members of the Education Committee threatened to resign if nothing was done to ease overcrowding (seating for 131, attendance of 220). The wooden structure itself sat up on stumps in a grassless, treeless five-acre white-clay pan; in the dry season it was unprotected both from the glare that aggravated the students' "eye blight," and from whirlwinds that sent the dust flying."[26] In the wet season from October to August, the Flinders River ran so high that students on the north side of town couldn't cross the water to attend school. But when tired nine-year-old Anna and her mother arrived in Hughenden after a long steamer trip north along the coast to Townsville and an uncomfortable day-long railway journey west across the Great Dividing Range, this Outback town of less than one thousand people was in the midst of a drought so severe that water was drawn from the railway well in the dry bed of the river.

"I was very well taught in the Hughenden school," Anna said, but the excellence of the teaching couldn't make up for the shock of the pioneer town and her father's absence.[27] Alice and Anna lived at the Atkin family's Royal Hotel during their stay, a move that lessened Alice's household duties but made Anna fearful of the sheep shearers from nearby stations who came in town to let off steam and ended up loud and boisterous until all hours at the hotel's bar.[28] Anna kept her father's picture tied to her pillow. She was lonely for him, a condition either caused or exacerbated by the attention her mother was getting. Anna discovered her kissing a local salesman. Another man, "a gentleman and manager of Winton Station," fell in love with Alice and followed them as far as the coast when the six-month appointment was up in December 1892.[29] As much as Anna disliked her parents' arguments, which had become as common in Australia as they had been in England, she had a fierce desire to see Alice and Geoffrey together. She did not know how to make things right between them, but she suffered in the way described by Olive Schreiner: "The barb in the arrow of childhood's suffering is this—its intense loneliness, its intense ignorance."[30]

They rejoined Geoffrey in Brisbane, the largest Queensland coastal-port city, where he was tuning and repairing pianos. Alice, rated as a "good teacher of infants" and "a very fair disciplinarian," on January 1, 1893, transferred her teaching appointment to nearby Woolloongabba at the same base salary of 110 pounds.[31] Each day Anna and her mother together took the horse-drawn bus to the school. Alice, as in the past, would make an example of her daughter. She used a rawhide strip after school to beat Anna for her grammatical mistakes, or, as Anna later wrote, "beat her irritation at the school system into me."[32] These lessons in corporal punishment, like the attempts at suicide, were another unfortunate example handed down from mother to daughter.

In February, 1893, just after they settled into furnished rooms, a record flood of the Brisbane River made parts of the city a lake with rooftops.[33] Most evacuees slept on the floor of a big church, but Anna and her mother were ensconced in luxury. Along with Mrs. Groom, the proprietor of their boarding house, they were welcomed into the wealthy Fenwick family's home on high ground.[34] From that house Anna could watch the bridge over the rampaging river. She saw a drowned man pulled to the bank. She saw half of the bridge, slammed continually by houses knocked off their pilings, break off in the onslaught.

They all waited nervously for Geoffrey, who had stayed dangerously long in the house he was helping to evacuate and protect. Finally he "tied a red cloth to a pole as a signal to the police boat" and came to safety.[35] But Anna, though excited and disturbed by the devastation below, was comforted by the security and unaccustomed luxury of the Fenwick house, remembering years later,

> My strongest impression of all this ruin and death is the memory of the clock with the chimes, the brass hot-water heater, and the fact that, as I lay on my extemporized bed on the sofa in the library, I read for the first time *Alice in Wonderland*.[36]

Three weeks later the river rose again. When the floods' devastation passed, Alice, Geoffrey, and Anna rented a small furnished house near the tracks. After months of being apart, then living in a boarding house, they finally had some privacy and a sense of themselves as a family again. With two incomes, they made a decent living, and Brisbane, larger and more sophisticated than Maryborough, provided diversions. Anna, feeling secure and settled, occasionally even negotiated parental accord and laughter by "extemporizing verses" and Alice paid her the compliment of saying that she "could get paid for that sort of thing on the music hall."[37]

To add to her delight at being with both of her parents, on her tenth birthday Anna had a party, rare and wonderful, with girls from school in attendance, gifts to open, and a whole tin of biscuits to eat. Shortly after, they moved to a bigger house with "the most beautiful jungle, with an orange tree, a lemon tree, a banana palm and two sorts of guava."[38] Her parents, free at last from the need to tighten their grasp on every pence, bought some fairly good furniture and household goods at the auctions and employed "a kind and charming servant" who gave Anna a bible.[39] It was a happy time.

Anna transferred to the Normal School, and found her writing talents blooming under an excellent English teacher. She made her first real friend, a girl "so lovely" that Anna never forgot her. She also brought home a gold medal for winning a public essay competition and she wrote poetry, making her father proud enough to send her poems to the famous Brunton Stephens for his opinion. Her mother did care enough about Anna's triumph to have the gold essay medal fashioned into a brooch for Anna to wear. But Geoffrey's pride Alice scorned and mocked. She made scalding remarks about Geoffrey's tendency to show Anna's poetry to his friends and acquaintances, once saying that "Mr. Pine," who had emotionally admired the poetry, "must have been drunk at the time."[40]

Alice, never happy too long in those days, had become completely disillusioned with teaching grammar under a school system she hated and for a supervisor with whom she repeatedly clashed.[41] When on January 1, 1894, the Department of Education attempted to transfer her north of Brisbane to the town of Paradise (an unwanted transfer sometimes rid the department of a troublesome teacher), she refused the transfer and gave her resignation a month later. Then with no warning to her husband, Alice advertised herself as "Madame Reprah" (Harper spelled backwards) and began giving physiognomy-based character readings in a storefront that, much to Geoffrey's chagrin and anger, she'd rented next door to his shop.

Anna was quite proud of her mother's participation in the craze for spiritualism and phrenology so popular in Australia in the 1880s and 1890s.[42] In her own way, Alice served as a combination psychoanalyst, contact healer, and fortune-teller. This character reading grew out of Alice's interest in the paranormal and her skill in intuiting the concerns of others. She had other abilities as well, such as knowing how much time had elapsed without consulting a watch, or knowing how far she had traveled along a given route. Alice claimed a "sensation in the back of her arms" gave her these latter abilities.[43] She had just begun communing with the ghost she said inhabited their house, and she had become adept at putting herself into trance-like states where she would hold a conversation with people from the past.

But Geoffrey's scorn and dismay knew no bounds, and Anna was once again witness to their dramatic scenes. Alice alienated Geoffrey in a profound way by setting up in his own territory and by positioning herself as far as possible from his rational, scientific mode of proceeding. Her business was, however, a very lucrative venture, something that she did not let Geoffrey forget. The additional income satisfied Alice's desire for finer material possessions, and, more importantly, it answered another need as well. Alice simply had more energy and creativity than her home and family could absorb. She liked to be out in the world, making things happen; as Madame Reprah she could do so.

When all the willing local characters had been read, Anna's mother closed her shop, left the afternoon sea breezes of Brisbane and went west over the hills to Toowoomba to give character readings in her hotel room during the evenings and lectures to the townspeople during the day. "She had the knack of going unadvertised to a new town, setting up her tent, and making money at once."[44] Anna was left in the charge of her father and their household help, Naomi, while Alice earned gold sovereigns and sent them home to Geoffrey.

Then the house with the garden was sold, along with the comfortable second-hand possessions they had gradually accumulated at auctions. Anna's just-settled life was disrupted again, at least the seventh move in four short but formative years.

While Alice lectured, her daughter and husband lodged with a Brisbane chemist whose "large, rambling house with a billiard room" was one of those homes which, as Anna later explained, taught her how other people lived. Geoffrey and Alice were not the kind to establish friendships with other families and visit back and forth. Those who liked Geoffrey probably found Alice overbearing; those who liked Alice probably found Geoffrey boring. Therefore the houses that Anna did have access to meant a great deal to her, though everything took a distant second to her relationship with her parents.

During this time Anna and her father regained some of the closeness they had earlier felt for each other. She made her father a solemn vow. Looking over the city one night as they walked together, enjoying the cool of the evening, Anna found herself choosing both a name and a vocation for herself.[45]

One Sunday night, walking on Wickham Terrace, we came to a point equidistant between the Church of England and the Presbyterian Church. Hymns were blaring out of both. My father put his arms around me, begging me with great tenderness to promise him that I would be a poet when I grew up. I gave him my word, and when my first set of verses was printed . . . I signed them 'Wickham' in memory of that curious and very emotional pact.[46]

Geoffrey had mailed her poems to one of Australia's famous "Bush School" poets, A. B. (Banjo) Paterson. Not deterred by the absence of an answer, Geoffrey went to the Scottish-born poet, novelist, and humorist, James Brunton Stephens, and asked him if Anna "would fulfill her [poetic] promise." Stephens replied, "She will be a poet on a condition you can hardly wish her since you are her father: she will be a poet if she has pain enough."[47] This assessment Anna would never forget.

When Alice took her road show all the way to Charter Towers, Harper family life changed again. Perhaps to socialize Anna to a wider circle, or perhaps out of necessity and propriety since Alice was leaving the area, Anna on October 13, 1894, became a boarder at the stately white stone All Hallows' School, a convent school known then as the "best academy for young ladies" in Brisbane.

This recommendation alone should have been enough to predict the fit between All Hallows' and Anna Wickham. In a way, Anna was not a "young lady." She was a complicated child eleven years old. She reveled in personal freedom, she was a voracious reader on her own, and she needed and wanted the company of her parents, not 130 other students. The fortress-like building with its towers dominating the Brisbane skyline was a far cry from the house and wild garden she had enjoyed with her family. Once through the massive gateway inscribed A.M.D.G., the abbreviation for Ad Maiorem Dei Gloriam (to the greater glory of God), she joined the twenty-one other boarders in a strict and steady routine of supervision from six in the morning until nine-thirty at night.[48] The weekends were quiet without the day students, but even those hours were scheduled, with Sunday afternoons set aside for writing letters home, which had to be read and approved by the sister in attendance. The whole and stated point of the education was to impart to the attending daughters of school inspectors, government officials, doctors, bank managers, journalists, contractors, and squatters "a form of education in which God is the centre around whom and in whom all life finds its meaning."[49] Admittance into the school was also an entree into respectability, since the fees were high enough to keep most out. Physiognomist Alice, for her part, was probably proud of paying the high tuition (somewhat less than £40 per year) though she cautiously reported her profession only as "a teacher, Charter Towers."[50]

Geoffrey, perhaps realizing the shock that sensitive Anna would feel at the change, requested that she be allowed to have an hour's quiet reading each day. The accommodation, however, made her feel isolated. She was also slightly embarrassed by how the flamboyant Alice, with her hair now dyed blonde and worn with a "fringe," differed from any run-of-the-mill mother. Anna was bored at the school's monotony, and taken aback both by the nuns' over-insistence on modesty and the curious girls' discussions of boys and nakedness. Other students had fun together and remembered their days at All Hallows' with deep and abiding affection. But Anna was lonely and she felt a misfit. She was able to confide in "the wise old reverent mother, Mother Mary Patrick," whose name would become synonymous both with All Hallows' and with a spirit of compassion, intelligence, and good humor. But even these private conversations in Mother Patrick's rooms could not assuage Anna's sense of loss and difference. The halcyon days of the ten-year-old passed into the more turbulent times of the preadolescent.

Despite the efforts of the nuns to instill Christian virtues, the girls at school were snobs. They constantly judged the quality of each other's dress, personal belongings, and community stature. Feeling outcast by this group she scornfully called daughters of "Irish publicans," Anna found one friend in Tickie Curr, a slightly older girl with religious inclinations who had come in with her sisters from an isolated sheep station. Anna fell "emotionally in love" with this social savior and good example.[51] During Lent they would "kiss the five wounds on the crucifix happily together."[52] Anna continued to experiment with verse and fill the chapel with her strong young voice, but she longed for vacation days and welcomed almost any interruption of the routine.

The school year's rhythm was broken once, however, by a visit to the side of what was fully expected to be Geoffrey's deathbed. Stricken with typhoid, he recovered only after Alice, summoned off the stage during an appearance at Charter Towers, was able to calm his agitation and hypnotize him into sleep.[53] (The Harper relatives were angry at Alice for being away and angry that her appearance at his bedside helped him turn the corner.) Afterwards Geoffrey went to Charter Towers with Alice to recuperate. When the holidays came, eleven-year-old Anna, unaccompanied but fearless, went north into the tropics to join them, holding her own in conversation with an attentive fellow passenger, Judge Paul, as the boat passed along the Great Barrier Reef.

When Anna was twelve, they had a seaside holiday, "in splendour at the best hotel" at Sandgate on Moreton Bay, fourteen miles from Brisbane.[54] Geoffrey and Alice together were not a "happy pair" on this trip, quarrelling so bitterly and violently that Anna trudged a whole day in the heat back to Brisbane in search of her mother whom she feared had left.

Yet despite her parents' arguments, back at the convent school Anna missed both of them and pined for family life. All Hallows' was no substitute. Tickie Curr understood Anna's passionate nature; Mother Patrick understood the poet in her. But apart from these two exceptions, boarding school reinforced her feeling that she was different from other people. They did not understand her, nor she them.

After Geoffrey's convalescence he and Alice decided to try their luck together again, this time in New South Wales. They would move south to Sydney and join Geoffrey's siblings Mary, Charlie, and Beatrice who had settled there earlier. The climate would be less demanding than Queensland's extremes, and the beautiful city curving around the deep blue harbor was vibrant. Anna's one good friend, Tickie Curr, had left the convent school to return to the sheep ranch and Anna looked forward to being in Sydney with her parents, saying, "I left the convent regretting nobody and feeling that nobody regretted me."[55] Her final entry in the All Hallows' register is May 15, 1896.[56]

Brisbane itself, where Anna and her parents had at least for a time lived together in a cozy house with a "jungle of a fruit garden," would become a place of remembered happiness.[57] The rest of Queensland is discussed in her poem, "Old Faith," one of the few poems the adult Anna wrote about Australia.

OLD FAITH

> I'll make a bond with Bundaberg
> And dedicate my powers
> To a young dream
> By Flinders stream
> And strength of Charter Towers.
> Then I will ask austerity
> From God—that prudent giver—
> Proud as a ring-barked blue gum tree
> I saw by Mary River.[58]

This poem is a shorthand version of the challenges of Anna's Queensland. "Bundaberg" was one of the towns where her father's music shop branches had failed. "Flinders River" was dry as a bone when she first saw it in Hughenden. Tropical "Charter Towers" was her destination when as a preadolescent she set out, unaccompanied, to join her parents. A "ring-barked blue gum tree" is a dead one, though one still standing with its bare branches raised. The most upbeat interpretation of these lines would be that Anna learned the value of perseverance, commitment, and austerity from her Queensland years. The darkest reading would be one that sees an innocent's potential constantly challenged by hazard and circumstance in a harsh land.

THREE

Life in Sydney (1897–1904)

This time Geoffrey was on the road. Alice gave up lectures for a time. Thirteen-year-old Anna attended school and lived at home. Her father, who had fully recovered from typhoid, worked as a business representative for W. H. Paling & Co., Ltd., importer of English and German instruments and the most prestigious piano and pianola company in New South Wales.[1] Her mother again was testing her mettle as a pioneer in a new line of work, selling policies for the Equitable Assurance Company of New York.

In an initial burst of fellow-feeling the family chose the same boarding house as Aunt Mary Harper. Mary, thirty-nine years old now, never married, had collected a few fine furnishings and counted influential people such as the Archbishop and the government astronomer among her friends. But cautious as always, she economized with a small and dark room at the back of the house. Alice and Anna lived in the expensive light-filled front room, irritating Mary with their excesses and their pet parrot who chewed the woodwork.

For a family who had been seven years in Queensland, metropolitan Sydney was an eye-opener.[2] All of Queensland had less than 475,000 people; Sydney and its suburbs alone totaled 410,000.[3] And Sydney society, to a much greater extent than Brisbane, was on the verge of closing itself off to newcomers in an attempt to conserve every bit of respectability and accumulated wealth hard won from an immigrant past. Michael Cannon, historian, notes that though in an earlier time the self-made man could become "somebody," after the 1880s Sydney "society" suddenly froze.

> The inheritors of the wealth built up by their ancestral convicts, roughneck squatters, gold diggers, smart traders, harsh manufacturers and crooked land speculators, settled down to the task of obliterating the past, repressing the present, and perfecting a new social image in which wealth, education at a church school, and embracement of a British-Australian imperialist outlook were the only acceptable qualifications for entry.[4]

Sydney's solid brick bastions were not within easy reach of the Harper family.[5]

For Geoffrey and Alice had made a substantial change in their attitude toward "the villa dwellers."[6] Propelled in part by Anna's adolescent desire to be more conformist, they themselves had begun to think somewhat wistfully about possessions, property, and stability. But their family life was as rocky as it had almost always been. When Geoffrey came home from his business trips, "there was the usual alternation of violent, brutal quarrels and a rather beautiful emotionalism." While Anna's father may have wanted a peaceful weekend of reading and cultured conversation, Anna's mother would have none of it. Gradually the situation escalated. Alice, suffering from a gastric ulcer, a lack of confidence in her own and Geoffrey's prospects, and the looming proximity of Harper disapproval, drank two bottles of Chlorodyne in another suicide attempt. She lived. Anna, meanwhile, took refuge in the attentions of admirers.

Shortly after their arrival, a young bank clerk who boarded in the same house began to turn his head toward Anna whenever she passed. Anna's father had always encouraged in her a companionable, rather than either a combative or meek attitude toward members of the opposite sex. He liked to see her as sort of an honorary fellow, having her hair cut short when it was not the norm, and teasingly saying to her, "I hate women, old girl, thank God you're not a woman, darling."[7] In Queensland her braids and pretty voice and grown-up mannerisms copied from her father and mother had won her some attention. In Hughenden she had made two "innocent, though sentimental, attachments" to boys, and with her girlish charm was "belle of the fancy dress ball."[8] When she had traveled at age eleven alone to Townsville, her conversation had charmed a distinguished elderly man also on board ship: Judge Paul solemnly told her she was beautiful and gave her two books, *Modern Science and Modern Thought*, and a volume of the witty light verse of Charles Stuart Calverley.

So even before arriving in Sydney she had begun to look in the mirror. She knew she had something, but was not quite sure what.

In general at that time Australian girls were more precocious than their English counterparts. Girls attended adult dances by age 13 or 14, married by age 18 or 19 and regarded themselves as "old maids" by age 23.[9] Assumed to be more frank and open, more robust, an Australian girl could have a bit of color on her face from the sun. The usual Victorian mysteries applied, however, and most girls were uninformed or misinformed about sex. At the same time, though, they were presented with a model that elevated childrearing and the wife-as-helpmate ideal. Anna's knowledge of things sexual was elementary, and Alice's tales of both dire childbirth and

> out-of-wedlock shame induced in her daughter a state of fear and repugnance toward sexual matters. While her giggling Brisbane convent classmates had huddled close to the window to watch a bare boy dressing across the quadrangle, Anna had hung back, uncomfortable. When the Hughenden sheep shearers had shaken the floorboards with their dancing, she cringed at "their brutal and massed masculinity."[10] Her father, however, had often included her in his activities and, in a sense, his friends were hers. In this way she had kept an even attitude, an almost "sexless part of me that is my mind" as she would later say in a poem.[11]

Geoffrey probably noticed that Anna was changing. Where once she would sit rapt as he explained a new idea, she now began to sigh with boredom when he read to her from Emerson's essays. But Geoffrey was too often on the road and when he was with his family there was a lot to be attended to. Alice, however, had her eyes wide open. Alice, who conquered in a man's world while accentuating her femininity in dress and appearance, had always tried (though in vain) to dress the young Anna in spotless pinafores and dresses and teach her both to sew a fine seam and to keep a clean house. Alice was ahead of Geoffrey in being the first to notice that Anna's taller, willowy frame, long, graceful limbs, direct and expressive gaze, beautiful eyes, and brown wavy hair were attracting attention.

Alice, with no extramarital loves of her own at the time, encouraged the young bank clerk's attentions toward Anna. She coached Anna how to respond as he brought flowers and chocolates. He followed the family on a trip through what D. H. Lawrence would later describe as, "sombre bush . . . and great spikey things . . . . tree ferns . . . virgin bush . . . lost, sombre, [until] the magical range of the Blue Mountains."[12] Once there, Alice looked the other way as the clerk taught Anna to play poker and to kiss. But when Alice thought it was time, Anna inexplicably says that her mother "brought things to the final quarrel."[13] The bank clerk's farewell letter, after Alice steamed it open, was returned as if unopened, inducing in Anna "a false attitude to love, which afterwards served me in bad stead."[14]

Mary Harper, two years older than Geoffrey and ever the big sister, could not have missed seeing the glances and the gifts, and probably felt acrimonious toward Alice's chaperonage. Perhaps she sympathized with her niece, having herself been disappointed in love. But as Anna's piano teacher and oldest member of the Harper family present, she also might have been expected to say something to rein in the situation. It is not clear from the record that she did so. Nevertheless, Alice and Anna moved to another boarding house.

Anna, meanwhile, had begun studies at the Sydney Girl's High School on March 30, 1897.[15] Her reading and study at the convent school at Brisbane paid off. It appears that she was one of thirty students whose performance in an annual competition won a scholarship, "tenable for three years," giving the chosen scholar "a free grant of text books and free education in a High School."[16] Opened in 1883, the school prepared students in Latin, Mathematics, History, Physical Science, Drawing, and of course English Language and Literature, Elocution, and either French or German. The school also prided itself on helping the less fortunate and hoped to inculcate this habit in the girls.[17] Students could go on to take senior and junior public examinations held in connection with Sydney University and some girls from the school went on to make names for themselves. But Anna's performance at the school was only mediocre. Living in boarding houses may have helped Anna develop her curiosity and her forthright manner; she was exposed to many different kinds of people, which probably led to her attitude of unflappability as a mature woman. But it was hard to study amid the noise and comings and goings of a boarding house, not to mention her teenage affairs. When Geoffrey came to stay, laughter and plans, alternating with recriminations and accusations, made life an emotional roller coaster. The young men who admired Anna put additional pressure on her time and attention.

At the new boarding house, a young dentist with a penchant for books on sex developed an interest in her. "With nausea" Anna later remembered the dentist as being "stupid, sensual . . . and [the author of] bad poems adapted from birthday books."[18] But Alice encouraged the two and they became engaged. Geoffrey, on the road and quickly losing influence over his beloved Anna, fumed at her choosing this wayward son of a Wesleyan minister. Luckily for Geoffrey, the dentist's sisters judged the innocent Anna to have "no principles" and the engagement was quickly broken.

Alice continued to encourage Anna's romances, either unaware or unconcerned that as Anna's mother, her now bright blond dyed hair, her sumptuous style of dressing and her unconventional habits of employment would be unlikely to encourage admirers for her daughter who could pass muster with the Harpers. When Geoffrey himself intervened with Alice over the issue of Anna's boyfriends, Alice denied any impropriety. When Geoffrey argued that she should stop overworking and instead supervise Anna more closely, Alice brandished her usual weapon: Geoffrey was unable to make enough money to keep them comfortably. She reminded him of the pain of her gastric ulcers, which would not have occurred, she said, if she didn't have to work.

At least, however, their living situation was improving, a condition in which Anna took tremendous satisfaction. She and her family had, over the years, developed a "ship coming in" mentality that helped keep them, and herself later in life, optimistic in times of economic want. With Alice's income from insurance sales and Geoffrey's income from the music business, they saved up "twenty pounds in gold, a very respectable sum." On Cross Street in Double Bay, an inner suburb on the south side of the harbor, they rented a house with fir trees by the carriage gate, carnation bushes blooming sweetly by the door, and a great deal of character in its wooden frame. Little bothered by having second-hand things, whether they were the dresses of society women or the furnishings of the recently deceased, Geoffrey, Alice, and Anna bid at auctions on paintings for the walls and set up their home.

On December 30, 1899 Anna finished her education at the Sydney Girl's High School. Though the family hired a "maid of all work," Anna was to do the housework and practice her music. Having made no lasting friends at the school in her three years there, and now in a new neighborhood, sixteen-year-old Anna became lonely in the extreme.[19] She was also diagnosed as "horribly overstrained and dyspeptic," the latter a condition generally described at the time as "lowness of spirits, general depression and feeling 'below par.'"[20]

Since the mid-1800s, people suffering from either the overexertion of "brain work" or the stresses of "the modern age" itself were treated with a variety of remedies: with phosphate pills, electric field treatments, or a complete rest "from cerebral activity."[21] It is not clear if her mother and father thought of Anna's work contribution as necessary for the household, or as therapy for her dyspepsia, or as simply the next step in her growing up, a way for her to contribute to the household economy while still leaving time free for her piano and singing practice.[22] But the work was not helpful to her state of mind. The repetitive nature of it coupled with her constant feelings of inadequacy made the tasks seem Sisyphean.

In general, Anna was prone to compare herself to other young women, her family to other families. Now with her mother's criticisms always sounding in her ear, Anna suffered more. She hoped that she would have a bright future. But though she had by this time begun to fulfil the musical promise seen earlier by many, by "belonging nowhere" in society she had no social outlet that would provide structure and feedback. Possessed of a conflicting attitude toward this idea of belonging, Anna both thought that having a social "set" would make it easier to get on in life, while at the same time she admired her mother's and her own independent spirits. So while such near-contemporaries as the future writer Vera Brittain, in England, complained of social rounds draining off energy and producing nothing, Anna had no such distractions.[23] She and her mother were not the kind to make afternoon calls or have an "at home" day; her mother was out selling policies.[24] This left Anna free to practice the piano four hours each day—pieces by Grieg, Schumann, Chopin, Beethoven and Mozart—but even these pleasures were cramped by the thought of Aunt Mary's corrections. If she was writing she was telling no one about it, and there was no teacher to bring out the best in her as "Miss Story" had done at the Brisbane Normal School.[25] She could sing true and with power but singing alone, as she used to do on the veranda in Maryborough, she longed for a listener who would recognize and encourage her talent anew.

Finally the Harpers decided her developing voice warranted professional opinion; they brought in a friend to listen. At least the partial verdict: too much volume. Anna felt her body freezing up over this criticism. And between Geoffrey's too-complimentary attentiveness to her talents and her mother's nit-picking mockery of her mistakes, Anna felt shadowed, hounded, and uncomfortable about her future, whatever that was going to be.

Anna seems not to have had a serious longing to marry young. Yet since she had no alternate plan her admirers kept her romantically entangled. The Harper aunts suggested she be apprenticed to a good draper, a job lacking in glamour but one through which some young people were rising into respectability through the ranks of business management.[26] This had absolutely no attraction for Anna. She began studying geology at the Technical College at Ultimo. Its museum exhibits—81,000 specimens of mineral and vegetable products and, fittingly for Australia, a comprehensive series of specimens of wool—fascinated her.[27] But even this seemed to be a dead end, satisfying for the moment, but with no outcome in mind.

Then Alice acted. She was irritated at the ordinariness of her life in Sydney and not as successful in the new life insurance business as she had hoped. On the road she had been the star of her own show. In Sydney, spending holidays with the Harpers, she felt too much a newcomer in Aunt Mary's territory. In Anna's words:

> My mother . . . underwent a nervous crisis, as always in periods of boredom. . . . She was under treatment . . . [and had been given] a sleeping draught containing one hundred and twenty grains of chloral. One night she went over to the wash-hand stand . . . poured the whole bottle into a glass and drank it off. I toiled up the hill to the chemists and found that forty grains was a poisonous dose. All night I kept my mother alive by rubbing the skin on her ribs, which gave her enough pain to keep her slightly conscious. I got our maid-of-all-work out of bed and made her make emetics of strong coffee and mustard and water. Next day my mother was very vigorous; she drank a bottle full of a strong solution of bromide of potassium, and a bottle of Stephens ink; she chased the fox terrier around the room with a carving knife, and then her rage abated.[28]

Alice's doctor (and she went only to the best) tried to convince the family that Anna would be better off away from her suicidal mother, perhaps with Aunt Beatrice who lived a short distance inland. He felt that if she did not, a nervous breakdown was imminent. But Anna felt she was needed at home, a pattern of assuming responsibility that for the rest of her life would drive her. In this case, she felt that no one could help her mother better than she.

Then, luckily, Alice drew in her breath, looked straight ahead, "bought a new hat and went without any introduction to interview the minister of education." She came home with a plummy job teaching elocution to students in the state and technical schools of Sydney.

Alice's business engines roared up. Her classes often had over forty pupils and the schools "paid five shillings per head for ten lessons." Her employment also turned out to have far-reaching consequences for Anna.

When Alice became ill one day, Anna, glad of the occasion for variety, was sent to teach some classes in her mother's stead. The work suited her abilities so well that while her mother continued to teach the older students, Anna, probably then seventeen, was put in charge of teaching all of the children under ten. Six of her pupils won medals in elocution competitions held in 1901 when the Duchess of York (later Queen Mary) traveled to Australia to open the first Federal Parliament. Mother and daughter raked in money at an astonishing rate, often making over two pounds an hour. Anna, finally over the shoals of adolescence, exulted, "Our life became a sea of half-crowns, and we used to bring the takings home wrapped in a handkerchief." By developing her confident (and lifelong) ability to coach speakers into a sterling performance, Anna began to come into that remarkable "presence" that all who knew her later remarked upon. Though she later said she regretted her temerity at making Shakespearean Juliets from ten-year-olds and training a child of three to sing in front of three thousand people, the work gave her purpose, self-respect, and a higher standing in her mother's too-critical eyes.

A happier young woman, she was now able to take a respite from home. She found her relief in an unlikely source. After chafing for so many years under the "vaunted Harper rightness" in music and deportment, after struggling under their too-metronomic musical tutelage and hanging her head at their lack of praise, Anna began to take the more relaxed Harper aunt, Beatrice, as a role model. Following the doctor's earlier suggestion, Anna accepted Beatrice's invitations to get away.

A photograph taken around this period shows Anna in a wide-brimmed hat, flowing dark skirt, and full-sleeved white blouse. She is seated comfortably on the grass, flanked by "Aunt Beat" and her father in chairs beside her. One arm casually rests across her father's knees. The other arm, crooked at the elbow, nestles on Aunt Beatrice's knees. Even the family's fox terrier cozies up at Aunt Beatrice's feet while Alice, standing in back, hands behind her skirts to hide the old burn scars, looks sadly distant from the group and apprehensively stares into the camera. Aunt Beat's gaze is looking lovingly down on Anna, who looks radiant from the physical contact and attention.[29]

Twenty years older than Anna and teaching music outside Sydney, Beatrice had a comfortable place "in small-town society." She kept a good house; there were no outbursts of violent temper. She was not ruled, as was her sister Mary, by a biting candor, but she knew that Anna would benefit from knowing how the social world worked. She taught her more about table manners and when to leave a P. P. C. card on visiting calls. She understood what Anna had been going through, and took Anna out. The bridge parties, dinner parties, tennis games, and dances gave the emerging "Miss Harper," in her best clothes, a chance at a social life. During her stays at Aunt Beat's, Anna was finally able to be a young person in a peaceful setting where people put her interests first. It was a great contrast to the silence of evenings in Sydney when Alice, exhausted by the day's teaching, would often retire at eight leaving Anna, when Geoffrey was out of town, to beautiful, warm, but empty evenings. Beatrice, who was later to return to England and then live out her days in Italy, was highly conscious of the genteel dress and manners befitting a serious music teacher. Yet she had enough of the spirit of youth and a genuine affection for Anna to see to it that her eighteen-year-old niece had fun.

Twenty-eight-year-old Leslie Parker was the best tennis player at Beatrice's club.[30] "He wore the right kind of tennis shoes, carried the best brand of racket, and, at the dances he organised, there was always a splendid kind of oyster pâte." Leslie himself was tidy, well-organized and, ultimately, ambitious to become a doctor. In addition, his was just the right family for her, given Anna's desire for normalcy at the time. His nine siblings, friendly and accepting of the gregarious Leslie's latest flame, worked in offices and in banks and were "all orderly and ordinary." His father, a pharmacist who oddly enough thought black pepper a cure-all, had been forced out of the previous town because he had been accused of mishandling the Wesleyan Chapel's books. Anna secretly called him "the old sinner" and then admired him anyway. Leslie's mother, whose society connections had kept her husband from ruin, carried on serenely. Watching the Parker women, Anna learned more about social niceties, began to read women's magazines, follow fashions, and sew "complicated little undergarments, and articles for the toilet." She didn't really love Leslie, but serenity, pleasure, and occupations for the free hours were attraction enough. She began to bring home suggestions to her mother about rearranging the furniture, stocking up on more and better table linens and toning down behavior to a Parkerish level.

Anna became engaged, and her father became distraught. Leslie's traditional diamond and sapphire engagement ring twinkled on her finger in a sort of insult to all that Geoffrey had stood for:

> the Parkers came to see us at our charming wooden house in Double Bay with the camellia trees, and my father wept because of them. Their ordinariness, which was such a relief to me, appalled him. Was this where I was to end, where he had begun, with Wesleyans? Wesleyans now depreciated, vulgarised, lacking the spirit and spunk of his forebears. I, who was to be his justification, who was to represent him, and establish his powers and his spirit among the people and in the world to which he belonged, here I was, imitating the Parker women, trying to keep my shoes on trees . . . [31]

When each of her stays at Aunt Beatrice's was over, Anna returned to her mother "with trepidation." Her fears were well-founded, for Alice did not like the changes in her daughter, seeing in them a rebuke and the Harper stamp. Even Geoffrey was dismayed at Anna's new attention to "little elegancies," the "fashionable and feminine clothing" such as her beautiful lace blouse, and her "desire to imitate and cultivate all ordinariness," which he saw as coming less from his sister than as a direct result of Anna's admiration for Leslie.

When the Harper aunts wrote to hint to Anna back in Sydney that her fiance had been seen with another woman on the club balcony during a break in the dancing, she was easily persuaded to give him up. Though Anna was now as tall as her tall father, Geoffrey's disapproval still hurt and his opinions began to matter more than ever.

She threw herself into her work with her mother when Alice, seeing a need to support orphan children, also saw an opportunity for the elocution business. They rented a vast mission hall and arranged to split the profits with the charity. The only thing lacking was a cohesive script. This Anna provided.

Anna, whose poems to her father had once been deemed so admirable by Sister Mary Aden that she was accused of "getting it out of a book," tried her hand at being a playwright. *The Seasons: A Speaking Tableau for Girls* was printed in 1902 by Pepperday, Sydney.[32] Anna was barely nineteen. The parents of all the pupils involved attended the performances and the teachers and the orphanage both came out considerably financially ahead.

Meanwhile, Anna had attracted another suitor. Oswald Phillips, a solicitor, was the next to be scrutinized by Geoffrey and Alice. They had fewer objections to him than they had had against Leslie. He was established, of "a credible class," and *not* a Wesleyan as Anna's two previous fiances had been. But Anna, apart from viewing him as an educated rare bird come to roost, seems to have felt no physical attraction for him at all.

Apart from the stir that Anna's various suitors made in the household, domestically things were also again changing. With her mother finally back at the top of her form, and money coming in at the rate of about 1200 pounds per year from the elocution work alone, Anna made the suggestion that her parents buy property. This was a good idea, as it turned out, since rising property values were providing the most common route up the Australian ladder of economic success.[33] They bought one house on Lower Moss Bay for rental income, and by 1903, another above Balmoral Bay (on Avenue Road at Mosman, an inner suburb) to live in.[34] Anna, who had loved the Double Bay house for its camellias, now found the Balmoral Bay house charming for its roses, its native crimson waratahs taller than her father, and the magnificent views of harbor and coastline. They bought a carriage and hired a groom who drove them to the elocution lessons. They also bought furniture more in keeping with their new address, hired a good housekeeper, and ate better than before. But living across the harbor from their usual rounds made the trip home longer. And though Anna was contributing in a substantial way to the well-being of the family, her work began to seem a toiling for daily bread, rather than the achievement of some lustrous goal. At times Anna was so exhausted from her teaching rounds that, sinking into the carriage seat and remembering she had left some of her pay on the classroom desk, she would wave the driver on and leave the money to the finders-keepers.

The year 1903 also, however, brought Anna a measure of success and friendship. The second of her plays for children, *Wonder Eyes: A Journey to*

Slumbertown, was printed in Sydney by Pepperday. Again her words were performed to great applause. Geoffrey would "come to rehearsals and cry with the satisfaction of it all."

Meanwhile, Anna was taking singing lessons and becoming more involved with music. In mid-1903 a gifted English cellist, May Mückle, appeared on the scene. Playing what was considered "a man's instrument" and in the company of tenor Edwin Floyd, May's life was to the impressionable Anna a glamorous succession of artistic triumphs, permitting the wearing of elegant clothes and providing access into European society. May had been touring with various other artists, including one of her talented sisters, and would later visit the U. S., Hawaii, and South Africa. She also composed for the cello. Outside the family circle, May was the first independent woman with whom Anna could identify and on whom she could model herself. Only three years older than Anna, she had a sound musical foundation and had fought successfully to establish herself.[35] Though it is not clear how they met, the two became friends, and before May returned to England in August, they visited the Jenolan Caves together.[36] Feminist May, whose encounters with male prejudice in the music community had turned her into a critic, warned Anna that "men would destroy and betray," another maxim that Anna would long recall.

When "strong and lovely" May left, Anna spent hours writing letters to her and dreaming of how she might one day "join my life with hers." The world seemed full of opportunity. After all, others were making their mark: Helen Porter Mitchell, an Australian from Melbourne incorporating the name of her birthplace in her stage name, Nellie Melba, had the world opera audience spellbound. Anna, encouraged to dream by the example of Nellie Melba, and strengthened by her friendship with May, began to work harder on her singing. The best vocal teacher in Sydney now told her she had a great voice. And her plays had been listened to by hundreds of people—albeit the entire casts were under the age of majority.

Her father, troubled by Anna's limited opportunities in Sydney, proud of her success with the printed plays, and disturbed by the ease with which Anna became romantically involved, decided that it was time to cut her loose from the family elocution business and return her to England "to make a success in one or more of the arts." Opera productions at this time in Australia were only very intermittently local ones; visiting companies provided the vast majority of performances. England was the natural place for Anna to continue her studies. Anna herself was fired with enthusiasm to go, if only to be with the remarkable May.

After a splendid vacation with her father touring the old gold-rush area around Tumut, Anna packed her crocodile dressing case and made ready for departure. After fifteen years in Australia she was leaving for a new life "back home" in England. Alice, who had bought all of Anna's clothes for her, packed sentimentally inscribed gifts for the Harpers and Whelans. She agreed with Geoffrey that for Anna's future it was good to be leaving, yet she obliquely urged her daughter to be on the lookout for a rich husband. Geoffrey meant for her to become a success at whatever she did, though he must have had a certain bias toward the writing life: He shouted, "*Punch*, Anna, *Punch*," when the ship pulled away, meaning that he wanted his daughter to write for that well-known English illustrated weekly.[37]

An allowance of four pounds a week was agreed upon to help Anna achieve her goals, whatever those might be. Would she be a Nellie Melba? Would she take the literary world by storm? In Geoffrey's opinion, she should "sing to the great heart of the people," advice that she much later admitted was fine but not quite explicit enough for a green, overconfident, sensitive twenty-one-year-old with little idea of how to get whatever it was she was after once the British tugs led the boat into harbor. Years later Anna writes a poem that contrasts the journey's "visible infinity" of blue sky and sea with the fascination of the immediate: "Only the ship is space to me, / The mode, the means of destiny."[38]

The years in Australia had given Anna the example of an independent, if troubled, spirit in her mother's incredible bravado and creativity. The years also provided her with a template for marriage that stressed competition and unrest. Though it was not yet evident that her father's zeal for learning had transferred itself to Anna (for she would become a lifelong, voracious reader and one who loved to debate the merits of a point), his ambition for his only child had discouraged her thus far from early and possibly unsuitable marriage.

The physical and social freedom Anna had enjoyed in Australia and the marvelous extremes of the continent itself seem to have permeated her. A strapping girl, her outsized voice and her independent thinking would mark her upon her return to England. She was on her way to becoming someone hard to forget (or to ignore) but it remained to be seen if she could make her mark in the arts.

FOUR

Singing, London and Paris (1904–1906)

O
n board the ship, with her obvious happiness, charming ten-
tativeness, growing confidence, and entirely new wardrobe
twenty-one-year-old Anna was irresistible. As the ship cut
through the seas she sang like a nightingale for the first-class passengers who
crowded into the second-class salon especially to hear her. She captured the
attention and affection of the First Mate. By Gibraltar, the boat's seventh
stop, she and an actress friend went ashore together and spent some of the
twenty pounds in gold that Anna carried in a belt around her waist.

When she left England fifteen years before, she had been a precocious,
somewhat timid child. Now London—"The Big Smoke"—as fellow
Australian Miles Franklin called it, was waiting. On Monday, August 15,
1904, Anna stepped off the deck of the *Ormuz* at Port of London, Tilbury,
England, fresh from her victories at sea.[1]

Hurrying cabs and snorting horses (there were more than 250,000
horses in London).[2] Heavy drays and puffing steam-trains. The few expen-

sive automobiles that only the rich could afford. The crowds of people. The glories of London her father had praised: Queen's Hall in Bloomsbury with an auditorium holding almost 2,500 people; The Royal Academy of Music then at Hanover Square and Tenterden Street, where Geoffrey's sister had trained; Fleet Street, where the presses of Geoffrey's old friend George Riddell pounded away under the shadow of the great dome of St. Paul's Cathedral; and the offices of *Punch*, in whose popular pages Geoffrey had urged her to appear.[3] Anna must have felt as though she would know the city intimately. The Royal Opera! The stages where May Mückle played! The very air must have seemed bursting with opportunity. What a crushing blow, then, to be driven to a modest address in Hampstead and to be talked down to like a child, treated as a colonial, and watched apprehensively as being the mercurial Alice's daughter who might or might not have inherited her mother's pretensions, aggressions, and sexual charms.

As if to forestall trouble, Anna brought her mother and father's gifts engraved "To the dear Home people from Geoffrey and Alice." Aunt Tid, Geoffrey's youngest sister, who was only ten years older than Anna and very pretty, came to meet her. Perhaps the Harper family thought the closeness in age would make Anna feel comfortable. But the meeting was not a success. Aunt Tid (Norah Patti Anglin) had been named after a leading soprano of the time and took music seriously. Though now thirty-one years old, with two children under the age of three, she had been a cellist in a women's orchestra, led by a mistress of King Edward VII.[4] Tid held conservative views, and in her opinion Anna was a wild card requiring scrutiny and caution. She treated Anna to a sandwich lunch at one of London's ubiquitous Aerated Bread Company (A.B.C.) shops, at which Anna scoffed, her spirits sinking steadily from the common surroundings and stilted conversation; Aunt Tid said that Anna's manner "made her feel like the niece."[5]

Norah Patti brought her to the Harpers' where the rest of the family had gathered to meet "this prodigy." Her grandfather Edwin was kind to her and playing "like Mozart" accompanied her singing of "O Divine Redeemer" and a song by Giacomo Meyerbeer to good effect. The rest of the family was skeptical. They admired Geoffrey, but their old animosity toward his wife was rekindled over Alice's too-successful foray into elocution. Anna, eager to impress the relatives, sang with her "affected habit of letting down my hair while I was singing," which was yet another reminder of her mother's theatrical influence.[6] Things went from bad to worse. After Anna passed out copies of her plays printed in Sydney she found one of them ripped to shreds in the lavatory. It was a bad omen. Still, the Harpers "knew a good voice when they heard one."[7] Norah Patti's husband, James Anglin, was even moved to tears that day by Anna's singing of Schubert lieder.

Eventually all agreed that Anna should take voice lessons and Anglin voted for a Royal Academy of Music education. In the end, however, the Harpers referred Anna to George Dukes, the bass-voiced son of a Cornish laborer, a student of Bouhy just beginning his career. Anna seems not to have been consulted about her wishes. They viewed her as someone they would shape as a favor to their brother and in spite of his uncontrollable wife; accordingly, they were strict with her.

The Harpers had no comprehension of how unsettling this situation was for Anna. From being a teacher of elocution, Anna became only a student with a voice teacher who bullied her about the operatic arias he gave her to sing. Power and decision-making had been stripped from her. She went from being an independent traveler who could order the family carriage, to being a chaperoned niece, at first not even permitted to go out into the city alone. She went from the house at Balmoral Bay to the cluttered, grimy home of Edwin and Mary, alternating with the crowded flat of the Anglins and their two babies. She was pushed to *work hard,* an admonition that had always had a bleakly discouraging effect on her art. But most of all, Anna felt out of place and not wanted by the family. All Geoffrey and Alice's inscribed words about "the dear home people" could not change the fact that they'd been getting on without each other for fifteen years. Sending the highly-strung Anna back to the fold may have sounded like the perfect solution to Geoffrey, alarmed by his daughter's romantic liaisons and pleased with her promise of success in writing or music, but a little more realistic thought might have shown him that the Harpers would chafe under the responsibility of an emotional young woman with plenty of ideas of her own. And that Anna would be caught in the middle.

Soon there was a minor explosion. Aunt Norah Patti, pregnant with her third child, was away from home in an attempt to rest. According to the story, Anna "pranced" into James Anglin's bedroom, an event that shocked him enough to make him flee the house, leaving Anna with the maid and reporting the matter to his wife.[8] Whether or not this was the impetus that sent Anna looking for new lodgings is not known. But the incident caused at least a temporary rift between Anna and Anglin, who with grandfather Edwin Harper had been her ally.

Ever since the cellist May Mückle had left Australia after her tour in mid-1903, Anna had been writing long letters to her. After a time with the Harpers, she visited May, hoping for a close bond with someone she adored:

> I went over to Maida Vale to see May Mukle [sic] in a dream of plea-
> sure and anticipation; with my over-emotionalism and affectation, I
> took off my shoes before going in to her room. . . . The whole fam-
> ily were immensely proud of May who had got into the news, and
> had made quite a reputation in London. The sisters felt that I . . .
> could in no way enhance that reputation. They began to ridicule my
> affection for May who had a new friend in a young ballad singer,
> Carmen Hill.[9]

Despite the warning bells that this reception should have sounded for Anna, she began to room and board with the Mückles in their house near the Regent's Canal. Anna, while viewed with alarm by the Harpers, was seen as somewhat superfluous by May Mückle and her friend; she felt very much a "rejected lover."[10] Yet she felt she must stay put. She was now in a house where the music never stopped. May was preparing for a 1905 South African tour. Someone or other was always coming for a lesson, or leaving for a musical engagement. Here Anna could practice Chaminade's "Amoroso" without worrying about waking sleeping babies or grand-mothers. She met, through the Mückles, consummate musicians such as the Goossens family, three generations of conductors, harpists, horn play-ers, and an oboist.[11]

Emotionally, however, her life was arid. She remembered with home-sickness the affection shown in Australia and forgot some of the trauma and felt more lonely than ever. In Sydney she had her parents, her work, and the admiration of her suitors. In London, at times, it seemed she had nothing. The wind blew, the temperatures dropped, darkness came early, and Anna caught influenza. "Lying gloomy and uncared for" in her room at the Mückles, who "had no time for students who were ill," Anna made one of those attempts at rejoining the bright crowds that sometimes come after the seclusion of the sickbed. She threw off her weakness and made her way by cab to hear a talk by George Bernard Shaw. Outside the hall a young man hailed her in the mistaken belief that she was someone he knew.

After the lecture they introduced themselves and had a conversation. William Ray had been a student at a lesser-known public school, a clerk in the Education Department and a stringer for London newspapers.[12] Sensing the wide-eyed aspect of Anna's personality, he played up his newspaper connection and was rewarded by an invitation to come to tea (an invitation that May Mückle saw as evidence that Anna was "fast").[13] He began to take her with him on assignments, no doubt impressing her and cashing in on the notice she attracted as well. Soon he presented her with a diamond and sapphire ring, her third engagement.

This was the first time Anna had become engaged to someone close to her own age. There was no Alice around to coach her in what to say and do, or to erect a wall of maternal protection and possession. Ray showed Anna no deference and was forthright in his desire for her, though she put him off. He was attractive to her, but there was little delicacy in William, and more than a little deceit. When Anna realized that William often misrepresented his career and family connections, she began to view him more realistically, but they stayed engaged.

It was through Anna that William Ray received his first big break writing for a news service. Russian emigrés, panicking and angry about the situation at home, were in 1905 and 1906 gathering in England and Europe to plan their own roles in the constitutional regime of their changing country. William was covering events for an American news agency, and Anna accompanied him to Whitechapel, an area of the city that at times seemed like a foreign town, given the language, dress, and customs of the recent arrivals. During one emotional night of speeches,

> A Russian girl in a nurse's uniform, with the red ribbon of the Revolutionists, was in a high state of agitation, tears pouring down her cheeks; she threw herself into my arms in a paroxism [sic] of emotion. William, who had gathered that she was an important figure in the revolutionary movement, told me to get her address. She was in charge of the Rothschild crèche off the Commercial Road, and close to the leaders of the movement.[14]

This useful contact put Anna in touch with leaders receiving Russian news hot off a revolutionary press in Paris. Their news she passed on immediately to William, who used it to turn his one month's trial employment into steady work. She also made some contacts within the movement who intro-duced her to theatre as she'd never seen it before.

Early in 1905, Anna went with Sasha Kropotkin and others to a the-atre in Whitechapel. All theatrical London was talking about the success experienced by Alla Leventon, known as Nazimova, then starring in *The Chosen People,* Evgeny Chirikov's drama that exposed and protested Russian anti-Semitic policies.[15] Nazimova, speaking in Yiddish, gave Anna a never-to-be-forgotten demonstration of how much the body and voice could convey, even if the words were not understood. "The best acting I have ever seen," Anna called it—and Nazimova was only a few years older than Anna. Herbert Beerbohm Tree, Ellen Terry, and many other theatre greats attended the party that Laurence Irving (who spoke Russian and was fascinated by everything having to do with Russia) gave afterwards. Nazimova, whose language was "the language of the soul," according to one reviewer, touched something deep in her English audience.[16]

Anna suddenly realized how an ability to act could help her singing to communicate with an audience. She decided to attend Tree's Academy of Acting, opened the year before by the highly successful fifty-one year old actor/manager. Once in the door at 62 Gower Street, she had to audition, not for Tree alone, but also for Arthur Wing Pinero, perhaps the first play-wright of the modern movement in English drama, and for Sir Squire Bancroft. For her audition she tossed off one of the poems she had been reciting since childhood, and made a sweet speech about how she had come all the way from Australia for the benefit of their teaching. The acad-emy audition was successful enough to earn her a place in the advanced classes and a scholarship for the tuition.

The school later became The Royal Academy of Dramatic Art, the foremost drama school in Great Britain. Anna's gravitation toward it was the first demonstration of her tendency to recognize and throw herself headlong into new movements in art, literature, and dance.

The academy was a good thing for Anna. Students in the class, Betty Kallisch and Carmel Haden Guest, wanted to be her friends.[17] Buoyed by this and the freedom of living apart from the Harpers, she forgot her sor-row over Mückle's lack of interest. She began to regain a little of her nat-ural curiosity and spirit. London began to seem hospitable.[18]

Meanwhile, William developed Anna's powers of resistance. When she showed him her Australian plays for children, he snorted in derision.

Though she was taking her singing seriously, William showed little interest and was in fact antagonistic when her studies interfered with the proposed marriage. His career, his interests, were to come first. If he wanted to listen to ragtime at the Savage Club, they did. If she wanted to attend a concert or opera, they didn't.

Then he made a gross tactical error. At his suggestion he and Anna strolled down Great Ormond Street to the rooms of Patrick Henry Hepburn, a City of London solicitor in his early thirties. Athletic, well-to-do and never married, Patrick had a thin, handsome face, keen, somewhat narrowed eyes, and dedication. At the time, he was dedicating himself to photography. He had met a fellow solicitor, W. Valentine Ball, in 1899 and shortly after they found lodgings together in Bloomsbury, "not one of the most delightful places in those days."[19] Patrick's rooms, only a few blocks from the scientific orderliness of the British Library, were a messy disaster. Not even seeing the dust and disorder, the piles of old papers and journals and clothing fighting for floor space, he "was making lantern slides [of ancient churches] with feverish concentration."[20] Anna was intrigued.

Soon after their first meeting she learned that Patrick's father, James Smith Hepburn, had died on February 28, 1905. Patrick and his brother Charles James Hepburn were coexecutors of the considerable estate, valued at £72,936, at a time when estates passed from fathers to sons without any death duties.[21] The big family home at 1 Elgin Road, Croydon, Surrey, had since been sold and most of the seven servants dismissed as his widow wanted a simpler life. Patrick himself inherited the family business, which primarily dealt in company law. Though a partner in the firm, Patrick had been up until his father's death little more than a glorified law clerk in his father's domain. Now he dutifully took over Hepburn Son & Cutcliffe, Bird-in-Hand Court, 76 Cheapside, London, though the law was of less interest to him than many other things.

In attempting to prove a theory about Romanesque arches, he traveled the length and breadth of England and made excursions into Normandy and Belgium. The photographs he took he made up into "lantern shows" and accompanied these with diagrams and suppositions. When Patrick was to give a lecture at Harrow School using this early version of a slide show, he invited William Ray, Anna, and his own sister, Nell.

Anna traveled to the lecture casting sideways glances at the poetry that Nell was reading as the train lumbered toward Harrow. The poetry had a sentimental border of cupids; Nell herself seemed ponderous, unsmiling.

Harrow School (founded 1572) has a venerable history and its pupils had included the poet Byron and the future leader, Winston Churchill. Anna expected good things of Patrick. But the lecture did not begin on time, Patrick had little stage presence, and he wore "badly fitting trousers." His involvement with the vaults and naves of his subject was so complete that the audience was practically forgotten. William and Nell sighed with boredom. But Anna, though accustomed to her father's meticulous attention to dress and her mother's consummate showmanship, was nevertheless touched by "this very inefficiency, by the appealing inadequacy, by the scholarship, the pains that had been taken, the effort that had been made."

Anna was making efforts of her own. She had come to the conclusion that Dukes's approach to singing was "brutal" and no good for her voice. Riding on the confidence she was gaining from acting classes and newsmakers, Anna auditioned for seventy-three-year-old Alberto Randegger. This Italian conductor, composer, and teacher, a naturalized British citizen, had won the respect of his adopted country and had been for years a professor at both the Royal Academy of Music and the Royal College of Music. He had written the well-regarded 1893 textbook, *Singing*, and any student lucky enough to train with him had an edge over the competition. Anna was ushered in wearing a new silk blouse sent by her mother, fresh gloves, and a hat, of course. She carried a sheaf of white irises, fresh flowers in the dramatic style of Nellie Melba. Despite her nervousness, she impressed Randegger with her personality and her singing. He started her on lessons in technique taught by his wife who soon told him that Anna would "set the Thames on fire in eight months." They reduced their fees on the strength of Anna's potential.[22]

Studying and practicing during the day, there was still time for a social life. One night soon after the Harrow trip, Anna and William joined Patrick for dinner at a restaurant in Soho (definitely not as trendy and upscale as it is today). Anna reports that she was as interested in her own beautiful mirrored reflection as she was in the posturing, attentions, and false bonhomie of William toward Patrick. But not completely distracted by her own reflection, she asked penetrating questions of Patrick and listened to the answers as she had done as a girl. Patrick, smitten, later "spent hours of that night walking up and down outside my boarding-house in his slippers," amazed at finding a woman so outside the common mold. Women in his circle tended toward what Victorian poet Elizabeth Barrett-Browning, in her work *Aurora Leigh*, called "the feminine arts." Outside his own family, most women Patrick knew couldn't follow an argument if it were wearing directions and a tall hat. Anna, trained by her father's dialectics, presented a worthy challenge to Patrick.

He had always been intent on proving himself. His family had been for generations involved in the leather and skin trade. His father, a company lawyer, had twelve children in all, and on Patrick had fallen the weight of first-born. For five terms, ending in 1886, he attended Charterhouse, a school founded in 1611. At Amersham Hall School, near Reading, he won second prize in the First Class of Mathematics in 1888. He knew that even such an admirable achievement as this fell short of the perfection his father expected in physical as well as mental arenas.

Thus Patrick had always driven himself hard. When he was ten years old he swam the dangerous tidal river at Littlehampton; as an adult he would break the ice to swim on Christmas day. He studied for the law at London University and earned a First Class Honours LL.B. degree, Clifford's Inn Prize, in November 1894.[23] He then allowed himself to take up with a passion the study of the solar system, the study of architecture, the expanded vision of telescopes, and the honing eye of the camera. Carrying a three-inch telescope he traveled to Vadso in 1896 and to Spain in 1900 to see the sun eclipse. In 1902 his interests took him across the English Channel to Normandy, where he photographed churches around Caen in his continuing effort to prove that the Gothic cross vault was developed from the Angevin dome.[24] He also pushed the physical limits of his powerful body. On his bicycle, he rode to York in a day. He sailed small craft, he climbed mountains in England and Scotland and Norway. In fact it seemed there wasn't much that Patrick Henry Hepburn couldn't do.

Now, though with his father's death in 1905 he had inherited family obligations, he was also free from his father's daily scrutiny and judgments. It was with a sense of lightness and anticipation that Patrick left the office each day, no longer having to fend off inquiries about how he was spending his time lately.

When Anna and Patrick walked around Bloomsbury, which had started as a suburb of London back in the 1600s, he pointed up at the architectural details of the houses they passed. When he took her to dinner he regaled her with a lecture on the mechanics of the human eye and she responded with full attention, knowing that more was being discussed than retinas. Patrick and Anna had begun to while away the hours without

William. The budding journalist became so upset at this that he wore out his welcome at Anna's relatives, the Anglins, by lovesick "moaning" and complaints about Anna's cruelty.[25]

In fact, it had been William who had pushed Anna into closer proximity with his friend Patrick. Ray had persuaded Anna, after visiting Patrick's cluttered rooms, to intervene. Anna responded with her ever-ready desire to help.

> Patrick was a hoarder, though at the same time he scorned property for property's sake. He had thrown away his diamond studs because of their association with some boredom, some banality, but had kept every pair of trousers he had worn since he was breeched, every theatre programme of every performance he had ever witnessed, every piece of string that had come to him round a parcel, and every envelope with every letter. He never allowed sweeping or dusting so the agglomeration was unbelievable.[26]

Anna set to tidy up the place. She made Patrick fashionable cretonne covers for his chairs. This strong organizational side of Anna was appealing to him. He photographed her sewing.

After that first dinner in Soho, Anna had said, "I like that man, though he will never know the first thing about me." She did not help matters by keeping mum about her aspirations and accomplishments. Although Patrick knew that his pretty dinner companion was studying with Randegger, she tended to avoid the topic of herself. She did not tell him that her father Geoffrey had sent her to London to make a success in the arts. And one wonders if they ever discussed William.

Soon Patrick was foregoing *The Times* on morning rides atop the bus to the city, the better to think of Anna. That she was engaged to another man does not seem to have deterred Patrick from actively seeking her out. It may have whetted his spirit of competition. Or, given the way Patrick could dismiss anyone who did not interest him, possibly Patrick did not see William as any kind of obstacle at all, but rather a convenient means to his own end. In the words of Soames Forsyte, author John Galsworthy's quintessential purchaser of beauty, Patrick came from a time and place in which "a man owned his soul, his investments, and his woman, without check or question."[27]

In the spring of 1905 Anna went to the country to rest her voice. Patrick came also, playing games with some children in a tower and showing Anna a chaste courtesy. The contrast between Patrick's interested but respectful attitude and William's manipulative behavior and sexual advances was becoming more and more evident.

Shortly after this, the strain of being caught between the attentions of two men pushed Anna to a decision. In a move worthy of her mother, she took three pounds of gold and departed for Paris. In the 1st Arrondissement she found a room in a small hotel off the rue St Honoré. She had no introductions; she had only the French learned in the stiff sessions at the convent school. But she aimed to concentrate on her voice with the "vague plan of going, like Bernhardt, to the Conservatoire."

After unpacking her few things she asked the way to the school. There she found a teacher, Monsieur Masson, who promised to let her sit in on classes while awaiting her audition for the Conservatoire, and to give her private lessons. She transferred her parents' four-pounds-per-week allowance so that it would be paid from a bank in Paris and then suddenly stopped short with the enormity of what she had done. She knew no one in Paris, her mind was in turmoil. Paris was supposed to be the ideal place for artistic freedom, but she had little idea of how to achieve it. She wrote to William that she was lonely and he ardently arrived at her door, having taken a room for himself in the same hotel.

In England Anna had only been "coldly interested" in William's advances. In France, she responded to his desire. When morning came she was frantic, sure that she would become pregnant from this, her first sexual encounter. Yet the dramatic possibilities of the occasion inspired both of them. By afternoon they were walking beneath the boughs at Montmorency, lovers in the flesh, if not wholly in the spirit (Anna was irritated at his timidity in the woods). When William went back to London Anna was all too aware of his "insufferable male air of disregarding me as soon as our lovemaking was over." She remembered his "nauseating habit of blowing his nose, and examining the result of this with ugly concentration."[28]

Anna was now a resident of the City of Light. She left the hotel and moved into a five-franc-per-day pension in the Clichy Quarter where the bedbugs were so bad that she slept on the floor. After deciding that any good artist had to live in the Latin Quarter, she rented a piano and supervised its move into a boarding-house in Notre Dame des Champs.

A poor, rather stilted audition crushed her immediate hopes of the Conservatoire; with characteristic drive, however, Anna succeeded in finding the right teacher for her project. Previously singing mostly works arranged for contralto, she had been trying to open up her voice and was now working to expand the upper range. Her new teacher, Jean de Reszke, had first-hand experience in changing repertoire.

Of Polish origin, de Reszke had started as a baritone, then retrained as a tenor. From 1884 he was the *beau idéal* of French and Italian operas and Jules Massenet had even created the role of Rodrique in *Le Cid* especially for him. Then in London in 1887 opera-goers drew in their collective breath as he sang Lohengrin, one of the great German roles created for the big and untiring voice. After several years of triumph in this new incarnation, singing Wagnerian roles for the Metropolitan Opera in New York, he had returned to Paris in 1902 to teach. Now this same de Reszke told Anna she had "the best voice he had ever had from England," put her in his Thursday master-class and gave her lessons in his private theatre near the Bois de Boulogne. "La Belle Anglaise," as the small boys now dubbed her, started making her mark, not only in her freewheeling and distinctive costume of large old brown felt hat and layered blouses, but in the world of music too. All she lacked "was social freedom." Instead her life continued to be circumscribed by the two men she had left behind.

William began frequent visits to France, taking her out of Paris for long, sexual weekends that, according to her own account, she entered into with the spirit of a student. But when he was invited to a literary gathering, he left her at home, ill-disguising his belief that she would not fit in.

A letter arrived from England. Patrick, who had spent the last days of summer at an independent observatory station in Spain at Alcala de Chisvert, overlooking the Mediterranean, had returned with good photographs of the August 30 eclipse. He told her that he had recently joined the prestigious Ward of Cheap Club. In addition to all this activity, however, he had been thinking, and had a request to make of Anna. He wrote politely asking if his sister Nell could come to Paris. His stated reason was that after their father's death she should have a change of scene. However, Patrick also wanted to get Nell away from a man Patrick felt was quite unsuitable on the social scale. So Nell came to Paris with her scratchy woolen "combinations" and conventional admonishments. She and Anna moved together to a rue Edgar Quinet flat located, aptly as it turned out, opposite a very dull cemetery. They then lived in Paris "by the light of

Croydon," never enjoying café life but instead attending the American Mission and supping tea at the crémeries.

Anna, who had never been impressed with Nell from their first meeting at the lantern slide lectures, found her a "fat, unintelligent and self-satisfied" villa-dweller.[29] Nell found Anna an unhealthy, eccentric, spendthrift prima donna who wasted francs on *fiacres*, those soon-to-be-extinct "open carriages drawn by sorry nags, and driven by *cochers* with red waistcoats and glazed hats."[30] But Nell, in a much larger way than the Harpers, assumed a "vaunted rightness," and she truly intimidated Anna with her relative sophistication, dowdy though it actually was. Even Nell's diction dominated her, with the result that Anna alarmed her parents "by writing to them utterly colourless letters beginning with the words, "Very many thanks."

They tried to help each other. Anna began to teach the heretofore-coddled Ellen how to clean the walls and to cook stewed chicken and rice. But Nell was a full ten years older than Anna chronologically, and much older in spirit. It was Nell who had given advice on the supposedly proper dress for the ill-fated Conservatoire audition, with the result that Anna had looked "respectable enough for a Church of England bazaar." As Christmas 1905 drew near the two women, exhausted by each other, returned to England for the holidays.

William and Anna exchanged gifts, but Christmas Day in London was a sad occasion for Anna. In the Foundling Hospital on Guilford Street was a chapel, once a very fashionable place of worship for Dickens and others, where the famous preached and hymns were played on an organ donated by Handel. In this Foundling Chapel, years before, destitute women of good repute stood in agonizing suspense as the luck of a draw decided whether their babies would win medical attention and a place at the home, or be turned away again to the streets.[31] Anna, overcome with emotion, observed part of Christmas Day there in the famous chapel, imagining herself giving "birth to a foundling" and being scorned by William who would find it "a pleasure . . . to let me down." Poverty and disgrace were as close for Anna as her own history. Overwhelmed by guilt and fear that she could bear a child she wept.

Two days after Christmas, Patrick, with William's knowledge and consent, and perhaps hoping to cheer her up, offered to take Anna to Oxford to see the colleges at that peaceful time of year. In an indication of her frame of mind, Anna "had a queer fit of trembling" during their stay. Back in London

Patrick walked her to her lodgings and they paused by Mecklenburgh Square's iron gates. There he kissed her and said, finally, that he loved her.

He also told her then that William had been keeping a secret. Patrick had been quietly giving William money to spend on Anna's behalf. William, however, had not spent it on anything for Anna, but had been using the money to further their relationship as lovers.

Anna returned William's letters and his Christmas present to her. She was enraged by his duplicity.

By the next evening, Anna and Patrick were en route to Paris alone. Patrick, cautious of propriety, spent the night in a different hotel.

Over the course of the next day she told Patrick the full extent of her involvement with William in Paris before Ellen's arrival. Disgusted by what Patrick had revealed about William's character, Anna was equally enthralled by Patrick's admission of caring. Then Patrick went back to London and Anna went on with her studies, but not before they agreed on marriage.

Anna thought that Patrick would want to wait a year or so before the wedding, given that she had just broken her engagement to another man. But in a letter he wrote to her on January 19, 1906, the only letter from him to her that survives, he makes clear his eagerness:

Madonna, and dear Love,

I got up early this morning to be at the office in anticipation of Gates, and get your letter before he should have a chance of laying his hands on it. And was well repaid for my trouble. I detect the Chaste in your opening remarks. Tour in Spain, indeed! I'm planning a longer and more pleasant journey than that. But seriously, I am very glad that the date is quite in our own hands, and that we can get married at any time instead of having an enforced delay of a month. When you come over we can at leisure consider the pros and cons as to the date.

I have just read in the evening paper that one Herr Sacco . . . intends to fast for forty-five days . . . if he accomplishes his intention . . . he will not leave [his fasting room] til the corresponding time on Sunday, March 4.

Think, by the time that hungry man has his next meal, you and I might be returning from our honeymoon!

Talking of moons, this morning, on my Citywards bus, I viewed the old moon . . . . It is new on Wednesday next, and a day or two after that I shall turn my money and before it's full, so I considered, you and I might be married.[32]

Patrick Hepburn attains his age of thirty three years on the 4th of February next, but I doubt if Edith Harper will ever reach twenty three.

. . . . I get lots of congratulations, but as nobody knows you yet, they're all on the wrong side. We must read over them together next week.

There are two crosses in the middle of our letter, one for duty and one for impertinence. I kissed the first once, and the other twice. Though you tell me the region it is intended for, and try as I may, I can't kiss that.[33]

They went together to Scotland to meet members of the Hepburn family and at a "most impressive family house at Bridge of Allan" were entertained at a party "to which the sons of important Glasgow merchants turned out in kilts." Since Anna had been introduced to Patrick at his disorderly rooms in Great Ormond Street, it came as a remarkable surprise to find Patrick so at ease in the heavy timbered halls where she felt so out of place. Nearer London they visited Watford, where each of Patrick's maiden cousins specialized in a different "hobby." The most interesting of them, Kate, did art photographs of friends nude and posing as mythological characters but she would never work on Sunday. Anna felt as distant from these cousins as from the kilts. In both places her trained singing voice went unheard as no one asked her to favor them with a selection. "Nobody took the faintest notice of me as myself, I was of concern only because I was to marry Patrick Hepburn." When they visited Worthing, however, Anna felt differently. To her future mother-in-law, Patrick's stepmother Ellen Jolliffe Hepburn, Anna wrote her first poem since arriving back in England from Australia. What makes Anna's writing of this poem odd and ultimately significant is that Ellen, in Anna's opinion, "plainly hated" Patrick.

After all the festive congratulations, the actual ceremony was quiet. Anna wore a plain white dress and a hat with pink roses, both of which Patrick gladly paid for since he did not want to wait for an advance of funds from Alice and Geoffrey. On February 4, Patrick celebrated his thirty-third birthday. On February 9, 1906, a year and seven months from the time Anna Wickham arrived in England to make a success in the arts, she and Patrick Henry Hepburn, Freeman of the City of London, were married.[34] In the austere elegance of the church of St. Margaret, Lothbury, one of those rebuilt in stone by Wren after the Great Fire of London, the tall and good-looking pair pledged their vows facing east toward the altar. Charles J. Hepburn, one of Patrick's brothers, and George Cutcliffe, Patrick's law partner, were two of the witnesses. After a "sober tea" with a few Hepburn relatives at the Thackeray Hotel on Great Russell Street, the newlyweds started off for their wedding night at Oxford, the town that had brought them together. William Ray appeared and tried to get into the cab with them but Anna would not allow it, nor would she speak to him. His bitter letters followed them on their honeymoon to Pau, one stop in their itinerary of twenty-two Romanesque churches in twenty-two French towns. As Patrick had hoped, Edith Harper did not reach her twenty-third birthday, though Mrs. Patrick Hepburn did.

FIVE

"Not a Single Crumpled Rose Leaf"[1]

Do you remember the summer
Before the boy was born?
You rowed me up the river,
Between the filling corn,
I see you now as you smiled at me
And handed me ashore
Then we were happier lovers,
Than in the year before.

We wandered in the orchard
Beside the river brink
I saw the young bronze apples
And lingered there to think.
'The child will be here in the autumn,
When fruit is red on the boughs.'
You asked me why I was smiling
As we went into the house.

(from "The Song of the Old Mother")[2]

Patrick, who had pushed himself physically all his life, expected that his extraordinary young bride would keep up with him, and she did. She made physical treks that would have daunted lesser mortals, including the honeymoon in which they visited twenty-two Romanesque churches, getting to one of which had them floundering hip-deep in unexpected snow. The happiness in the first year seems to have come from a sense of adventure shared. They did much together, and what was not done together seems to have been done with the happiness of the other in mind.

On February 24, 1906, fifteen days into their marriage, they bought Emile Zola's *Le Rêve*, inscribing it "From each to each / from both to both," signing their names and dating it "on the fifteenth day of the 1st year of grace."[3] They took many books with them on their honeymoon and read to each other and alone.

Disagreements were few. On their wedding night Anna had been surprised that Patrick wanted to make love, since he had remained in her mind not only a sort of respite from William's advances but somewhat of a father figure. Anna was aware that Patrick (though from a courageous background that traced its lineage to Charlemagne and Robert the Bruce), was not easy or comfortable in his relations with women. One of his fellow solicitors had a daughter whom Patrick had admired; one of Patrick's cousins could never look at him without blushing. But he had not been sufficiently drawn to either of them. His mother, Ellen Gertrude Hepburn, nee Clay, had died when he was only nine years old and as the eldest male he had been deferred to all his life by most of the women in his family. So Anna might have been correct in seeing Patrick as uncomfortable about women, but she did not correctly read his desire. Patrick was taken aback by her surprise, but they quickly recovered.

Only once, on their honeymoon, was Patrick overcome by fear at this new state, marriage, asking Anna, "This is all very well, but how are we to meet the ordinariness of life?"[4] Anna was puzzled at this melancholy aspect of Patrick that she had never seen before. In this he showed more common sense than Anna who, it appears, did not know enough to fear the ordinary.

Once back in Bloomsbury they found "the sweetest pleasure" in making a home for themselves. Patrick found the move itself gravely unsettling, requiring as it did the shedding of years of accumulated things. He negotiated a lease that for £100 per year gave them three floors of rooms at

22 Tavistock Square (the square where Charles Dickens had written *Hard Times*, and not far from No. 52 where from 1924–1939 Leonard and Virginia Woolf ran their Hogarth Press). Anna and Patrick stayed at the Thackeray Hotel during the transition.

Each made contributions toward the other's happiness. Anna, who realized that Patrick found painful her discarding of the nonessentials at Great Ormond Street, took special care in selecting the "newest fabrics . . . [and] plain papers of a low tone of green . . . to put him in a condition of elegance."[5] Patrick purchased a huge filing cabinet and organized his scientific papers. Anna catalogued them. They saw themselves as a forward-thinking couple open to new ideas and resolutely rejecting a Victorian atmosphere. Knickknacks, variegated wallpapers, and potted palms had no place in their decorating scheme. If there was some lingering disorder, in their opinion this was offset by the presence of "the best books" that would make their home the equal of the best.[6]

The honeymoon had set the tone for the first months of the Hepburn marriage. For the most part, Patrick established the pace and the agenda and Anna met his expectations, throwing herself with vigor into all he proposed. She was busy, adored, and all possibilities seemed open to her and to them. Anna had the attitude that together, combining their strengths, they might make a career, achieve something admirable.

Patrick seems to have left the organizing and running of the house to Anna—understandable, since this is the way he was brought up. Patrick, of course, was accustomed to being surrounded by women who took it as their right to have servants and who, as Anna said, were able to give instruction in chilling monosyllables. But Anna, young, impetuous, and naive in the ways of running a household, was decidedly experimental in her organization. She employed a Dutch cook, then a Chinese cook, then a pensioned seaman who scrubbed out even the coal bin.

This was really Anna's first foray into gracious living. The rooms she'd had in England and France were not her own. Most of her earlier life had been spent in temporary surroundings. In Australia, up until the time of the house at Balmoral Bay, her suggestions for amenities were vetoed. At last, with her mother half a world away and with Patrick's proud acquiescence, she was fashioning a place for them both.

Along with many other of the well-off in Edwardian England, the Hepburns had the opportunity to indulge themselves. Patrick was making four hundred pounds a year on investments and was drawing twelve hundred pounds per year from the firm. Financing their trips to France, Rotterdam, and Amsterdam was no problem. Nell, who had once said of Anna, "She fascinates everyone but me," was not shy about saying that Anna had married Patrick for his money.[7] But Patrick, initially, at least, took great pleasure in Anna's expenditures for the house and paid for their trips without a qualm.

The spheres of business and family were kept separate. Perhaps this was not so much Patrick's wish as it was expedient appraisal. Patrick had even before their wedding taken her to his office in Cheapside. Known as one of the "oldest and quaintest" of the buildings in that area, one of its walls had withstood the Great Fire of London.[8] They had entered through a little passage (that also led to Simpson's restaurant) and in the privacy of the evening hours, Patrick showed Anna what provisions he had made for her in his will. But before they began their honeymoon trip they had also visited the office to receive congratulations. At Anna's instigation they uncorked a bottle of champagne from Simpson's to celebrate. At this, Cutcliffe, the resentful junior partner, had bent toward Anna and with oily surface goodwill admonished the new bride, "Now the less you have to do with your husband's business the better."[9]

None of Anna's relatives, who had made so many decisions for her when she first arrived, had attended the wedding and in these first months of her marriage they were conspicuously absent. But for entertainment she and Patrick played the piano, sang, read, and often spent Sundays visiting Hepburn relatives. Anna chafed at their formality; her verdict might best be summed up in the words of a later poem, "The Dull Entertainment:" "Here is too much food / For the talk to be good, / And too much hurrying of menial feet, / And too kind proffering of things to eat.[10] She found most of the Hepburns tiresome. But eighteen-year-old George Hepburn, one of Patrick's stepbrothers then between leaving Westminster and entering Technical College, enlivened their household for a time with his youth and good spirits; Anna liked him because he was bored with Hepburn family life and because he was reading *Das Kapital*.

Anna was still singing, encouraged by the fact that even so great a star as Nellie Melba had not had much of a career until she married. Patrick, however, had given up photographing churches since it was enough to see them with Anna. He continued to take pictures, however: "barges on the Thames, oaks in Epping Forest."[11] And one photograph of Anna, crowned and nude beneath a diaphanous drape, indicates an interest in subjects closer to home.

Anna conceived almost immediately. Patrick was tender since the doctor was worried about Anna's extreme sickness. Then, as if to top the first shock of unintended pregnancy, a second shock came. Mother was coming to visit.

Alice had cabled ahead about her trip, and Anna couldn't sleep the night before from sheer dread. In the carriage on the way to Tilbury to meet the ship Anna was so sick that she lay on the floor. When the ship docked,

> my mother greeted us in full tragedienne: "Anne, O Anne," she called from the rail of the steamer, straining towards me, her eyes full of the most devastating emotion.[12]

Anna saw her mother's arrival as completely shattering the peace of life with her husband. She had maintained a correspondence with her parents. She wrote long letters to her father full of the events surrounding the Russians and the exciting events she saw unfolding around her as news stories. Geoffrey, always triumphant at any connection to England, was especially proud because his Anna was part of the excitement. But from Alice, the news had been less heartening. "Dear Ede," she would write, and then begin "hysterical" outpourings of Geoffrey's offenses. Alice, though she would drink the occasional bottle of ink, was against alcohol, and she saw Geoffrey's drinking as evil and out-of-control.[13] Alice's letters were a sort of poison for her daughter because, as Anna states, "I was very attached to my father and fears about him took the strength out of me."[14] Now Anna would have to face her mother's real-life repertoire of emotional outpourings, threats, warnings, and unexpected acts. She would be upstaged in her own life; Alice's personality would work to ensure that.

Her mother swept into 22 Tavistock Square, all blonde curls and flowing trains and sporting the persona of "worn-out woman" needing assistance from her newly wealthy daughter. When that didn't work, Alice became a door-to-door bookseller and tried to persuade Anna to give her the names of Patrick's relatives so that she could make sales. Alice suggested that Patrick pay back the money they had spent on Anna's fare and lessons. "In short," said Anna, "she raised all the hell she could."[15] In a loud scene, with Anna hysterical and Alice unrepentant, Patrick finally asked Alice to leave. His action, however, caused the first rift between Anna and Patrick and marked a shift in the marital balance of power. Anna, distraught as she was over Alice's excesses, still retained a daughterly love, and the mix of shame and relief she felt at Alice's dismissal by Patrick registered deeply.

Alice, unfazed, went to live in Hampstead with a friend from her school teaching days. Anna and Patrick tried to get back into the state of marital bliss that had prevailed before Alice's arrival. Thinking that a brief vacation would bring the situation back in tune, they planned an outing.

Neither Patrick nor Anna had the least inclination to moderation. They went sailing the River Bure at the Norfolk Broads, visiting a church two miles distant from the shore where they had tied their small craft. Anna trudged along after Patrick, and all might have been well except that the dingy capsized when they attempted to get back to the boat. Anna was plunged into the water. A passing barge rescued her, but the shock of the experience, coming as it did on the heels of the upsetting incidents with Alice, proved to be too much.

Anna and Patrick returned to Tavistock Square and on September 2, 1906, she went into labor. When the pains were at their worst, Anna asked Patrick for a drink of brandy. He said, "I'd rather see you dead than drunk," which Anna said later was a "particularly horrific remark given that his own mother had died from complications after childbirth."[16] Hours later a premature daughter was delivered; the baby cried, but lived only a few minutes, and Anna was never allowed to hold her, never gave her a name. Even years later Anna lamented that she had not pressed hard enough to see the child but had let the little one go without ever seeing her face.

Alice, meanwhile, had stayed in Hampstead, enjoying a social life and the pleasures of London. When Patrick's relatives, realizing that Anna's mother was still in town, conveyed an invitation to the annual Hepburn garden party at the wonderful ivy-covered house of the Watford cousins, Patrick made clear that he didn't want Alice to come. He had learned of her most recent venture, a physiognomy parlor at the bottom of Regent Street, and he appreciated this as little as Geoffrey had once done. Finally, however, Alice set sail for New South Wales, to Wagga where she and Geoffrey had recently transferred.

During her mother's stay in England Anna had conceived again, but had miscarried. This second miscarriage had made Anna determined to go full-term with her third pregnancy. About the time of her mother's departure, pleading fatigue, she encouraged Patrick to go alone on a planned Easter cruise around England while she went to Margate. There she reveled in her condition and her freedom from exertion, and worked on harmony exercises at the beach. Her mother cabled Anna from the port of Marseille, "Luck in Thirds" and her concern seems to have cheered Anna considerably, coming as it did from a distance.

Patrick, who had never been as driven as Anna to have children, nevertheless felt pleased and proud when the great day, November 3, 1907, came. For her part, Anna said that this single day was "the happiest of my life."[17] Anna went through twenty-three hours of labor, "which I bore with all the patience I could summon. I read Shakespeare as long as I could, in defiance of the pain."[18] She had intended to go through childbirth without drugs, but gave in to her doctor's direction and took chloroform in the last stages of labor, "though it had been my ambition to sing as the child came into the world in emulation of the Mother of King Henry the fourth of France."[19] When she awoke, with Patrick's pride and the eleven-pound baby to keep her company, a new era had begun for her.

They named the baby James Geoffrey Cutcliffe Hepburn after Patrick's father, Anna's father, and Patrick's partner. And Anna threw herself into motherhood with an absolute passion.

"An Admirable Mother" (1907–1909)[1]

THE FOUNDLING

There is a little naked child at the door,
His name is Beauty, and he cries,
'Behold, I am born, put me where I can live.'
The old World comes to the door,
And thrusting out a lip, says only this,
'It is true that you are born, but how were you conceived?'

There is an owl upon an elder tree,
Who opening an eye, says only this.
'That is a lovely child!'
The old World said again,
'Yes! but how was he conceived?'

There is a gust of free wind
And high cloud voices call.
'What can you ask of Love but conception?

Men are born of blest love,
Of evil love is death.
There is but one pure love, the love of Child,
And that is sweet as a pine forest, clean as the sea:
Old World take all your children in.'[2]

Motherhood unleashed a philanthropic energy, a social conscience in Anna Wickham. Where did this come from? Her mother and father had always been generous to passing beggars or neighbors in need. But the influence of her father and mother can not totally account for Anna's new enthusiasm, though Alice's work with the public and Geoffrey's reading of philosophy certainly set the stage. Patrick, of course, had been raised to feel that his position required a certain obligation to society, but this was certainly not to be effected in a hands-on way. Anna's enthusiasm and concentration on motherhood *was* a hands-on affair, and it responded to a national focus on "motherhood" in medical, legislative, and social circles. Her work was also a compassionate response evolving from her earlier fears about being pregnant out-of-wedlock and her current joy at finally becoming a parent. Anna, much as she earlier took to heart the white and black circles demonstrating saints and sinners, now was converted to motherhood. She turned her home upside down to accommodate baby Jim and rushed into action to help other mothers.

Evenings at home were much different now. Anna, instead of being Patrick's conversational dinner companion, lay their baby Jim on a chair beside the table and focused her attention on that universe. Patrick wanted her to continue to be charmed by his talk of lantern slides, cycling exploits, and his growing interest in astronomy. She let her mutton get cold while attending to the baby. Anna knew she had to use the "nursery system"—nothing else would do for a Hepburn baby—but she co-opted the system by first reading all the baby lore she could get her hands on and then herself training their most recent cook—a fast learner—to be the nurse. The nurse turned out to be somewhat "waspish" in character, but since to Anna the worst nurse was one "overtrained . . . dull, and a poor chief friend for a little child," waspishness was probably preferable to dullness.[3] Not only did Anna take on this self-education and training, but having learned so much she branched out.

Anna focused her energy on motherhood and infant mortality, both much discussed in 1907. In the late nineteenth century, proponents of a vigorous imperialism had waved a red flag of warning. The nation's birth rates were declining and infant mortality rates were rising. Economically based arguments held that the population of a country was its "capital," one of the "national assets" on which the future depended. Thus not only middle-class proponents of the education of mothers, but also socialist advocates for improved working-class conditions and adherents to eugenics (improving hereditary qualities) all eventually converged on at least one salient point: the importance of mothers to the health of children. Laws were passed to improve conditions for childbearing and childrearing by providing meals for the needy, school medical inspections, and training for midwives. In 1906, the same year that Anna and Patrick married, the first National Conference for the Prevention of Infant Mortality had been held. Volunteer societies pooled the talents of doctors, clergymen, social workers, medical officers, and concerned ladies and gentlemen to spread the gospel of improved child welfare, household sanitation, and cleanliness. These volunteers fanned out into the slums posting notices of meetings, distributing leaflets on clean milk and breast-feeding, and offering prizes for healthy babies and infants, while in their conferences and in official enquiries they gave evidence about what they saw and learned.[4]

One of the societies that formed was the St. Pancras School for Mothers that opened in June 1907 in Chalton Street, Somers Town, only blocks away from what is now the new British Library and just an easy walk from Anna and Patrick's flat. The Babies Welcome and School for Mothers, as it was called, became influential far outside of its borders. In addition to influential support, it possessed a thoughtful and compassionate spokesman in Dr. Sykes, Medical Officer for St. Pancras, and a program that actually succeeded. Anna became a supporter.

In general the "Motherhood" movement, in the quest to improve infant health, wanted to educate mothers. Too often, however, its class-directed efforts (not many talked about ignorant middle- or upper-class mothers) tended to blame working-class mothers while paying little heed to poverty and other factors that hobbled the mothers' lives.

The new center in St. Pancras was "more comprehensive and firmly rooted in the realities of working-class life."[5] For example, it focused on making sure mothers were fed. The school's Medical Officer, Dora Bunting, felt that "women don't think enough of themselves." She came to the conclusion that women stinted on food for themselves to give more to their families, and even "didn't think of themselves worth cooking for, and only cooked if husband or children would also be there to eat."[6] Accordingly, in the school's cheerful dining room Bunting made sure that nursing mothers were given healthy meals and that the aim was for "friendly conversations" rather than intimidating and obtrusive instruction. The Welcome, as it was known, did provide mothers lessons on nutrition, cooking, sewing of baby clothes, care of babies, and consultations. But it regarded an open atmosphere as all important, and reasoned that the more mothers were drawn to the center on their own initiative, the better the chance of their profiting from the encounter. (The school also reached out to men with "Fathers' Evening Conferences"; coffee served and smoking allowed.) In these ways the Welcome stood in contrast to many other societies or official agencies whose representatives had an insufferable air of superiority and would, to the great hostility of families affected, barge into a family's home for an "inspection" without so much as a "by your leave."[7]

Simply by virtue of being a solicitor's wife Anna was welcomed into the organization, but her fellow committee members, although themselves a varied lot, probably initially had no idea of the complex view this young woman would bring to their proceedings. Some of them, like the Countess Russell, were aristocratic. Others, such as the Reverent D. Ensor Walters, had a religious bent to their helpfulness; Alys Russell, married to the mathematician and philosopher Bertrand Russell, took up positions more radical. Lady Henry Somerset was a temperance leader; Mrs. Humphrey Ware was an anti-suffragist.

But Anna was herself a descendent of a working-class family. Her grandmother Whelan, widowed at a young age, had successfully brought up three children in poor circumstances and had ultimately triumphed in the raising of a fourth child who had been born out-of-wedlock. With this example always in her mind, Anna held that many working-class mothers were remarkable for their tenacity, courage, and ability to cope with scarce resources. In this she would have been in direct opposition to some in the eugenics camp (those alarmed at survival and growth of poor families and who held that "the birth rate was declining fastest in the classes [i.e., the educated and well-to-do] whose contribution to the race and the nation was most important"), and she certainly opposed the view of many would-be educators who placed blame on "maternal ignorance and negligence."[8] Like Arthur Newsholme, a Medical Officer of the period who after careful statistical analysis saw "conditions of poverty as having a large influence" and who argued "against simple generalizations about the incapacity of working-class mothers," Anna felt that struggling mothers needed both aid and education.[9]

She became very active in the School for Mothers work. While she instructed mothers in "mothercraft" she also felt "that there might well be something that I could learn from poor working-class mothers."[10] In a lecture she gave (probably to prospective volunteers or perhaps to the staff) she skillfully defended the mothers with reason, fact, and example, conceding points where necessary and ultimately making the case that,

> We women who have the means to be good housekeepers and managers should co-operate with the mothers who are at a disadvantage.[11]

In another lecture Anna was asked to discuss, "The Effects of Gifts on the Recipient." Many of those in social work wanted to make sure that any help given to the poor or struggling would be "constructive" and not "destructive." In her lecture, Anna distinguishes between two types of giving, "One . . . buried deep in parenthood, the other . . with the sense of property." Anna called the second type "gifts of propitiation," given not for the sake of the recipient, but only as a byproduct of the purchase of some advantage (social, political, or spiritual) for the giver. This type of gift-giving she saw as dangerous and destructive because it often required the recipient to "subscribe [or pretend to subscribe] to a creed or to a system." Anna thought that gifts given in great kindness, "with tenderness and wisdom," and with the object that people "might become vigorous" were the best gifts.[12]

It must have been around this time that Anna raised eyebrows all around by an unusual action that backed up her contention about gift-giving. Marasmus, a condition of progressive emaciation in the young then responsible for many infant deaths, was linked to problems in the milk supply. Realizing that mothers might not have the equipment to boil and thereby purify the milk, in a moment of inspiration Anna hired a taxi, purchased shiny new saucepans and distributed them in the tenement houses—probably all done with a theatrical flair that would have made her mother proud. It was an original act. As her son Jim Hepburn would later point out, it was a gesture very characteristic of Anna, something no one else would even think of doing—and for that reason she would feel quite pleased; it wouldn't be lost on her that she was making this double contribution. . . . On the one hand, she'd make a point with her associates; on the other hand, she would genuinely feel that to get a clean saucepan would be pleasing and helpful to a working-class mother.[13]

Knowing that intense need existed in the "most appalling slums" only a half-mile away near the King's Cross Station, Anna took herself, in her elegant rustling black skirts, to where she could have an impact: helping children.

Anna, after she had become adept at caring for babies, even took sickly babies into her own nursery, hoping that the good food and healthy conditions there would renew their strength. Years afterward she realized that she may by that action have been putting her own infant son James at risk, but at the time it was impossible for her to see a pressing need and not respond to it.

Anna became friends with Miss Emily G. Colles, a woman ten years her senior who from 1908 to 1909 was "Lady Superintendent" in charge of the School for Mothers. Anna found it satisfying that Miss Colles was cousin to a peer and had a brother who wrote reviews of musical performances and was later music critic for *The Times*. Emily herself was soon to be an author when in 1912 she wrote *The Pudding Lady: a new departure in social work*.[14] As Anna had done with Tickie Curr and with May Mückle, she took Emily as a role model; as she had joined those earlier models in their respective passions for religion and for music, she now exalted Emily for her self-sacrifice and dedication and knowledge of the motherhood movement.

Miss Colles may have initially attracted Anna by her social involvement but it was her pottery making, her singing, and her appreciation of poetry that kindled in Anna some old dreams of a world outside of the regulated Hepburn environment.

For the regulated Hepburn environment was beginning to seem cloying, cold, discouraging, and even obstructionist to Anna in various ways. Patrick continued to instruct Anna in table manners. Anna's grandmother Harper had died a week after baby Jim's birth, but Patrick had for some months earlier been gently discouraging contacts with Anna's relatives. He had read her plays for children but had not been any more encouraging about them than William Ray had been. He accompanied her sometimes to singing engagements, but choked the air in the cab with his billowing pipe smoke. In the summer of 1908 when baby James was crawling about, Anna wanted to introduce him to the shore and rent rooms with the shush of the tide within earshot. Patrick, who would not hear of such a plebeian outing, arranged for a nursemaid for James and took Anna away from London. They traveled six weeks in all, mostly in Scotland, and by the time they returned Anna was "uninvigorated and almost sullen. My mind felt debauched by having its attention constantly directed, and its powers unused but absorbed."[15] She found she was slipping into a place where her sense of herself "became fretted and unharmonious." In a chance encounter on a railway platform a coffin being carried by shocked her into thinking "our love is dead."[16] Her health declined from episodes of bronchitis and dyspepsia so that she went to doctors and tried diets ranging from raw beef and coffee to lettuce and beans.

During the preceding months Emily Colles had become more and more a part of home life at Tavistock Square. Her presence continued to be both stabilizing and destabilizing. It is not clear if she actually lodged with them or if Anna brought her there so often she became like a permanent houseguest. But the three of them were on very easy terms. Though she was dismayed when they smiled at each other, Anna encouraged Emily in duets with Patrick, whom she had taught to sing. She mocked Emily for her "badly fitting blouses" but admired her for her silken social ways. Emily entertained Patrick in a way that Anna was no longer willing to do but their interaction opened up the void Anna may have been sensing. Ultimately, she used Emily as a confidant and wrote poems about Patrick "which were a confession of the entirely bogus quality of that relationship."[18]

What Anna may have suspected, but ignored from the time of the stillbirth, was impossible to hide from the spirit of her imagination: Their marriage, their relationship, had become unsatisfactory. Anna had thrown herself into mothering James, working with the School for Mothers, and even taking sick slum babies into her nursery. Yet motherhood and its related activities were not enough to keep her content.

> In spite of my interest in the child, I began to want to follow my own devices. I needed to talk to Patrick as well as have him talk to me. He became disturbed and disoriented by the rapacity of my call on his intellectual cooperation. He liked to instruct me and tell me what he knew, but when my curiosity passed the bounds of his knowledge he was discountenanced and at a loss. Our life was easy, but without ambition or plan. I felt like an eternal pensionnaire at a creditably equipped seaside boarding house.[18]

When Anna and Patrick met, he was—as he was trained to by his public school background—unconsciously displaying a new type of man to Anna. Anna had never met someone who sounded, acted, or moved as he did. Quite distracted and pleased by her own accomplishments at that time, however, it only came upon her gradually how different Patrick's history was from her own. Patrick had grown up with a green lawn, garden, and seven servants. He had been brought up under the assumption that he would take his place in the Hepburn constellation, not in the leather and skin trade that had established his forefathers, but in the law, following in the footsteps of his father and grandfather. Though Patrick had told Anna about his family, it was his photography, his astronomy, and his bicycle treks across the moors that kept him and Anna talking for hours on end. Since Patrick abhorred "swank" above all, and since he wanted to fashion an identity for himself outside the confines of his own family, he had often downplayed his heritage. So the ancestral home, the party in Glasgow with kilted businessmen, the visit to the busy maiden aunts, the history-filled halls of his practice in the city only slowly made their combined imprint upon Anna. Only gradually did Anna become aware of the depth of difference between her freer colonial upbringing and the rigorous standards of conduct and propriety that Patrick had been held to. At first, exhilarated by Anna's youth, her mixture of deference and amusement toward him, he was all for playful behavior. He had not objected when on the train Anna trailed violets in his moustache; he frolicked with children in a country church tower when he was bursting with undeclared love for Anna. But with the birth of his firstborn son following only a few years after the death of his own father the sum total of Patrick's heritage hit him full force. There were certain standards.

For Anna, it was shortly after baby James's birth that the strain of living up to Hepburn standards (good, not ostentatious, a distinction very difficult for a girl whose mother had always picked out the clothes for "her baby" and had chosen unconventional household furnishings) had begun to show. She had not immediately recognized in the symptoms of "fatigue and suppression" any deep disturbance because, as she said, "I had my mind's surfaces arranged in the pattern of a devoted wife."[19] But she had begun to deeply feel the lack of a creative outlet. She had her singing, but her acting and writing abilities were not being used. She remembered her mother, whose volcanic energies unleashed destructive fire into the family circle unless they were put in service to some major purpose. Anna had always felt that it would have been better for her as a child if her mother had been on the stage.[20] Perhaps this is why at the time or even before the School for Mothers work had become a passion, Anna had trumped marriage routine with a surprising card she had kept hidden in her hand.

She wrote a sort of study in madness, a dramatic monologue on the nature of hysteria;

It concerned the shooting of a lover, by a woman who had been outraged in every part of her mind and heart.[21]

Without telling Patrick anything, she auditioned for an agent and was offered a job performing the piece at a theatre in Manchester. After panicking thoughts, she began to see that what for her was merely taking an initiative would seem to others a rash and renegade act: who would take care of the baby—did she want to leave Patrick—would he accept an actress as wife? She took three-month-old James with her and went to the agent to back out. They released her of course, but she was mortified to hear the agent's associates coarsely joking that the baby she carried in her arms was his. The study in hysteria was put aside and Anna redoubled her efforts at motherhood. But however briefly it had surfaced, a covert current of unhappiness, and perhaps some deeper disturbance, had made itself felt.

Sex was an overt problem. Though Patrick and Anna were still lovers enough that Patrick "bought stockings and, dressing me, kissed my feet," Anna was not interested in "erotic calisthenics," thought that sex should be "pleasureless," and wanted to have a family. Patrick, at least as Anna explains him, seems to have thought it was a "duty" that sex be frequent and wanted "love experience" only to make up for having lived a relatively chaste life; his desire lacked passion, she thought, and babies interested him little. Anna felt that her days were "deficient in my intimacy with my husband."[22] She later mused in her autobiography, echoing what was being said by Margaret Sanger, that

My proper function as a woman was to accumulate energy, hold it still in me, and transmit it to my husband by the techniques of love so that he could shape our family's future with the welded power of the two of us.[23]

Anna continues, "But I was not suitably mated. . . ." Even so, in January 1909 she became pregnant again. Her health was not good and they feared there might be, as was said then, a hole in her lungs. Patrick, who along with many medical experts at the time saw travel as a cure-all, arranged a trip to Madeira for Anna. He had not learned his lesson from the Scottish fiasco, which was that Anna had traveled so much as a child that she did not share his joy in seeing new horizons. In addition, a trip meant more time away from her fifteen-month-old son. The trip did do some good for Anna, however, though nothing like what Patrick may have imagined, or ever learned of afterward.

The night before departure she and Patrick had walked around the ship taking the air. Suddenly in front of them was a woman, the daughter of a fellow solicitor and the only girl ever to interest Patrick before Anna. In a great show of pleasure and "what wonderful luck," Patrick agreed that of course Anna would travel with their party of three (parents and daughter) to quaint Portugal. If changing her destination were not enough, Patrick left behind his bowler hat in Anna's cabin as another, wordless, chaperon.

But by the time the ship was underway the next morning Anna met a "fine, witty, horse-racing Irishman" on deck. Snubbing the oh-so-correct party of three, Anna joined the Irishman for lunch at a distant table. Though "the solicitor and his family could not have understood what the Irishman and I said to one another, . . . rocks and stones must have understood my laughter."[24] One of her later poems, "There came a lazy Celt, / Sunny and gay, / And he caused black ice to melt / With the things that he did say" probably recounts this episode. It ends with the Celt singing: "O! Shelter in me, Sweet, / And let me give you rest, / For I love your hair and your feet, / And your pleasant moving breast."[25]

Before the ship docked to discharge its Lisbon passengers Anna had declared her freedom from the staid spirit of the Hepburn milieu. Alone in her cabin, she masturbated to imaginary scenes of lusty seduction.

> On the return cruise the Irishman was on the ship and we laughed together again. He was not in the least physically attracted to me, and would have found my erotics amateurish. I coveted the professionalism of a woman of the streets and longed to travel on with him for some wildness and emancipation in Dublin. Ruefully, I took the train to London.[26]

Back in Tavistock Square toddler James and husband Patrick welcomed Anna back. She, however, was cool, and took advantage of Patrick's workday absences to knit a fine pair of green socks and send them to the Irishman. Then she banished "lust and tenderness" from my heart and "set myself to my duty as wife and mother."[27] With a second child on the way, Anna and Patrick decided that a move out of the confines of Bloomsbury was in order and began the search for a new home.

SEVEN

"I tried to build perfection with my hands" (1910–1912)[1]

J ohn, Anna and Patrick's second son, was born on October 25, 1909, at 49 Downshire Hill, Hampstead. Though the Tavistock Square flat had been attractive for its relative closeness to Patrick's professional life in the city, for the children they wanted something more. Hampstead's hill location overlooking London, the cleanness of its water and air, and the park lands of Hampstead Heath drew them there.[2] And in a cozy Regency house they found a place that would suit them, a house beloved by its inhabitants then and now, set in a half-acre of land enclosed by a handsome weathered wall with roses clinging to the brick.[3] The cherry trees, old residents from the time when much of Downshire Hill was market gardens, bloomed frothy white in the spring. Anna, who shared the Victorians' fascination with fairies, saw plenty of imaginative potential in the boughs.

The three-story house, nestled below the street, was early nineteenth century, of local brick. Stuccoed in a light cream color, with iron balustrades at the French windows and a collection of tall chimney pots striving up from the slate roofs, it connected with the village by a sort of bridge. The front of 49 Downshire Hill looked south out into the garden. The back of the house was on the street side and an enclosed entryway, in appearance much like an expanded sentry box, extended from the back of the second story to the sidewalk. There were only a few bedrooms, not a straight door in the place, and, as Anna wrote,

> My house is damp as damp can be,
> It stands on London clay.
> And if I move unthinkingly
> It shakes in a most alarming way.
> Mayhap it will all come down on me
> One day.[4]

But its thick walls, low ceilings, and sturdy board floors, the privacy of its garden, and the sunlight that shone into the rooms in the mornings convinced Anna and Patrick to take it. They could sit before a magnificent fireplace that covered twenty-five feet of the east wall of the living room, fill the shelves with the books and journals they had collected and enjoy the house's charm.

The Regency houses in Hampstead's South End neighborhood were and are a varied and handsome lot. The area has a reputation for attracting people who respond to beauty. Only a few streets away in John Street/Albion Grove (in the next year to be renamed Keats Grove) was the house where in 1819 a consumptive John Keats had, after his breakfast, set a chair on a grassy spot under a plum tree and wrote his "Ode to a Nightingale." On Downshire Hill and nearby lived, or soon would, artists who were helping to change the course of painting in the first part of the twentieth century, such as the organizer of Post-Impressionist shows, painter Roger Fry, and artists Mark Gertler and Isaac Rosenberg (the latter also to emerge as the writer of some of the most powerful poetry of World War I). At 47 Downshire Hill the studios of the Carline family were soon to attract Stanley Spencer and his contemporaries studying at the Slade School. Gaetano Meo, Italian artist and earlier a favorite model for the Pre-Raphaelites, lived just down the street. No. 49 Downshire Hill put Anna in the middle of a vibrant artistic community with the added attraction of the Heath just a few minutes away. For from No. 49, looking one block down the gentle slope of the street, they could see the steeple and clean-lined facade of Hampstead's St. John's Church, and far beyond that, the spire of St. Michael's, Highgate, marking out the Heath's expanse between.

Once the hunting grounds of King Henry VIII, later the thin glacial soil of much of Hampstead Heath provided a grazing common and thus early protection against development. Eventually public love of the space and private beneficence combined to set aside the nearly 800 acres comprising what is now the largest park in any metropolitan area in the world. Painters such as Constable had found inspiration in the curved hills and open, ever-changing skies. Dickens wrote of it. The site of pleasure fairs, it once accommodated 100,000 visitors on a single holiday. At other times it was so peaceful that strollers on the hill crests could hear Big Ben to the south, tolling the hours. The mirror-like waters of the Hampstead and Highgate ponds, reservoirs of the River Fleet, reflected the willows' first bursts of spring green and their long-lasting cascades of autumn gold. For Anna and Patrick the Heath was everything they needed—a place for the children to play and wide-open spaces for walking, swimming, and stargazing.

Having early been firmly told by her husband's partner to keep out of the family law business, Anna had instead in their first years of marriage focused on fine-tuning Patrick's other pursuits. She organized his slides, had his journals bound, and suggested ways to polish his lectures, once writing one for him. (She even would have had him run for politics, but Patrick found politics a dirty business and refused.) In seeking to push and encourage Patrick, Anna was destined to be thwarted. First of all, Patrick found it condescending to be "encouraged" to do anything; he had been an achiever before Anna came on the scene, and he continued to pursue his interests. Raised to a life of self-denial in the midst of comfort, Patrick reined himself in on certain expenditures, for example, on clothing purchases. But in photography, scientific discovery, and athletics he found pleasure and in these he set himself few limits and needed no encouragement from Anna. Secondly, when Patrick did take up Anna's suggestions, he would embrace them thoroughly and take credit for the ideas.[5] During this period of time Anna felt, more often than not, a sense of frustration in their dealings with each other. Marriage, she had hoped, would be a partnership, a striving toward goals together. Patrick, however, had his own agenda.

The Hampstead Scientific Society had just acquired an eight-inch reflecting telescope for its observatory on Hampstead Heath.[6] Within months Patrick was instrumental in setting it up and the telescope was in place to allow fascinated observers to follow the path of Halley's Comet across the 1910 night sky. In January his paper on "certain peculiarities of illumination of the moon's disc when in eclipse" had appeared in the Journal of the British Astronomical Association (B.A.A.). Later, during the apparition of Mars, he set up a camp bed at the observatory, only sleeping between observations.[7] In April of 1911 he was elected a Fellow of the Royal Astronomical Society; in October, he became the director of the Saturn section of the B.A.A.; six months later, when in mid-April of 1912 he was in Chartres making photographs of an eclipse at the central phase, his paper on an earlier solar eclipse was published. Other papers, on Venus and Sirius B, later appeared.

The introspective brooding that Anna felt had assailed Patrick after their first son's birth had spun itself out into a torrent of investigation. Patrick's childhood astronomy had begun when through dint of long pleading and personal scrimping he had bought a three-inch Wray telescope. The years from 1910 to 1912 were crucial ones for Patrick as an astronomer, for in 1911 he purchased a twelve-and-a-half-inch Calver from his mentor Arthur Cottam, F.R.A.S., and in 1912 added a twelve-inch clock-driven equatorial reflector so that many of his observations could be made from the privacy of their own garden. His continuous activity was the marvel of his fellow astronomers who talked with awe of his ability to go to the office during the day and make observations at night.

He also was experiencing difficulties, however. The first was the death of his aunt Mary Elizabeth Hepburn (nee Duncan), widow of his uncle William, on January 27, 1911 at her nearby home, 13 Well Walk, Hampstead. Patrick had admired her and in fact she seems to have been a point of pride for the family who was conscious that hers was "the best ordered of the Hepburn houses. Mary had never in all her history run out of her special brand of champagne."[8] She was just one of his father's generation dying: two of Patrick's Hepburn uncles died in just the three years after he and Anna married, and his flamboyant aunt-by-marriage, world traveler and author Jane Ellen Duncan, was buried in Naples, Italy, in May 1909. For a man convinced of the importance of history, the loss of these upholders of hereditary glory must have been considerable.[9] Then in June of 1912 Patrick received word from the Sudan of the death of Jonathon King Hepburn, his twenty-seven-year old unmarried stepbrother, a Forest Service Inspector at Wau, on the Blue Nile. Jonathon had been Patrick's cotrustee in overseeing the money bequeathed for the care of their sister

Frances, slowly dying of a disease of the spinal column.[10] Patrick would now have more of the responsibility. His supportive family structure was diminished at the same time the pace of his other activities was increasing.

Where did all this leave Anna? It left her alone. According to son Jim's later account, even when the family took meals together, Patrick often had a scientific book propped in front of him at the table. His life was a series of briefs, wills, contracts, letters, and meetings followed by celestial observations, mathematical equations, writing, and meetings. And in 1912–1913 more meetings, when forty-year-old Patrick, who had been in the Livery since 1894, was elected "Master" of the Curriers' Company, one of the City Companies so important in London's history.[11] This was in addition to his Freemasons' meetings; he was initiated in October, 1910. In his free time he welcomed visits from his siblings and step-siblings. Where did all this leave Anna? Disaffected.

After her 1908 sojourn in Portugal, Patrick had met Anna's return train in Victoria Station expecting to find a loving wife restored to health and compliant mind by days of rest. He would have been better off to have sent himself on a holiday. For he found Anna a sardonic and cold young woman who had resented his manipulation of her journey and read the class-conscious H. G. Wells on the beach at Mount Estoril. To top it off, if he had only known, she had become infatuated enough with the Irishman to knit him green socks.[12] Though the shipboard infatuation had quickly passed she had restarted her relationship with Patrick, not with lust, love, or tenderness, but with "duty" foremost in her mind. That Anna later wrote with happiness of the 1909 move to the Downshire Hill house is probably because there she first realized that she might go her own way and pursue her own interests as Patrick was avidly doing. It was while she lived at 49 Downshire Hill (from 1909–1919) that she became a poet.

Anna was fighting the loneliness of a lady living in a new place with only a few social connections other than her husband's. Her grandfather, Edwin Harper, then nearing eighty, lived nearby in Maitland Park Gardens. She did see Auntie Gert, who had married a baker and painted lampshades beautifully, and even Aunt Tid, who brought her three children to play in the garden. But Patrick most often discouraged contact with her relations and preferred that she move in his family circle.

She tried her best. In the summer of 1910 Patrick's cousins Eleanor, Kate, and Margaret organized the annual Hepburn garden party at Watford. Against the backdrop of a huge ivy-covered porch four long rows of adults assembled for a photograph. Of the few children pictured, two of them were residents of Downshire Hill: Patrick settled sunny-haired John on his knee while Patrick's sister Nell (now happily married to her beau from the Choral Society) held three-year-old James tightly in her lap. Anna is seated far from Patrick but in the same front row, wearing a heavy dark coat. She would later write in her autobiography that she came to see Patrick's ultra-correct manners as "a little too good to be perfect. He never looked really happy in God's world and in his care to be correct . . . he looked almost as if he were suppressing a hiccough."[13] This seems to be the predominant mood of the guests in their high white collars: chin-bumping ruffles for the women, starched bands stiff as iron for the gentlemen.

Anna hoped to keep their children joyful and free of a too-strict mechanistic discipline. When it had become apparent that Jim was going to speak with a stutter (later overcome by acting classes), Anna felt that this indicated that her own earlier approach to child-rearing was too intense. She relaxed and instead of an instructional tack she organized games and reading in the nursery, and "happy treks" on the Heath.[14] She sought to understand them and to stimulate their senses. She would improvise poetry for them on the spot, and composed poetry about them also. John she called "The apple-blossomy king."[15] Though in one poem she says that he was "born of sorrow" (unlike Jim who was "born of my content"), John as a toddler comes into most of her poems as a golden child, inventive and imaginative, defined as an artist just as surely as she sees the civic planner and tireless worker in first-born Jim.[16]

Much of Anna's time was spent running a household, dealing with the children's nurse and the cook, the cook-general, the maid, and the gardener.[17] That her and Patrick's upper-middle-class household had servants was normal for that time (when 46 percent of the population—most of them women—were working in domestic service).[18] But though Anna had once thrown her cook's dinner out the window to make a point and assert authority, she really was unable, in most cases, to see or treat her servants as anything but people with personalities, potential, histories, idiosyncrasies. She wrote the servants into poems; she undoubtedly gave them more than Patrick would have condoned, in fact she called their home "a servants [sic] Paradise."[19] The exception, as earlier mentioned, was nurses: those she scorned as "an ugly noxious race, / Soft in the head, and hard in heart and face."[20]

Even the everyday running of a household with a husband who took no notice could be an enervating and unrewarding task, but Anna's job was compounded by health problems—bouts of bronchitis and her unspoken complaints: "intellectual, and emotional and erotic frustrations."[21] But her occasional feelings of distaste for Patrick had not yet turned to fear, and her anger at him could change by nightfall "to charm and endearments."[22] She could occasionally call up the memory of their first months together, "How kind he was to me, how utterly devoted to my happiness, and when I was weak he carried me in his arms."[23] Her chief relief was the antics of her children, with whom she continued to feel delight. But, like her mother, she had an abundance of "initiative," a fine mind too little used and a store-house of suppressed energy.

She continued to keep her hand in the School for Mothers and her work there provoked her into at least one poem about the death of children and the hard-heartedness of a class-based outlook. In it she disparages the upper class who "whispered apart" saying, "Seeing that the man is poor, and the woman sick, / It is well that the child is dead." Anna saw tragic nobility in the lower-class, powerless, grieving mother who, "being sick gave only her love."[24]

The idea of class was never too far from her mind. The visits to and from the Hepburn family had created in Anna a special kind of anxiety. She obsessed about their finesse with champagne and camembert and tried to find the same "right" kind of paint that they used. She feared she was not "dustless" and orderly enough for their critical eyes, though Patrick himself had never minded dust and accumulation and had appreciated Anna's taste in furnishings. In tiny script she obsessively filled up a "Where is it" book with the location of every item in her home.[25] She wore stays, following the fashionable silhouette, though she felt her body "crushed" by them. Her days she found too much occupied with being "a lady" and "buying fine clothes, and fittings for the house."[26] She saw how overattention to a household could kill the imagination, as in these lines from her well-known poem, "The Fired Pot,"

> And I have watched the women growing old,
> Passionate about pins, and pence, and soap,
> Till the heart within my wedded breast grew cold.[27]

But there seemed no respite for her.

During the baking heat of the summer of 1911, Patrick, pursuing once again his ideal vacation, took Anna to the steep rocky cliffs of Sark, an island in the English Channel, when she would have liked to be at Brighton with their sons.[28] In 1912 they did all go to Rye for a vacation that was more Anna's style, staying in a house with a clear sea view. But, inexplicably, instead of Anna's accompanying the boys to the beach every day, the boys remember it was the servants Lizzie and Ellen who took them on the little railway that led to Camber Sands.[29]

Probably in late 1912 or early 1913 Anna went to Ceylon to meet her father and travel there. By February 9, Anna and Patrick's seventh anniversary, both Geoffrey and Anna had returned to England (Geoffrey gave his niece Miriam, Aunt Tid's youngest daughter, *Wuthering Heights* for her ninth birthday on that same day). Hardly anything is known about the Ceylon trip except that to a friend Geoffrey expressed a profound disappointment in his daughter.[30] Perhaps Anna, pressed more and more into an appreciation of Patrick's hereditary line, had become ashamed of her father's work. Perhaps she was even angry that neither she nor Geoffrey had made the "success in the arts" that he urged her to achieve.[31] But Anna also says that she told her father that her situation was affecting her creativity: "Observe this atmosphere / I can't write here."[32]

Several lines in Anna's "Inspiration" probably sum up the tenor of Anna's struggles during those years:

> I have tried to build perfection with my hands
>> And failed.
> Then with my will's most strict commands
>> And naught availed.[33]

In a photograph taken in 1911, Anna's full dark eyebrows form a frame for her large, wide-set eyes. Long dark hair, fitting her face like a scarf, is gathered at the nape of her neck. Her mouth has a slight smile and the lips are parted slightly. An embroidered satin jacket falls in folds off her shoulders and there is a soft look about her. Are the dark circles under her eyes a matter of photographic atmosphere or a symptom of fatigue? We don't know the occasion for the photo, but what is clear is that another Anna Wickham is emerging, a very different woman from the one in the garden party picture of 1910 where her voluminous dark coat, floor-length skirt, and high-necked blouse gave little indication of imagination, movement, vulnerability, or risk-taking. By about 1912 the satin Anna Wickham, casting off her committee woman, dedicated-solicitor's-wife persona, has made a radical change.

Anna's youthful interest in poetry had been rekindled initially by Emily Colles, her friend, the supervisor at The Mothers' Welcome. Anna had been moved to poetry by her love and appreciation of motherhood and had begun a poetic discussion of marriage. Now Anna took on religion too, proposing to start the "Church of God in Life."[34] Much as her mother would later cable her father from the United States saying that she was going to establish a new religion and would Geoffrey like to be a disciple (the answer was no), Anna found the religion of the Anglican church and the Wesleyans, the religion of the Baptists and the Roman Catholics, in fact all the Christian churches, deficient. In poetry, she worked out the intellectual underpinnings of a creed, though she did no proselytizing. Her point was simple: religion housed in buildings was dead. Christ, for whom she could argue forcefully, was and should be a god of the streets—in the people and for them. And chance and change (she wasn't her father's evolutionist daughter for nothing) were to be the solace of mankind—not his or her ruin.[35]

Anna decided to have a selection of all the poems she had been writing made up into a book, her first book of poetry. It would be a departure from any run-of-the-mill solicitor's wife's thoughts and, whether she knew it or not, would establish not only this difference but make evident the growing distance between her and Patrick. That Anna knows this is risky business is shown in the poem "Divorce." The sheltered valley of a lonely love is "smothering," but on the "rock heights" of desire there is either "victory or quick death." Whether or not Anna is speaking biographically in this poem, she draws a compelling picture of the pain of someone trapped in an unfulfilling marriage, making this poem a frequently anthologized one to the present day.[36]

Anna took twenty poems to the Women's Printing Society Ltd., a firm busy with, though not limited to, women's issues of the time, including suffrage.[37] (Their male detractors criticized them in *Print: A Journal for Printing-House Employees* for not paying "a fair wage" and for taking jobs away from workers in the Compositors' Union.)[38] Anna's poems were set into a slim volume with no frills. No devices enliven the dun-colored paper covers, only the words:

SONGS
JOHN OLAND

Why a man's name and why this man's name? Of course it had been quite common in the nineteenth century (witness the Brontes' first efforts and George Sand's choice) for a woman to choose a masculine pseudonym. And perhaps Anna thought the idea of a male hand penning such poems as her "All Men to Women" would be more convincing to her readers. But it is likely that Anna wanted the protection of a pseudonym not only should the verses fail but should they succeed. Chary of trouble with Patrick, who as his various club activities increased seemed more and more insistent that his wife keep a fairly conventional profile, she might have seen a pen name as an essential maneuver.

Whatever the reasons for her decision, her choice of name works on several levels. When May Mückle had come to Sydney on tour she left her cello behind for a time while she and Anna explored the subterranean wonders— the "fluted columns, glorious draperies, coral bowers and fairy grottoes"— of the Jenolan Caves in the Blue Mountains of New South Wales.[39] The pen name John Oland, commemorating that subterranean visit, is symbolically significant of Anna's beginning to address the deep and complex issues of her life.

The book probably was printed in 1911, though this has proved difficult to verify.[40] 1911, the year of Grace Wiederseim's *Ducky Duddles*, Beatrix Potter's *The Tale of Timmy Tiptoes,* and Frances Hodgson Burnett's *The Secret Garden* was also the year for such tomes as *The Woman's Book* (everything a woman ought to know) and *The Fifty Year Diary*, both of which seemed to speak to a public full of faith in information and confidence in the future.

But poetry, as well as much else, was about to undergo a revolution. A generation of people who had inherited Tennyson, embraced the, Brownings, and wrestled with Matthew Arnold would soon see changes in the appearance, the sound, the rhythm, and even the subject matter of poetry. The appearance of Anna's experimental little book (some of it "free verse," a term borrowed from the late nineteenth-century French *Vers Libre* movement) before the First World War places it in the vanguard of early modernist poetry.

Anna, though she does not forgo such old forms as the sonnet, ballad, and blank verse, with their specific and predictable meters and/or rhymes, is working in a new spirit. "A little growth" she begs in the last line of "Song of the Low-Caste Wife." She accuses "the blood of old kings" (the upper classes—and Patrick) of possessiveness, saying: "Your people thinking of old victories, lose the / lust of conquest, / Your men guard what they have, / Your women nurse their silver pots." And in another poem, "Surrender," her passionate metaphors ("I am myself earthquake and eclipse / And all thick darkness and rending grief") are ones that even "rocks and stones" could understand. Patrick had never taken her verse writing seriously. Her Australian plays for children he had seen as sweet and harmless exercises for the elocution classes. He perhaps had been ignorant of much of what she had been writing recently. So the publication of these new "songs" was not only an irritant to Patrick, busy with his own pursuits, but a threat to his control as Anna's desire to maintain an independent spirit appeared in print.

As Patrick's resulting demands for conformity increased, Anna reached a dangerous impasse. When her mother came to England for a visit Anna kept the arrival a secret, though she installed her in a room in the house next door. "The shades of the prison house" were closing in on her as Patrick increasingly frowned and looked suspiciously at any lighthearted-ness on her part. When Patrick brought in an astronomer friend to dine with them she played the compliant wife, all the time straining to under-stand how her life once so full of promise and surprise could have come to such a lonesome pass. In her poem, "The Explainers," she frets, "They have given every star its place, / They have made a wearying diagram of what was boundless space."[41]

EIGHT

May, 1913

Patrick's astronomer friend came to dinner. And again. And the more he visited the less attention he paid to the movement of stars, charmed as he was by the enigmatic woman that was his host's wife. There was some tension brewing in this Anna, some emotions that were being almost painfully held in check, yet she presented a serene face. Their household seemed to lack for nothing and she had pride in the shining silverplate and the beautiful garden. But at times she spoke as though she envied the beggars on the Heath their freedom and their lack of possessions. She dropped a hint that it was through her prodding that Patrick had begun to go to the same tailor as the Prince of Wales. But her own dress betrayed some dichotomy of spirit. Sometimes she dressed in beautiful fabrics in jewel-like colors, other times, with a hem undone, a slip trailing, the buttons off her reefer coat, she was more than casual, almost aggressively careless about her appearance. In the astronomer's opinion, she seemed starved for intellectual companionship, though she and her husband read together on a Sunday, could quote some of the same sonnets, and snapped up the newest books the moment they came out. Patrick had written to Anna about this new acquaintance when she was visiting Colombo. The astronomer, as heir to a large fortune, had a private observatory and the means to make things happen, both of which Patrick thought worth mentioning to Anna.[1]

It was when the astronomer came for a time to stay at 49 Downshire Hill that the trouble began. Though Patrick was oblivious at first, Anna was not. But she sought to ignore the man's interest in her and kept up the conversation. In one instance she quoted some lines of her own poetry as she took the guest on a walk across the Heath. As the astronomer was also a poet (though "a bad one," Anna later said), this provided a strong point of common interest. Later they went together to the Egyptian Gallery of the British Library and also stopped in so that Anna could introduce the astronomer to her mother, recently arrived on a visit to England.

The astronomer was warm toward her mother, "yellow hair and all" and Anna appreciated this, especially in light of Patrick's view of Alice. Patrick had developed such an antipathy toward her that Anna had thought it best to conceal both her mother's arrival, and her lodgings, improbably, right next door.

Anna had not meant to entice the astronomer. She later said, "I wanted some one, any one, to exchange lyrical ideas with me." She had become so lonely that she even took her sympathetic servant as a confidant, a breach of decorum that she knew Patrick would abhor if he knew.[2]

Eventually, "Mr. Carrington" attempted to take Anna in his arms. He yearned to set up "a new culture" in a nearby village and knew she was just the one to help him do it. When that didn't move her, he wrote to her proposing they go together to Spain. But the pages of his ardent suit fell into Patrick's hands.

When, years before, Anna had made what she called, "the most disastrous decision of my life," letting Patrick send his sister Nell to live with her in Paris and essentially become a chaperon protecting Patrick's interests, the result had been that Anna was unable to pursue the bohemian life and had been stifled by Ellen's sense of what was right and correct.[3] Now Patrick, who saw himself as one who had rescued her from her family and herself, turned a cold and appraising eye toward her with Mr. Carrington. It seemed to him as if she were again veering too much toward freedom. Patrick's monitoring was meant to keep her more and more chastened. He had no intention of letting his charming, captivating, troublesome, and worryingly restless wife harm her reputation—or his. Patrick also knew the law: adultery in women was grounds for divorce, though a man's adultery had to be "combined with cruelty or desertion."[24] And the father had a right to the children.

In the ensuing confrontation Anna told Patrick that her mother was next door. Patrick rushed over with his rival's letter, convinced that he would discover the truth from Alice. Alice, however, read it and concluded no adultery had taken place, an opinion that Patrick came only grudgingly to accept. But his accusations had already been made and his charges had wounded Anna who had been "so much Marguerite that I was frightened of so much infidelity as lunching alone with Mr. Carrington in Soho."[5] She was beside herself:

> The storms that rose in me from my husband's injustice had an added abandon from the nausea I had experienced in his embrace. I had been accused of desecrating my home—my children's home, the home that I loved and of which I was proud. . . . [6]

Patrick and Anna continued fighting. On a Friday evening in May, 1913, Patrick attempted to drag Anna into the house from the garden where she had earlier been singing "Home Sweet Home" at the top of her lungs. In the uproar, Anna says, she put her fist through a glass door. A doctor was called in to dress the cut that Anna received in trying to resist, but she did not tell him that she had gotten it in self-defense.

The events of the next few days moved quickly.

Patrick ordered her to stay at home. On Saturday morning she saw an opportunity and rushed out, intending to go to friend Philippa Nevinson in Golders Green. Policemen were called in to bring her back. In the afternoon Anna escaped, seeking refuge with a friend, but the woman, "a Russian woman painter who had been ten years a prisoner in Siberia" alerted Patrick, who burst in with two doctors trailing behind. Anna's general practitioner, one of the two, insisted on certifying Anna immediately. The other doctor, however, a specialist who knew and admired Anna's book of poetry, successfully argued against taking the case before a magistrate that night. They both ignored Anna's request to have a woman doctor be brought in to assess her. On Sunday Anna suggested desperately to Patrick that they go down to Bloomsbury and look at the rooms in Great

Ormond Street where they had first found happiness. But once there, Patrick, probably grimly offended at her rising panic, left her and went to his office to work on some business. She became distraught and followed him. They returned home together that evening, Patrick repeating, "It's one of your [mental] symptoms that you think I don't understand you."

On Monday Anna left a note for Patrick:

> I can't stand this any longer. You put a person of my temperament on a sofa, rob me of initiative and then, by suggestion, give me every kind of mental aberration under the sun. I have only an ordinary attack of 'wanting to write songs' (laugh if you will), to all this you add domestic ferment, and now you call in two medical spectators. I am a lot saner than most people. I can't stand it any more, goodbye.[7]

When Patrick found the note he acted quickly. The tension had been building for years. As did her mother, Anna required an outlet for her energies outside the narrow sphere of a solicitor's wife. But her recent activities had gone beyond the bounds of acceptable behavior as far as Patrick was concerned. In his opinion a respectable woman didn't write verse exposing the tragic underpinnings of a marital mismatch; a respectable mother didn't take such an active hand in the raising of her children, but left them more often with nursemaid and nanny; above all, a respectable wife didn't go about having her husband's friends fall in love with her. It was all too much. Patrick was about to "discipline" her in a way in which many Victorian husbands would probably have been in complete sympathy. He had always been a stern and uncompromising father, and now he saw himself as protecting the children from a wild influence. Patrick Hepburn, principal of his law firm, rising astronomer, aspiring Freemason, Master of the Curriers' Company, the eldest of the Hepburn sons, could not stand by and watch his carefully constructed achievements come to nothing because of his woman's libertarian tendencies. Though he might frame his actions as meant to protect his wife from hurting herself through intemperate displays of emotion, what he was really doing was attempting to stop the disintegration of his married life. "You'll never leave me will you? It would be such a shock to my family," he had said before their marriage.[8] The meteor he saw headed toward him now was one he had always feared. So while Anna went off on Monday, May 26, to the School for Mothers' meeting, Patrick set in motion the awful late Victorian "madness" machinery.

That same evening Anna dressed herself in her "evening gown the colour of arterial blood" and sang at a concert organized by Selina Humphreys. Afterward, Edward Garnett, writer and well-known publisher's reader recently moved into Number 4 Downshire Hill, brought the impassioned vocalist home to meet his wife, Constance Garnett, translator of Russian plays and novels. Anna demurred when asked to sit down, but still they talked about myths as she was obviously "putting off the moment of going home."[9] The Garnett's son, David, came into the room just to see the face that went with such a beautiful voice. He then walked Anna across the road, deeply disturbed when she told him that she feared her husband was about to have her put in an asylum.

A doctor waited, appropriate papers in hand. The children had been sent next door. In a car outside were two mental nurses, alerted to expect powerful resistance. Instead Anna went quietly. Sensing the danger of her own position, Anna vowed to remain calm and only said to the nurses, "Which of us two is crazy?" when her mother—who had sided with Patrick—came running to the car to play, characteristically, to the fullest her part in the farewell scene.

NINE

"I Got My Courage" (1913)[1]

FAITH

I keep a bird in my heart,
He lives on sorrow,
His name is Faith.
He is so quick a conjurer that he can borrow
Flesh from a wraith.

He swallows the harsh weeds of pain
And gives me scope,
To tend my little garden-plot again
And wait for Hope.[2]

The last long glow of the spring night had faded before the car left 49 Downshire Hill and rumbled up Spaniards Road toward Epping Forest. Still dressed in her red concert gown with the silver corsage, Anna sat determinedly quiet between the two nurses as the lights of Hampstead were left behind. From the moment she realized that Patrick was serious about putting her away she swore to herself that her behavior would give no one grounds for keeping her locked up long. By the time the car turned into the gates of Brooke House she was resolute: she would give her "protectors" no evidence to use against her. A little over seven years after Patrick had walked Anna down the aisle of St. Margaret's, his pledge of love had come to this, a private asylum for those who could afford the best.[3]

Ducking under the ivy massed around the "great dark door" Anna was ushered along the corridors, the nurses' keys to the locked ward jangling. First left alone in her room, "my long, slim body quivering with apprehension," she was then joined by a woman with a candle who kept watch as the tension of the last troubled days brought exhausted sleep.

She had committed no criminal act; she had harmed no one, including herself. But the law, particularly The Lunacy Act of 1890, permitted her commitment.[4] Anna, from her hours of childhood reading in the pioneer town of Maryborough, or traveling unaccompanied on the coastal steamer along the Barrier Reef, or escaping from her overbearing Harper relatives on arrival in London, had always relished her freedom. Now she had lost it. "It was not even as if I was serving a term of imprisonment and knew when I was to be released," she later wrote.[5] Her fate would be decided by experts, and those experts, she knew, had been chosen by Patrick. Patrick felt that her belief in herself as a poet was one of her symptoms, as was the idea that he did not understand her. Now any opposition would also be read as a symptom, and to compound this problem, with the administration of sedatives even aspects of her own behavior might lie outside her control. She did not know how difficult it would be to keep her initial resolve to stay cool. Just to get through the weeks of hell that followed would require the full exercise of Anna's mind, will, and imagination.

Mental hospitals at the time differed greatly in type of care and size. The public London County Asylums in Hanwell, Horton, and Long Grove had each well over 2,000 beds each. Two out of the three had been established just since 1902, pointing to an alarming increase in the rate of people committed. Anna had the bad luck to have her sanity questioned during a time when people were being judged in droves as asylum material. And if she had been sent to one of these places, one can only guess what would have happened to her. As it was, the following months were horror enough.

Brooke House, a forty-bed facility at 1-9 Upper Clapton Road, Upper Clapton, was originally the manor house of a wealthy cleric's small fifteenth-century estate east of London. A minister of Henry VIII rebuilt and enlarged it, but it was poet-statesman Sir Fulke Greville, Lord Brooke, who named the house in 1621. In 1774 a Dr. John Monro licensed the property as a private mental hospital.[6] By the time Anna walked through its doors, it had seen almost one and one-half centuries of "the Care and Treatment of Ladies and Gentlemen suffering from Nervous and Mental Disorders."[7] There were no paupers here. But whereas some licensed houses took only "quiet or harmless cases," Brooke House did not have these restrictions. As Anna stated, "even the sanest of inmates had tried to shoot a bailiff." Behind the elegant exterior hid a world of hurt.

The Tuesday morning following her arrival Anna was examined, sedated, and kept in bed. On Wednesday, May 28, 1913, she was officially admitted.[8] For a few frightening days she was not even allowed to get up, but through her drug-induced haze she must have heard the regular nightly "dismal howlings" of a manic in the isolation ward. Then Patrick came to call. To Anna's supreme, but concealed, outrage, he read to her from one of his new papers, a proposal to integrate the various scientific societies in the South of England. She also felt that his mood had improved, being now possessed of "a new look of efficiency, and a new officialdom: he was the husband of a lady who was out of her mind." It was when Anna decided to hide her real reaction to Patrick that she felt "a return to normality." She managed to write a letter to him the next day telling him not to worry about her, and to go on the vacation his doctor recommended. But the vacation was to the island of Sark and Anna secretly dreaded that he might fall from its steep cliffs and never return to release her.

A few days after her arrival she was informed that the next morning she would "be allowed to get up," an occasion that would also carry the privilege of being able to "walk about the asylum." This must have been a very mixed blessing. In the so-called nursery wing, senile patients and "one or two young deficients" were ruled by nurses who punished the troublesome by sending them to bed at 6 o'clock. In the day room one woman lay in a stupor "from constant masturbation." Another woman talked over her shoulder to Napoleon, while still another woman, a former doctor, nightly gave birth to hundreds of infants and then "periodically she slaughtered her progeny." Others wandered lost in a world of their own, amidst the terrific odor caused by the incontinent. All in all a "sad little society."

To a certain extent Anna could keep to her own society if she chose. Her private room, which cost Patrick fifteen guineas per week, was clean and comfortable as a "railway hotel" and included a fireplace and writing and bedside tables. There was a sitting room nearby to receive visitors. From the barred bathroom window Anna could glimpse the street, a balm to her restricted soul. But the bath itself was shared, and the nurses were accustomed to using the tub for washing "the faeces-smirched night-gowns" of patients. Anna, who had been drilled by her mother about rigid Board School standards of cleanliness, found herself cringing in disgust as flecks of excrement settled on her skin during the bath. And one fellow patient, "old Emma Hoff . . . showed her confidence in me by using my room as a water-closet."

Anna's medical treatment focused on keeping her quietly occupied, and a daily routine developed. She wrote letters, knitted, took her medicines, one of which was a tonic containing quinine, which caused a buzzing in her head, and walked in the garden. In late afternoon she took tea with those others able to behave themselves properly. Evenings, she was "encouraged" to play the piano in the common room and to sing, which she did, but she makes no mention of whether the tennis racket Patrick brought her was ever used on the court where the rest of those patients considered "coherent" played.

It is not known whether her mother stayed long in London, but if she did, Anna didn't record any visits from her. She was allowed to telephone her sons, repeating with serious seven-year-old Jim and four-year-old John the nursery rhymes she had taught them so well. Patrick's visits, however, caused concern. Though Anna had long ago given up Wesleyan-style repentance, she was developing what might be seen as a highly unusual confession of sin. For her, the worst acts were those subservient and supplicating: "I most offend my deity when I kneel," she has written.[9] If she would not kneel to her god, she certainly was not going to buckle under pressure from mere mortals. Anna had made the decision to act cool and controlled. She knew there was one Hepburn woman "long shut away" in a succession of private facilities; she did not intend to be the second.[10] Nevertheless, when Patrick later returned from his Sark vacation suntanned and rested, Anna capped their increasingly difficult conversation by calling him a "swine" and thus incurring his rage and two more weeks in the asylum so that she could learn to "protect" herself and govern her speech.

On her own, Anna had obtained an algebra book, finding that the concentration involved in the solving of these problems kept her from plunging into despair. Other privileges were extended at appropriate intervals. First was taking tea with the doctor's wife, a woman who told her helpfully and ignorantly of another unhappy wife who "shot herself through the head." Next were outings, always, of course, accompanied by a nurse: "solemn drives around Epping" in a closed carriage, a stop for a cream bun in a shop on the High Street and once, "Oh blessed relief," a performance on the music hall stage. But Anna kept her sanity primarily by interesting herself in the other patients.

One, a former painter, had rubbed all her hair off her head and had become "oblivious" of her surroundings. Her rantings had alienated her family, and she spent her days fretting back and forth. Anna spoke sharply to the woman, listened to her story of thwarted lesbian love and then dictated a reasonable letter to the woman's brother, "without hyperboles about hell and damnation." As the woman became more reasonable Anna took her along on the supervised outings, and asked permission from the doctor "to get her some Harlene which I rubbed into her head, and her hair began to grow." Anna's interest in the woman prompted the doctors and family to a more sympathetic attitude and finally a transfer out of the private asylum. Much later Anna would write,

> The last time I saw her she was living under . . . much happier circumstances in a doctor's house. She had grown her hair. She was not a lunatic but a moral and nervous breakdown. The only thing I had done for her was to interest her. It was a relief to me to have something to do with my energy.

Of male patients important to Anna, first and foremost was "George Morris," formerly a medal-winning student at the Slade School, who won Anna's affection and interest by introducing himself with the words, "Your husband must be a great fool to let you come here." They became firm friends as Anna considered his hearing of voices and his "spirit companions" no more disturbing than were Martin Luther's. Though Anna did not act on the new and troublesome "crude desire" that often assailed her in the asylum, she did use these "negligible contacts" with Morris and others to write about love.

Two doctors on hand explored Anna's state of mind, probably contributing to Anna's life-long aversion to anything but self-analysis. The first doctor, the senior man, had an unimaginative view of a woman's role in life: "Mrs. Hepburn," he told her, "there is always something to do in the house." The second doctor, a Scotsman appreciative of the nurses' sexual aspects and himself a bit attracted to Anna, brought her a paper and pencil when he heard that she wrote poetry. Anna pretended to be uninterested, but his act was probably a catalyst for Anna's life-changing transformation in the year to come.

This doctor had asked Anna to repeat to him the poem, "Nervous Prostration," which she had shouted at Patrick from the garden:

> I married a man of the Croydon class
> When I was twenty-two,
> And I vex him, and he bores me
> Till we don't know what to do!
> It isn't good form in the Croydon class
> To say you love your wife,
> So I spend my days with the tradesmen's books
> And pray for the end of life. . . .[11]

The poem is explicit about Anna's dilemma: she was married to a man so unlike herself that she felt she was slowly dying inside from the lack of sympathetic mutual understanding and expressions of love. A later poem also adds that she felt Patrick's psychological domination of the family was harming the children as well:

> I had two lively children in my youth . . . .
> [the man's] solemn constancy [or "solemn will"]
> Prisoned us round—until the boys
> were mechanised past any
> natural joys
> And I was maddened—impotent & ill.[12]

The doctor, by giving her the means to write out her pain without trying to obtain the poems as evidence or use them in therapy, gave Anna confirmation and recognition of her talent and freedom to use it. Once she stamped down her fears enough to write, for Patrick had considered her poetry trouble and symptom of illness, the verse poured out of her, "just as a rush of oil."[13] By the time she would leave the asylum, she had written eighty poems that she secretly carried out with her.

For finally her time was up. The law required that asylums have visiting inspectors. This commissioner said of Anna's story: "Well, I think this is the tallest order I ever heard," and released her pending the completion of a satisfactory probationary month. On September 17, 1913, Edith Alice Mary Hepburn, female, patient #53827, was released, "recovered," to begin life again as a free woman on the outside, and a soon-to-be-free woman on the inside.[14]

Taken in total, Anna later felt that the experience "ruined" her and in effect ruined her family. Whether or not poetry, an admirer's attentions, or her own emotionalism caused Patrick to put her away, it was now evident to Anna that she was in a marriage built over a fault line and that quakes would not only be periodic, but serious. The conflict of their temperaments, their aspirations, their backgrounds, and what they held important—he the phenomena and rules of the physical and social worlds, she invention, and the investigation of people and ideas—would make for many future disagreements. Likewise their desired outcomes differed: she, trained by her mother and father, at this time expected and needed both catharsis and conversation (though as she aged her objectives would change). He, on the other hand, drew back coldly from the emotionally demonstrative experience and was obsessed with his scientific pursuits. Anna had married Patrick with stars in her own eyes, though, on their first meeting she had said, "that man will never know the first thing about me." His "'gentleman' manners" (to respect pride, nurture hope, and never exploit prerogative) she never doubted.[15] Patrick had sadly failed her in devastating her pride, trying to cut off her hope and self-satisfyingly availing himself of the laws' inequities.[16] Now, having been locked up and lorded over she must have been shell-shocked as any returning soldier would be. Yet hope had not deserted her in the long months of her sorrow and anger. Now she was about to enter zestfully, one might even say vengefully, into the new "modernist" spirit abroad in the land. David Garnett would fall in love with her, D. H. Lawrence would become her intellectual sparring partner, and young painters Nina Hamnett, Mark Gertler, and others would become her new friends.

TEN

A Changed Anna (1913–1914)

No sleepy poison is more strong to kill
Than jaded, weak, and vacillating will.
God send us power to make decision
With muscular, clean, fierce precision.
In life and song
Give us the might
To dare to be wrong. . . .[1]

Anna stepped down from the carriage after an uncomfortably awkward drive with Patrick from Brooke House. They must have seemed like strangers to each other. And after weeks of only telephoning the boys, she yearned to hold them in her arms but James, especially, held back.[2] Lizzie, the servant who had become Patrick's mainstay, was touchy, even a bit resentful at the mistress's return. The apples were red in the orchard, the sun still strong. That night, Patrick resumed some of his old fondness as he took her into his arms and said, "It's good to have you back." Anna, who wanted to hear him ask forgiveness for causing her asylum sufferings, heard in these words only his relief that physical needs would again be satisfied. Without desire she submitted, but took deep and lasting umbrage at his insensitivity and his ignorance of her feelings.

In the asylum Anna took a lot of time to think about the previous few years. How had things turned out the way they did? In her attempt to be a perfect wife, obligation and responsibility had ruled and had left behind the impetuous Anna. A new spirit had been building in Edwardian England and she was not aligned with it. While 5,000 suffragettes had marched through London's summer streets to protest the jailing of women working for the vote, Anna's big event had been the customary Hepburn garden party.[3] Worker strikes, modern art, the great Liberal victory in General Elections—challenges to society had been proceeding apace. Meanwhile, Anna had done volunteer work that Patrick approved of, taken care of her two children, run the household and the choices "betwixt the baked and boiled," and tried to be a supportive wife to a man with the makings of a scientist.[4] But her own singing had been discouraged and her first poetry published to his irritation and distaste. Except for the friendship of Emily Colles, who had perhaps enjoyed Patrick's company as much or more than Anna's own, her involvement in the wider world had gradually shrunk. She had told her father "my genius / must be miscarriage / I said, 'Observe this atmosphere / I can't write here.'" She told him that she had resigned herself to devoting more of her time to Patrick's astronomy and to her sons' welfare. But she was no more contented with this than her father had been.[5]

In the asylum she had witnessed the extremes of human behavior in the other patients: wild, frenetic activity, on the one hand; a blasted uncomprehending, sometimes drugged inactivity on the other. Dealing with those extremes and with her own fears and shudderings had actually deepened her physical and mental strength. Her asylum stay had reacquainted her, in the persons of George Morris and others, with the artistic world and with behavior outside the iron template of the villa dweller. In addition, she had come full-face with sexual desire—her own and others. What sort of road would she choose, now that the doors had opened and she stood once again gazing across the lawn and into her beautiful garden?

Arrangements had been made to keep Anna subdued. Lizzie had supervised the boys, who were never told reasons for their mother's absence.[6] In addition, Lizzie bossed the other servants and had taken over for Patrick, who preferred to be thought a dunce at household management (though on his scientific expeditions he operated quite successfully). Together, Lord of the Manor and faithful servant had developed a system in which Lizzie would be bursar and Anna supplicant, money a humiliating pound at a time, as needs arose. A policy of metaphorically placing her "on a sofa" and "rob[bing her] of initiative," was still in place and would continue.

At the end of the probationary month Patrick said, in response to Anna's timid inquiry about her fate, "They can't do anything to you without *my* permission." But the doctors found Anna "recovered." This verdict was given in writing on September 17, 1913, sixteen weeks after her commitment. The cloud of uncertainty that had followed Anna broke to a dazzling blue. Patrick, by turns surprised, bitter, and resentful, would in the years ahead see a changed Anna fight her way into a new life, a modern life.

It was a new era at 49 Downshire Hill. Her energy "had been stimulated by . . . incarceration." She gave her own garden party, invited the politician Israel Zangwill, and dressed up her boys and one of their friends so that the tussah blouses spelled out VOTES-FOR-WOMEN.[7] With arms linked the boys passed up and down among the guests with the message for all to read. Her own personal campaign would concentrate on expressing herself and on making friends among the new artists, the poets trying out new images and rhythms, and the novelists who would shove over the barriers of polite imitation of their predecessors. She would free herself of Patrick's domination. As she would write in her poem, "Gift to a Jade,"

> For love he offered me his perfect world.
> This world was so constricted, and so small,
> It had no sort of loveliness at all,
> And I flung back the little silly ball.
> At that cold moralist I hotly hurled,
> His perfect pure symmetrical small world.[8]

She kept Lizzie on because it was good for the youngest son John, but raised "so much hell" that she regained control of the household money. She discovered a new disregard for Patrick's money. Perhaps seeing so much of it go for her asylum upkeep disabused her of his attitude that money was important. She took a new look at the house and "painted out" the Victorian Liberty wallpapers and bought Cubist paintings for the walls.[9] In an earlier time, seeking to keep track of the sheer number of things in their household, Anna had filled page after meticulous page in a standard Victorian "Where is it?" book. Now she tossed aside her striving for order and her youthful admiration for such Hepburn concerns as neatly compartmentalized sewing boxes, special champagne, signature dinner gongs, and immaculate white paint. She began singing again at home, "raising my invincible voice in free and self-invented song."[10] She took over the main care of the boys and resumed "our games and our readings . . . and our happy treks abroad." Patrick, meanwhile, who had during their 1906 engagement proudly shown Anna the provisions he had made for her in his will, made another Last Will and Testament.[11] In this one Anna would receive money from a trust unless she formed some other alliance. If that happened she would be cut off, or, as the will states, it would be "as if she were then dead" and the will's other provisions would be activated.

Anna went to The Poetry Bookshop recently opened by poet and editor Harold Monro at 35 Devonshire Street, a five-minute walk from the British Museum and from Patrick's old rooms on Great Ormond Street. "Have you any free rhythms?" she asked him. Black-browed Monro looked up at the sound of this resonant female voice and responded with interest, "We've all been trying to write them." Anna passed him the modest pamphlet of poems written by her friend, John Oland, but Monro quickly guessed that the real author was standing directly in front of him in a lovely hat. He took, eventually, an amazing fifteen poems (he generally did not print that many from one contributor) for publication. So began Anna's rejuvenated career.

Anna offered to buy Patrick a sextant with the money she would receive for the poetry but he declined. He was not about to allow his wife the pleasure of this purchase, since it was deeply ingrained in him that financial flow in a marriage only went downhill: from man at the peak, to woman in the valley. As Patrick's disapproval of her deepened, Anna looked about for support.

In the asylum her curiosity had been piqued by a small dark-haired woman who was employed as a companion to one of the patients. Corky, as Anna called her, was not well-connected in any way and had no advantages of education, but through her desire to have a life of adventure had acted Shakespeare, performed in a musical group, and written short stories.[12] In the asylum she had adventure and a money-making enterprise as companion to the woman doctor who regularly murdered imaginary offspring. The latter must have been good fodder for future stories, but to alleviate the heavy daily mood she and her lover Manuel, a Portuguese, would sally forth to the handsome rooms of Frascati's restaurant on Oxford Street after meeting under the lamppost opposite the asylum. These meetings Anna had watched from barred windows, wondering at the vagaries of life that put Corky in the mainstream of nightlife and people, and herself in the choking atmosphere of the asylum.

Remembering Corky, who by then had left the asylum and was looking for new work, Anna summoned her to an interview. "Would she like," Anna inquired, to be "lady's help" for the sum of twenty-six pounds per annum? The arrangement proved entirely satisfactory, for though Corky then did nothing for her keep she was happy to forego a salary and live rent-free in leafy Hampstead with small sums for pocket money. Anna, for her part, received a bulwark, a second in defense against Lizzie and Patrick's officiousness. "There was no emotional relationship between me and Corky," Anna said, "[but] she amused me, she rested me, she accompanied me everywhere."

Anna had never been short of admirers. From her teenage years people had always found her commanding height, her beautiful shape, her voice, her curiosity, and her commentary compelling and exciting. Her way of "smiling down" in greeting (according to Oswell Blakeston, who wrote about her years later) could be overwhelmingly positive and powerful.[13] In the asylum, fellow patient George Morris had been only forthright in saying what many thought. Now Anna and Corky made a handsome pair and "the gentlemen who did not fall in love with me fell in love with Corky." For her part, Anna kept things on a fairly chaste level: "A pressure of the hands, a kiss snatched behind a door" but the contacts helped her to renew a sense of self that had been eroding and must have also given her a secret satisfaction against what she called the "wedded gloom" of Patrick. Though Corky soon left for Paris, and then marriage, her lighthearted companionship contributed importantly to Anna's recovery and reinvention.

The men provoked no such lasting appreciation in Anna but they did, however, function in an important way. For stimulated by her own freedom in the glorious London fall and by the desire of these men Anna began writing verse at an unprecedented rate. "The machinery of my phrase making," she said, roared into action, and she promptly sent the poems to her father who responded that his daughter who had been dead had only slept. From the eighty poems smuggled out of the asylum, the number grew at a tremendous rate. Of course, it can be a mistake to constantly read Anna Wickham's life into her poetry, assuming that each time she says "I" she means it personally.[14] She herself says that her poems were often "imagined" from other people. Still, a poem like "Song" is illuminating of the change that desire and appreciation brought to Anna, regardless of the identity of "my love."

> I was so chill, and overworn, and sad,
> To be a lady was the only joy I had.
> I walked the street as silent as a mouse,
> Buying fine clothes, and fittings for the house.
>
> But since I saw my love
> I wear a simple dress,
> And happily I move
> Forgetting weariness.[15]

When Anna's poetry debuted, June, 1914, in Harold Monro's magazine *Poetry and Drama* it made a very favorable impression. Monro's quarterly focused on poetry, criticism, and reviews but included art (often woodcuts), dramas, and writing on theatre.[16] The *Morning Post* of June 25, 1914 singled out "Miss Anna Wickham," as seeking after new truth and beauty. The reviewer praised her "strangely-enhancing poems" and favorably cited her "Cherry-Blossom Wand." Newspapers, too, had picked up her poetry: *The Daily Mail, Daily Citizen, Daily Herald*, all carried her poems, which surely must have driven Patrick to distraction, disdainful as he and many of his class were of any kind of attention from common journalists.

Besides her galloping charge into the fields of poetry and her sideways glances of flirtation, Anna found in the world of art another fascination. As a girl she had been given some Japanese prints, and as a student in Paris she had been attracted to the free-wheeling artists quarters in Paris.[17] Since their 1909 move to Hampstead, they had been neighbors to many artists at a time when painting, sculpture, and drawing were expanding beyond representation and toward the abstract. But previous to the asylum her actual contact with artists may have been confined only to the Russian painter who had betrayed her whereabouts to Patrick. Now, however, as Anna delightedly realized that "An artist does not imitate, he discovers," she began spending time where the artists spent time, to discover the discoverers, so to speak.[18] The Domino Room of the Café Royal, with its marble-topped tables and red velvet chairs and banquettes, had from the 1890s been a home away from home for artists and writers from Whistler to Augustus John, from Oscar Wilde to A. E. Housman. It was still the place to find the best and the brightest, along with "nostalgic expatriate Frenchmen, plotting foreign anarchists, raucous bookmakers, shady-looking crooks, con-men, pimps, blackmailers" and even members of the Royal Family.[19]

Slade students, too, were among the clientele. The Slade School of Art, which Anna had learned more about from the admiring George Morris, was then under the leadership of artist Henry Tonks who believed, in contrast to stodgy Royal Academy of Art precepts, in the importance of drawing from life rather than either drawing from models or copying existing works of art. He inspired other soon-to-be-noteworthy figures to join the Slade. Roger Fry, for example, lectured in the History of Art. Only months before, the avant-garde artists at his Omega Workshops had begun producing exuberantly designed and colored ceramics, furniture, carpets, and fabrics. Also at the Slade around this time students such as David Bomberg, Mark Gertler, Wyndham Lewis, and Stanley Spencer were readying themselves for stellar careers. An ebullient atmosphere prevailed. The high spirits carried over to the Café Royal, and when that closed for the evening, to Madame Frida Strindberg's Soho cabaret club, The Cave of the Golden Calf. Jacob Epstein, Lewis, Charles Ginner, Spencer Gore, and Eric Gill had been employed to paint and decorate that low-ceilinged room to evoke the wild, the natural, and the ritualistic. Artist Nina Hamnett, for one, found the whole scene "agreeably gay and cheerful."[20]

This lively and spontaneous young woman, then twenty-three years old, with a "tall, boyish figure and attractive, laughing face" was one of the Café Royal crowd that Anna, then twenty-nine years old, became close to. Hamnett, daughter of a military officer, had spent her youth chafing against restriction. Not until she became an art student, first at the Pelham School of Art (1906–1907), the London School of Art (1907–1910) and then, when her parents refused to pay any more fees, at evening Life classes at the polytechnic at Turnham Green did she begin to come into her own. A tiny allowance from two sympathetic aunts plus a £50 lump sum from an inheritance had recently enabled her to rent rooms near Fitzroy Street, "the forum for all that was newest in English art" and home to the immensely popular leader of the English modern movement, Walter Sickert. Hamnett chopped off her long hair into an attractive cap style and painted a self-portrait that shows her confidently at her easel. She lived with a freedom that Anna admired. On a five-day trip to Paris she had made the most of her time. Jacob

Epstein was there attempting to finish carving on the enormous stone tomb at the grave of Oscar Wilde. Each day Nina had gone to the sprawling Père Lachaise cemetery with Epstein, fellow sculptor Constantin Brancusi, and a few others, to uncover the Wilde Monument which French authorities had deemed obscene. Now back in London, she was working as hard as she played. Though she would not have her first solo exhibition until 1918, she already had exhibited a watercolor of a child at the Walker Art Gallery in Liverpool and was attracting admiration not only for her fun-loving disposition but for her paintings and drawings. She had also begun work at the Omega Workshops applying designs and meeting the astonishing variety of people that walked through the Omega doors at 33 Fitzroy Square to work, to buy, or to see for themselves this innovative experiment. But then influenza struck. She was ordered to stay in bed and it seemed she would have to return to her parents' home and give up her hard-fought independence. Anna, hearing of her plight, and remembering lying "gloomy and uncared for" at the Mückles' when she herself was ill with influenza at age twenty-one, took her to Downshire Hill, gave her a room overlooking the garden and tended her though the illness.[21] Nina watched from the window as Anna walked in the orchard with D. H. Lawrence who had sung hymns "for hours in the drawing room;" Frieda Lawrence and Katherine Mansfield, who were also visiting, kindly conversed with Nina at her bed-side.[22] Hamnett and Anna continued to be friends even into the 1940s.

D. H. Lawrence, Frieda, and Anna would also spend a lot of time together, though only over the course of a short time. But before seeing how that relationship evolved we must first look to David Garnett, the Lawrences' golden boy back in 1912, but by April, 1915, angry and hurt at things Lawrence said and did, forsaking their company entirely.[23]

David (Bunny) Garnett, the twenty-year-old son of Edward and Constance Garnett, had been struck by his first glimpse of Anna who, only hours before her commitment, had joined his parents for coffee:

> a very beautiful woman, tall and powerful, with shining dark eyes, abundant dark hair parted at the side that fell in a wing over her ear. She had rather heavy features with a rich warm complexion like a ripe nectarine. . . . I was fascinated.[24]

David Garnett was the one who eventually saw her to her door, reluctant to have her go inside and face her husband. Garnett saw her as a woman entering a trap, about to be imprisoned by a dangerous tyrant with "Victorian views about the position of women" and he urged her to hide herself; Anna told him that it was for doctors to decide the question of one's sanity and that surely they couldn't keep her long.[25] When the next day his mother had called at 49 Downshire Hill, Constance was given the distinct impression that it was none of her business what happened to Mrs. Hepburn. Constance told Patrick that perhaps Anna was tired, and that she would be welcome to rest at a seaside cottage owned by some of her friends. The offer was brushed aside, though Patrick allowed that his wife was a genius.[26]

Garnett had, through his youth, fallen in love often, and had a strong, sentimental nature. A fourth-year botany student at Imperial College and a traveler who spent a boyhood school term in southern France, he had twice been to Russia and had also vacationed in Germany and the Tyrol. Nevertheless he remained, in a way, innocent. Anna's story had all the elements that he was highly susceptible to: a beautiful woman, an evil conspiracy, the chance to rescue, and the chance to be admired. Above all, perhaps, it contained an opportunity for him to prove himself and to push into the adult world of his parents. When David accidentally ran into Anna on the street months after she had been released from the asylum he was, if anything, more attracted to her than before and she responded to him also.

David Garnett was an exhilarating person to be with. He had energy, a tendency to quickly assess a person's worth, and a boyish enthusiasm and desire to champion difficult causes. The latter he inherited from his parents who were often involved with political refugees and were associated with the Fabian Society. Edward and Constance also preferred to live outside the social swirl of London literary circles, but instead kept the Cearne, their countryside house of rough-cut stone, as a haven for themselves, family, friends, and an astonishing parade of Garnett's "discoveries" who were to become literary greats.[27] David grew up accustomed to seeing his mother at her desk alternately "eager, frowning, puzzled or amused" as she translated classic Russian works (over seventy volumes) and his father stretched out in a wicker chair reading manuscript after manuscript for his publishers.[28] Edward was a responsive reader and editor for the likes of John Galsworthy, Joseph Conrad, D. H. Lawrence, and others who often came for weekend visits. Thus David sailed in an imaginary sea with Joseph Conrad manning the sails in a wash-basket boat. Ford Madox Ford (then

Ford Madox Hueffer) astonished him by suddenly crouching down like a frog and giving chase, leap after leap. Ford also took him and his parents to tea with Henry James, that chronicler of European and American society, who was dressed in a tight fitting pair of knickerbockers and an equally tight black-checked coat. On another occasion young David performed a comic Friar Tuck in a home-produced play in front of an audience that included G. B. Shaw.

David had, in addition, the whole of the countryside for his play and a vivid cast of neighbors and village dwellers for his examination. And as a young boy on trips to London, even the unnerving aspect of a visit to the dentist, for example, could be sweetened by the prospect of visiting his grandfather, Keeper of the Printed Books, superintendent of the great domed Reading Room of the British Museum. His grandfather lived in the keeper's official residence on the museum's east side. On certain days the family would be allowed to play on the lawn. Other days, grandfather Garnett would open a private door and they would glide into one of the great exhibition halls. Through a long passage was his grandfather's office, and while his work was being done, David would be given books and turning the pages, would see the passage of Japanese sailboats and other exotic fare. Once he marched with his grandfather right past the knees and saluting arms of museum guards into the inner sanctum—the blue-painted dome of the Reading Room, where you were supposed to be twenty-one—unless you happened to be the grandson of the very man who was preparing the very first catalogue of the treasure-trove of books (he got through the letter "s" before retiring).[29]

So David Garnett was, despite his youth, a storehouse of tales and a keen observer. When he and Anna met again he could see that despite her forays into cafe society she was still at odds with her life. Like the woman/vixen in Garnett's later award-winning novel/fable, *Lady into Fox*, she had not suffered herself long to be petted and brushed and kept captive before her nature had asserted itself.[30] It was Anna's "feeling of suffocation" in her marriage to a conventional husband that had prompted her to produce her first poems, David felt. Though he admired the poems he saw now a chance for her to escape from unhappiness.[31] Anna and David began taking walks on the heath at night.

Their long walks ranged far and wide in topics for discussion. David's comments would often produce a delayed reaction in Anna; at their next meeting she would push across the table pieces of paper . . . . On them were poems she had written since our last meeting. Sometimes something I said struck her and instead of replying she would reach for a pencil, scratch a few lines & push them across the table. . . . her thoughts and feelings were her poems. A stream of good & bad ones flowed through her.[32]

The relationship's intensity mounted at the same time Anna's involvement with the art world grew. She commissioned John Flanagan, the painter, to do a portrait of the young John, with his hair a corona of gold on a background of emerald green. It was with Anna, Garnett says, that he met poet and essayist T. E. Hulme (published in the *New Age*), Henri Gaudier-Brzeska, Jacob Epstein, and a number of other young painters and their mistresses and models at what were known as very bohemian gatherings. They would meet at the Café Royal. The night that they joined the new Crabtree Club, artist Augustus John's less-than-satisfactory replacement for the bankrupt Cave of the Golden Calf, painters Mark Gertler, David Bomberg, and John Flanagan all stumbled back to Anna's to sleep it off together three in one bed.[33] Anna's poem, "The Cherry-Blossom Wand," which she was by then singing to Garnett, summed up her spell: "So I will drive you, so bewitch your eyes."[34] David was a handsome, passionate man in love with her and he begged her to leave her husband and go off with him.

An unhappy marriage, a younger man wooing an older woman? Garnett could not have missed the parallels between their situation and that of his friends D. H. Lawrence and Frieda Weekley, who Edward and Constance had supported in 1912 during the first difficult months of that affair. The same brick wall that confronted Lawrence and Frieda would lay ahead for Anna and David. The presence of children and the certainty that the children would go to Patrick just as Frieda's children remained out of reach, physically, and when the divorce went through, legally. David knew the magma-deep love Anna had for her children would not permit such a separation. He also was not yet ready or able to support a wife. No matter what Anna's affection-starved self might be screaming, she would not leave her children; and she and Garnett would not permit themselves to be lovers while she remained with Patrick.

From a marriage Anna had expected, based on her parents' marriage and her own hopes, liberty, an intelligent companion, children, and a certain amount of power. Now, though she had recently been deprived of her liberty, and her power too had been challenged, she could not give up her flawed marriage. She still admired Patrick's intelligence and the strides he was making in the field of astronomy, and she was unable to imagine a life without the happiness her children provided. She was also undoubtedly a bit afraid. At this impasse, she and David gradually split. David realized "that she would be no happier with me than as she was. It would only be exchanging the misery of living with Patrick Hepburn for the misery of living without her children."[35] He continued to try to see her, one January day in 1915 venturing to her house with a new plant to give to Jim. Even a year after their relationship ended Frieda wrote in an April 19, 1915 letter to him, that it was "Anna whom you loved . . . hopeless in it from the beginning." But actually by March, 1915, David had already moved on and was able to write in his journal,

> I went to the Café Royal . . . . Anna and Mrs. Kenelm Foss came in after about half an hour so I talked to them. I felt so warm to Anna but queerly for the first time without that awful pang.[36]

With the impossibility of their relationship, David had begun to find other friends. Increasingly Garnett was drawn into the Bloomsbury set, that charmed and tumultuous group named after a London parish, which began with a general interest in literature, art, and philosophy but, after 1910 and the influence of art critic and painter Roger Fry, woke up the English art world to Post-Impressionist ideas about form, color, and mood.[37] The cohesive circle, with a core related by family and marriage, included Vanessa Bell (married to Clive Bell), her lifelong companion, painter Duncan Grant, the writers Leonard and Virginia Woolf, biographer and critic Lytton Strachey, economist, art patron, and collector John Maynard Keynes and others. The artists of the Bloomsbury set founded several exhibiting societies, among them Bell's own Friday Club (est. 1905) and the joint-effort Grafton Group (1913–1914), and were apologists for radical ideas in art, though those ideas were likewise challenged by Wyndham Lewis, T. E. Hulme, and others. Anna's sympathies were more with the challenging camps, while the young Garnett was increasingly drawn to the Bloomsbury group. To the Bloomsbury group, beauty was considered a higher concern than utilitarianism—an idea that surely would also have rankled with Anna, concerned as she was with the social good. And over D. H. Lawrence's objections, who feared and loathed the group's homosexual elements, David felt finally that he was at home with this group's ideals, aspirations, and activities.[38]

The split between David Garnett and Anna Wickham illustrates that the new spirit abroad in Edwardian England had many manifestations. She, as Garnett wrote years later, chose to align herself with the tribes of Chelsea, Slade students, their mistresses, and models. She preferred the hard up to the well-off and the struggling, doomed, and unknown to the successful and fashionable, Bohemia to Bloomsbury.[39]

The final wedge between them came because of the war. Patrick was away on a Royal Astronomical Society expedition from Greenwich to Minsk, in Russia, to view and photograph a solar eclipse. Thus it was left to Anna, on the morning of August 4, 1914, to announce the news. Anna had the boys Jim, age seven, and John, then age five, summoned to her bedroom where she gravely told them, "my boys, your country is at war." As days went on, the word was that the war would be a short one; "over before Christmas," was the often-repeated byword. Anna was not opposed to the war initially. But David made his mind up that he would not fight. He volunteered his services to the Friends War Victims Relief and left England soon after. Later he would follow the Bloomsbury group's stand as conscientious objectors. By 1916 he would move to Charleston, a house outside of London, with Virginia Bell and Duncan Grant, as a farm laborer.[40] Despite political and other differences, David Garnett continued to admire Anna Wickham's verse and over sixty years later he would edit her *Selected Poems*, saying that her work was not only "redolent of the warmth, the slow appreciation and humour of the woman I was in love with" but also distinguished by "individual feeling, her power of putting down no more than she wanted to say, by her avoiding the poetical and conventional . . . by a felicity of phrase."[41]

These years of 1913 and 1914 were, for Anna on a personal level, a time of concentrated change. She had not left her husband. But she had struggled free from Hepburn dominance, with its long-standing Victorian biases toward wealth, comfort, and family tradition. On an artistic level, one of the most important events of these two years was the publication of her poems by Harold Monro, a man who was dedicating the better part of his energies to poetry. This tale, with all its twists and turns, gets a chapter of its own.

ELEVEN

Anna Wickham and Harold Monro (1913 and beyond)

The story of Anna Wickham and editor/publisher/poet Harold Monro is a long and complicated one, beginning within a year after Monro opened his one-of-a-kind Poetry Bookshop that gradually helped birth a time of "poetry intoxication."[1] Anna became one of Monro's most important poets, and Monro was her steadfast champion.[2] She took part in all the enterprises Monro offered: little magazines, anthologies, book publications, rhyme sheets, and poetry performance space. Ultimately the two survived not only the growing pains of Anna's publication in the U. S. and the planned for (but possibly never executed) joint visit to the heiress Natalie Barney's Paris salon, but also irritation, perturbation, denunciation, and embrace. But the tale starts with a mystery: just how did the two come to find each other?

When The Poetry Bookshop was officially opened for Monro by Henry Newbolt on January 8, 1913, poets, writers, and others who loved literature had quickly become familiar with the narrow Georgian-era house.

Upstairs in the attics, poets could rent cheap lodgings. On the ground floor, the small selling room of 12' by 12' was lined floor to ceiling with oak shelves that carried poetry: poetry in periodicals, pamphlets, chapbooks; fat volumes of poetry bound in leather and gilt-stamped, thin volumes of poetry in cloth covers; lives of the poets, literary criticism and, on a large table of oak (the massive furniture all built by Arthur Romney Green, who shared his friend Monro's ideals), the latest publications issued by the bookshop. Monro himself was a poet, though he did not find his strongest voice until toward the end of his career. But he believed from the start of his career that a "new age" was dawning when people would shed their exhausted beliefs and traditions and "live more joyously and rationally" as a result of a better understanding of both natural law and the self.[3]

Normally little mystery was involved in a writer's coming to Harold Monro's shop. The little haven was advertised, written about, much discussed, and frequented by those who quickly came to appreciate the warmth, atmosphere, and dedication to poetry that they found there. The mystery here lies in how much each of the main players in one particular drama, thirty-four-year-old owner Monro and thirty-year-old Anna Wickham— recently released from an asylum for supposed nervous disorders—may have already known about each other.

Anna had been able to write during her stay in the asylum because of the intervention of one of the doctors, a Scotsman who was attracted to Anna and fond of poetry and had supplied her with a paper and pencil. Given Patrick's extremely negative reaction to Anna's poetry, the behavior of this doctor showed courage and/or that there was something unusual about this asylum.

Now halfway up a dingy Bloomsbury street, off the clamor of Theobalds Road, Anna found, a few days after her asylum release, the center of poetry in London. Why Harold Monro, whose own poetry had by that time been published by Elkin Mathews (*Poems*, 1906), Constable (*Before Dawn [Poems and Impressions]*, 1911) and his own joint venture, Samurai Press, would have been attracted to Wickham's poetry is easy to see. In the poems he had written or would write were themes of longing, love of freedom, anti-clericalism, loss of religious faith, love and passion similar to those in Anna's poetry. But those initial moments must have been freighted with tension—Monro's head bent over the pages, Anna uncomfortably picking up books from the table or scanning the shelves—"I wasn't cross, only shy and nervous like you"—as she would once write to Monro.[4]

Monro may have been nervous and shy, but he was a man fighting for a vision just as Anna was making a new way for herself. During the years Anna had been raising her first two children, Monro had spent several years of wandering and thinking, trying to achieve discipline either through short-lived group work such as the Samurai or in various European "crank settlements," as he called them. He had come to the conclusion he must "do something" about what he saw as the abysmal state of poetry in England.[5] He felt that people needed poetry and he would help make it available to them. He assumed financial risk and editorship for a revamped London journal, *The Poetry Review*, under the auspices of the staid Poetry Society. But only six months before Anna met him he had founded his own journal, *Poetry and Drama*, a quarterly focused on poetry, criticism, and reviews but including art (often woodcuts), drama, writing on theatre, and even a ticket for admittance to a Poetry Bookshop reading.[6]

Though he was now making headway with his shop, he often felt alone, having to be responsive to the dictates of commerce, the demands of family, and even the aching unresolved issues of his own desires. When Anna walked in—a woman who seemed to many people larger than life and possessed of a clear, decisive wit, a way of mocking that seemed to give her a higher moral ground, yet open about her "inadequacies"—he must have seen the possibilities of a friendship with a woman who was his equal.

When the fifteen poems he gathered (from work written after her self-published *Songs*) debuted in *Poetry and Drama*, June, 1914, they made a very favorable impression.[7] The *Morning Post* of June 25, 1914 singled out "Miss Anna Wickham," as seeking after new truth and beauty. The reviewer praised her "strangely-enhancing poems" and favorably cited her "Cherry-Blossom Wand." This poem did become a lasting favorite of poetry readers. Flirtatious, confident, mysterious, the poem was sung to a tune that Anna composed and that many people, eventually, heard her sing. If one poem could be said to have made her name in the 'teens, it was this one which Monro, a music-lover and concert-goer himself, chose and published.

A year or so before, in a lecture at Cambridge, Monro had defined the contemporary poet as one that "caught the spirit of Darwin, that spirit that had so altered our attitude, and rendered obsolete so many ways of talking about life."[8] Anna, of course, had been schooled in Darwinian thought by her progressive father almost from the time she was able to take words in. And she did have a way with words in poetry, here in "Envoi":

> God, thou great symmetry,
> Who put a biting lust in me,
> From whence my sorrows spring,
> For all the frittered days
> That I have spent in shapeless ways
> Give me one perfect thing.[9]

The acknowledgment that something was missing in Anna's life would have touched Monro. In his poetry, for example, in "The One, Faithful," he writes about the need for the solace and understanding of friendship. In his poem, "Officer's Mess," there is a painful longing for friendship that is not of the bottle, or fickle and short-lived. Anna's tone may be more demanding than the tone Monro generally uses. And she also feels free to address a God that Monro, as early as 1908, has given up on, though he felt the loss of his faith profoundly.[10] But this type of engagement with an issue is exactly what Monro, according both to his own admission, and to conclusions by scholars who have studied him, looked for again and again in his interactions with people and only too rarely found.

Monro had had homosexual loves and encounters since his school days. It had not stopped him from marriage, however, first to Dorothy Browne, the sister of one of his best friends, Maurice. During that marriage, that lasted at least in name from 1903 to 1916 and produced a son, Nigel, he and Dorothy lived at least part of the time in Ireland, where rain, isolation, and the married state drove him nearly to suicide. Monro, remembering the long walks and intense conversations of his school days, confided to his journal, "Why did I surrender my dear, dear freedom?"[11] Among the poems Anna showed him that first day in 1913 was "Divorce," lines of which might have been written expressly for Monro:

> A voice from the dark is calling me.
> In the close house I nurse a fire.
> Out in the dark cold winds rush free,
> To the rock heights of my desire.
> I smother in the house in the valley below,
> Let me out to the night, let me go, let me go.[12]

Whatever their problems with marriage, however, both poets had a deep need for love. In the poem, "Unto Her," Monro spoke of "Peace and eventual Heaven in your mind; / And in your body, that one place I have sought, / A tranquil lodging for my stormy thought," while Anna wrote in "The Wife's Song,"

> I would carry you in my arms,
>   My strong one,
> As if you were a child;
> Over the long grass plains by the sea,
> Where dunes are piled.[13]

By the time Anna met him, Monro may have already taken on as his shop assistant, Alida Klemantaski, seventeen years his junior. She seems to have loved Monro almost from the day they met and when Monro's first shop assistant left, Alida made herself indispensable. She had ambition and taught herself many things, from bookkeeping to hand-coloring book covers and rhyme sheets. Harold came to love her idealism, her innocence, and her tender ministrations, but she didn't understand Monro's sexuality. This made Monro guilt ridden, while Alida compensated for her lack of understanding by abhorring anyone who dwelt on sexual matters. Mrs. Hepburn, she wrote to Monro, was one.

> Mrs. Hepburn drives me mad. Bodies seem lovely things till she comes & makes [crossed out] strives to make one feel that sex is the only thing that matters & one act between a man & a woman, all that life means, & defiles the body with her thought. I hate having to come in contact with her & only want to get away & hide from everything. Dearest, forgive me writing of myself. I meant to say many other things, but again I haven't managed.[14]

Klemantaski's general attitude toward sex—fearful, frightened, or holy—isolated her from some of the bookshop's patrons. In letters to Harold she railed against those who made sexual advances, or those who did not fit into the "lady" category and who "would enjoy anything from a man."[15] Klemantaski's letters expressing a smothering love of Monro and a vitriolic antagonism toward those people or things that she thought threatened Monro's stability or their combined happiness (they only married in 1920 at the urging of one of Monro's friends). But since Monro always maintained an existence apart from Klemantaski, including lunching and dining almost daily with writers and artists and going to the continent without her, Anna's friendship with Monro flourished to the extent her husband and family life left her time to be with others, to the extent that Klemantaski's objections were brushed aside and to the extent that Anna's caustic opinion of Alida was disregarded.

Anna's poetry was well-respected by Monro for what he called her "rare power of condensing a troublesome problem of social psychology into the form of a lyric."[16] He liked her "chiefly conversational" style, and the variety in the moods of her work. He noted with satisfaction that "there is plenty here to shock those mild beings who delight in the thrill of a good shock," but felt that she was certainly more than "a brilliant writer of psychological gossip." He admired her "frank sensuality," and advised men, in particular, to read her poems in order to appreciate, "a woman whose intellect controls her senses, and whose love-poems are as natural as daylight or snow."

Just as it was no secret that Alida Klemantaski "loathed" Anna (as one of Wickham's sons has said), it was no secret that Harold Monro had "a great feeling for Anna both as a poet and as a person."[17] Before long his diary began to read, "Tea with Mrs. Hepburn." She could match his sadness and bitterness, she could jolly him along in letters, excuse his dourness to others, even eventually "drink level with him and understand, what was more, why he drank himself," as Penelope Fitzgerald says.[18] If Monro took her into his confidence when he himself had a nervous breakdown in August of 1919 and spent time in a sanatorium at Caterham, her understanding may have been especially helpful.[19]

Not that Anna did not become irritated with him. Later still she complained that in his fear of the censors (a force to be reckoned with in those days of the ordered destruction of D. H. Lawrence's *The Rainbow* and James Joyce's *Ulysses* and a printer refusing one of Charlotte Mew's poems) Monro was printing her so "innocently" that her reputation would suffer permanently.[20] In a poem, "To Harold Monro," she even accused the bookshop of "filching" the fees due to her.[21] When Monro wanted to bring out a "Collected Edition" in 1927, Anna found it irksome that he did not want new things from her: "He thinks I should have died in 1915," she wrote Natalie Barney.[22]

But back to the issue of how Anna Wickham and Harold Monro first learned of each other. Not just anybody could open a bookshop—even in the great city of London—devote it solely to the sale and cosseting of poetry and expect it to be and stay a going financial concern as it did (with ups and serious downs). It might not have been possible without the almost tireless energy of Alida, of course, who kept the place going during the First World War and even kept it open after Harold's death in 1932. But even with her assistance it could not possibly have been done unless the owner was lucky enough to have a private income. This was exactly the case with Harold Monro. Five generations of his family (his father the engineer was an exception) had nourished a business that was stable enough to provide Monro with an income sufficient for a modest, but decent living.[23] This business was none other than Brooke House, the private asylum belonging to the Monros since the late 1700s, and where Anna, just before coming into Harold Monro's shop, had spent a long summer.

Works about Harold Edward Monro, which detail his publishing and poetic career, only touch on his connection with Brooke House. Joy Grant calls the asylum by name; Ruth Tomalin gives an idea of how much income Monro derived from the business.[24] Dominic Hibberd, Harold Monro's biographer, notes that when Monro ordered his affairs before his World War I service began he made a visit to Brooke House as part of that planning. By 1928, Hibberd's biography states, Harold was a trustee and had regular meetings with the trustees and with Dr. Johnson, the Brooke House physician in charge.[25] But in 1913, when the license for the private asylum was held by Mr. H. T. Monro and two others, Harold may not have had as much to do with the business, though even then a Dr. Gerald Johnston was resident physician and coholder of the license.[26]

If Monro had a close relationship with the doctor at the asylum, that doctor surely knew that Monro had opened a bookshop devoted to poetry and he may have thought that Monro would be interested to hear of this most unusual woman hospitalized, at least in part, for the egregious sin of writing her heart out in poetry. The doctor, after giving Anna the means to write, may have mentioned the publications of the bookshop. Then again, at that time, Monro may have simply collected his share of proceeds from an asylum trust, may have had no communication with the doctors running the business, and no interest in the place other than as a producer of his yearly income.

So did the doctor tell Anna of this bookshop, happy that his fascinating patient might find a supportive and interesting society there? Did Monro tell her of his interest in Brooke House?[27] If the doctor never told Monro of the new patient, would Anna herself have told Monro where she had just spent her summer? As a matter of fact, how many people knew that Anna had been hospitalized?[28]

Harold Monro has taken some criticism, including self-criticism, for rejecting early poetry of T. S. Eliot and Edward Thomas.[29] (John Drinkwater, poet, playwright, actor, and friend of Monro sheds light on this by explaining, "although he was often unaffected by good work he never liked bad."[30]) Some have faulted him (he gets praised for the same reason) for attempting to walk some sort of middle line in poetry—always scanning the horizon for the poet who will speak to the people without offending too many of them.[31] If Harold Monro took Anna's poems without knowing where she had written them, he risked no more criticism than was usual in the press. If Harold Monro, however, knew that Anna had recently been released from his asylum, and if he thought her stay was widely known, he opened himself up to further scrutiny. Was he irresponsible in publishing the work of an asylum patient? Was he generous in promoting such work? There was already interest in the intersection of art and madness; for example, the psychiatric clinic doctors at the University of Heidelberg had begun assembling drawings and paintings by patients in German, Swiss, and Austrian asylums.[32] Was the venerable Monro asylum, often in the forefront of developments, part of this trend?

From their early meetings ("tea with Mrs. Hepburn"), the relationship between Monro and the modern-thinking Hampstead poet grew less formal and more direct. "Mrs. Hepburn" came to insist that he address his letters to "Anna Wickham." She felt free to harangue him about small matters (the deportment of his clerk, for example). She sometimes regretted his reserve and felt he should publish bolder, riskier works. She shrewdly assessed and disapproved of Alida's attempts to restrict his freedoms. Monro, who over the years probably heard, read, and edited well over a hundred of Anna's poems, probably came to know her as well as any of her fellow poets did. It seems almost certain that the asylum, Brooke House, would have come up in their conversations eventually.

The question of how much Harold Monro and Anna Wickham knew about each other when they met is still a literary mystery. The Hepburn sons were told it this way: Harold Monro saw her poetry, liked it, and encouraged her to write.[33] Anna just says that after her release, " . . . I heard of the Poetry Bookshop."[34]

TWELVE

Anna Wickham and
D. H. Lawrence (1915)

Anna Wickham's poetry had been published in Monro's *Poetry and Drama* in June 1914. Only two months later, England was at war (the account of Anna and Patrick during that conflict will be in the next chapter). Though the war was expected to be over quickly, by the spring of 1915 it was evident that the war might be long and burdensome. Early policy measures, such as control over telegraphy and foreign grain purchases, were not enough. Economic management had to become government directed, and the munitions industry must come under a ministry of munitions. The Liberal government, which had been in power, made way for a coalition headed by Asquith. Society in general began to feel the pinch of manpower shortages and disruptions of various kinds. Even though measures such as rationing for civilians had not yet begun it was *not* "business as usual."

Yet even while war's demands on the country became heavier, changes close to home were cheering, almost triumphant, for Anna. As Patrick had feared, and she had hoped, her career as a poet was launched. It was undoubtedly a personal triumph for her when *The Contemplative Quarry*, in orange paper wrappers with black lettering and black decorative border, came out in May to such good reviews. Monro, too, must have been pleased by this, for though within the length of a chapbook (being less than forty-eight pages), apart from the *Georgian Poetry* and *Des Imagists* anthologies, it was his Poetry Bookshop's biggest book so far.[1]

Probably the second most rewarding event of 1915 was getting to know two people who, for a short time, were her neighbors: D. H. and Frieda Lawrence.

In the Lawrences' parlor in their home just across Hampstead Heath, Anna felt at home. She felt that she was back "to the thrift, pride and diligence" that had built her grandfather's house.[2] And like the small houses of her childhood, like the sitting rooms of the up-breeding workman or small bourgeois, it contained merit-conferring articles of property. On Lawrence's wall was a blue Persian rug. It was his totem symbol.[3] Anna could also, however, understand how he wanted to escape his working-class background, to create a new man. For the five months, August through December, 1915, that Lawrence lived in Hampstead, they had a rewarding friendship.

Lawrence's poems had appeared in Ford Madox Ford's *English Review* and, in the U. S., Harriet Monroe's *Poetry: A Magazine of Verse*. In anthologies, too, his poetry was represented in influential places. His work would appear in Amy Lowell's Imagist anthologies. And a friend of the arts, Edward Marsh, had asked Lawrence for his poem, "Snapdragon" for the first *Georgian Poetry 1911–1912* as well as for two Lawrence poems for the second *Georgian Poetry* (1915), published by The Poetry Bookshop. Though he had not yet attained his reputation as one of the best-known and most provocative writers of the twentieth century, Lawrence was making headway.

He had recently been living with his wife, Frieda, in various cottages in the country, working on new novels. He hoped to follow up on the critical success of his 1913 *Sons and Lovers*. But in the country he couldn't even buy a typewriter ribbon, much less find contact with writers and prospective disciples. He and Frieda decided that 1 Byron Villas, Hampstead, was what they needed.[4] At the edge of the Heath, the area called The Vale of Health was thought to be good for people who, like Lawrence, had lung trouble. Frieda would also be close to her children and Lawrence to his publishers.[5] In this empty lower flat, for the first time in their life together they could set about furnishing a home, finding secondhand furniture, hanging gifts like a gilt mirror from neighbor and fellow writer Catherine Carswell and installing other items to establish comfort. This produced in Lawrence a "gay and careless mood," at least according to Carswell. To Bertrand Russell, however, Lawrence wrote: "very dislocated and unhappy in these new circumstances . . . delivered up to chairs and tables and doormats."[6]

Anna Wickham herself was not in a mood to focus on her domestic satisfactions; she was after the life of the mind and was writing "at the rate of a hundred lines a morning, with only half an eye on the kitchen and nursery."[7] But the Hepburn home, well-stocked, well-furnished, and located just one block off Hampstead's High Street, was a source of comfort to the Lawrences. On her Broadwood piano, Anna played works by Grieg, Schumann, Chopin, Beethoven, and Mozart and she accompanied Lawrence, who liked to sing, on any hymn he chose. Besides the music there was the attraction of servants to cook, attend, and help keep order. And in wild disarray there were books. Everywhere. An accumulation on every floor of the house and spilling out of the long shelves. Books on science, books on music, complete works of Robert Louis Stevenson, Rudyard Kipling, Sir Walter Scott, and the eighteenth-century politician and writer, the Right Honourable Edmund Burke, who wrote extensively on issues of emancipation. There was poetry from Tennyson to Yeats.[8] The latest in little magazines, such as *The English Review*. Karl Marx. *Pilgrim's Progress*. Foxed and bumped Bibles. The Hepburn family histories. *The Holy Roman Empire*. In her ordering phase Anna had organized the volumes by a letter and number system of her own devising. The books had the marks, if not the location, of all this obsessive attention, and the sweep of their range made a great welcome to any booklover crossing Number 49's bridge and threshold.

Though Anna seems not to have met Lawrence before the summer of 1915, David Garnett had often talked to Anna about Lawrence and Frieda and the days he had spent with them in Germany in 1912. He and Lawrence had collected plants on their walks in the mountains, and Lawrence had often held forth on his expanding ideas. Lawrence and Frieda in love had deeply impressed him. In telling Anna about all of this he probably also, however, had shown his impatience with some of Lawrence's more recent ideas, which included formation of a society of people who could "hope" (the aim was rather vague, but the thrust was away from bellicose England). Then in April, 1915, only a few months before Lawrence and Frieda took the Hampstead flat, relations between Lawrence and Garnett had broken off.[9] So, though Garnett did visit them once in the fall of 1915 on a break from his Friends War Victims Relief work, it was Dolly Radford who introduced the Lawrences to Anna, this striking woman that they had only heard of.

Anna knew the facts of Lawrence's past: how Lawrence had gone to meet a Professor Ernest Weekley and then, within a month, fled to the continent with Weekley's aristocratic German wife, Frieda. She also knew that Lawrence and Frieda had married in the summer of 1914, several months after the decree absolute of Frieda's divorce, and that Frieda had lost custody of the children. Extremely sympathetic to this situation, Anna opened her home to them and they opened theirs to her.

Anna recognized energetic and courageous Frieda as "the tent pole of this new Goth's dwelling," housing a man who "might well be emperor of Rome, if he found the right javelin, and was allowed enough time."[10] Lawrence and Anna could talk to each other. If Anna would not fall in with some of his ideas, she had a quick intelligence that understood and responded to his rapid-fire images. And as a poet who was experimenting with both formal and free verse she appealed to Lawrence.

Born within two years of each other (Lawrence was the younger), both had loved poetry early on, both appreciated music, and though nature may have figured more prominently in Lawrence's work than in Anna's, both found beauty in green and growing things. Both were enamored of the world of ideas. Both had overwhelming feelings for their mothers (Lawrence's had died in 1910) and in general, both writers had outsized passions and outspoken natures. And if Anna was in (unexpressed perhaps) turmoil from the asylum experience, Lawrence too was in turmoil. In trying to make his living from writing, he was often hard up and forced to think about money, even to the point of making appeals for funds. A year spent increasingly in the company of Lady Cynthia Asquith, Lady Ottoline Morrell, and Bertrand Russell had left him feeling more and more distanced from his roots, and yet increasingly dissatisfied with the upper classes too. Anna, though her surroundings were elegant enough to feed Lawrence's social-climbing instincts, had the added advantage of understanding his background.

Like Anna's mother, Lawrence had trained in the Board School system. Anna well understood that in terms of social acceptance this meant that during his teaching years he was in a sort of no-man's land. Raised above his pupils, but far below not only those who ran the system and hired him but also the "public school" networks that educated the upper classes, Board School teachers like Lawrence existed in a social limbo, misfits who felt the sting of not belonging anywhere. Yet this not fitting in actually provided a sort of creative freedom that Lawrence may not have understood as well as Anna's mother had. As Lawrence came to be identified as a writer he had moved up in the English caste system and, for example, stayed at Lady Morrell's country house and corresponded freely with the Asquiths. That accomplished, he then had to face their judgments, as well as thank them for their help.

With the Board School as the opening topic of conversation, he and Anna strode across the broad reaches of Hampstead Heath. Anna said at times she felt the two of them were "like a pair of cold children shut out of a tenement together, while the elders were out in their uncultivated manner hunting up food."[11] Though Lawrence was slight of build and always weak in the chest, he was a demon for walking. He and Anna covered miles of the Heath together, deeply occupied in talk. In his anger, humor, or sense of mischief, Lawrence was nothing if not intense, and Anna enjoyed this intensity. On one walk her sons eight-year-old Jim and six-year-old John waylaid the pair. Tired of having the red-haired man divert their mother's attention, they pelted him with snowballs from their hiding place behind a tree.

It is not recorded anywhere what the boys' father, Patrick, thought of these rambles. But perhaps Lawrence makes clear what he thought about Patrick. In *The Captain's Doll*, a short novel published in 1923, well after he knew Anna, "Captain Hepburn" is an astronomer with an "air of aloofness and perfect diffidence that marks an officer and a gentleman."[12] With his aristocratic bearing and his "beautifully modeled" features he is "a perfect portrait of an officer of a Scottish regiment." One of the women in the story, Mitchka, is afraid of Hepburn because he is "like a closed road" in his self-sufficiency and ability to compartmentalize his life. This Hepburn, who after his military service finds his calling in astronomy, says, "It's been an immense relief to me watching the moon. . . . I look right out—into freedom."[13] The description of Hepburn's telescopes surely came from seeing Patrick's. Likewise, the character Hepburn may well have been based on Patrick. The character Hepburn suffered through the love of, first, his mother, then his sister, then a girl known all his life. "Then my wife: and that was my most terrible mistake," Lawrence has Captain Hepburn say after her untimely death from a fall, "a caged wild bird . . . suffering." Of course, these loves would also describe Lawrence's, but they resonate with the real Patrick Hepburn as well. Lawrence, in his writing, probably traded on his knowledge of Patrick Hepburn in a way that would have alarmed the private side of Patrick and irritated Anna's idea of what was good form where her husband was concerned.[14] Though Anna felt justified in criticizing Patrick, she did not like others to do so.

If Patrick was still making Anna suffer through his silences, she now had someone close by with whom to talk about ideas. As Anna said, "In Lawrence's room I was at home again after my escape by marriage into the fecklessnesses and disorders of the descendants of the Tudors, the Stuarts and the Patron of Hereward the Wake."[15] With some people Lawrence dominated, or tried to dominate conversations. With Anna, however, there was usually give and take. She felt the relief of the interchange of ideas with him. After years of listening to Patrick's facts and observations, she felt Lawrence "relieved me of the burden of my mind and at the same time tried to reveal what was in his mind to me."[16] Their talk was "never of personalities," never of "coal-mining" nor "aunts and uncles." But the conversations were "communion . . . profound and exceedingly serious." Lawrence never tried to approach her sexually, a fact that years later Anna said she was rather offended about, but he did insist on two things: "that I should talk to him, and sing hymns with him, the lovely hymns of our grandfathers, the weavers, the little farmers, the rather larger shopkeepers, the millers. These songs scented with the courage and tenderness that is in English land."[17]

In addition to times in the long, sunny drawing room at 49 Downshire Hill and their walks on the Heath, they would also meet at Dolly and Ernest Radford's, 32 Well Walk, Hampstead. The Radfords had known D. H. since 1909. Dollie kept the Lawrence of radical ideas on a short leash and succeeded in making him talk about "fields and gardens and country manners."[18] Not quite as decorous were evenings at 1 Byron Villas when the "meeting" spirit would prevail and Lawrence would rail at his friends, holding forth, as Anna said, on the bipolarized Absolute. The casually, comfortably dressed Anna sat near Mrs. Carswell, neat in her "evening dress, her party shoes laced to the knee with yellow ribbons."[19] Others also were in the audience. As Lawrence grew more and more pedantic and prophetic both Frieda and Anna grew increasingly uneasy— Frieda because Lawrence seemed to be unmannerly to his guests, Anna because Lawrence seemed to be sounding off like a Board School teacher. But his stridency came from his real agony over events in England.

In 1915, Lloyd George, who would replace then-Prime Minister Asquith by the end of 1916, was convincing opponents that the war was a "crusade."[20] The trench warfare particular to this war was taking its deadly toll. Big guns, rifles, and trench conditions decimated the ranks. Men were needed to replace the fallen soldiers. Poet Robert Graves, then just out of Patrick's alma mater, Charterhouse, and intending to go to Oxford, was instead commissioned to a Special Reservist detachment of Welshmen where he learned about war, firsthand. Rupert Brooke, friend of Edward Marsh and a poet who had charmed readers with his poem, "The Old Vicarage, Grantchester," died the same year. By June 1916 Harold Monro of The Poetry Bookshop would be called up despite his poor health; because of the war, he had in December 1914 already ceased publication of his little magazine *Poetry and Drama.*

Along with the war came changes in attitude. As the country became more nationalistic, anti-German sentiment troubled the lives of German shopkeepers, waiters, intellectuals, and writers. Zeppelin raids, one of which Lawrence witnessed from Hampstead Heath and later reproduced in *Kangaroo,* exacerbated the situation. The country began to see things in terms of "the enemy" instead of "the house of Hanover" with its royal ties to England. Since Frieda was German, Lawrence had a special worry. His politics shifted and he began to lash out at England. He remained a pacifist.

Those who were halfhearted about Lawrence's ideas eventually found themselves frozen out; those like Bertrand Russell who disagreed found themselves on the point-end of a signed poison-pen letter.[21] On the other hand, those who seemed to give some promise of understanding Lawrence were asked to contribute. During his stay in Hampstead he decided to start a paper, *The Signature,* with friends Katherine Mansfield and John Middleton Murry. Violently opposed to the war himself, Lawrence hoped to gather sufficient support to issue the magazine regularly. Subscribers such as Anna Wickham paid a half-crown for the short-lived journal.[22]

Though Anna might have had work that would have fit *Signature,* the paper was strictly the mouthpiece for the three who had begun it. But Lawrence did appreciate Anna's work, copying it out by hand to send on to editors.[23] The first of these was Edward Marsh of *Georgian Poetry.* Though

Edward Marsh was employed by Winston Churchill and hemispherically opposite to Lawrence on the issue of the war, they had social ties, mutual friends in society such as Lady Cynthia Asquith and Lady Ottoline Morrell, both supporters of the arts. Marsh liked Lawrence, occasionally helped him financially, and for a wedding gift thoughtfully sent the Lawrences the *Complete Works* of Hardy, which was helpful for the project Lawrence was then working on.[24]

Lawrence wrote to Marsh in September, when Anna was already planning her second book of poems:

> Dear Eddie, I don't believe you've seen these poems by Anna Wickham (Mrs. Hepburn). She is just bringing out a book, with Grant Richards: either in December or February. . . . I think some of these poems *very* good. You may like them for the *Georgian Poetry.*[25]

Anna's work had, as recently as June 1915, appeared in the *Egoist,* which only the month before proudly brought out an Imagist issue. And Lawrence's "very good" was the equivalent of another person's pages of praise. But Edward Marsh did not use Anna's poems, though much later yet another of his contributors quotes her from memory.[26] In all of the anthologies—five volumes over a period of ten years that sold well and brought financial rewards to the contributors—Marsh used the poems of only two women, Fredegond Shove and Victoria Mary Sackville-West. Though purporting to look for "new" and "modern" writers, *Georgian Poetry* was very much the child of a single parent, Edward Marsh, and in terms of policy and selection, the favored child was, undeniably, male.

Not really deterred by Marsh's rejection, on October 26, 1915, Lawrence sent five of Anna's poems to another place where he had been published, in Chicago poet Harriet Monroe's *Poetry.* Monroe used the poems in the January 1917 issue of her magazine. Not only did Monroe print the poems Lawrence sent, but she made only minor changes in Anna's work, which was quite the opposite treatment that she gave William Carlos Williams, who would go on to become one of the most respected poets in the U. S. One of the poems chosen, "My Lady Surrenders," has the type of effective catachrestic ending Wickham uses occasionally, while "After Annunciation" is a gentle, spare address from a mother (possibly, but not necessarily, the mother of Jesus) to a child.

Poetry was just the sort of exposure needed to bring Anna Wickham's poetry before an intelligent reading audience far beyond its origins in the middle of the United States. Harriet Monroe sought to print verse more than the mundane fare then printed primarily as filler in American newspapers and general-interest magazines. A woman with a mission, angry that poets had to subsist on what she called "a bread and water prison diet," she felt that donors, press, and public "respectful" toward painting, sculpture, and architecture were "contemptuous" toward poetry.[27] With Alice Corbin Henderson, and later Ezra Pound as "foreign editor" beating the bushes for good material, she succeeded in finding stable financial support in five-year pledges from wealthy Chicago philanthropists, lovers of the arts, women's clubs, and individual artists. (The magazine continues today.) Monroe confounded those who had expected "a worthless assemblage of petty rhymesters under soft feminine editorship."[28]

How Lawrence could have roused himself at this time to help along a friend's career is quite amazing. For he was in the midst of a censorship battle. On November 3, 1915, a magistrate's warrant suppressing *The Rainbow* had crushed Lawrence's hopes for that book, at least in England. Despite protests all copies were ordered destroyed on charges of obscenity. It was a cruel blow, made all the more so because Lawrence's publisher did not defend the book.

Lawrence had already been seeking to leave England. After spending time in lines in the foreign office "shed," he had then called on Cynthia Asquith to help cut red tape so he could get a passport. Ultimately, however, instead of New York, Florida, or Spain—destinations they considered—Lawrence and Frieda were forced by the war to stay in England. They did, however, leave London. By December 31, 1915, Lawrence had transferred the lease of 1 Byron Villas, sold or given away all the furniture, and decamped with Frieda to Cornwall, angry and bitter.

Despite Lawrence's help in getting Anna published, she seems to have been able to appraise him coolly. Though she admired his fire and found talking with him an immense relief, eventually she felt that his writings exuded "a sort of miasma of menace towards women who detach any considerable portion of their energy from their purely sexual function."[29] Although in their conversations the two were on equal footing, and she remembers Lawrence as "kindly" in not insisting on a monologue (as if she would have permitted a monologue without interrupting), Anna recognized that in his writings there was "some madness of preconceived truth" rather than the more measured "observations" that came out in his conversation. The on-the-page Lawrence was different from Lawrence on the Heath. In conversation on their walks she was able to get through to the "real man" without fighting through the thicket of pretensions and edicts. She could laugh at his exaggerations and still maintain the fondness that existed between them. Anna and Lawrence could range wide over the Heath in their walks, discussing "the granular quality which is the nature of cause" and other things. Still, it was a friendship that does not seem to have continued after Lawrence's stay in Hampstead.

Lawrence did continue to write to fellow Hampstead resident Catherine Carswell after he left for Cornwall (Carswell's lawyer husband vetted Lawrence's work for actionable writing). But Anna, who saw some of those letters to Carswell, said that she would have been impatient with some of the phrasing: "I congratulate myself that Lawrence would no more have thought of writing like that to me than he would have thought of offering his Mother a bad half-crown."[30] Coming out of similar backgrounds, Anna had a unique perspective on Lawrence the man. Anna would not brook Lawrence's pretensions, just as she could not resist taking teasing aim at his sexual bluster: "Had I married you, dear, when I was nineteen / I had been little since but a printing machine / For before my fortieth year had run / I well had produced you a twenty-first son."[31] At times she seems to have grown truly impatient with Lawrence's cock-of-the-walk attitude, calling him in an unguarded moment, the "Universe's gigolo."[32] Still, during the months when he lived in Hampstead she gave comfort and attention. Her husband, with no say in the matter, gave Lawrence the basis for a future character. And Anna's travels in Ceylon and her early years in Australia may have even given impetus to the Lawrences' later decision to travel to those faraway places that seemed to speak freedom and new beginnings.[33]

THIRTEEN

The Hepburn Family during the War (1914 and beyond)

As I stand at the bottom of the hill I am conscious of a faint insistent rhythm. It is a drum and fife band in the distance. . . . Soon there is a swaying on the crest of the hill. This becomes a ribbon of marching men that the street lamps mottle with shadow and light . . . in some way the sound of the music and the marching feet have a certain quality of silence. The sound and the scene no longer appeal to the eye and the ear, but only to the mind. They become like things vividly thought. . . . The march seems like the march of ghosts. . . . I am left in the street with tears in my eyes.

Anna Wickham in "The Night March"[1]

In the night march of recruits through London, Anna says that seeing the recruits, their instruments, the horses that stepped to the music, and the civilians walking along beside them connected her in some way to ancestors who had fought long before. This was not a comfortable connection, however, for filtering through the scene of fanfare were "the powers of death and hell."[2]

But Anna lived in a time where English imperial power, though waning, continued to arouse deeply patriotic feelings about the sanctity of country. These feelings had been always encouraged by her father and mother who, though living lives of self-exile, held England dear. When Belgium had quickly fallen to German attack at the war's beginning, Anna had agonized over that fall not only because journalistic accounts reported and sometimes embellished stories of German horrors but because she too had a Belgian connection in that her grandmother Whelan had lived there until age 15.[3] Add to this mix of family influence the long discussions both with friends David Garnett, who was against the war and determined to stay out of it, and D. H. Lawrence, who was raging against carnage and bull-headed nationalism, and it is no wonder that Anna was stung to tears by the night marches moving past no. 49 Downshire Hill and onto the Heath. Just as much of the world was dividing itself up into belligerent camps, England too was sometimes a divided place, where conflicting arguments swirled and passions were strong. At the end of 1915, about the time the Lawrences were packing for Cornwall, the latest national political argument—over whether service should be voluntary or mandatory—was reaching a conclusion. Anna had cause for concern.

In the opinion of Lady Cynthia Asquith, friend of the Lawrences and daughter-in-law to Prime Minister Asquith, the last dregs of the voluntary system "had become almost sickening, with an attitude of 'Come along *willingly!* or we'll fetch you.'"[4] In at least the first 1916 rounds of conscription Patrick Hepburn, forty-three years old and a married man, would have been exempt. He knew, however, that boys of fifteen and men in their sixties, the latter often veterans of other campaigns, were lying about their ages in order to fight. The casualties at the fronts, the shell-shocked, gassed, wounded, and maimed soldiers who were coming home to be tended, all these left manpower gaps in the trenches dug in the mud of France to hold off the Germans who themselves were dug in across the ravaged moonscape of no-man's-land. The war machine needed men. The inevitable moment approached when Patrick Hepburn, from a clan where the pikes had often been raised in battle, would have to decide. Should he, could he, stay on at his law office? There, even in the best of times, he felt cut off from his scientific interests and the physical side of life. And now the call to service was strong. He enlisted. On January 25, 1916, roughly a year and one half after the guns first sounded, Patrick was given a commission in the Royal Naval Air Service. By February 2 he had completed initial training in the Kite Balloon section. By February 14 sub-lieutenant Hepburn was on his way to the British East African campaign against German East Africa, whose defense was being so brilliantly conducted by General von Letlow-Vorbeck.

At home, there was suddenly a silence. So many arguments, so much tension and contention, so many struggles for supremacy and freedom to act, now, suddenly were over. The battles of marriage had been pushed off the map by a larger struggle, which itself would have a profound effect on all members of the Hepburn family: Patrick, in uniform, one man among many; Anna, suddenly a woman with no wall to push against and the world outside altering daily; the boys, children in a time of war.

With enlistment began the complicated dance that Anna and Patrick stepped to during the war, a dance of separation and embrace. War brought them temporarily closer, though never completely healing the personal wounds of 1913.[5] But it is possible that the separation may have begun on a very bitter note for Patrick, a bitterness caused by Anna's next volume of poetry.

During 1915, about the same time that Lawrence was encouraging Edward Marsh, of the *Georgian Poetry* anthologies, to include Anna's poetry, Anita Bartle Brackenbury, Anna's friend, neighbor, and an enthusiastic advocate of her poetry, wanted to introduce her to the publisher Grant Richards and push hard for publication of a book to follow Anna's *Contemplative Quarry*. Mrs. Brackenbury (she was also known as Miss Bartle), who never believed that "less is more," was an eternal optimist who had been plying Grant Richards with ideas for anthologies and even offered—he demurred—to have his horoscope read. During the war, because she appeared to be from South America, she had had to defend her British "right of abode" in a hearing. "She announced in court in a strong Chilean accent that she was a natural born British subject." Which was true, but she offered as evidence her parentage, when at the time "ladies didn't announce in public that they were illegitimate."[6] Anita's court ordeal, an illness she was suffering from, and her generous nature brought out Anna's tender side and she wrote a number of poems praising Brackenbury. The poems alone might have irritated Patrick, but even if Anna had been neutral, which she wasn't, Anita was just the type to set Patrick's teeth on edge: she "knew everyone," was vocal and energetic, had a reputation as a lesbian and, sin of sins, she admired Anna. Anita had sheltered Anna when she needed it, offering a place where rest, "dreaming," "laughter," and "weeping" were permitted.[7] Anita's husband, an inventor, also admired Anna, and Anna felt affection for both husband and wife and their son, Peter, and daughter, Marigold.[8]

Anna became as close to Anita as she had been in Bloomsbury to the social worker/artist Emily Colles. In poems, she responded gratefully that Anita's garden, "dug deep for flowers, / Through sunny self-forgetful hours" had provided "care / And loving" during a "summer when my life was cold."[9] It is also possible that Anita, at no. 14a Downshire Hill, may have been the neighbor who provided lodgings for Anna's mother during the turmoil of 1913, a further link of friendship and loyalty.

To Grant (Thomas Franklin) Richards, Brackenbury sent a manuscript of Anna's work selected from the last year or two. Richards found the title, *The Man With a Hammer,* distasteful, suggesting instead, "Man's Woman in Revolt," but thought most of the poems were wonderful and "ought to be worthily published."[10] Poet and publisher met face-to-face in his office, 8 St. Martin's Street, on Friday, September 24, 1915. Two weeks later an agreement was drawn up. By November 9 the pages of the book were already in galley proof, indicating his enthusiasm and his desire to go full-speed ahead, though only a year before a more cost-conscious Richards had admitted, "I am afraid of poetry at present."[11] But he had been in publishing long enough to know a moment that must be seized, and he made sure to ask Anna Wickham to give him a recent photograph for publicity purposes.[12]

From 1897 (and until 1948), Richards, the temperamental and highly individual publisher of novels, poetry, and nonfiction volumes on literary and social criticism, travel, gardening, and cooking had sought out such singular writers as George Bernard Shaw and A. E. Housman and had founded the World's Classics series in 1901. He was ultimately, if not always immediately, innovative; for example, he brought out James Joyce's *Dubliners* in June of 1914, though the book was first offered to him in 1905.[13] Though his business dealings often resulted in a stymied cash flow and even several bankruptcies, by 1915 Richards, "with a gleaming monocle, and behind it a shrewd inquisitive eye," had embarked on what would turn out to be his two decades of general publishing success.[14] Though he published some works only for the bottom line, his pride, as Anna discovered, "rested on the works of fiction and poetry that launched or furthered the careers of their authors."[15]

His objective for Anna Wickham's book was the big Christmas bookselling season. Snags arose, however. A hoped-for preface by the physician and sex expert, Havelock Ellis, whose popular writings were having a liberating (or scandalous, depending on your point of view) influence, never materialized. There was a wait for the dedication (not surprisingly it was "To Anita Bartle Brackenbury"). These problems pushed back the publication date. In addition, letters would arrive from Anna or Anita altering lines of poems. Richards finally put his foot down and prohibited further changes, saying, "I know enough about the poetical temperament to know that with a volume containing 100 poems one can think of a new alteration every day in the week."[16] Another delay was caused by the shifting number of poems to be published; Anita would add poems and Anna would take them out. The major culprit was the poem "Nervous Prostration" ("I married a man of the Croydon class") that had simultaneously figured so prominently both in Anna's troubles with Patrick (she had tauntingly yelled it at him) and in her salvation at the asylum (it so impressed the doctor that he brought her writing materials). The big question was whether or not this poem should be included in the book. In or out, out or in, Anna could not make up her mind. Finally, by November 18, the dangerous poem was included. Then wartime labor shortages at the printers in Edinburgh delayed page proofs until December 4 and it became apparent to the irritable Brackenbury and the defensive Richards that Christmas availability, the hoped-for target, was a fading hope. A few advance copies arrived in Richards's Leicester Square office on December 15 but it was not until the 21st of January, 1916, that the book came out, probably meaning a significant loss of potential sales.

The poem "Nervous Prostration" appeared on page thirty-six of a ninety-six-page book; buried, but perhaps not deep enough for Patrick's tastes. And the first lines ("My Dear was a mason / And I was his stone") of the book's title poem must also have glared accusingly at him, though the total effect of this poem is softer than its opening. With Anna's new book, the recently-named Junior Warden, Freemason Patrick Hepburn, a man of "the Croydon class" who would have liked a woman who complemented his deeds instead of competing with them, once again found his wife in the limelight and himself in the searchlight. There is a chance that in the two years since Anna had begun to fashion a new life for herself he had grown used to her outspokenness. It may be that he was too preoccupied with his astronomy work, his briefs at the law office, and his charitable committee work to be much interested any more in what Anna did. And, of course, given his sophisticated literary tastes, he was perhaps able to separate the male subject of many of the poems from any identification with himself. Nevertheless, facts speak. A few days after Anna's *The Man With a Hammer* came out, Patrick had volunteered for the war and what would turn out to be lengthy separations from England and from Anna.

The Man With a Hammer contained 167 poems.[17] The price was 2s. 6d. net. and the size listed as Crown 8vo (7¹⁰⁄₁₆" × 5³⁄₁₆"). With a gray linen cover and indigo all-caps title, author's and publisher's names displayed on the spine, it is obviously put together with the respect that Richards gave poetry and literature, the pride of his publishing heart. He advertised the volume as "very notable . . . a poet in revolt . . . against the stupider bonds of convention, of domesticity, or ordinary urban and suburban life. The work has an atmosphere of its own: it has beauty often; always it has force."[18] The content of the book as a whole lives up to the comprehensive aim of Anna's poem "Resolution:" "I will not draw only a house or a tree, / I will draw very Me; / Everything I think, everything I see!"

The poems cover the territory. Striving after expression is one theme. Weariness is another. She writes of the attraction of religion ("Supplication") and of the power of nature to heal ("The Stormy Moon"). In "Definition" she advances a dialectic to the questions "what is a wife," "what is a mother"? She writes of the power of love to renew ("The Fired Pot"), and in "Song of Anastasia," the overwhelming satisfaction of purely sexual desire well-met: "Let love be fierce as lightning, and as brief / As summer-hail, that is a storm's relief." In "The Sad Lover" she describes how bitter it is when love has gone, for "As a dead miser yearns / For earth-stored treasure" there is "no splendid hour." She establishes both male and female personas, but allows other poems a genderless lyric musing, a narrative line or a well-formed argument.

The main subject of the volume is love. And if a poet does his or her best work on issues most difficult, then the strength of these poems about love makes clear that Anna is tackling the subject she most needs to wrestle with. Though certainly not each of her poems about love is fully realized, there is a subtlety and an almost breathtaking quality about the best of them. They also have a freer quality, as a whole, while the poems about social reform, appearing toward the end of the book, appear more obedient toward form and have a more strident tone. And about war? In her earlier *Contemplative Quarry* Anna had written

> War brings her sword to ravage and destroy,
> That through the smoke of the consuming real
> Man sees a clearer and more sure ideal.[19]

Plenty of poems about the war were being written by men at the front and published in these years for an eager public. But in this volume there is not a single one.

On his first tour of duty Patrick was gone for eight months, returning only when the war in British East Africa wound down. During his absence Anna circulated as much as she liked among the cafe tables and gatherings of those friends in the art and literary world who remained in London, certainly much more than Patrick would have approved of. But Patrick was out of the country and society itself was changing as chaperons went the way of the dodo. The tête-à-tête, though still of gossip interest in society, became common. There was a feverish desire to connect with other human beings, and again quoting Cynthia Asquith, whose diary offers a unique window into the period, "I have got extraordinary zest for human being intercourse just now, could spend the whole day in interviews. Is it in spite of, or on account of, the war."[20]

Anna may have had a love affair with her rejected journalist of 1905, William Ray, before the war was over. Later in life, during an agonizing period of self-analysis, she would condemn herself for having "played the whore" but it is not clear whether she was disgusted with herself for sexual excess or for choosing a "bore" to have a fling with. Certainly she kept up the flirtations that, she always maintained, allowed her "to imagine" in poetry, but the leering of a randy soldier, as another section of "Night March" shows, is not the kind of attention she is after.

She read her work at Harold Monro's Poetry Bookshop on February 8, 1916, to a crowd of fifty. This was an outstanding turnout and excellent publicity for the new book. A few months later, May 11, 1916, she, Harold Monro, Alida Klemantaski, Mrs. Matthay, and E. J. Dent read from behind curtains (this was before the Sitwells' *Façade* using a related strategy) the Gordon Bottomley play *King Lear's Wife*. The popularity of these readings points again to Anna's inherited and cultivated talent for the theatre, but because son Jim objected, Anna turned down another offer for theatre work on the grounds that it was not good for the family.[21] She did, however, work in munitions for a short while, perhaps sometime during the period from spring 1915 through 1916 when, in response to severe labor shortages, society women began assembling parts for respirators to help protect soldiers against the poison gas used in battle.

Many in London, for example the Omega Workshop, were mobilizing support for Belgian relief. When a group including The Duchess of Norfolk, one lady, two countesses, and one doctor banded together to provide additional relief for children in Belgium, Anna served as Honorable Secretary for this "English Committee for Assisting the Vestiaire Marie-José (A Society for providing Milk Food and Clothes to the Babies behind the firing line in Flanders)." With plenty of illustrations and sixteen color plates, *Princess Marie-José's Children's Book*, sales of which would provide funds for the project, was published in December 1916. Anna provided Chairman-Editor Mrs. Carmel Haden Guest, her old friend from drama-school days, with two poems, "The Bad Host" and "Baby Marigold," to go with drawings by W. K. Haselden and Daphne Allen.[22] Israel Zangwill, H. G. Wells, John Galsworthy, W. H. Davies, Violet Hunt, Walter de la Mare, and many others contributed to make a colorful, in many ways charming, book, but when the nationalistic poems celebrate the English "Tommies," or soldiers, and prophecy "a storm of . . . doom" for the "gross people called Hun," and cheerful rhythms are put to the words "They marched with elation / To murder a nation, / But they dug their own grave in the sun," the effect is chilling rather than warming and one doesn't imagine these contributions being good bedtime stories. Anna's two poems, however, do entertain rather than propagandize, especially her verse-tale of the antisocial little three-year-old "Achibald Percival Minns," who ignores the guests at his birthday party and is punished by the ultimate: no tea.

Volunteer work, writing, and socializing may have taken up a good many hours, but it appears that Anna's main focus during Patrick's absence was time with her sons. Jim was eight, John was six. With that intense concentration so easily summoned by children, Jim would bend over the morning newspaper, imagining his father's fate in the advance, retreat or fixity of the lines on the war maps. John was intensely proud of his father in uniform, so much so that he had to be reproved occasionally for "swank."[23] Watching their father enlist and serve, in fact, probably formed the template for war service that they would eagerly fit themselves to in 1939.

Anna did not shield them from the impact of the war, although for a very brief time she took them to live in a cottage in the Oxfordshire countryside, perhaps somewhere in Watlington.[24] One summer of the war they went to Rye to "take a break from the Zeppelins and the austerities of wartime London" and "lodged at the Hope and Anchor, a pub at the seaward end of Watchbell Street."[25] From across the channel at night came the "faint thunder of the Allied guns laying down a preliminary barrage to the second battle of the Somme." Young Jim joined a scout troop and he and the local boys were led by a retired Captain Corry, "marching through the Sussex lanes" singing a lively tune with the refrain, "He's got a pimple / On his whee-o, whee-o." Jim played with John in the ruined Camber Castle, or John pestered the shipbuilders with questions. Anna visited with friends she had made in Rye in previous summers and rested as she knitted a big square shawl. When the boys were put to bed, in her sitting room she talked deep into the night with the woman who tended the bar and came pouring her heart out to a receptive listener. Generally, however, Anna and the boys stuck it out in London, through air raids and shortages.

Though air raids may have become more associated with later wars, the 103 raids on England during the 1914–1918 war killed 1,413 people and injured thousands of others. The first of these came on May 31, 1915, when Patrick was still at home. This and the following raids came during daylight hours, but for a year toward the end of the war they were conducted only under cover of darkness. London defended itself by "balloon aprons" and fire directed against the tormenters in the sky but the eerie Zeppelins and other aircraft struck terror, and almost a sort of awe, into the people on the ground. The usual procedure at no. 49 was to race the 100 yards down the street to shelter in the imposing police station building until the "all clear" sounded. Yet even terror had its limits. On one occasion Jim was just about to finish his homework for Heathmount, his Hampstead preparatory school (where Evelyn Waugh was a few classes ahead of him), when the siren sounded. With three Latin sentences left to translate, he looked at Anna, she looked at him, and they finished the sentences together before finally closing the door behind them.

Even on days when no threatening aircraft inescapably dramatized the war, war was present in what Anna would have called her "domestic economy." Patrick's salary as a member of the R.N.A.S. would have been much less than he was making as a solicitor. Then too the country had suffered steep price increases as a result of personal stockpiling, panic buying, and

the almost inevitable profiteering. These increases were followed by com-
modity shortages, especially after the German submarines began attacking
even merchant vessels after the autumn of 1916. Finally, compulsory
rationing began in London in time for Christmas 1917.[26] Ration cards,
then ration books, were issued and Anna, like everyone else, was faced with
small sugar rations and the need to carefully plan out meat meals and keep
an eye on the amounts of bread and butter consumed by the household.[27]
Dining out was likewise met with restrictions on numbers of courses, portion sizes, and hours of sale. One such now-puzzling order stated that "No
Meals will be served over 1/3 per person. No Individual customer shall be
served at any meal whatsoever, which begins between the hours of 3 p.m.
and 6 p.m., with more than two ozs. in while of Bread, Cake, Bun, Scone
and Biscuit." Alcohol, which not only depleted supplies of valuable grain,
but also was judged to lessen the population's capacity and desire for work,
could only be bought between certain hours, though this rule was somewhat circumvented by private clubs that served alcohol to members. And
presumably the private clubs did not play moralizer by pasting up the war
posters that advised women customers to remove themselves as, or from,
temptation by "not remaining on the premises longer than is necessary for
obtaining reasonable refreshment."

Even dress became a political statement as wartime posters sternly
admonished all riders of the Underground and the buses with the message:
"To Dress Extravagantly in War Time is Worse Than Bad Form. It is
Unpatriotic." Anna, very relaxed about her clothing, may have welcomed
this order as an imprimatur. Probably the greatest difficulty was attempting to keep the help she needed to run no. 49. Anna, as one relative has
said, did not do housework, she organized it.[28] Yet, a servant's desire to
leave household service she understood. Anna was in laughing agreement
with one departing maid who was quitting her to go to work in munitions
because household service was "so chronic slow," that "I might as well be
married and have done with it."[29]

British wartime propaganda spread the word that it was important to
"keep the home fires burning," notwithstanding the fact that coal, too,
came under rationing, and in some houses more than one meal was eaten
while wearing a coat. Compliance and attitude were important, as Jim and
John, aged eleven and nine by the time the war ended, knew. The importance of "remaining steadfast" and defeating the intended effects of the
German blockade by "putting up with the inconveniences which became

increasingly manifest" was the way young boys could make a contribution to the war effort.[30]

A close sense of comradery between Anna and her sons came from this threat of the enemy at the gate. This was heightened by their combined solidarity in the face of a father's absence. But there was also a large measure of fun. To Anna's young sons "a devoted mother," she was "a tremendously stimulating person to be with."[31] The boys knew that their mother was an artist, for she read her poems to them and at least once Jim was allowed to go with her to a Poetry Bookshop reading. But in addition Anna was their leader, the idea woman, the challenger, the instigator. "We all looked to Anna. . . . We were sort of a cooperative and we did things together. . . . We thought that Anna could achieve anything. And that was the way of it."[32]

Mother and sons would go on excursions into the nearby countryside or into the city. On one occasion never to be forgotten by young Jim, they packed a hamper and sat on the spring-green bank of Welsh Harp, the beautiful reservoir lake of popular Victorian music-hall songs. Munching on their picnic sandwiches made with margarine, Jim felt the joy of self-sacrifice and told Anna patriotically that margarine really *was* superior to butter.

"She would have a lot of friends around and a lot of people always calling at our house," said Jim later, of this time when so many activities began or ended at no. 49.[33] Since Patrick's absence Anna had reconciled with the Harper relatives, and Norah Patti and husband James Anglin brought their children to Downshire Hill for a wonderful time chasing around the garden.[34] Harper aunt Gertrude Chesters and cousin Peggy came too, going home delighted at having seen Mrs. Patrick Campbell, the famous actress, and Anna at the piano with the renowned May Mückle playing cello.[35] During a time of hysteria about spying and revolution, young Chesters also was recruited to stay overnight as moral support to Anna while the latter passed worried hours in the possession of what she thought might be secret Russian spy intelligence. The next day Anna passed the story to *Daily News* magnate Alfred Harmsworth, Lord Northcliffe, who then offered Anna a ride home in his car. After stopping to buy a meat pie they ate it together at the kitchen table, but this was probably Anna's only contact with the "father of yellow journalism."[36]

Her circle, later expanding to encompass those in theatre and dance, was becoming the way she wanted it. Where at one time she had rather hoped that Patrick would make friends among the peerage, she seems to have given up this social aim and decided to be content with as wide and as varied a circle of friends as she could bring together. Enjoying the character of her maid as she did the discussions on literature, inviting in the Harper relatives with neighboring and visiting artists, she ran a loose confederation of people who interested her.

Patrick's absence also allowed her a more complete freedom to write as and where she pleased, and her continued publishing successes had given her a momentum. She began to allow herself room when hit by what her family began calling "a creative mood." This meant she might compose poetry in bed, or at the table in "a workman's shirt," as she says in her poem "A Woman in Bed," or even in the bath.[37] She was just as likely to find a poetic subject in a bus going by or an airplane overhead as in a flower, bird, or ancient myth. The boys knew that these bouts of creativity meant that the daily schedule went out the window and that the claims of the poem would come before the claims of the household. Once Anna had the first line or two of something—and she is a poet of very strong and memorable first lines—she would have to continue. Sometimes, no doubt, she finished up a poem out of sheer fatigue or irritation at interruption. (Then when she would read publicly she had a disarming way of commenting while at the podium: "Rubbish, but there it is," "Not much sense but some rhythm," or, more optimistically, "Now here's an intelligent bit.")[38]

Patrick returned from British East Africa on October 11, 1916. His long moustache was gone and his lean face appeared even leaner under his uniform hat. Disappointed at not having climbed Mount Kilimanjaro, but otherwise fine, he was stationed in England for a while. The months away had worked a mild magic on them both. Anna, like so many young wives during the war who feared the loss of their husbands, decided to have a child, becoming pregnant in February, 1917. Patrick, for his part, was "not so silent" as he had been.[39] In the time he was away he had felt himself utilized to the utmost, which, rather than making him feel depleted, seems to have opened some shut place in him and, in a way, introduced him to himself.

It was not every man who could serve in the air. The records are full of reasons a man could be turned down: "he is not sufficiently robust constitutionally," "nervous temperament," "lacks common sense," "unable to stand the strain of . . . a high altitude," "he himself is of opinion that he will never make a pilot," and finally, "is drinking too much and useless as a pilot, incompetent as an officer and entirely lacking in qualities which make an officer [appointment terminated]."[40] The Royal Naval Air Service, newly formed in July 1914, was seeking an exceptional type of man. "Quick, keen and alert" was their ideal.[41]

One of Patrick's cousins felt that the Royal Naval Air Service "ought to be honored to have him."[42] While Anna felt that this showed family hubris, Patrick's record shows that his military superiors probably would have agreed with his sisters' opinion. The record lists his impressive accomplishments. From his training as an astronomer he had "theoretical and practical knowledge of meteorology and other physical sciences." He had "knowledge of theoretical navigation" and "knowledge of signaling." He "spoke and read French, Spanish and German." He would prove to be "especially good on survey and map work." In addition to these attributes his officers might have seen indications of Patrick's other qualities, the ones that had attracted Anna too. He was intelligent, and it showed in his face. He was remarkably fit due to his habit of looking for hardship in ice-cold swims on Christmas Day; strenuous bicycle treks in England, Scotland, France, and Belgium; sailing adventures on the Broads; and mountain climbing in the Lake District and elsewhere. As Anna knew, he expected to lead. He felt duty-bound to serve. He was a stickler for detail and had trained himself to think ahead.

Finally, Patrick was in a position where he could shine. Never overly appreciated by his father or at his public school, now his science was of practical use in determining positions and mapping them and in making weather observations to be relayed down the line. His habit of conducting astronomical observations at night while heading the law office during the day had prepared him to go without sleep when necessary, and his physical conditioning to handle the temperature and altitude extremes of balloon ascents to 5,000 feet.[43] Though considered too old to be an airplane pilot (most were under thirty), his deliberate coolness to the triple threat of enemy fire intended to puncture his balloon, send it up in flames (the observer was supposed to parachute if there was time), or kill him with a well-placed bullet, was the quality probably most admired in a British officer. The balloon observer could be a sitting duck in the swaying wicker basket high above the ground crew who were to defend him with antiaircraft guns or by rapidly changing the balloon's elevation to foil the air attack or long-range shells. Photographs from the era show the terrifying sight of a plummeting balloon, its 20,000 cubic feet of hydrogen a mass of flame.

The balloons were normally positioned behind friendly lines to be as far as possible out of reach of long-range guns. From the heights, the observer could often clearly see fifteen miles (the horizon was about sixty miles) into enemy territory. Using the naked eye and, if the weather were calm, looking through high-powered binoculars, observers could mark the range and effectiveness of their own guns. They could assess road, rail, and air movements in and out of the enemy zone and estimate numbers of enemy infantry and calvary and artillery. They could check the effectiveness of their own camouflage. For observers stationed along the seacoasts, as Patrick often was, the watch was for submarines—swift and deadly foes not only to war vessels but to unprotected merchant ships.

Telephone lines running along the steel tethering cables connected the balloon observers with the crew on the ground. But this fragile link could easily be broken. High winds could buffet a balloon, in the worst case breaking the tether, sending it soaring off into the clouds. In fact, Patrick's reputation for coolness was made for life when he found himself in exactly this situation and survived a loop-the-loop:

> Going up at Richmond to a "blimp" stationary balloon with mechanic to make some repairs, they were caught by a line squall and the balloon was torn from its moorings and turned completely over. The occupants managed to hold on; the balloon righted itself and came down safely in Suffolk.[44]

His presence of mind in such situations won him respect and admiration. And perhaps the very exercise of all his faculties, and the reputation it brought him, allowed him to shed, for a time at least, the "remoteness" that his children and others saw in him. Freed of what had become his hated law office routine, he went into the field with confidence and probably brought it back home with him as well.

During Patrick's time in England he even flew a few hours of missions and when reviewed, August 21, 1917, at Milford Haven, Patrick was "very strongly recommended" for promotion, having "proved himself a keen and capable officer . . . zealous, capable and hardworking." By October, he'd been made Flight Lieutenant. To add to his full cup, on Friday, November 16, 1917, Anna and Patrick became the parents of their third boy, Richard, a blond-haired charmer with a rose-bud mouth who would win fame for his sweetness even among the more judgmental contingent of the Harpers.[45] But time with his family was short. On November 24, 1917 Patrick boarded the *Queen II* for Kite Balloon bases in the Mediterranean.

On December 1, 1917, he was directed to Taranto, Italy, a port city in the heel of Italy's boot. His posting was probably part of a direct response to the beating that Italy, in the war since mid-1916, had been taking as the Austrians pushed them out of the north and down to the Piava River in the Lombardy Plain. The frightened allies, needing to keep Italy in the war and seeing the real danger of collapse there, sent in British and French troops and support provided by balloon sections such as Patrick's. These reinforcements, the splintering of the Austrian empire and the pullout of German divisions to bolster lines at the Western front saved Italy to fight again. Patrick's later postings at Gibraltar and Malta gave him more leisure, at the former enough time to begin learning Hebrew from the books in the local padre's library and work on translating the Book of Psalms.

As the war continued into 1918—Russia involved in her own revolution; France trying to adjust after a 1917 troop mutiny; Germany near the end of her resources; England exhausted with effort and the Americans troops injecting desperately needed support on the Western Front—a huge British offensive from the Somme to Cambrai had been launched March 21, 1918. At the same time the Germans advanced in a drive that saw three positions, Péronne, Ham, and Chauny, evacuated by the Allies. On the second day of fighting, March 22, George Hepburn, Patrick's youngest half-brother and the one he and Anna were closest to, died. Serving with the 98th Field Company he was killed in action at Driencourt, near Péronne, France. It was a harsh blow and the closest sorrow for the Hepburn family. Of Patrick's four male siblings, now only William Clay and Charles James, remained. The Royal Naval Air Service had time and again found him "very keen," "a capable officer" who had "proved himself" to the point where he was even "strongly recommended" for promotion to Flight Commander. Then on April 1, 1918 the Royal Air Force was established and Patrick's experience in charge of Kite Balloons in both patrol and convoy duties made him an ideal candidate. In quick order he was named to No. 1 Balloon Training Wing and promoted from Lieutenant to Captain. On April 24, 1918, he was appointed Acting Major, R.A.F.

It may seem impossible to us now, but England's R.N.A.S. and its precursor the Royal Flying Corps had at the beginning of the war managed to scrape together only about sixty aircraft, some pulled from the civilian sector. Initially the craft were used almost entirely for reconnaissance in cases where static troop positions made calvary patrol impossible. Only gradually were airplanes used to make bombing raids. "Captive" balloons such

as Patrick Hepburn manned, by observing and thus inhibiting troop movements, have come to be seen by many as "a decisive factor in creating and
maintaining the stalemate that was characteristic of the Great War." Their
use in directing the artillery shells made them a deadly handmaiden.
Changes in methods of war, however, made them all but obsolete by World
War II; Patrick's posting had been with a unique and fleeting part of aerial
history.[46] Now he was a founding member in what would be another chapter in the history of military aviation.

Anna seems to have more than accepted the propaganda blitz regarding the duty of those at home to uphold the soldiers. She took an obvious
pride in Patrick's service. Though only one letter remains from their correspondence, what it shows is a woman writing encouragement to her husband far away. Her four-page letter, now missing one page, was dated
September 5, and probably reached Patrick when he was stationed at
Gibraltar. In the letter there are the usual health concerns, but also a warm
account about the children's pets and the family's visit to a museum exhibit
where they saw aeroplane models and submarine models, and, she writes,
"I wanted you very much to explain things [to the boys], Pig iron . . . ani-
line . . . and all that." She assures him she is with him in spirit. Her tone is
sympathetic, supportive, and humorous. It lacks any direct expression of
passion, but displays fond affection, being addressed to "My dear old
Friend," and signed "Your old Girl." "Your old Girl," a sort of alumni term
from her Australian school days, was, at this time, thirty-five.[47]

Patrick, skilled and lucky, escaped the war physically unscathed.
Emotionally he may have suffered, but the results of that had not shown yet.

Anna does not record what she was doing or feeling on that momen-
tous Armistice morning, November 11, 1918. But just-turned-eleven Jim
was vividly, open-mouthedly aware of the significance of the day. He was
then the youngest boy enrolled in University College School (probably
thanks to Anna's poetic reputation with Headmaster Guy Kendall, previously form-master and advisor to the same Charterhouse Poetry Society
that had fostered Robert Graves's writing talent). Jim remembered the day
opening, as was customary, with all the school gathered for prayers and
announcements in the great hall before being dismissed to classes. At
eleven o'clock, however, another assembly was called; this to announce the
cessation of hostilities, in effect the end of the war that had begun over
four long years ago. All were dismissed, and across the city of London, a

realization that the world of exploding shells and forced absences, unanticipated death, and strange transformations was over. So many losses, so much longing.

Patrick was finished with the military by March 1919.[48] Almost immediately after his return to Hampstead, Anna became pregnant. The house at no. 49 Downshire Hill, which held so many memories good and bad, began to look awfully small for their growing family.

A new house was in order. They would move to the top of the hill that overlooked all London, Parliament Hill, where Patrick would be nearer the stars and Anna could still walk on the Heath to her heart's content.

FOURTEEN

"O Give Me Back..." (1919–1921)[1]

Pregnant Anna, toddler Richard, and Jim, John and the (former) R.A.F. Major Patrick Hepburn turned the key on no. 49 Downshire Hill and headed for their next Hampstead house. The lantern slides, the masses of books, the charts and photographs, dresses and linens, pots and pans, chiming Asselin clock, and all of the paraphernalia accumulated over thirteen years of marriage had all been packed up and carted down the steep High Street and back up the winding climb of Parliament Hill. At no. 68, Parliament Hill, they would be only a stone's toss from the green of the Heath and from there to the summit was just a few bounds of a deer or the mad dash of a rabbit.

The hill, though with an ancient history, may have been named as recently as 1605 when dissidents who plotted to blow up the Houses of Parliament supposedly watched from this summit to see if their plan succeeded (it failed). Back of the summit to the west and north, the oaks, ash, and silvery beech formed a cool fringe. The spires and domes of Highgate rose beyond the low ponds to the northeast. Miles to the southeast the bells of Big Ben counted out the hours for the kite flyers, the sheep tenders, and Sunday painters at their easels aiming for just the right luminosity in their oils of the distant dome of St. Paul's. From the summit practically the whole of London could be seen, and writers from Addison to Pope to Keats to Coleridge had once looked out on the view.

Anna and Patrick, except for a two-year period, would live their life together at no. 68. Essentially, they owned the house, built in 1877, but leased the land under a long-running agreement with the ecclesiastical council of the Church of England. The agreement offered more security than the Downshire Hill rental. The house offered more space.

Built into the hillside, the "semi-detached" villa was three-storied and also had a full finished basement that let into a long sloping walled garden in back. Facing the road, the high house of red brick with bow window and sparkling white-painted trim rose up to the gray slate roof with no softening of front lawn or garden. It almost gave the appearance of a tower. The tall front door opened onto a vestibule where a grand open staircase rose to the floors above. On the ground floor were three rooms, generously proportioned. The dining room windows looked east out over the brick garden wall and down a slope of the Heath; the drawing room overlooked the street and faced into the setting sun. Patrick's long and narrow study was lined with shelves already producing that soft and comforting hue of fine books well-handled. On the floor above would be Patrick's bedroom, Anna's bedroom, a nursery for Richard and the baby to come, and a bathroom big enough to hold court. On the top floor of the house were four rooms where the oldest boys and the servants would sleep.

On the lowest floor, the basement, the cook would hold forth in the kitchen over the Eagle coal-burning range. Through the connecting doors the maid would bring toast and tea to the family in the breakfast room where they could look out on the garden. The scullery and coal room were separated from the pantry by a dark narrow passage that led to the side door, outside and next to which was the door to the servants' toilet. Anna may have loved and appreciated many of the servants who worked for the family but the biases of her society were reinforced in the architecture. Lesser facilities, even down to lesser hardware on the doors and windows, clearly demarcated rank in a house of the 1870s, at least a house where social pretensions were of importance. From the servants' bell in the dining room, to the separate entrance for the tradesman, this house and its neighbors were built to cater to those who wanted to indicate a certain hauteur. This display, however, seemed to be of less importance to Anna and Patrick than the excellent location that suited their hopes.

Before or about the same time that they purchased the house Anna and Patrick were untangling the puzzle that returning soldiers and officers and their families faced: how to live now that the war had ended. Widespread unemployment meant bitterness on the part of many ex-servicemen who came back to find difficulties in getting a job.[2] Patrick had the law firm, but his client base had shrunk. After demobilization, Anna urged Patrick to become part of the Meteorological Service then just being established, so that in weather forecasting he could follow the natural bent of his interests. But Patrick's partner had held together the practice during the war years and wanted to retire. If Patrick pursued his new career the firm that his father had built up would close. After some deliberation, family loyalty and a fear of living on a meteorologist's salary convinced Patrick to continue in the law. But if Patrick could not break away from the profession he disliked, at least no. 68 Parliament Hill, quiet at the end of a street, further away from the bustle of the town and with open skies above, was a choice site for observations. He set up a "foot-reflecting" (meaning the glass was a foot in diameter) telescope in the garden and began to publish and lecture again, at one point preparing a huge chart with 10,000 dots pasted on it to help people understand just how vast a sum was one million, and how long were light-years. Later, in 1920, Patrick was allowed by the Astronomer Royal the unusual privilege of using the Greenwich Observatory's twenty-eight-inch refractor telescope on Sunday nights to continue his observations on the rings of Saturn. He and Anna had astronomers Arthur Eddington and James Hopwood Jeans to dinner.

Anna herself had a visitor—one who would help the household finances. Joan, the barmaid from Rye who had talked long into the night with Anna that summer of 1917, came calling with news. As barkeep at an inn in Kent, Joan had been surprised one evening to learn that the very disgruntled youngish man drinking whiskey at the end of the bar was the heir to Leeds Castle. As the evening went on, and continued at her lodgings, a fuller story revealed itself. The man, Fairfax Wykeham-Martin, had quarreled with his father before the war and been cut off without a penny. Working as a cowhand in Argentina, and in wartime as a stoker in the

Royal Navy, he then returned to the castle hoping to regain a place in his father's affections and largess. The reconciliation failed and he had come into the Goat and Compass that night full of anger and bitterness. Joan, however, remembered Anna well, and remembered too that Anna's husband was a lawyer. After visiting Anna, Joan went back to Fairfax Martin with the assurance that something could be done to help him. It wasn't long before Patrick had devised a way for a small regular income to come to Fairfax Martin on the strength of his prospects.

When Fairfax Martin did inherit the castle it was a great delight to Anna that this "best bit of business" since Patrick took over from his father was the unlikely result of her broad connections. Patrick went time and again to the castle, often with his sons, as he remained the family's solicitor and became a friend. Fairfax Martin allowed Jim Hepburn the thrill of driving his motorcycle. Prince Henry, youngest son of King George V, came to the castle fishing on the same weekend as Patrick and gave the Hepburns one of the twenty-pound pikes he caught: Patrick had it stuffed and mounted for Anna's dining-room sideboard.

It was a full life at no. 68. Anna's pregnancy was proceeding. She hired a Swiss nurse, Yvonne, for the baby-to-come. And on December 10, 1919, Anna gave birth to a red-headed fourth son, named George in honor of Patrick's much-mourned stepbrother. The baby was baptized George Whelan Hepburn (Whelan after Anna's mother's side) at All-Hallows, the Anglican church on nearby Severnake Road.

As a baby he was a special favorite of his father. When people had complimented Patrick on their first baby, James, he would modestly say, "well, there aren't many that could beat him." Now, whether it was pent-up emotions from the war, the idea of his brother's namesake, the longer view of the experienced father, whatever the reason, Patrick was with this child, "almost lunatic with joy." Anna was thirty-six years old, Patrick forty-six, James almost a teenager, John ten, and Richard almost two.

Thus began a period of relative domestic quietude. The arguments between her and Patrick were probably fewer than just before the war. He spent much time at his office and, as before, occupied himself with other interests, but he was also able to enjoy the young men his sons were becoming. Besides the trips to Fairfax-Martin's castle, he took them sailing far northeast with cousin Will Clay on the reed-surrounded lakes of the Norfolk Broads (where he and Anna had once capsized in the dingy), took them on a westbound train to Watford to see the site of the Smith cousins' water-powered paper mill, and brought them fireworks to set off in no. 68's garden for Guy Fawkes Day.[3] They went on walking trips and bicycle jaunts, and Patrick taught them too from his considerable knowledge.

This time her domestic situation suited Anna. Though many of her poems are about the impossibility of writing while balancing a child on each knee, there was a side to her that not only appreciated being needed but that actually reveled in the chaos of motherhood. Her babies, her young sons who were showing promise in school and sports, her fanciful choice of domestic helpers (at least one a ballet dancer), and her husband, whose energies were successfully directed outward, all combined to produce in Anna writing that was very different from the acerbic lyrics of her first books.

"The Comfortable Palace," a prose work never published, is a myth-like piece about an earthly paradise. There are lovely details: babies cry one-half hour every day in the garden and it is like "music on the cornet."[4] There is much singing. There is no hurry. There is one rule: children must be on time for dinner but adults can be late "if they are reading or finishing an argument." Swans, who are the equivalent of servants, and perhaps are of the "mute" variety, are "always there when they are wanted" and they bring food just at the thought of it. The dead are dressed in beautiful lilac linen.

The King himself is often gone but palace management is by his aunt, The Kind Fairy, and his wife, The Good Queen. This fantasy piece of blissful domesticity is far from an anxiety-racked domesticity where the father has "mechanized" the children so that there is no natural spontaneity or gaiety. This is a household run with a free, light hand, a place of love, help and engagement, pleasing in every way. Was Anita Bartle Brackenbury's influence showing? Or perhaps Anna had reconciled with the motherly aspects of herself. At any rate, relative domestic tranquility may have played itself out in better rapport between herself and Patrick. Or vice-versa.

That the Hepburns' marriage was a tempestuous one might have been predicted from a comparison of their personalities. What is interesting is the course the marriage took, surviving (for better or worse) at each turn and influenced by affection, law, circumstance, and will. After the first months of bliss passed (1906–1907) and children came, the family held together to care for each other. When Anna or Patrick may have preferred divorce (around 1911), it was uncommon and the sheer unpleasantness of courts and evidence may have been too much to contemplate. Finances alone would have made this a difficult choice. When Anna's independence became too threatening, the asylum (summer 1913) was Patrick's answer. The law allowed her to be put there, but regulations also sprung her from her prison. When Anna was released from the asylum and worked on a new life for herself, war (1914–1918) intervened, giving her and Patrick a breather from each other. Now, with the war over came a period of domestic reconstruction and reacquaintance, for Anna and Patrick a second chance at a good marriage made visible in the small forms of their two new children, Richard and George. "O give me back my rigorous English Sunday," Anna had written in "The Fresh Start," and if we can look beneath the irony, she does have joy in household and motherhood, this time not in a social "School" as she had in 1907, but in her own home. Moreover, still seeing motherhood as one of the important jobs in a society, she added her own particular view: she would raise "artists," not just children.[5] Passion in love was the only item that she might have to do without.

Anna had the help of two young women in marshalling the children into a system of order. They succeeded somewhat, though the children made unexpected forays. Richard, dressed only in a short t-shirt, one day unlatched the door and led his naked baby brother onto Hampstead Heath for an outing, only to be captured by an alert policeman who brought them back to Anna, one adventurer under each arm.[6] Poppy Vanda and her half-sister Rita Reece, the helpers, came to Parliament Hill because of the strength of Anna's personality. Poppy, as she was called, had walked up and down in front of the Hepburn home until one day she achieved her objective, meeting Anna. (There were only three people in the world she wanted to meet: Anna, for her poetry; Yehudi Menuhin, for his violin playing; and Anton Dolin for his dancing.)[7] Poppy brought a bright spark to Anna's life; perhaps it was she and not Anita that Anna had in mind when she penned "The Comfortable Palace," perhaps it was some composite of the two. At any rate, Poppy helped Anna, Anna inspired Poppy, and the friendship that developed between the two would eventually bring Anna, in the twenties and thirties, into the world of dance, theatre and, even later, to a contract with BBC television. Meanwhile, they worked together to control the little "bandits" who had stolen Anna's heart. And her time. For as she would soon write to the American Louis Untermeyer,

If the baby playing "Typewriter", would only let me write
I might compose him something on the Spirit of Delight
Something as accurate and rhythmical as Shelley's
But if I turn my back, my young fill their small bellies
With ink and safety pins and tacks,
That I forget emotions and my facts,
You see I've lost my sense of rhyme
By this time![8]

In fact, Anna was preparing a new book to be issued by Harold Monro's Poetry Bookshop. Grant Richards, who had brought out Anna's *The Man With a Hammer* in 1916, had been chomping at the bit to get another book. When he saw her work in the Belgian children's anthology he had written with congratulations. He had hoped to bring out her next volume in the winter of 1916–1917 but she never delivered a manuscript to him then, having instead only recently delivered her third child into the Hepburn household. She had given Richards a play to read entitled "In the Stranger's Orchard," but it only "puzzled" him and he did not elaborate. By 1921 Richards complained that on several occasions "Mrs. Hepburn has telephoned saying she was sending material for a new book, but it never comes."[9] However, at least once Richards had broken an appointment with Anna; though he apologized by letter afterward, his brusque and demanding manner had by this time alienated her. He had been dismissive of her attempts, with Brackenbury, to plan a separate Australian edition of her work since of course he wanted to sell sheets from his own print run to any interested foreign publisher. And his attempts to find an American publisher for her book had not met with success.

On the other hand, Harold Monro was always attentive. He had never slackened his commitment to poetry, as Richards would do in times of financial trouble. He kept alive the sound of poetry despite personal and national crises. Readings had continued at his Devonshire Street bookshop, or at large halls rented for the purpose, until by the mid-1920s listeners could boast of having heard the best: among them W. B. Yeats, Robert Bridges, Ford Madox Ford, W. W. Gibson, Rupert Brooke, John Drinkwater, Siegfried Sassoon, Edith Sitwell, Ezra Pound, Harriet Monroe, and T. S. Eliot. Some authors declined to read their own work but let Monro or Alida Klemantaski read for them. Alida read "The Farmer's

Bride" for Charlotte Mew (when its self-effacing author was asked if she were Mew, she replied, "I am sorry to say I am").[10] Most women were not as reluctant as Mew to read. From one-fourth to one-third of the readers in a given year were women.[11]

Themed readings using the works of many poets were held: under the umbrella of "Impressionist Poetry," Blake was juxtaposed with contemporary figures such as H. D., F. S. Flint, and Robert Frost.[12] There were evenings devoted to modern French poetry, to modern American poetry, and one to the Italian Futurist poet, F. T. Marinetti. Other readings focused on a single figure from the past. Monro, for example, read Byron. On July 7, 1921, Anna read thirty-two minutes of Robert Browning (Monro always kept track of the length), including "The Bishop Orders his Tomb" and "A Pretty Woman." Usually she read her own work.

The records kept by Harold Monro and Alida Klemantaski show that Anna Wickham read nine times from 1914 to 1924, but she probably read more often.[13] That Monro gave poetry a place to be heard added immeasurably to the understanding and appreciation of poetry and encouraged the writing of it. In giving Anna a place to "publish" her voice Monro gave her an additional way to come before the public. In turn, Anna's voice and her stage presence, coupled with the provocative material and style of much of her poetry, contributed much to the excitement surrounding readings at The Poetry Bookshop, which were held from shortly after the bookshop opened and until at least 1931.[14]

War poetry, after the Armistice, had suddenly became "dud" as people wanted to forget about the last five years.[15] Harold Monro knew that some of the poetry Anna was writing reflected her love of home and children and her interest in folk-tales and myth. In his January 1920 issue of *Chapbook* he had already printed "Due for Hospitality" and "The Little Old House," a five-stanza tribute to old Shropshire values of hard work, diligence, thrift, prayer, and love. Though Anna owed Grant Richards a first look at her next book, this "right of first refusal" clause could be circumvented by making a book less than forty-eight pages.[16]

That is just what The Poetry Bookshop did, producing a book of fifty-six pages but, abiding by the Richards' stipulation, containing only forty-seven pages of text. Anna called it *The Little Old House* and dedicated it "To Alice and Geoffrey Harper" (wishful thinking or final tribute in this coupling of names, for her parents' marriage would end in 1923). *The Little Old House* was issued in April of 1921 and priced at 2s. 6d.[17]

Reviews were lackluster. Her first book with Monro, *The Contemplative Quarry*, was now out of print, but critics who remembered it found this new work "more conventional," though "yet still showing signs of a rebellious temperament."[18] *Country Life* praised it as "beautiful and accomplished" but "a little deficient in character and originality." *The Daily News* said it "lacked strength of imagination or thought" and was too sentimental, a feeling echoed by another reviewer who called it "harmless if garrulous sentiment."[19] It appears that Anna agreed with the book's detractors. Though she later thanked Harold Monro for his "exceedingly successful publicity campaign" she wrote to Louis Untermeyer that the volume was not a "book" but a "domestic exhibit."[20] That she can see its cloying sentimentality speaks to her critical faculty, but it does not explain why she let the volume be published when she had other poetry that exhibited some of her old fire. Perhaps she wanted a break from turmoil. *The Man With a Hammer* may have provoked so much domestic upset that she wasn't taking any chances close to home. Another explanation is that Monro picked the poems and it was he who wanted a book that focused more on domestic content.

The most surprising twist in her publishing career, and the one that was about to occur, took place almost without Anna's lifting a finger. People in the U. S. were beginning to be curious about her poetry and they came looking.

Back in August 1915 Irish poet and playwright and close friend of James Joyce, Padraic Colum, had reviewed Anna's *Contemplative Quarry* in *Poetry*.[21] He wrote, "Here is woman claiming experiences for herself, songs for herself. The intention of the writer has put her emotions awry, and her songs are hard and twisted." He saw her work as "provocative" unlike the "innocence" of Frances Cornford and the "belatedness" of Edward Shanks, both of whose books he also reviewed.

In the U. S., in September 1917, Anna's poem "Host" had appeared in an eclectic little magazine, *The Lantern*, Oakland, California, edited by Theodore F. Bonnet and Edward F. O'Day, that published such British writers as A. E. Housman, Siegfried Sassoon, W. H. Davies, and Lawrence.

Anna's U. S. appearance had attracted the attention of Louis Untermeyer. Untermeyer made his living designing and manufacturing jewelry in Newark, New Jersey. He was a social liberal, a poet, editor, and a forward-looking anthologist who, though a year or two younger than Anna, introduced her in a 1920 anthology as "one of the most individual

of the younger women-poets." (After the two writers finally met in person
in the 1920s, Untermeyer called her "a magnificent gypsy of a woman,
who always entered a room as if she had just stamped across the moors."[22]
He continued to print her poetry in almost every anthology he published
in his long career.)[23] His request for biographical information led Anna to
write to him on June 10, 1920:

> Mr. Monro has sent me your note saying you have no autobiograph-
> ical details of me. I have hesitated for some time not knowing what to
> send. I was born in Wimbledon Surrey in 1883. It was always my
> father's ambition that I should be a poet. I went to Australia at six,
> returned when I was twenty one. Studied for opera in Paris . . .
> Married had two sons. Tried very hard to be a housekeeper, got so irri-
> tated that I wrote 900 poems in 4 years. My attempt to organize a
> house ended in my writing the revolt of women.

Rhetorically, and quoting someone, she asks Untermeyer, "'What does
the sociologist need but frank biography?'"[24] and continues, almost as an
observer of her own behavior, "I think it is interesting that a long domestic effort should have caused an explosion in free verse. It unites with my
theory of oppressed peoples & my theory of war."

Back on the subject of biography, Wickham tells Untermeyer that she
now has four sons, three unpublished books, and is making "a second
domestic attempt," which she is afraid "will break down in another flow of
verse." She ends by saying that she would be "writing poetry this morning"
if she could think of something 'aimiable' [sic] to say."

Untermeyer felt that Anna Wickham's poetry would speak to readers
in the U. S. Women had just won the right to vote; Charleston fringes
were flying. America was opening up to a modern world, watching films
and stage stars, "motoring," dancing to the Victrola, playing auction
bridge, and still reading. The end of the war had provoked a recurrence of
fascination with Europe, especially France.[25] American writers and the
American public were eager to connect with their counterparts across the
sea. Untermeyer counted on this climate of the 1920s as one conducive to
an appreciation of Anna's poetry and knew that the combined effect of
Contemplative Quarry and *The Man With a Hammer* would show her
range and ability best. He saw her as one of six "unaffiliated" poets who
were "sufficient answer to those who contend that the age we live in is

hopelessly prosaic." With Anna's permission, Untermeyer supplied several titles for poems that were untitled. He wrote a forward that must have gladdened Anna by its acute understanding of what she was trying to do in poetry. He called her "a psychologist" whose "fretted energy" produced a "harsh" and "astringent" poetry that illuminated the struggle "between dreams and domesticity."[26]

Publisher Alfred Harcourt, on the strength of Untermeyer's enthusiasm and another reader's report, sent a letter to England indicating his interest in a combined U. S. edition. Anna referred him to Grant Richards. Richards, who after only a short period of gloating to Harold Monro that "we might between us clear up the poets of the country" began peevishly lecturing Harold as to who owned what rights to Anna's work.[27] "My agreement with her leaves me a free hand," said Richards and issued directives about who should be doing what.[28] Letters went back and forth across London and across the Atlantic from November, 1920, until a three-way agreement was signed on February 28, 1921, by Grant Richards Ltd. and Harold Monro and the American firm. The agreement with Harcourt, Brace and Company set royalties at 10 percent on the first 2,500 copies and 15 percent on copies over 2,500 (the book sold for $1.75).[29] By the time the two Englishmen shared the royalties (Richards winning big since the book he had published had so many more poems than Monro's), monetary gain to Anna was slight. But the public that the book gained her was another story. It was the first time that her work had been published in a country that was not at war, and its reception shows that the timing was almost perfect.

The book came out in early fall 1921.[30] Reviews popped like champagne. A few notices, most notably one by Ivor Winters in *Poetry*, were negative. A minority felt that what she produced was "not poetry," a fairly common charge about modernist work by critics fond of rhyming iambs. Most reviewers liked her ruthless honesty of expression, wit, control of form, "music," and her willingness to tackle subjects of social, cultural, religious, and spiritual importance. They praised her exact language (a little *le mot juste* trick she picked up from the French via F. S. Flint's Imagist poetry) and they found its "harsh" quality to their liking.

A clipping service sent the reviews to Anna who had them pasted into a large scrapbook, filling many pages.

Untermeyer saw to it that the book was promoted and reviewed. *Vanity Fair's* July, 1921 issue gave a full page to ten of Anna's poems. On

September 3, Joseph Wood Krutch reviewed the book in *The Evening News,* while Herbert S. Gorman did so in *The New York Times Book Review and Magazine*. Krutch saw Wickham as one of the few capable of being a confessional poet without being a bore, and liked the way she juxtaposed restraint against moments of sudden, fierce intensity. He described the "long, cool blade" of her poetry as giving "new point to the attack upon conformity."[31] Gorman found her strong in "thought content" and "absorbing" subject matter with a "unique" "method of work."[32] Anna had asked Untermeyer to place in the front of the book "A Note on Method," which he did. This poem made clear her far-reaching objective:

> Here is no sacramental *I*.
> Here are more I's than yet were in one human.
> Here I reveal our common mystery—
> I give you "Woman."
> Let it be known for our old world's relief,
> I give you woman—and my method's brief![33]

Mark Van Doren, on October 26 in the *Nation* characterized her poems as "passionate and ascetic" and her muses the kind to "whip her to intellectual appetite and artistic execution." In short, a "prophetess" whose "demon is unrest."[34] He felt that her marriage with wit would have made her "at home" in seventeenth-century England, a reference to the so-called metaphysical poets such as John Donne, George Herbert, Andrew Marvell, and Henry Vaughan then being much discussed because of the work of H. J. C. Grierson and T. S. Eliot.

Meanwhile, poems also appeared in *Current Opinion* in August and October 1921.[35] Of the six poems printed there, "Soul's Liberty," is probably the most overt statement of Anna's complicated attitude toward war. The poem is against social materialism as being an overconcern with property and thus destructive to "soul's liberty." And just as the physical buildings of the church, those "silly objects of desire," are a hindrance to seeing God's presence "clear and high above the town," so "war and fire" strip away all but essentials.

All in all, 1921 was a wonderful year for Anna. One book published in England, one in the U. S., considerable attention paid to her poetry and relative health within the family. The drought that had afflicted England, when "no rain fell for six months . . . and the green fields were burned browned, while shrubs and even trees wilted and died . . . a desolate sight," had lifted about the same time her U. S. book was published.[36] As the year drew to a close, however, personal disaster struck. The Hepburn children were quarantined when scarlet fever was diagnosed in Richard.

Anna was always sensitive to her children's feelings, though she might sometimes chafe under their shenanigans. A sick child or a fearful child might count on a poem from her, and the children had favorites they would ask for again and again. The rhyme and rhythm of this poem would fit it admirably to be sung, and perhaps it was:

> I'll give my lad a pretty ring
> I'll cull it from the bushes,
> Ten dewy drops on a green grass string.
> I'll go and ask the thrushes
> For goldy notes from their browny throats
> To make a drink for my baby,
> That he lose the pain
> And smile again
> And live as blithe as maybe.
> Laugh with thy mother, little knight,
> For hither comes the starling,
> His legs are yellow as the sun's light,
> And he shall dance for my darling.[37]

On December 31, after nineteen days in the Fever Hospital on Lawn Road, Hampstead, four-year-old Richard Hepburn died of septic scarlet fever. Anna had gone home after having been told that the crisis was past. It would have been only a matter of days before the quarantine on their home was lifted and things could get back to normal again there in the "Comfortable Palace" at the top of Parliament Hill.

FIFTEEN

Paris, and Return (1922–1926)

In England was "the smell of the sickroom," the pitying eyes of neighbors and friends, Patrick's grief, and the responsibility for two other sons.[1] As soon as she could manage, Anna left London.

Seventeen years before, Anna, "*la Belle Anglaise,*" dressed in her long skirt and pretty layered blouses, had used her schoolgirl French to find her way to the forbidding Conservatoire. At that time she was running away from romantic entanglements and intent on developing her singing voice to its potential. This time, however, Paris would be her refuge from grief.

She took fourteen-year-old Jim with her. They crossed the Channel on the night ferry to Dieppe and then went by train to Paris. First registering at a hotel on the rue d'Odessa in the heart of the crowded Montparnasse quarter, they then went out into the reassuring morning bustle to get something to eat. Anna spied one of her friends, the English painter Lett Haines, standing on the street corner and so they all sat together at a small table of the Café de la Rotonde. They watched the passing parade and talked. Anna's long-range plan was for Jim, who had already missed weeks of school because of the scarlet fever quarantine, to miss the remainder of the

159

year. He would improve his French and keep Anna company. Patrick would visit them occasionally.

Was the trip her idea or Patrick's? Was it an irresponsible running away, an irresistible reaction?

Anna was, as her son Jim later wrote, "devastated" by Richard's death. At home she had nursed him tenderly "with the whole of her energy," but knowing that septic scarlet fever was usually fatal. He was moved to the fever hospital as his case worsened, but then the crisis passed and he had steadily begun to improve. Anna was unprepared to be stopped at the door of the ward and told that she had lost her boy.[2] When the necessary arrangements and rites had been seen to, those painful days when one proceeds without hardly being conscious, she had taken stock.

From Anna's earliest years, mourning had been a part of her family's mythology, not rare, of course, in the Victorian age of black-bordered note paper and set mourning routine. Her family's mourning, however, was not so bounded by custom. Her mother's earliest memory was that of being shut out of the Whelan house to play in the street while the rest of the family went with her father's coffin to the cemetery. The story had been told to Anna again and again. And as a young child Anna had gone out in the night with her mother to the dark edges of the 1,000 acre Wimbledon Common to search the stars for the eyes of the infant that Anna never knew, the little brother who had died before she was born.[3] Anna also was aware that her father had more than once run out to bring back Alice after she had gone alone at night to the boy's grave to weep. As an adult looking back, Anna resented having been captive audience to her mother's emotionalism. Yet at the same time she admired Alice's ability to release those emotions.

After Richard's death Anna turned her back on any extended formalized expression of grief. As a poet she had "all the words of my language" at her disposal and, for example, would later use poetry to come to terms with her mother's death. But in this case a more tacit mourning seems to have kept her from breaking down. She did not isolate herself. She did what she had done before: surround herself with people. Her past had taught her that being with people, going places where you could have a conversation, watch something amusing, or engage in a debate or a flirtation, held sadness at bay. Just as in Sydney, when her stay with Aunt Beatrice Harper had protected her from her mother's unbalanced state, or when the gaiety and intellectual parrying at London's Café Royal had given her spirits a needed release after the asylum, so in Paris Anna would take the same cure and wear the pain away gradually, day by day. Jim would be her ally, her surety, possibly her excuse. They would keep themselves in the company of those in the arts who had flocked to France from all points of the compass.

Many of those had settled, or would, on the Left Bank. Enough Americans to populate a small town of the big names of twentieth-century writing: Ernest Hemingway, Gertrude Stein, Sherwood Anderson, Ezra Pound, H. D., Henry Miller, Djuna Barnes, Anaïs Nin, Zelda and Scott Fitzgerald, and John Dos Passos among them. Enough Irish and English writers to make the islands tilt at their leaving, including the well-known James Joyce and Ford Madox Ford, or the lesser-known individuals such as Tommy Earp, Richard Aldington, Mary Butts, and Radclyffe Hall. Journalists from all three countries. Russian writers and mystics. Exiles from all over Eastern Europe. Painters, sculptors, actors, dancers, musicians, and composers freeing themselves to work and play in Paris, "City of Light," and city of book stands along the quays. City of favorable exchange rates and wonderful food. City of freedom.

Man Ray and his young assistant Bérénice Abbott photographed the scene. Publishers of magazines and small-press owners capitalized on the concentration of talent and enjoyed themselves: Margaret Anderson and Jane Heap of *The Little Review*, Robert McAlmon (*Contact*), Alfred Kreymborg and Harold Loeb (*Broom*). More than a few wealthy women, Peggy Guggenheim, Bryher (Annie Winifred Ellerman), and Natalie Barney, were there, or would come, intent on furthering the arts and, if it happened, their reputations. Those others who had flat wallets found the economy merciful.

After World War I, and before England went on the Gold Standard in 1931, living in France meant living better than one could at home. Douglas Goldring, contributor to the little magazine *Coterie* wrote:

> After the Armistice those who could do so had every inducement to cross the Channel. London was grim, gloomy, depressed, shabby, overcrowded and expensive . . . drinks were dear, pubs opened late and closed early.[4]

Cafes such as the Rotonde, the Dôme, and Café Parnasse were easy meeting places and even working places; a writer could scribble the day away, piling up coffee saucers, and still have money left over for a good dinner. The atmosphere, according to English journalist George Slocombe, had not reached the fever pitch of the later 1920s and the pace was pleasurable:

> The terraces of the cafés on the famous *Carrefour* were smaller then, less intimidating, more intimate. The boulevard was less garishly lighted, the cars parked in front of the cafés were rarer, the curious spectators less numerous. As midnight approached the street grew empty, a village-like hush fell upon the quarter. One sat . . . in a murmurous silence overcome by the pleasure of reunion with old friends met there by hazard, after long absence and journeys in remote places, as at the cross-roads of the world, overcome by the gentle inebriety induced by well-cooked food, and good wine, and wild talk, and the immense liberty and delight and satisfaction of being in Paris. . . .[5]

The scene was not without hazard, however. Aldington, who had published and favorably reviewed Anna's poetry in 1915 during his editorial stint at *Egoist* and who would regularly publish her work in anthologies called the Parisian cafe:

> an admirable invention of civilized life, but it must be used with caution, as the Frenchman uses it. It is so pleasant, so easy, so attractive, so perpetually varied, that quite insensibly it comes to occupy too much of the time of the unwary.[6]

As many were to find, to their peril, the cafe could soon take up the better part of a day or—even if one were to accomplish something while working there—could still lead on to champagne nights requiring a good part of the next day for recovery and a good part of the next bank-draft for restitution.

Aldington also noted another hazard that trapped the unwary. In a city attracting talent by the trainload, an "almost frantic competition for notice in an over-crowded market" developed. An "inevitable overvaluing of spurious novelty" was the result of such overcrowding.[7] At least in one friend's opinion, Anna was not one of those posturing for attention, not one who "contrived to catch the public ear."[8] Her unorthodox methods of recording poems anywhere, a holdover from the Café Royal days, must not have counted as showmanship to the friend, although it certainly made an impression on almost everyone else.

Anna had not yet been published in France but she arrived in Paris with a reputation of favorable reviews for *The Contemplative Quarry and The Man With a Hammer*. Perhaps some people had seen *Dial*'s dissenting December verdict, scolding that her lines only "infrequently" rise to the "perilously beautiful plane that is authentic poetry" and as a result dampening book sales among the more traditional of *Dial*'s 14,000 readers. But Anna's "pugnaciously modern personality" (the reviewer's verdict) would not have attracted those traditionalists in any case.[9]

Within a few weeks the January, 1922, number of the *Liberator* arrived from the States. Anna's "The Singing Wives" appeared, along with poetry by the Jamaican, Claude McKay, and by Chicago's ("Big Shoulders") Carl Sandburg. The magazine was hardly as radical as its predecessor, *The Masses*, but editor Max Eastman still managed to produce a credible vehicle for the Left and Anna's poems were quite at home there. *The New Republic*, a liberal weekly, also carried poems by Anna for three issues running (January 4, 18, and 25).

The winter days were full. Reading occupied a good part of Anna's days and she soon discovered Sylvia Beach's companionable Shakespeare and Company bookstore, just about to set everyone talking by publishing the banned *Ulysses* for James Joyce.

Writing was also a part of Anna's Paris, perhaps in the "bursts" she was subject to in England, or on a more scheduled basis. In her large and elegant hand she wrote twenty-three poems in a "Lorraine" brand school notebook and labeled it "Paris: Feb.–March, 1922."[10] But at cafes she wrote "on the café tables, on the backs of menus, on the waiter's apron, anywhere . . ." reported new friend poet Edna St. Vincent Millay, "ten thousand poems a day . . . many very bad, naturally, but some splendid."[11]

She saw old friends such as the painter Nina Hamnett, and met new people such as the South African writer Beatrice Hastings. Natalie Barney, who would later play such an important role in Anna's life, was probably just a new acquaintance, one among many, or perhaps their paths never even crossed at that time. Anna met with Ezra Pound, the American poet who had made his mark in London and now expected to conquer Paris, one morning on the terrace of the Café de Dôme and she spent part of one lengthening afternoon writing a poem about him.[12] She was also getting her thoughts together to answer the three questions about poetry that Harold Monro posed to "twenty-seven ladies and gentlemen," that number including T. S. Eliot, who was publishing "The Waste Land" in his

Criterion, and Ford Madox Ford, to whom so many looked for leadership in literature.[13]

The winter passed. Anna had decided that Jim's education should include French lessons at the Berlitz School and guitar lessons with a tutor but that he should be free to explore on his own to a considerable extent. In the evenings he would often take in the Cirque de Paris or see a film. Their lives took "parallel courses which, however, converged at frequent intervals."[14] One wonders if they talked much about the loss at home that had sent them together to Paris. Certainly Jim was old enough to think about these things in a deep way.

Anna, as she would do with all her children, included Jim in her circle of friends.

Nina Hamnett, Anna's friend from the Café Royal, had been in Paris for almost two years. Anna arranged for her to paint fourteen-year-old Jim's portrait in the dulled and muted tones Nina favored.[15] He sat for her in the Montparnasse studio she had taken over from Modigliani after his death.[16]

Quiet pursuits were balanced by more lively entertainment. With such a group of people, in such a time of relief after the war, a spirit of exuberance prevailed. There was a mock duel "over some real or imagined slight to Anna." Tommy Earp, poet, critic, and ex-President of the Oxford Union strode with the art dealer Van Loo through the tall iron gates of the Luxembourg garden and under the trees they fought it out with their clattering wooden swords. The encounter ended in the boulevard St-Germain at the Café de Flore, where offended and offending alike celebrated in a flush of pink champagne.[17]

Another time Anna watched Jim defend himself against Aleister Crowley in a game of chess at the tables of the Dôme. Crowley, the painter, mystic, magician, and sexual experimenter, had come from his Sicilian "Abbey" for a few months' stay in Paris. Later his drug-taking, satan-worshiping practices would lead to his being hustled out of France by the authorities. He was already self-advertised as "The Great Beast" and possessed a sensationally unsavory reputation. Crowley, probably feeling himself indulgent and generous, had suggested a match. James Hepburn later wrote:

> . . . the game started, and Anna and Crowley continued their conversation while a circle of friends and acquaintances gathered to listen to the discourse. Crowley rather casually made his moves without

much consideration. Suddenly I saw that I had checkmate in two moves. He was furious, Anna delighted.[18]

Many of the Americans who met or heard of Anna around this time liked her work, which seemed to them bold and fresh and "defiant." Poet Elinor Wylie, in *The Bookman,* had chosen Anna's "The Winds" for a "best poems" feature.[19] Harriet Monroe published more of Anna's work in the July 1922 issue of *Poetry.* Alfred Kreymborg picked out one of Anna's poems for the August issue of *The Measure,* a magazine of consistent importance to American literary history.[20] Maxwell Anderson prepared a "Mazurka," which he dedicated to Anna in *The Chapbook,* October 1922.

Anna also met Americans such as poet Edna St. Vincent Millay and Griffin Barry. Anna's son Jim was impressed both by Millay's closetful of beautiful shoes and by Barry's athletic, easy ways. With both of these new American friends, Anna talked often of poetry, politics, and the theatre.

Griffin Barry, who would later father two children with educator Dora Russell, wife of the philosopher/mathematician Bertrand Russell, was then in Paris as a foreign correspondent. His idealism and his wide experience attracted Anna. His grandparents had lived in Pennsylvania and he was born and lived in Wisconsin until age seventeen, then lived for a time in California, briefly attending Stanford University. In 1915 stationed in Liége and Antwerp with the Commission for Relief in Belgium, he had seen close up the effects of war.[21] By 1916 he was in Russia as special assistant to the American ambassador, and then missed the fall of the Tsar only because he was "riding in hay carts through Kazan, looking after German and Austrian civil prisoners."[22]

These Belgian and Russian connections piqued Anna's interest. In addition, they were almost the same age. Some people, like red-haired friend and fellow *Daily Herald* reporter George Slocombe, saw Barry as "vivid and gracious."[23] Others thought he was mousy and vindictive. In most books about this period he rates only a footnote, sometimes not even that. The fact is that Barry attracted a lot of people. He was bisexual, as were many of the Paris crowd. Millay was one of his companions in 1921; they had spent time in March, 1922, together in Vienna, as Ernest Hemingway wrote Sherwood Anderson, though Millay's biographer, Nancy Milford, notes that by that time they traveled together only "for convenience."[24]

Griffin could actually quote lines of Anna's poetry to her, a fact that she must have appreciated. He encouraged her to work and won one of

Anna's highest accolades when she called him a "disciplinarian" who moved her to write poetry. It is not clear if his "deepset blue-grey eyes" and his "permissive attitude toward love," influenced her as much as they later did Dora Russell.[25] He gave her a photo of himself in April, 1922, that she later pasted in the family album. He felt, as Anna did, that a society where the artist or writer was often penniless was an unjust one; they stayed friends for a number of years.

According to Slocombe, Wickham was one of the individualistic women of Montparnasse who had "found their vocations."[26] Slocombe described her as being "tall, gaunt, bronzed, she looked . . . like a figure modeled by Epstein," and it is true that Wickham was photographed, quoted, and noticed by many, not only for her poetry, but because of her striking features, conversation, and manner and her interest in other people.

Millay was one of those that Anna spent time with. Red-haired, green-eyed Edna St. Vincent was already a poet, playwright, and actor (Provincetown Players) by the time she and Anna met. Like Anna, she had written poems even before she was of school age; her poems, also, had lines so memorable they begged to be repeated. They were both known to have an almost intoxicating effect on people. Millay had a reputation as a lover and a rebel, despite that from early April on she saw Paris in the company of her mother.

Millay had heard about Anna Wickham the year before from the critic Edmund "Bunny" Wilson, who had discovered Anna's verse in 1921 and liked it. Her own opinion of Anna was likewise favorable:

> awfully interesting . . . great big jolly, untidy, scathing, tender and brilliant . . . I like her tremendously. She's a thrilling person. Beautiful in a way: Magnificent big head, and sweet, fine eyes. She is married to an astronomer named Hepburn, and has three boys, the oldest fourteen.

Millay also described her as "the most *essentially motherly* woman I ever met."[27]

Millay, in this remark, zeros in on a significant aspect of Anna. Slocombe, too, found this "maternal" quality in her.

All the years that Anna had spent studying motherhood, lecturing, and talking about it, being a mother, watching motherly women such as Anita Bartle Brackenbury, writing about motherhood, and now suffering through the greatest of its losses—the death of a child—had brought this maternalism to a fine level. Even her impassioned love of her own mother, though it had often led to situations too oppressive to be tolerated, had lately been acknowledged when Anna dedicated a work "To My Mother, 'First love, and dearest love; Wake, it is morning.'"[28] So it is evident that at this point in her life (she was thirty-eight), motherhood was part of her core identity. She will later write to a friend that "the childhood of my children" was the happiest period of her life.[29]

What is interesting and unusual about both Slocombe's and Millay's admiration of Anna's maternal side is that they discuss it in terms of her poetry. Slocombe states the contrast in terms of female and male. He sees her writing, on the one hand, as done with "calm virile strength and integrity," but portrays her "maternal" person, on the other hand, as "a vast serene, benevolent goddess."[30] (Incidentally, he also sees her as someone who thought men [as opposed to women] could do no wrong, a viewpoint that at the time, he felt, led her into "strange and capricious admirations.")[31] Millay, in a sort of related judgment, is struck by the difference between Anna in person and Anna in print. She sees Anna, in print, as rebellious, freedom-seeking, and feminist. But in person, Millay reported, Anna could be "curiously reactionary in comparison with her books and, as noted (a matter of "astonishment" to Millay), "motherly."[32]

If Slocombe and Millay had known Wickham over a longer period of time they might have seen that Anna deliberately tried to tend her "maternal" side. Nina Hamnett had felt her warmth when Anna cared for her during sickness. Epstein benefited when Anna had bought him a block of stone to carve.[33] The tired women of the London slums had seen it in action when Anna delivered clean saucepans to them. And certainly in years to come many people would find in her a stimulating encouragement, though she would become equally noted for subtle putdowns, stinging rebukes and, later, even physical violence. Whether it was by instinct or intent, Anna sought to keep mothering, sex, poetry, politics, and her other interests encouraged, permitted, fostered. It was a difficult balancing act, one that had, and would again, fail her.

Slocombe's and Millay's observations also serve to highlight Anna's theorizing about men and women. Even in her earliest book, *Songs*, she had been musing and making arguments about men, women and creativity. Certainly she was in the early- to mid-1920s in the process of formulating and articulating her later opinion that "female fertility" had been (unjustly) denigrated by "world teachers:"

> Buddha leaves home the night his first child is born . . . Jesus denies
> his mother. Karl Marx exalts economics above the womb. Rousseau
> makes foundlings of the increase of his wife.[34]

She felt this "exaltation of male fertility above female fertility" might be
responsible for the sorry state of a world with "so little hope." And in a very
Jungian vein Anna would write that in "the house of the soul" there is a
marriage of female and male principles; the "whole creative consciousness
of a pure artist" was, in her opinion, "bisexual."[35] Certainly the seeds of
these ideas were present in Paris that spring of 1922.

  These two developments in Anna's thinking (the importance of the
maternal and the necessity to think in terms of bisexual creativity) were
something that Patrick would find very difficult to accept. He recognized
and appreciated Anna's "mothering" quality but, at least according to
Anna, wanted the bulk of it for himself. Mothering was not, however, an
aspect that she wanted to entertain in connection with her husband.
Though Patrick, as the eldest of his siblings may have been "a lonely boy,
lonely in the midst of a large family," Anna wanted to steer clear of this
need.[36] She did not want to be "a substitute for a life-starved man's dead
mother," as she bluntly stated.[37]

  Anna does not record what Patrick thought of principles of bisexual
creativity, or of her circle of friends, widened by her visit to Paris, of lesbian
and homosexual writers and artists. But the difficulties that lay ahead for
their marriage may be an indicator. Trouble of some kind was brewing, if
slowly. When she returned to England Patrick was suffering from "black
moods" frequently enough that Anna came to the conclusion that he was
"suffering from melancholia."[38] Anna probably came back from Paris more
than he could handle.

  For five months, Anna and Jim had been away. They returned to
London, probably in early June, to the big house on Parliament Hill, to the
toddler George, to twelve-year-old John (who would start at University
College School in the fall), and to Patrick, who would soon turn fifty.

  R. D. Smith, editor of *The Writings of Anna Wickham* and author of
that volume's lengthy, well-researched biographical essay on Wickham,
writes that when Anna got home from Paris she decided to "become a
model housewife."[39] Son Jim felt, too, that "for long periods, after the
death of her third son . . . Anna suppressed the creative impulse, giving priority to the demands of her family."[40] This may be overstating the case.

It is true that Anna had no books published during this time. Through Bartle Brackenbury Anna sent a manuscript to Grant Richards in February, 1924.[41] His rejection of this inconsequential work, "The Venturous Shepherdess," satisfied the right of first refusal clause in Anna's contract, therefore making it possible for her to send manuscripts elsewhere. There is no evidence that she did so.[42]

But she was active on other fronts. Poems appeared in *The Liberator* (April and July, 1923) and in Harold Monro's *The Chapbook, A Monthly Miscellany* (March and June, 1923) and *The Chapbook, A Miscellany* (October, 1924 and 1925). Editors asked for and printed her work in some interesting anthologies, among them *The New Poetry* (1923) put together by Miss Monroe and Alice Corbin Henderson.[43] She received a wonderful, intelligent review in *The Bookman* by poet Marguerite Wilkinson, who appreciated the tensions and paradoxes in Anna's body of work. She compared Wickham's intellect and poetic approach to zigzagging lightning and continued:

> To acclaim love and to doubt it, to defy man, as a feminist, and then to offer him the specious homage of precedence, to inveigh against the church and then to pray reverently to the Mater Dolorosa in one and the same book—surely this is to offer a series of unusual contrasts in thought and emotion.[44]

In addition, Anna read at the Poetry Bookshop and attended many of the readings; probably it was here that she finally met Harriet Monroe, on vacation in the summer of 1923 from her native Chicago.[45]

Her outsized character alone might have kept her in the public eye. A laudatory "Personalities and Powers" column included a nice ink drawing of Anna's increasingly well-known head.[46]

The usual round of family matters and entertaining was taken up again, but increasingly Anna and Patrick went separate ways. Patrick was often at his law office and doing astronomy (he continued to travel observing eclipses). He was also still clerk of the Curriers' Company and had begun serving a six-year term on the British Astronomical Society Council. But he was good with the older boys, taking them sailing on elaborate outings that began with a ride in a private railway carriage. It may have been around this time that they also began Alpine and Lake-District climbing trips together. Still, beginning in 1925, he consistently spent the Christmas holidays away from his family.

Anna tended the young George, with whom she felt a specially close connection. She, too, went traveling, including one journey of several weeks during 1924 taken to give Jim a look at Genoa, Leghorn, Elba, Rome, and Venice before he began working as a railway cadet (his father and cousin had decided Jim should work his way up to senior management.)[47] Later she took all the children on another journey—George so young that his passport photo was taken on the lap of his nanny, Rita Rees. They went to tennis matches and boxing exhibitions, for Anna was an avid fan of both. She knitted bright red socks for a tennis umpire (a photograph and caption made the evening paper) and could discourse on a jab.[48]

She kept up with friends. Griffin Barry, for one. He had come back to England in late 1922 and with him she attended a gathering of socialists. At a party afterward H. G. Wells and all of but one of his guests cooled off under the water hose; Anna was the one who smoked on calmly.[49]

Though with some she might have kept up an imperturbable face, she could be loud. She had developed an interest in dance and arranged lessons for Jim, already a good ballroom dancer, with Seraphine Astafieva, a Russian dancer who ran a ballet school in Chelsea. Together with her new young friend Poppy Vanda, Anna sometimes watched rehearsals. She was there on a June morning, 1923, when Anton Dolin, later a lover of Serge Diaghilev and a principal dancer with Ballets Russes de Monte Carlo, threw a fit. Dolin had discovered that he was not going to be allowed to do his solo. Raving, he threatened to withdraw from an upcoming program.

> The climax was reached . . . when Anna Wickham was present. This made me show off more than ever. I flung myself on to the studio floor, knocked myself against the wall, and finally hit myself over the head with a tambourine. Anna, a member of the Hampstead set and a brilliant poet, understood my tantrums. "Knock your bloody head my lad, it's good for you! Go on, knock it!" cried Anna.[50]

Anna's understanding did not, however, extend to her husband's actions nor did she, at that time at least, recognize how she and he together tortured each other. "Genius in women / raises hell in men," Anna would later write, but other troubles seemed to be pursuing them as well.[51]

These new problems seem to have begun at the time of George's birth, when (using the then-new psychoanalytic vocabulary) Anna described Patrick as "megalomanic and proud." According to her, the doctor in attendance even warned her that Patrick was behaving oddly, saying that Patrick was acting "rash," and might endanger his business. Shortly after the war, when Anna was hosting a party and Patrick returned, in a burst of jealousy he lunged for her sheer blouse and ripped it, declaring to her embarrassment and the dismay of the guests, "You might as well show everything."[52]

It was probably around or shortly after Anna's return from Paris that Patrick began to take offense in an unsettling way when she offered to help with the accounts, though it was clear he was feeling burdened by them. He accosted her sexually in the basement passage, something that was out of character with his normal behavior. He waved a gun around.[53]

She seems not to have known what to do, though she comments that if she gave him "tragedy" his tempests would subside (a pattern she saw often enough with her mother in her childhood). She felt that speaking to his relatives would be utterly useless. She may have been wrong about this. There had grown up a warm relationship between Patrick's half sisters and the boys. They taught Jim the catechism, provided weekend getaways, and may have listened to Anna, whom they increasingly saw as a good parent. Cousin Will Clay and others were possible confidants. Her own parents, besides being half a world away, were themselves preoccupied. They had divorced on March 3, 1923; Alice immediately remarried in New Zealand and Geoffrey also found a woman who seemed very good for him.

Almost without warning Patrick, as the boys remember it, drew up papers in 1926 for a marital separation. (Divorce in England was still unusual and always messy.) Though no document has been traced, according to the Hepburn family it included both a clause that mandated Anna keep away from Patrick and provided financial provisions (£400 per year). If she approached Patrick the allowance would be cut off. The very first night of their living apart, however, Patrick came by to visit and to converse with Anna; no voices were raised.

The boys did not know why their parents were separating. Anna did not confide in them, or in anyone else who has recorded it for posterity. But Jim stated that the effect on Anna was twofold:

> She departed from the family home with meager financial provision, from which she had to support herself and her three sons; she was, in a sense, released from what she would have regarded as obligation to her marriage, and so was free to pursue close relationships outside it.[54]

What caused the formal break? Was her perception of Patrick's melancholia more than he could stand, being a proud man and distrustful of advice? Had one of them had an affair that disrupted the delicate balance of the home? Was it because of long-standing incompatibility and divergent objectives in life? Had Richard's death been too much for them to face together? Were simmering financial difficulties putting pressure on the relationship? And had Anna asked for the separation? Was it intended to be the first step toward a divorce, or merely a breather or a scare tactic? Anna would tell Natalie Barney that she was thrown out for wanting to write for the stage. But what is clear from other later letters is that Anna, though she might complain about Patrick herself, did not allow others to. She retained a certain loyalty toward the man who was still her husband and the father of her sons.

The separation began a time where Anna was often at her wits' end about money and lodgings but became part of Natalie Barney's circle in Paris, joined the P.E.N. Club in London, and began to take an almost dictatorial interest in her sons' careers. As for writing, she put much of the following two or three years into letters.

With her parents Geoffrey and Alice Harper in 1890, probably just before departure from England for a new life in Australia.

Miss Edith Harper, eighteen-year-old elocution teacher and voice student in Sydney, Australia. June 17, 1901.

Anna Wickham, back in England, enacting some sort of ancient story.

Anna Wickham, poet.

Twenty-four-year-old Anna Wickham with first son James Hepburn, 1907.

With two eldest sons, James and John, 1915.

When third son Richard died at the end of 1921, Anna took her eldest son, James, and fled to Paris for a six-month stay.

Anna Wickham, 1911, about the time of her book, *Songs*, which she brought out under the assumed name, "John Oland," and had printed by The Women's Printing Society.

The Poetry Bookshop, 35 Devonshire Street. Harold Monro, Anna's first publisher, created this haven in Bloomsbury London, which meant that there was always a place to meet and hear the best poets of the 'teens and 'twenties read their works.

Brooke House, the asylum in Upper Clapton where Anna suffered and wrote in the summer of 1913. When released, she vowed never again to let her husband have such power over her. She sought out other writers and artists and managed to change her life. (Hackney Archives Department.)

Anna's husband, Patrick Hepburn, enlisted in the Royal Naval Air Service in World War I and performed the dangerous work of balloon observer.

A letter Anna wrote to Patrick, then in the Royal Naval Air Service.

Harold Monro. (By permission of the British Library. Additional Manuscript 57768.)

Natalie Barney. (Courtesy Special Collections, University of Wisconsin-Madison.)

George Hepburn, around 1931. Anna's youngest son, away at school, at times corresponded with his mother in verse.

Dancers John (left) and James Hepburn in their 1932 "Double Act."

Anna at her desk at no. 68 Parliament Hill, the house where she lived from 1919 until her death in 1947. (Hulton Archive/Getty Images.)

The state of Anna's kitchen was infamous but the kitchen wall, decorated with poems, was famous. The next issue of *The Picture Post* contained a letter from a clergyman who was highly offended by Anna's housekeeping. (Hulton Archive/Getty Images.)

Anna and May Lawrence (later Henderson) at a Hampstead pub. (Hulton Archive/ Getty Images.)

SIXTEEN

"I have a skin for what is false in you"[1]

S o said Anna Wickham about Natalie Barney, the woman who meant more to her, with the exception of her mother, than any other woman in her life. They began their friendship in 1926, the year that Anna and her husband separated. Anna's infatuation with Natalie was brief but the passion was long, if that is not a contradiction.[2] The friendship after the storm of love was even longer. Anna Wickham adored Natalie Barney; their interactions and their correspondence track a fascinating international literary era in Paris. They admired each other's writing though they quite frequently disapproved of each other's behavior. They kept in touch for twenty years. Through Natalie, Anna experienced the literary attention she craved, though it was not without cost.

Natalie Clifford Barney (1876–1972) was American by birth, Parisian by inclination, independently wealthy, a leader, a lesbian, a writer, "captive" to no one, and a connoisseur of beauty, intellect, and originality who attracted famous and creative people to her weekly Friday salons.[3] Sylvia

Beach, proprietor of the Paris bookstore and lending library Shakespeare and Company, said Barney was "charming, and, all dressed in white and with her blond coloring, most attractive. Many of her sex found her fatally so."[4]

Barney had very early won a name for herself by making things happen. She possessed a rare combination: knowledge of herself, a strong will, and financial resources. "There she is . . . a most deluxe edition, limited to a single copy," is what another contemporary had to say about her.[5] She had the skill to organize, one that Anna had always admired. As a woman, she was a practiced and creative seducer; as the host of an international literary salon that would last for over fifty years, her place is probably unequaled. By the time she met Anna she had already accomplished a great deal. And she was charming and still handsome, to boot. Djuna Barnes pegs her sardonically and sexually: ". . . a witty and learned Fifty, and though most short of Stature and nothing handsome, was so much in Demand, and so wide famed for her Genius at bringing up by Hand, and so noted and esteemed for her Slips of the Tongue. . . ."[6] Natalie Barney's first biographer, George Wickes, notes that "her wit was the articulation of an original mind that quickly seized the complexity of an idea, and her charm was an intuitive response to people who interested her."[7]

"When I met you I feared to drown of happiness," Anna wrote. "I had so much pleasure from contact with your mind, from your society & from the observation of your spirit."[8] Anna paid Natalie her highest compliment: "I can imagine from you," she once told Barney. And no wonder. Natalie led a fairy-tale existence and, moreover, she played all the parts: the well-dressed princess (couturier Paul Poiret), good fairy godmother, sophisticated seducer (sometimes for evil, sometimes for good), monarch of her own domain, benefactor, tight-fisted financial advisor, and stalwart knight or prince or troubadour.

Barney's beginnings in America and Europe had prepared her for the life she chose. Raised in Cincinnati, Ohio, until about age ten (she was born in Dayton), her family lived as did many wealthy households at the time: city society (Washington, D. C.) in the fall and for Christmas; grand seaside dwellings both in summer (Maine) and winter (Florida); plenty of European visits. Her father, Albert Clifford Barney, had inherited the family firm producing railroad cars, which he then sold to the Pullman Sleeping Car Company for an immense sum. Her mother, an accomplished artist studying under some of the best painters of the day, sought to paint well, entertain in her own way—turning her head from society's strictures—and avoid having marriage thwart her desires. Thus Natalie's mother set for her daughter an example of confidently going after what she wanted.

While still a student, Natalie knew she would be a lover of women, and later she thwarted her father's wish that she marry, once by deliberately choosing as a fiance a man her father never would accept: the infamous Lord Alfred Douglas, lover of Oscar Wilde. In 1900 her book of poems, *Quelques portraits-sonnets de femmes*, was published in Paris; these poems written to women sent her father scurrying to buy up all copies to keep his daughter's lesbian orientation under wraps. At the turn of the century she persistently wooed a famous courtesan, Liane de Pougy. The woman finally accepted her and even wrote a best-selling book about the affair titled *Idylle saphique*.

Albert Barney died in 1902, leaving Natalie a fortune of $2,500,000 (augmented by $1,500,000 when later her mother remarried) that would make her financially independent for life. She went to live in France.

At Neuilly, then still a village outside Paris, twenty-six-year-old Natalie sometimes hosted as many as 200 people in her house and garden, gathering artists, writers, and musicians with sometimes fabulous entertainments thrown in. In another extravagance inspired by a mutual attraction to the poet Sappho, lovers Natalie and Renée Vivien (British poet Pauline Tarn), in 1904 thought of founding a colony on the island of Lesbos.[9] The plan did not work out and the affair ended badly. Some thought Barney's behavior may have even driven Vivien to an early death.

In 1909 Natalie moved to a house at no. 20 rue Jacob in the St-Germain-des Prés quarter, today a pretty area of mostly narrow streets, fairly low apartment buildings, small hotels, and well-kept shops catering to the table arts and antiques sectors. The move, at that time, may have brought her closer to the disapproval of some members of an older society living in the neighboring Faubourg St. Germain area to the west, but it satisfied her wish to live in the thick of things in "the most artistically active part of the sixth *arrondissement*," the Left Bank later to become famous with American expatriates after World War I.[10] The Sorbonne, in what was known as the Latin Quarter, was slightly south and east of Natalie's new home, the shady park of the Luxembourg Palace was south, and if from her house she turned north onto the rue de Seine, walking a short distance she would run smack into the Institut de France, the domed building that houses the Académie Française, keeper of the purity of the French language. Across the river and to the east, one day Natalie's serene gray and white portrait done by artist Romaine Brooks would hang at the entrance to a suite of rooms at the Musée Carnavalet.[11] But that would be many years in the future.

When Natalie moved her belongings in under the dim, gated archway of no. 20 rue Jacob and then across the sunny courtyard and in through the double doors of the ivied *pavilion*, who could have guessed that she would live in this rented home almost until her death in 1972?

She never cared much for the finest furnishings (she used her mother's castoffs), and a spotless household was never the object. The rooms were meant to be used, but were not to be the focus: it was living that mattered. In the same way, her wild and unkempt garden might have provoked a look or two of dismay from the fastidious. But the point of the garden and trees was to provide a casual foil for the nineteenth-century structure that it surrounded: a temple to friendship. This *Temple à l'Amitié* had five steep steps leading up to a classical porch complete with Doric columns and triangular pediment. Inside, the walls curved attractively and furnishings of a daybed, chairs next to the small mantle, and some decorative objects and chandeliers made the place cozy, though the building itself was in a dilapidated state. In this unusual temple and rough garden, together with the house (free-standing but for the fourth wall that abutted onto an apartment building), Natalie reigned however she wished, serving and served by the artists, writers, musicians and others who mattered to her. That some of her employees fled her surroundings, that some people would not have received her in their own homes or cared to read what she championed or would not have been caught dead in her salon, was not a matter of much concern for the "wild girl from Cincinnati."[12]

The Friday salon at 20 rue Jacob (5:00 to 8:00 p.m.) began in October 1909 when Barney was about thirty-two years old. The early gatherings sometimes had more than one 100 guests. The later, smaller and more famous Fridays were held in the two ground floor drawing rooms. "Unless there was a poetry reading or a concert or some special occasion, there were never more than twenty people in her salon. After all, there was not room for great numbers, since everyone sat around a large mahogany table . . . of course, . . . only the intimate members of the circle stayed longer than half an hour. . . . In warm weather . . . tables were put up in the garden."[13]

As Shari Benstock points out, Barney "clearly saw the danger of forming separatist groups and made her salon an eclectic, international, and multisexual meeting place." Benstock also notes that:

Natalie Barney never used her salon to further her own career as a writer, nor did she set herself up as the center of the salon. Her purpose was to bring people together, to foster the work of other artists (many of whom were women), and to embrace the cultural life of the Left Bank community. Barney's was a feminist effort that would eventually become an endeavor on behalf of lesbian literature and art.[14]

Contemporaries of Barney's sometimes stressed the more aesthetic aspects of the surroundings themselves. One of those attending Barney's salon writes about her "Fridays":

Miss Barney's house was at the end of a cobbled and shady court. The salon had Irish lace curtains, and was crowded with pictures and statues and books, by or about Natalie's famous friends. It was also crowded with her famous friends. This *pavillon* was a *pavillon* des muses, but Dolly [Wilde] impudently re-christened it a "Musée de Province."[15]

In addition to the quality of the social and cultural aspects of the salon, critic Karla Jay points out the temerity of an "American upstart" even having a successful salon in France. Jay attributes the success of the Barney salon to two things: first, the financial freedom accorded to Barney because of her inherited fortune, and secondly, the aftermath of the Dreyfus affair that, having polarized people's opinions, then created a need for a more politically neutral meeting place for the intellectuals of the time. Jay also analyzes how Barney's position "as an outsider in every sense of the word" did not pose the "threat of disrupting French familial values from within."[16] In short, she was not a French Protestant who might challenge French Catholics, nor was she politically motivated to choose sides; finally, she was not a woman seeking to marry into an established French family. As Jay notes, she filled a gap in French circles for "salons that would once more be politically neutral turf so that any battle within could be waged on the artistic front."

If politics here are taken to mean those associated with governmental activities, then Barney's salon usually *was* politically neutral (exception to this is Barney's pacifism during World War I). But if sexual politics are taken into consideration, then Barney's salon was less "neutral" than "expansive." She did not hesitate to champion the lesbian life openly.

Natalie could be gracious, curt, frank, evasive, challenging, and attentive—a combination refreshing to anyone tired of stuffy society or bored by the usual remarks. In 1910, not long after her move to rue Jacob, Remy de Gourmont, a leading critic in the Symbolist movement, made her reputation. He had been won over by Natalie's successful efforts to bring him out of a social self-exile begun years earlier as a result of health problems. In admiration, he began not only to write personal letters to her but also launched, under the heading "*Lettres à l'Amazone*," a public appreciation of her in *Le Mercure de France*, the journal he had helped to found.[17]

New admirers crowded in. A good many of those admirers were women. She was now relaxed about her identity as a lesbian and many others were equally open in her company, following her example. She seems to have initiated quite a few women to lesbian love and was very forthright in her admirations. Everyone knew the power a set of dominant eyebrows or the sweep of long eyelashes could have over Barney (some people, including, later, Anna, seemed to relish describing such features for her).[18] Barney thought that being a lesbian was a "perilous *advantage*" [emphasis added].[19] She saw lesbianism as a natural state offering, according to Shari Benstock, a "double confirmation of woman's separateness and wholeness."[20] Natalie certainly did not hold one view, common to her day, that loving women was "inversion," or a kind of curse to be regretted. Nor did she feel that woman-to-woman marriage was the answer, as did her British contemporary, Radclyffe Hall. For Barney had a low opinion of marriage:

> *Marié: n'être ni seul ni ensemble.*
> Married: to be neither alone nor together.[21]

By late 1926 Natalie Barney had decided to form her own *Académie des Femmes* (Academy of Women) to highlight the talents of women of letters and to introduce French- and English-speaking women to one another. Madame Aurel, Colette, Lucie Delarue-Mardrus, the Duchess de Clermont-Tonnerre, and Rachilde were to represent the French; Gertrude Stein and Djuna Barnes, the Americans; Mina Loy, the English; and one male, Ford Madox Ford, also from England, a skillful editor, promoter of literature, and a fine novelist, was thrown in for good measure.[22] The academy would then be an on-going venture, the aforementioned being only the first wave. Offering select guests a particular "Friday," Natalie would establish an in-home "conference" not only celebrating the accomplishments of living women she admired, but also giving center stage to retrospectives of poet Renée Vivien and playwright/political activist Marie Lenéru. Though men had always attended Natalie's salon and were welcome now (the list reads like a Who's Who of important personages), Natalie wanted to challenge the male dominance of the arts so characteristic of French intellectual and artistic circles. Perhaps this stemmed from her father's aggressive tactics aimed at silencing her voice. Perhaps she took a cue from the Académie Goncourt that "in a counter-blast" was also founded to protest the exclusiveness of the Académie Française.[23] (In fact the academy did not admit a woman until Natalie's friend, Belgian-born novelist Marguerite Yourcenar, was elected in 1980.[24]) Or maybe it was truly to honor women's achievement in the arts. Regardless of the spoken or unspoken reasons for its creation, the Académie des Femmes did successfully recognize female achievements in the arts, giving women a privileged place and providing an audience for their works. If Barney's preliminary introductions to the honored writers also honored herself by quoting snippets from letters praising herself or brashly reminding the honored ones of their loveable "faults," well, this was classic Barney; never become sentimental, never get so close to a person that you couldn't reserve a little cold-eyed judgment, literary or otherwise.

Natalie Barney asked Lucie Delarue-Mardrus, one of Barney's friends and former lovers (Barney had convinced Lucie's husband to look the other way during the affair), to do translations. She also asked her to serve as the "présidente" because, as Barney quite accurately summed it up, Mardrus shone in a crowded room, gave astute and loving introductions to the writers, and managed a fierce command of an audience.[25] But of course it was really fifty-year-old Barney who ran the show.

These literary gatherings were held at 20 rue Jacob, the two-story house set back on a cobbled courtyard that was becoming so important in Natalie's life that Anna Wickham would once write to her: "It is not *true* that you miss no place or no person, You dare not leave Jacob St."[26] The neighborhood, earlier the site of a great abbey whose church still remains, was vividly associated with Racine and Voltaire and others of the greatest names in French seventeenth- and eighteenth-century literature. It was in "the heart of the intellectual and artistic quarter . . . whose traditions are associated with the classical divisions of learning—philosophy, letters, the arts—rather than inherited titles and property."[27] And writers in the sixth *arrondissement* who were important to Barney had sought the perfect word:

Remy de Gourmont writing at a breakneck pace; a few attics away, Colette penning her school-girl chronicles.

How did Anna become involved with Natalie Barney and her literary "Fridays"? Although some sources say Anna briefly met Barney in Paris, 1922, Anna wrote in 1934 that she met Barney "eight years ago."[28] Nineteen twenty-six is the year of the first correspondence and, of course, is the same year as Anna's marital separation from Patrick Hepburn.

Lucie Delarue-Mardrus was probably instrumental in bringing them together, or at least she records the first of Wickham's appearances in the Barney milieu.[29] At a gathering given in honor of Barney at the Caméléon, a popular nightspot in the Montparnasse quarter, Anna stood for some time in silence at the fringes of the party. Then she read a stirring sonnet in English and went back down the stairs without chatting or even introducing herself to anyone. This all proved so intriguing to Delarue-Mardrus, a gregarious woman, that the next time Anna attended she tried to start a conversation with her. Anna wouldn't say a word of idle chatter but instead "came to the middle of our group," and "grabbing nonchalantly a piece of her poorly combed hair," proceeded to recite "as if for herself" bits of poetry.

Anna's not conversing didn't put off Delarue-Mardrus, who had traveled extensively in Asia and Africa, been married to J. C. Mardrus, a noted translator of *1001 Arabian Nights*, and prized a "*curieuse personnalité*."[30] By the time Delarue-Mardrus, who already had seven books of poetry to her credit, had seen Anna three or four more times, she made inquiries of others and learned that this enigmatic visitor also had a poetic vocation. Someone then passed along Anna's books. Delarue-Mardrus translated many of the poems, a job for which she was well-suited, having studied English from childhood in Normandy and Paris and having, from the beginning of her own career, eagerly practiced and experimented with poetic forms. She undoubtedly showed the translations to Natalie.

It should be remembered at this point that Natalie, besides her social skills, was also a writer, an idiosyncratic one. For one thing, she primarily wrote in French, her language of choice, though not the language of her home country. For another, her way of skipping from genre to genre; in 1902 *Cinq petits dialogues grecs*; in 1910 a collection titled *Actes et entr'actes* that included short formal verse plays with feminist themes; two more books of poetry (one in 1910, one in 1920); and several collections of aphorisms (*Eparpillements,* 1910 and *Pensées d'une Amazone*, 1918). The latter two books were collections of Natalie's thoughts and a symbol of Natalie's achievements in that most fluid and spontaneous of genres: conversation. So when Natalie and Anna met each other, it was as equals in the field of writing and kindred spirits in the love of good conversation. As it turned out, they both would develop and maintain a lifelong appreciation for each other's work.

Barney was impressed by Anna's poetry and poetic reputation. Late in her life she would call Anna, "that great poet."[31] But Barney, at five-foot-two, probably found Anna physically compelling as well. The English poet's tall form, large head, striking features, hair in a careless chignon, and her musical, but powerful contralto voice made a striking contrast to the smaller figures in the salon. And as a mother and, at least legally, a wife, she functioned, for Barney, as a contradictory emblem of wildness and domesticity. Barney may have also noticed (Delarue-Mardrus whispering behind a hand), that at the time Anna had an expression of a "tall young girl who, often scolded and beaten, still fears more physical abuse."[32]

In 1926, separated from her husband (quite literally "neither alone nor together"), Anna was in deep need of affection and by her own admission, longing for some sort of "refuge." As far as any explanation for the separation, the only written one Anna ever gave was, "I was thrown out of my house for attempting to write a ballet for Diaghilev."[33] She was free from what too long she had seen as "the wedded gloom" of Patrick, but life without him presented myriad complications, too. Anna, understandably, was often in emotional turmoil. "I need to cry," she had written Natalie from London one Friday in 1926.

Not the least of Anna's complications was where to live. In April, 1926, according to Anna's P.E.N. membership application, she was renting "Prospect House," an interesting tower home reached by going up a winding brick alley from the very top of the High Street in Hampstead. In the next year and one-half she and her sons would live in at least five different houses, apartments, and rented rooms. At times she would come to Paris for several weeks. Once, from a person she never identified, she received a cable asking her to come to America and provoking much inner debate about what to do. (She didn't go, and in fact she never did travel there, despite her fondness for Americans in general.)

Certainly there were other problems besides where to live. The family did not have the domestic help they were accustomed to, the housekeeper having stayed with Patrick. Anna's energy sometimes was overwhelmingly taxed, coupled as her new responsibilities were with the sicknesses that would sometimes visit the family. In one dreadful period still to come she and the boys would all have influenza at the same time. Her old nemesis, bronchitis, would raise its ugly head for months at a time several winters running, with one especially bleak period in March and April 1927.

But if health concerns passed, the miasma of financial troubles settled in for the duration. Funds became for Anna a daily struggle, once becoming so severe that a son remembers her donning a ragged dress and using her acting lessons to good advantage, singing to a theatre queue and bringing in £12. Griffin Barry wrote with tenderness and thinly disguised physical longing, telling her to not to worry about repayment for the present (they loaned each other money), and sympathized with her lack of funds for "shoes and bus fares."[34]

From 1926 through 1928 Anna would constantly have to reshuffle her finances to handle expenses for food, clothing, and shelter, not to mention school fees, transportation money (Anna never had a car and never learned to drive), and medical expenses. Still, on what she called Patrick's "alimony" the family managed to live exuberantly, if not richly. It was during these few years that Anna and her sons began to earn the reputation summed up in the phrase "La Tour Bourgeoise." There was nothing bourgeois about the sometimes nomadic, always interesting life they lived.

Jim, John, and possibly George, went with Anna to Paris in 1926 and while there they all had separate portraits taken by a photographer soon to achieve real and lasting fame. Bérénice Abbott, an American who had taken on accents as local coloration, worked in a studio at 44 rue du Bac only a short walk from Natalie Barney's home. The portraits she did captured John's, the middle son's, alert, somewhat wary, grace as well as Anna's quiet solidity and somewhat humorous resolve.

Jim was soon to leave his work with the Northern Line railroad and night classes at the London School of Economics (playing rugby for the University College School "Old Boys" and cricket for the Hampstead Cricket Club on the side) in order to teach fencing and continue taking acting and dancing classes. He would soon go on the stage. John was finishing up at University College School, by most accounts a brilliant boy, with friends such as the budding poet Stephen Spender, who wrote a poem to him. George, or "Rastus" as the family continued to call him, was just a kindergartner as Anna began shepherding him through these frequent relocations. Though Patrick would take George to the zoo and once to the

Lord Mayor's Show (Patrick's City of London connections giving them a coveted window seat on the parade), most often he was just with Anna. Too young to go with the older boys, and sensitive to the way Anna and his brothers had begun to loudly and argumentatively discuss the best course of action for this and that, George and his mother formed an unusually strong bond.

Anna of course was not unique in being a mother/writer. Alice Meynell had had a busy domestic life, Rebecca West raised a son, to give only two examples. Another of Barney's friends, Mina Loy, was mother to such beautiful daughters that together the family turned heads when they walked down the street. But Anna was no less remarkable with her sons. Good looks, tall strong physical frames, beautiful voices, alert intelligences, they would have stood out in a crowd wherever they went. And from the time Anna was, as she said, a "nursing mother of distinction" to this time when the two oldest were creating their careers and the youngest was providing her with his excellent company, everyone who knew Anna knew of her sons and her pride in them.

Some of the more published women writers who did not have children loomed large on the literary scene, Virginia Woolf being probably the most famous example. Closer to Anna was the poet Charlotte Mew, who never married or had children. But Anna had always relished her involvement in her children's lives. If there was less time for writing she would turn that very problem into poetry, as she did in the poem "Dedication of the Cook" and her poem, "New Eve," with the lines, "Why was I born beneath two curses/ To bear children & to write verses?"[35] But now that she and Patrick were separated, how would she find time for writing? How would she make her living?

Forty-three-year-old Anna had, like most solicitor's wives, never worked outside the home for a living, but instead had an active social life and worked for social, political, or religious causes. Unlike most solicitor's wives, Anna wrote poetry. This brought her a fair measure of recognition but little income.

Anna had wanted to work in the past. She turned down roles in the theatre, for example, because she felt she should be with her children and she also knew that Patrick would consider it beneath the family honor. As she later told Natalie Barney, she had "three generations of working women" behind her.[36] She was proud of their resourcefulness—her great-grandmother's connection with the Royal Court of Belgium, her grandmother modeling for artists and later housecleaning in the homes of the well-off, and finally, her mother who taught in the schools of England and Australia and set herself up as a lecturer, healer, and character-reader. But Patrick had a pride in "keeping his women" that Anna felt proved a source of financial loss to herself.[37] Patrick's allowance (intended to be £400 annually), was probably intended to keep her comfortably, but Patrick was sometimes either unable, or unwilling, to live up to the terms of the agreement. "The first time he cheated me I was amused—but this is wearisome." And when Anna attempted to argue with him about the reduced support he cut one install-ment of the allowance almost £14 for breaches of "civility."[38] Her sons felt the amounts he paid were "meager." At first prompt with the payments, later Anna commented that Patrick was "not so agreeable" as he had been. Perhaps Anna's journeys to Paris had made him angry or even frightened him. At any rate, Anna's financial situation gradually plunged. In the next few years her aging wardrobe went from simply being untidy to being what she called the "John the Baptist" look until she, who always admitted being "womanish" about clothes, was humiliated to find herself being "remem-bered" as someone elegant. "That was before I started writing verse," she sighed to Natalie.[39] Soon she would be having to think in terms of shillings and pence instead of pounds, and having to budget money for stockings and borrow a coat from Natalie for a Paris occasion. More than once Anna writes on "the wearisome theme of chemises."[40] At times, she told Natalie, she wanted nothing more than to go off by herself for two years, or flee oftener to the diversions of Paris. But responsibilities dictated that most of the time Anna would stay put in London.

When Anna returned to London (probably home in time for the General Strike, May 3 until May 13, 1926), she sublet 19 Heathcote Street, a Bloomsbury house that Alida Klemantaski and Harold Monro rented out for the spring and summer months.[41] The boys were fascinated by Alida's aquarium in the front window, but it was a short-term rental and the family was soon on the move again. Anna tried to focus her energies.

Into this whirlwind of discomfort and uncertainty rode Natalie, the undisputed leader of what Anna Wickham called "a Holy Island for the Imagination of Women."[42] Natalie's comfortable circumstances, her hos-pitality, and above all her appreciation for Anna's unique poetic voice gave Anna hope, pleasure, and support. She engaged Anna as no one did before or after. Barney brought out all of Anna's passion because for once there was an individual who not only appreciated Anna's work but would also give her a place to shine. The "disciplinarian" (as Anna described it) in Barney disapproved of Anna's excesses and said so but the literary critic in Barney engaged with and approved of Anna's work.

"When I climbed into your camp for refuge . . . I found it," Anna said.[43] In 1926 Natalie's "camp" was a lively and varied circle of Americans, English, French, and Italians, some of whom lived in Paris, some of whom just showed up when they visited or were passing through. Anna was first introduced to Natalie's circle as a woman who had been a virtual prisoner of a well-born man.

Anna had probably fallen in love with Natalie on an August night in 1926, though the details are not known.[44] Probably shortly after Anna first discovered how much she felt for Barney, Barney went with Romaine Brooks, her lover, to Beauvallon on their yearly respite from Paris.[45] From that time on Anna entertains Natalie with letters and poems. Wickham the woman might have been suffering, but Wickham the poet, inspired by Barney, took these concerns and transformed them into poems and letters.[46]

By September Anna was back in the suburbs northwest of London, staying at an address at 67 Carlton Hill though relying on The Poetry Bookshop for letters from Natalie and the rest of her mail, a system that kept "breaking down," because of the shop's September opening at its new premises, 38 Great Russell Street.[47] By November 1926 Anna triumphantly writes Natalie, "tell Romaine . . . that 'Charlemagne' (Patrick) has been vanquished"; Patrick may himself have taken rooms off Tottenham Court Road while Anna stayed, perhaps off and on for a little while, at Parliament Hill. (In the spring of 1927 she would move to 51 Willow Road, Hampstead, sharing a flat with a young novelist named Ruth Brockington.)[48]

Anna saw in Natalie so many attractive things. Anna loved the American side of Natalie, forthright and lighthearted, her continental polish, and the fact that she had Jewish ancestors. Anna had a variety of nicknames for her: "Captain" Barney for leadership in her "camp" of refuge; "Joshua" for the person that brought her walls tumbling down; and simply "natalie" for the woman whose arrival in a room created a *frisson* and raised the level of the gathering, as Anna said it did one night when they were listening to an old Russian woman singing folk songs at a cafe.[49] And on two fronts, lesbian and artistic, Anna accepted Natalie's leadership. It was quite a switch for someone who was capable of silencing conversational competition by acidly observing, "There is only room for one leading lady here."[50]

In December, 1926, Anna mailed Natalie a love poem:

> My heart is fire for the beauty of snow
> For the white of my belovéd, and her pure behest—
> For her wise cold, her virgin "no"
> To amourous importunate request.[51]

By the time Anna came onto the scene, Natalie had been involved for almost ten years with an American-born painter, Romaine Brooks. Brooks and Barney would together build and share a vacation home on the French Riviera, also staying together in Italy for part of each year, and they were well-matched in matters of wealth and talent. Natalie drove Romaine to distraction with her many sexual affairs, swearing immortal love one moment, absenting herself the next, but their partnership lasted fifty years, ending only when Brooks could not forgive the notoriously experimental Natalie a last added relationship in old age. Natalie believed in fidelity of friendship, which she saw as lifelong, rather than sexual fidelity, which she might well have summed up as folly and waste. At the time Anna met Natalie, the involvement with Romaine must have been clear but it did not stop Anna, who may not have perceived, until later, both how deep and how broad was the scope of Natalie's affections, including not only Romaine but many others.

A letter written in early 1927 asks Natalie to "notice" Anna's feelings. "I know you don't like emotionalism and I respect that," Anna says, and so she seeks instead to reach Natalie through imagery.[52] "I want you to become aware of it, as you are of any other natural object, as for instance the yellow legs of the starling." Anna then describes a sort of kinesthetic uncoupling as illustration:

> I love your splendid courage & your magnificent good sense—in a way that could make my bones disarticulate & fall in a heap at your feet. Now nothing remains to be said.[53]

Around Easter, 1927, Anna tells Natalie all about Patrick's recent coup: his borrowing of a dirigible from the British government from which to view and photograph a solar eclipse. But this kind of ordinary slice-of-life topic was being overshadowed, already by March, with Anna's mounting semi-humorous campaign against the contenders for Natalie's time and attention. Her poem, "Resentments of Orpheus," mentions [Ford Madox] Ford, Mina Loy, [Gertrude] Stein, the "false lightnings of Tonnerre [Madame Clermont-Tonnerre (Elisabeth de Gramont)], friend and lover of Barney," the "yarns . . . of the unmitigated [Djuna] Barnes," and [Mina] Loy. With an iambic tetrameter couplet she capped off her poetic diatribe: "Let smokes of mediocrity / And such slow fires envelope thee."[54] Natalie must have liked the poem. She copied it over in her own hand. For Anna, Natalie was probably the subject of a lifetime, a female muse as important in her control and influence as Patrick had been important in his.

Natalie Barney's confidence, her irrepressible inventiveness, her salon, perhaps even her dictatorial pronouncements, certainly her appreciation, practically drove those close to her to distill the experience into art. As earlier mentioned, Natalie's early lover in Paris, Liane de Pougy, used their affair as the basis for what became a best-selling novel, *Idylle saphique* (1901). Other writers, poet Renée Vivien and Lucie Delarue-Mardrus, novelists Ronald Firbank, Radclyffe Hall, Colette, and Djuna Barnes all used their contacts with the American heiress as springboard to treatments of lesbian life in poetry, novels, plays, and other works. Not all of the portraits are flattering and even those that are, are not flattering all of the time. In Hall's *The Well of Loneliness*, Barney (in the guise of Valérie Seymour) comes across not only as a good listening ear in time of trouble but also as a killjoy and a woman whose light desires (for a lemon squeeze and some cold chicken) are at odds with the misery around her. The female members of Natalie's circle, lesbian or straight, appeared in a light, mocking satire by Djuna Barnes called *Ladies Almanack*, a tale that reportedly reduced Natalie to helpless laughter and which she helped pay to publish.[55] Romaine Brooks painted portraits of Natalie and of several of the rue Jacob visitors. Many of Barney's friends, Una Troubridge among them, kept up long-lasting correspondence. Anna under Natalie's spell was no different. When in Paris, Natalie's house drew Anna magnetically. When in London, because for Anna travel was now the exception rather than the rule, the post had to suffice.

In poetry and in letters Anna showed her passion and feelings of love and tenderness toward Natalie. Her wit shows to good advantage in letters that would continue for twenty years. She wrote giving an insider's take on literary and artistic circles and, to a lesser extent, intellectual and political ones. In the letters she is forthright on what it means to be an artist, especially a woman artist.

Only a few of Barney's letters to Anna survive (the rest were destroyed in the aftermath of a World War II firebomb that hit 68 Parliament Hill) but these show that she appreciated Anna and was happy to do things for her on the few occasions she was allowed to do so. Though we are missing Natalie's letters we can infer from Anna's replies some of the gossip, the worries, the criticisms and the kind attentions, the plans and (from some gaps) when one of the two might have been too busy, too involved with someone else, or too resentful of some breach of etiquette to write.

From London Anna wrote of the literary and the personal. When her P.E.N. membership came through she went "electioneering" to drum up a good attendance for the James Joyce dinner, crowing over her success in getting out writers who couldn't usually be bothered, saying "Arthur Symons is going & folk who have been slumbering for centuries."[56] (This was significant because the then 62-year-old Symons, who had attended in years past The Rhymers' Club, edited *The Savoy*, and written poetry in the decadent spirit, had undergone a brief nervous collapse in 1908. Even though he had earlier recovered with the help of his friends, Anna may have felt a personal triumph in seeing him accept the invitation.) She signed, along with practically every writer from Lascelles Abercrombie to W. B. Yeats, the protest against an American, Samuel Roth, who was without authorization republishing Joyce's *Ulysses*.[57] She dined with friends such as Violet Hunt, and made plans to visit Middleton Murry's second wife, then recovering from pneumonia. Periodically, however, her own family required all she could give. In January, 1927 Anna, Jim, and John all had influenza and had moved back home temporarily to get through the illnesses (Patrick "living in town"). Probably sometime soon after, early in 1927 (the date is based on a letter from March 14, 1927, saying "your selection of [my works] was perfect"), Anna came to Paris to be feted at Natalie's salon.

There are at least two accounts of Anna's day. Delarue-Mardrus remarked that "even though we were celebrating her, she seemed to be thinking of other things."[58] Harold Acton also wrote a description that provides most of the details for the following.

When the assembled group quieted down that day, Natalie began her introduction to Anna, this speech punctuated by loud applause as she talked about Anna's multiple roles as author, spouse, and mother of sons (a *demi-revoltée*).[59] Her poems, said Natalie, had unfurled on the banners of feminist causes; they had been used for the Women's Movement anti-corset campaign. "Her lungs filled with country air" (presumably making her more fit for battle) Anna had fought against "puritanism and other Anglican vices," and Natalie explained that Anna had especially led a charge against "matrimonial servitudes that shut in the bourgeois of the Croydon class."[60] Anna was both "pelican and nightingale" Natalie told the listeners (i.e., she had the sweet and haunting nocturnal poetic singing of the latter and the penchant for self-sacrifice of the former, as the pelican was thought to take blood from its own breast to feed its young).[61]

To illustrate her claims about Anna, Natalie had chosen for the day's reading some poems that showed the poet's life as wife and as mother. "The Fresh Start," "The Walk" (a seldom-anthologized monologue in which a controlling man orders a woman to follow his will and instructions), "Definition," "Envoi," and several couplets taken from selected poems. "The Fresh Start" was translated by Abel Doysié and the couplets by Natalie herself (who was very pleased to have achieved Anna's rhyme in French) but most were translated by Delarue-Mardrus, who admired the psychology of the poems and Anna's ability to excel "at singing her worries."[62]

Not all the audience were enthusiastic. Sherwood Anderson (reported by *The Bookman* in 1922 to be a man of "gorgeous vanity") had, according to Harold Acton, misunderstood Gertrude Stein's invitation and thought the afternoon had been scheduled to honor him. Probably piqued, he said that Anna, the featured guest, had "fortified herself with garlic and wine in advance" (probably true) and was simply "a derailed freight car."[63] Anderson attended with Acton, a much younger man just beginning his career as a poet, novelist, critic, and writer of historical studies and memoirs. Acton enjoyed the spectacle. Anna's poetry, he thought, went over well and translated better. He caught the "sheepish," probably slightly skeptical, expression on Anna's face when someone "compared her to Blake." According to Acton she was heartily congratulated (too heartily for Acton's tastes) afterward, and had "smiled defiantly throughout" (an observation much different from Delarue-Mardrus's). From that afternoon on, Anna had her voice recognized and won for herself a good spot on the "carte du Salon de l'Amazone etre 1910 et 1930" that Natalie Barney later would draw to illustrate the many and varied people who made her Friday salon a crackling showcase of controversial and highly original works. Anna, who often just titled a short poem "Song" was so identified on her 20, rue Jacob placecard and also on Natalie's map of artists who had already, were, or might in the future show the world a new way of thinking.[64]

Once back in England, Anna resumed the flow of letters. (Barney kept them, although we have no way of knowing if she kept every one. There are 140 in the Natalie Barney collection.) In the late 1920s, Anna sometimes wrote so frequently that she fretted about "importuning" Natalie rather than pleasing Barney. Sometimes she sent a letter each day for several consecutive days. She had been married to Patrick Hepburn since 1905 and, with the exception of six weeks of her institutionalization in the early 'teens, and the World War I years, had lived with him, if not always in harmony. But when they separated, Wickham was, apart from caring for her youngest son, George Hepburn, free to go her own way. Since money for travel was a problem, Wickham kept in close touch with Barney by mail.

The tone of Anna's letters to Natalie varies greatly over the years; sometimes the letters are self-absorbed, other times kindly and affectionate; on occasion they are threatening or slightly incoherent, or angry either in volcanic-like flow or erupting geyser; at their best they are confident and forthright. Penned most often on Lion Brand embossed stationery from Dickinson, written in English, usually in Anna's most beautiful flourishing hand (she had a crabbed or erratic script only on occasion) and punctuated with dashes of varying lengths, the letters themselves are often marvels of metaphor to describe daily events. She even felt free to use religious metaphors with Natalie, something not all members of the circle would do.[65]

Some of the letters are what Anna humorously called "Des Cartes à l'Amazone," a play on words reflecting Anna's reading in philosophy at the time. These postcard poems and notes she hoped would eventually rival Rémy de Gourmont's earlier *Lettres à l'Amazone* and she reportedly copied these postcard communications into a large blank book that she carried in a leather case. But the book and case she later left by accident on a train and much to her dismay it was never recovered.

The most remarkable aesthetic aspects of the Wickham/Barney correspondence are its intensity and its poetic richness. These aspects, along with the enduring, though at times sporadic quality of the correspondence, indicate the complex nature of the relationship.

Notice my feelings, she says to Barney, who has told her that she does not like "emotionalism." "You are a baby about your work" she scolds when Barney shrinks from the business of getting work published. "Your reference to my husband is bad mannered . . . we will not mention him," she orders when Barney presumes to criticize Patrick (Anna wants to reserve that right to herself).[66] Pound is "every sort of idiot" she comforts

Barney when Ezra dashes cold water on Barney's idea to have an international magazine. There are many quotable moments in the correspondence and her personality comes through clearly. Events themselves are not always so clearly described. This, along with the fact that not all the letters can be dated, makes reconstruction of certain happenings difficult.

The letters are significant because the poet's unmistakable sensibility and her affair of the heart and mind grasp the reader's attention, while important and not-so-important literary figures, fashionable cafes, dusty drawing rooms, whispered rumors, plots, failings, battles, publishing coups, and familial loves shuttle back and forth almost in silhouette, creating theatre. And because Anna is both showing off for Barney and allowing herself the expression of a full range of emotions, the freedom in the letters contrasts with the other genres in which Anna works. In her poetry she usually seeks to control the line, regardless of whether she's working in a strict metrical pattern. In her 1935 partial autobiography (not published until 1984) there is a psychological crafting of the total, so that events mirror one another, and certain themes repeat. But in the letters to Natalie, Anna is like a circus act without a net. In fact she says that "the man in the baggy trousers" (herself, the clown) "is best on the trapeze."[67] It is for Barney that Anna swings out again and again on the thin bar of language, ready for the huzzahs of success but willing to go through the whole act just for the sheer joy of the air whizzing by and for the delight when the swing reaches the top of its arc.

In June 1927, Natalie met a young Englishwoman, Dolly Wilde, a niece of the famed Oscar, and by July their affair had begun.[68] While Anna might have initially seen her as a "cadet," a minor, youthful player in a woman's game, Natalie was fascinated by Dolly's sometimes acid wit, good looks, and devil-may-care attitude, quickly easing her into a very close relationship, an off-again on-again rival to Romaine. Certainly Dolly would soon push Anna off center stage, and behave in such a way that Anna even put a curse on her that Natalie begged to have lifted years later when Dolly was really suffering.[69] Letters indicate that Dolly Wilde's excesses (and Natalie's too-understanding correctives, palliatives, and complaints) irritated Anna immensely. Though she could forgive Natalie many things, Anna would never forgive Natalie for this particular affair. "Alright to have courage like Dolly—but how about a spot of judgement," Anna responded to one of Natalie's tales of woe-in-love.[70] Serves you right for not visiting the [Oscar] Wilde Memorial with me, Anna said, now you have to "look at its [Dolly's] legs & have it call you Little Jack Horner at dinner."[71] And in the thirties, when Natalie persisted in bending Anna's ear about the latest exploits of "puppy Wilde," as she was known when it suited her, Anna, probably with great inner delight, had a calligrapher prepare in elaborate script, a formal "Certificate," fining Natalie the sum of £.9.4.6. "for mentioning a mistress to her true lover."[72]

Anna usually tried to get along with the members of Natalie's immediate company, her poem "Resentments of Orpheus" not withstanding. She thought, though, that too many of Barney's set were jealous and self-serving people, not above devising "set ups" to throw one or another from favor and privilege. She once commented that Romaine had "more muscle than judgment," but she admitted that Romaine had "certain powers of left and right over me."[73] Romaine "hated socializing," did not like Barney's gatherings, and rarely attended them. This and other aspects of her somewhat crusty personality appealed to the rebel in Anna, that side of Anna that could write, "I never had pleasure in coquetry except at its death."[74] Delarue-Mardrus, on the other hand, irritated Anna by publishing in *La Grande Revue* an April, 1927, article appreciative of Anna's work, but insulting to Patrick and remarking that leaving the "elegant prison" of 68 Parliament Hill had left her in despair, without money, and "a drunk." And with Isadora Duncan, who was in Paris then working on her memoirs to obtain badly needed cash, Anna truly had a "not very happy passage."[75] Probably one of the few fashionable women to still wear her hair long, one night in Paris Anna came up to Delarue-Mardrus, her "forehead bent down lower, sad, even sinister . . . holding in a paper, without saying a word, her hair forcefully cut off by Isadora Duncan."[76] Delarue-Mardrus says that "perhaps the poetess had feasted more than one should have, thus feeling too weak to resist the attack against her hair." To fault Anna for this hack job seems absurd, given another occasion in 1927. At that time Duncan's then-lover, Victor Seroff, witnessed Isadora hounding another young woman, Alice Spicer, to drink wine to the point of sickness.[77] Then Isadora had waded into the dark sea threatening suicide.

These and other episodes show that in 1926 and 1927, Anna had landed in a milieu that was diametrically different from the crémeries of her Paris youth. When Anna was a voice student in Paris taking lessons from de Reszke her exploits were rather mild, first entertaining her lover William Ray on the weekends and then regularly suffering the disapproval of her future sister-in-law, Ellen Hepburn, for other things. In 1922 when she visited Paris, though the atmosphere, full of youthful energy, had a tonic effect on Anna, it must be remembered that she had recently suffered the death of her third son, Richard, a death that was unexpected since the child was thought to have passed the crisis point in his illness. Accordingly Anna held back from involvement to a certain extent. This time too Anna was probably under the pall of her recent separation from her husband of twenty years. But since she and Patrick had stumbled up and down so many hills of marital discord, this time in Paris was different. It was exciting. It was liberating. Yet it was also unsettling, so often subject to that "mob" mentality, as Anna called it. At times the reach of Natalie's circle of friends extended even to London, as in an event where Anna's "reputation" was being called into question around the time that Barney began her affair with Dolly Wilde. According to Anna, she had been trying to get her feelings off her chest regarding the Delarue-Mardrus article. In the course of letting off steam, she was involved in some sort of incident at the "Curzon Hotel" involving mostly theatre people from the Provincetown group. Later defending herself to Natalie, Anna accused Mary Vorse (a good friend of Griffin Barry) of having "planted" a woman and stolen money in order to disgrace Anna.

Delarue-Mardrus's article, favorable concerning Anna's poetry and sympathetic concerning Anna's domestic affairs, nonetheless had called Anna a "drunk." To this charge Anna continued to allude. In June, 1927, she poked fun of Natalie's then well-known aversion to the use of alcohol by saying, "I should be glad to know your intuition of the number of times I have been drunk in the last fortnight."[78] Another time Anna scoffed that she was so short of cash that the only beer she would be buying would be a bottle of stout for each time "a certain indigent friend" came to dinner.[79] To the stolen money charge mentioned above, Anna resigns herself to the fact that it is on its way to becoming "a piece of literary history," at least, she said, according to literary tastemaker Edward O'Brien.[80]

Anna appreciated Natalie's ease in finding new friends and lovers and artists but resented it when Natalie so obviously chose favorites or held others up as stellar examples of good taste and manners. Likewise, she hated it when Natalie criticized, which she frequently did.

In the period from 1926 to 1928 Anna came to Paris roughly two times a year, according to Anna's son Jim. During that time Natalie kept attempting, as Anna said, to "civilize" her in manners of dress and deportment, tactics Anna met in two ways. In the matter of dress, though Anna would not shake her habitual untidiness, she was touched by Natalie's gift of clothing (a handbag, a coat, money to buy fabric to "construct a black dress") and sent her appreciative words. But Natalie's trying to rule over her behavior brought, first, measured thanks, then, controlled exasperation and finally, anger that deepened the more Natalie persisted.

This may have been because Natalie could have used a little civilizing herself, not only in the giving of unsolicited advice, but also in the matter of keeping appointments. A favorite device was to overschedule her time, an irritation suffered by anyone who had Natalie for a friend in those years. She would make too many appointments, show up and stay for only a few distracted minutes, slipping out the door leaving disappointment behind. "Let him who has not cursed her for such things throw the first stone at me!" said Delarue-Mardrus.[81] Especially, time alone with Natalie was at a premium (unless you happened to be the favored one of the moment).

Barney had a smooth, and beautiful, social veneer. This had first kept her out of direct conflict with her father, then permitted her to live the life of a debutante for a few years and finally enabled her to build a large and quite diverse circle. Anna was clearly aware of the advantages such a veneer conveyed, but her mother's dominance and her own decades-long irritation with the Hepburns' socially coded ways meant she had no patience when Natalie tried to use her social graces to manipulate her. Anna was constantly sounding the gong both when she felt Natalie was putting on airs to impress her and when Natalie's criticisms were meant to "improve" her.

Sometimes Anna's humor came to the fore on those occasions. Once responding to what she saw as Natalie's finicky tastes Anna responded mildly, "I guess you wouldn't like the man's birth marks—or [you would] know that his aunt hasn't learnt the uses of the fan." In the same letter Anna goodnaturedly thanks Natalie for a small favor but backhands her for feudalist attitudes:

> I will say that your way of doing business makes me feel like a twelfth-century peasant being dragged out of bed to go on a spot of road mending. Quant à moi. You can take your medi-aevalism with you to the devil
>
> Yours affec[82]

Wickham is conscious of the contrast between Barney's wealth and stability and her own lately unsettled life. In late 1927 Barney has obviously either mocked or berated Wickham for her behavior and appearance and her living arrangements. Wickham deals with each in turn:

> You have suggested to me that I had not the tact nor social equipment to deal with men like T. S. Eliot.

Wickham responds that George Bernard Shaw answered her recent letter, which to her was proof that she could operate at a high level. Natalie criticizes her for her clothes, or as Anna states it, "you found your argument on the fact that I have no chemises."[83] Anna, short of cash and ready to spend what money she had on other things, defends herself by telling Natalie, "Master you should understand asceticism if you are a Jew," a barb aimed at Natalie's airy dismissal of her background. For though Natalie had a Jewish background, she paid it little heed, a lack of interest that Anna, who kept up with Israel Zangwill's Zionist plans and knew and appreciated a great deal about many religions, could not understand.

Probably because Anna was herself vitally aware of the precariousness of her current social and financial position she is incensed by any of Natalie's criticism of her life. She feels she has succeeded, despite Patrick's financial obstructions and her own physical and emotional health concerns, in keeping her family and herself going during the period of marital separation. Thus when Natalie criticizes her situation by calling it "disorderly," Anna takes aim and fires:

> I come to you after fifteen months of brilliant extemporisation—when I have built a city from three eggs cups & a straw & you tell me my life is disorderly.[84]

Natalie's criticisms especially hurt Anna because she held such reverent attitudes toward her often arrogant muse/model. So it is a relief when, in the letters, Anna throws off that reverent attitude. Anna often wrote to Natalie in what she called the "wife" role, a "relation of the spirit"; when writing in those roles she exercised what she termed a wife's right: "full freedom of invective."[85] Thus when Natalie was being aloof, Anna wrote sarcastically. When Natalie spent her time with other friends and lovers, Anna responded with a poem indicating that Natalie was wasting her time, since those involved were hardly to be taken seriously. "Full freedom of invective" was displayed nowhere as strongly as in Anna's letter in which she expresses her wrath at some other members of Barney's circle, calling them "light ladies" and tartly observing that she "cares nothing for the opinion of mobs."[86] When "the mob" tells Natalie "horrible . . . abortions of truth," Anna wants to comfort her, but "the way to express my truth to you is to take you in my arms & hug you—hug you like a grisly—& there are miles & your prejudice in between."[87]

Natalie was accustomed to having women angry at her and emotional with her. One imagines her reading Anna's most cutting barbs with only "that laugh, low and a bit rusty . . . with which she underlines all disagreeable things said to her."[88] The love sections may have pleased her more, as in Anna Wickham's poem, "Fear of Humour," indicative of her thwarted desire:

> When I mock beauty with burlesque,
> With poor impertinent grotesque,
> I'm afraid.
> But how else were desire allayed
> And all my hunger stayed?
> Love touched my backbone with his fist
> And laid her fingers on my wrist.
> Yet all my body is unfed,
> And I mock beauty, or lie dead.

In this poem, with its shifting possessive pronouns, Anna shows how love (male and female) has left her wanting. Judging from her other poetry and her autobiographical writings, this torment, this unfulfilled longing was with her from childhood and continued into her marriage. With Natalie Barney, however, Wickham gave unrestrained voice to her longings and yet realized, at the same time, that in her urge to captivate Barney she was pushed over into an excess that failed to win Barney as a long-term lover and at times even strained the friendship between the two. Thus Anna often resorted to mocking love so that it would not consume her. Too often for Anna there was no emotional release of what she terms "my passion . . . deeper than bone."[89]

But when Anna writes Natalie a horrific poem about sows and teats saying "this is mad and you have maddened me," even the cool Natalie must have shaken her head.[90]

The biggest issue between the two women was over what constituted acceptable behavior. Probably because Natalie wouldn't give Anna "rendezvous," Anna once came—and went—undetected in disguise at Le

Sélect. This must have later made Natalie at least smile, given how she her-self had liked costumes in her earlier years, dressing as a page and having her photograph taken.[91] Natalie's "lady-in-waiting" once threatened to throw Anna out of 20 rue Jacob for some infraction, and when Natalie pre-tended surprise and a sort of my-hands-are-tied attitude, an incensed Anna said, "I should be ashamed to crow on a dungheap as ill-governed as your household."[92] On another occasion, having learned that Natalie Barney's nerves would not stand the sound of tearing paper, Anna "tore up two tele-phone books and an entire file of the *Nouvelle Review Française* into small bits before Natalie leapt from the couch and had the butler thrust her out."[93] Like Dolly Wilde, though less frequently, Anna could be outra-geous in a way that Natalie could not tolerate, yet admired just the same.

Similarly, Natalie sometimes acted in ways that totally disappointed Anna, the most profound concerning the appeals trial of charges of obscen-ity involving Radclyffe Hall's controversial novel, *The Well of Loneliness*, which, as mentioned above, had a character based on Natalie Barney. In a long letter dated December 15, 1928, Anna wrote regretting that Barney can't come to London for Christmas, but rejecting her excuses for not doing so: "I have a skin for what is false in you. And I am constantly in pain." Anna has "received instructions" (how to help Hall?) three hours late. In addition to criticizing her for this, Anna feels that Natalie should have come to London to defend Hall and lesbianism:

> You should have been in London during the week of the appeal. Your kingdom is threatened. You don't want the kingdom, but it has been yours and you should defend it.[94]

Natalie, whose father's favorite city had been London, did not go.

If blunt expression is a mark of true friendship then Anna and Barney were truly the best of friends. Anna could say, "Stop treating me like an ine-briate." Natalie could criticize Anna's work and get in return a funny reply from Anna in the style of a questioning brogue, "Is it me you will accuse of forcing a rhyme . . . ?"[95] When Natalie has criticized Anna and Dolly, Anna says tongue-in-cheek that they should join with Dolly in a song of repentance to the tune of Hymn #49.[96] Or Anna would make suggestions for alternate forms of address, saying in one letter that perhaps Natalie should sing, "Anna, poor woman" rather than the usual, though implied, "Anna, old inade-quacy."[97] But at times there seems to have been real malice in the exchanges.

In one letter several years after their meeting, Anna sends to Natalie a sepia-toned photograph, probably taken in her twenties. Seated, her long dark hair flowing down her naked back, Anna wears a sort of crown and looks down at a large clear-glass object next to her. She is draped in a gauzy fabric and through it you can see her beautiful nude body.

In this case, Anna was wounded by Natalie's honesty. Natalie had obviously written back and commented about the toll the intervening years had exacted on Anna. Anna writes a reply: "I lay & cried about [what] you said about the decay of my beauty . . . I have never been so hurt about anything."[98]

During the period Anna was separated from Patrick, probably one and a half years, or at most two, by her own account she experienced "the depths of undiscipline and bad taste."[99] At times, as far as Natalie was concerned, she was considered to be obstreperous in the extreme. In 1928 the relationship between the two women was rocky indeed. In January Anna had expressed violent feelings for Natalie. By February this particular storm, emotional and poetical, seems to have spent itself though a February 12, 1928 letter, in which Anna says that she must "resist" what she calls spiritual impregnation by Barney, shows that Anna is still very vulnerable. "I have touched the depths of undiscipline & bad taste," Anna cries out about this period; "my soul would have died." But allowing her to get through it, she said, was Natalie: "I have used you, as a woman in labour uses a roller towel tied to her bed-end, to pull on."[100] A weaker woman than Natalie might have been pulled into the maelstrom with Anna, or cut off relations entirely. To her credit, and in her own fashion, she served Anna well during this time. Perhaps it was sufficient for Anna to know that the letters were passing to that "genius" who she so admired.[101]

The drama continued. In the spring of 1928 Anna had serious asthma. "All hell's dryers & bleachers in my lungs," she wrote to Natalie.[102] By May 1928 Anna was in Paris and being very demanding—not that it seems to have done her much good—of Natalie's time and attention. Anna had holed up at a hotel with the specific intention of producing verse, but the scratchy, uncontrolled quality of the script might indicate more than exhaustion from intense poetic effort. Still ill from her lungs and staying inside? Drinking? Perhaps a severe emotional crisis? Anna asks for "someone to come round for poetry" so that she can conserve her energy ("I can make a washing-list & I can write verses but I can't do them both in the same fortnight").[103]

Writing at a breakneck pace, she had been told that Natalie would send someone over to pick up the poems Anna is producing but would see Anna in person only on her own terms:

> Anna, I gave you rendez-vous this afternoon for tea at Select—You said you would be good if I went there—I can't see you except when I give you the day and hour.[104]

Wickham pens a note on Barney's paper and returns it, rejecting the offer in this way, "I would give all the five oceans of tea for an hour of your attention and work the world up into a syllabubs [a kind of frothy dessert] for the service of your ears & eyes."[105]

By the time she left Paris Anna had been troublesome enough to ask Barney to meet her in forgiveness, though if they met we do not know. "I ask all that may be entreated that I shall never be ugly to you again" and, possibly shortly after that, "write to me that you forgive." Anna says that some of the "abominable nonsense" of the last "year or more" actually pulled her through a difficult time made bearable by the "dope of inventing as I did for you."[106]

One person who speaks of Anna at her worst was the person Natalie trusted most. On June 8, 1927, probably a year or more after Anna and Natalie became close, Natalie added twenty-five-year-old Berthe Cleyrergue to her household staff.[107] The young woman, through competence and personality and discretion, became the one to carry out Barney's directives. Berthe, who for example adored the drug-addicted Dolly Wilde and even nursed her through one of her suicide attempts, had a low opinion of Anna Wickham.[108] She thought Anna ugly, ill-dressed and without manners, self-respect, or any redeeming quality except that she "wrote poems and I think she was a well-known poet."[109] Berthe noted with disdain that Anna would "sit near the gutter and wait for Miss Barney," and thought Anna crazy and even dangerous. Late in life she recalled acting under orders not to admit Anna (who came when she wanted to) unless Natalie expected her.

Berthe of course was not yet employed by Natalie on such earlier occasions as when, for example, Radclyffe Hall, Mimi Franchetti, Anna and Natalie had comfortably dined together in August, 1926.[110] She was not there on the occasion of Anna's "Friday" literary gathering. And since Berthe spoke only French she could not ever know what transpired between the two women in English, except by conversation with French speakers and the evidence she herself saw. Berthe thought Natalie was not moved by Anna's letters. And there were times when Natalie clearly was not answering Anna's letters (Anna commented on the silences) or ignoring some (Anna marked one of her envelopes: "Please read this"). But the several extant letters from Natalie, in addition to the fact that most of Anna's letters are an on-going conversation between two people, show that Natalie was keeping up with Anna even if she didn't always like what she heard.

As many have pointed out, Natalie's life was accompanied by none of the guilt that troubled others. She herself makes much of the fact that her friends were often lifelong. Yet though Natalie could be intensely kind, and tried to be helpful in the extreme to people such as Dolly Wilde, she was above all a realist who never allowed a friend to be a burden. In just one example, when Remy de Gourmont gave Natalie the sterling publicity that made her reputation, after her efforts to draw him out reduced the shame he felt over physical disfigurement due to illness, he remained "grateful, devoted and uncomplaining to the end" though Natalie found less time for him as her life became busier and new admirers crowded in.[111] Thus it is not surprising that in times of Anna's deepest need, Barney would distance herself from any displays distasteful to her.

Anna's greatest attraction for Natalie may have been that she was a writer who, from the very beginning of their relationship, ardently admired Natalie's writing. In an early letter to Natalie, Anna praises a poem, saying she wishes Natalie had said the poem to her.[112] She liked Natalie's works and corresponded with her as artist to artist, sending Natalie her precious "last but one" copy of *The Contemplative Quarry*, out of print by that time. Anna, in her quest for the quintessential Barney, translated Gourmont's *Lettres à l'Amazone* in five days, so eager was she to know more about her friend; then she planned to do the *Pensées* "far more carefully" with help from a translator. She later attempted to find a publisher for one of Natalie's more arcane works. "No one can appreciate your work as I can," Anna said, and she may have been right. Many of the people around Natalie were more interested in Natalie's physical embodiment while Anna, perhaps because most of the time she had *only* Natalie's writing to sustain her, equally and also appreciated Natalie's work. Because Anna read so widely, was quite critical of her own work, and was adept at traditional themes and forms in English poetry and at least conversant with those of French poetry, she could appreciate Natalie's poems. The disjunctive or insouciant elements of Natalie's aphorisms did not put Anna off. Admiring adroit brevity as she did, Anna admired the succinctness of Natalie's wit.

Even when Anna was most angry she did not attack Natalie's talent and was always generous with her praise. Anna could and did quote Natalie lines from her own poetry. She wrote Natalie asking for copies of her poems by title. She would pass on compliments of Natalie's writing (such as "magnificent writing" from one [unnamed] contributor to the *Philosophical Review*) with as much pleasure as if the compliment were for her.[113] She encouraged Natalie on her plan (never executed) to bring out a bilingual literary magazine. In fact, it was probably Anna's suggestion, "Why not make an anthology of your representative women," that spurred Natalie, who was notoriously relaxed about getting published, to bring out in 1929 the wonderful book that, more than any description can, gives us the flavor of Natalie Barney's salon at its most woman-centered and ambitious best.[114]

When Natalie brought together this volume, *Aventures de l'esprit*, it included a section on Anna as one of those twelve women in the arts Natalie Barney found "representative of contemporary and cosmopolitan literature": Lucie Delarue-Mardrus, Anna Wickham, Colette, Rachilde, Aurel, Mina Loy, Elisabeth de Gramont, Djuna Barnes, Gertrude Stein, Romaine Brooks, Renée Vivien, and Marie Lenéru.[115] In the "Forewarning" to *Aventures de l'esprit*, Barney states that she did not intend "to spread the epidemic of memoirs. I reveal certain aspects of kindred writers." Her goal was to choose writers (men were also included) "who, through native excellence put to the hard test of time, are propelled by their own force and transcend time." In *Aventures'* seven-page introduction to Wickham, titled "English Bohemian Life and Anna Wickham," Barney writes about English pubs and drinking, militant English women, and the contrasting "health" Wickham brought to London with her "lungs filled with country air."[116] Barney depicts Wickham as successfully combatting "puritanism and other Anglican vices" and, quoting from eight of her poems, calls Wickham "the English Verlaine."

This is significant in two ways: first, because Barney "deeply admired the French Symbolists: Baudelaire, Verlaine, Mallarmé," and second, because Verlaine consumed alcohol not as a "necessity" but as a "supplement." Since Barney at that time felt alcohol was "the enemy of the human race," her comparing Anna with Verlaine may have been her attempt to come to terms with Anna's relaxed, though not usually excessive, attitude toward drinking. The comparison to the French poet becomes important again, years later, when in a self-critical poem Anna agonizes over the body of her work and yet knows, "I have lived five years longer than Verlaine."[117]

The final aspect of the Anna-Natalie relationship that has provoked curiosity is that of financial assistance. Natalie had a lot of money.[118] A lot of the people that Natalie knew, did not. How did this play itself out?

In some cases (Dolly Wilde, Djuna Barnes, and others), Barney financially subsidized the publishing of works important to her and/or put considerable effort into seeing them through the press, and/or arranged for prepaid subscriptions to pay costs.

Natalie was generous at times, but according to composer Virgil Thomson, reminiscing in 1972, she was "not an easy touch. No, no, no."[119] Similarly, her occasional gifts to Anna, modest for Natalie's spectacular means, were given in a way that did not offend Anna's sensitive and proud nature, for as Anna once told her, "My good dear, . . . I want to keep myself."[120] A few pounds here and there enabled Anna to buy "a clockwork train for George" at Christmas, possibly a membership to the Aristotelian Society, second-class fare to Paris, and other small items. One wonders if Natalie wanted to include Anna in a plan she and Pound developed where people would purchase "shares" in a writer or artist. Not as preemptory as it sounds, the plan was intended to allow the recipients time for creative efforts (in the most famous instance, to permit T. S. Eliot to quit his work at the bank and concentrate on producing more masterpieces such as *The Waste Land*. Eliot was ruffled by this and quickly declined, just as surely as Anna would have if the plan had been proposed in her time, because her pride *and* her confidence would not have permitted it.)[121]

Yet there was some sort of poems-for-money arrangement, even if the amount involved was just a token. It caused problems, for although Anna liked the "disciplinarian" side of Barney, she hated to be told what to do. In January 1928, Wickham's anger surfaces:

> For the love of God don't tell me to write poetry. It maddens me—
> If you want me to write poetry let your will sleep in the storm of
> my energy—Don't ride all over the battle field—Stand on your hill
> & confer.

In a letter headed only "Tuesday," Wickham writes Barney that she has finished twenty-eight of a projected 302 poems "[since] I owe you three hundred & two francs which is always a bond." This amount, of course, was a very small sum, serving as a symbolic value, perhaps even as a joke extended over time. Obviously, however, Barney had given her some kind of financial assistance which Wickham wanted to repay but was finding it difficult: "Hail Columbia—How the hell can you expect me to try & do business with you when your cook gives me back my cheques," Wickham writes. "You have powers of life & death over this poetry," she says, and adds, "though you didn't want to buy this often it is cheap."[122] Wickham's important American publishing connection, Louis Untermeyer, once asked Anna if Barney "owns" the poems. Wickham wrote to Natalie that she answered Untermeyer, "Louis, she does," proving, she says, "my passion is deeper than bone."[123] It seems unlikely that Wickham really regarded Barney as having ownership and publishing rights of the poems she wrote for her; it is more likely that Wickham just wanted to pay tribute to Barney by reporting the conversation with Untermeyer. In any event, Wickham may *say* that Barney "owns" the poems, but she never views the poems as off-limits to her reading repertoire. In November 1927, Wickham had written, "I read poetry about you at the Bookshop yesterday—even our little poetry." And even as late as November 1946, Wickham gave a reading at the Poetry Society and "read one or two poems from the post-card series."[124]

Natalie's financial assistance, then, was small, but done in such a way as to spare Anna's feelings at a time when she could ill afford to repay even small sums. Anna was grateful. But direct financial help was truly not what she wanted. Far better, she wrote, if Natalie could help by selling copies of Anna's *The Man With a Hammer* and other works, a sale that "will not only leave me with my dignity" but provide a needed ten pounds.[125] Anna adds, "Doris Stephens has promised to make a market for these books at the National Women's Party, 21 First St. N. E., Washington D. C., Secretary Miss Paul—She says I can sell them . . . first editions . . . of my first book *The Songs of John Oland.*"

This practical assistance would have taken Natalie's time and energy but required none of her money. It is not known if she did it.

As R. D. Smith has said, "Anna was fascinated by Natalie, though never subdued by her."[126] He calls the relationship "mainly long-distance passion." But just what was the extent of the relationship between the two women?[127] In one poem, dated July 8, 1927, that begins "Will there be a lovely art / Equal to her eyes & heart," Anna says, "I only kissed her bed."[128]

On February 6, 1928, Anna writes a poem in the first person with the lines: "Since I threw Sappho / in my Holy Night."[129] In a response to Natalie in October, 1936, Anna almost triumphantly confesses, "I haven't seen you for five years, you haven't touched me for ten, & yet a few phrases from you & I am down with desire as definite as an attack of malaria."[130] The wording of this declaration is interesting: it is the "phrases" that Anna is unable to resist, attuned as she always was to Natalie's art, and of course to Natalie's appreciation of Anna's art.

Unfortunately, most of the Barney side of the correspondence no longer exists. During World War II, a firebomb struck the attic of 68 Parliament Hill and many of Wickham's papers and correspondence were lost. The few extant letters to Wickham from Barney, originally held by the Hepburn family but now in the British Library, testify to Barney's enduring regard. "Anna, dear and incorrigible Anna," writes Barney in a letter dated only "November," thanking Wickham for poems and saying she awaits the receipt of more. And on April 24, 1934: "I'm always glad to see your writing because it has conveyed so much to me that is new and inspired. . . ." On October 11, 1934: "Why no more letters or poems? How are you? and "la tour bourgeoise?" Again on November 4, 1934, "we *all* send love to you and good tidings—and I relish your mind and existence."[131]

For her part, Anna had paid Natalie her supreme compliment. "I can imagine from you." But though this gift resonated deeply and happily with Anna, "imagining" from Natalie also made Anna extremely vulnerable.[132] Natalie had never intended to be, promised to be, or lived as the exclusive muse for any scholar, writer, or artist. And Anna, if we look just at the signature on her letters, put Natalie into more roles than anyone would be comfortable filling (husband, wife, mother, and child).

What must have been freeing for Barney, who was always trying to encourage "an authentic female voice" in other women writers, was that Anna was a poet who from the very first had dealt often with female experience, sometimes in a humorous vein, sometimes with suffering that came out of the depths of her experiences and those around her.[133] She did not have to be encouraged to write her experience. The female voice for Anna was only one motif in her considerable repertoire but she used it so well that she earned the apt sobriquet "Song" from the woman who mattered most to her: Miss Natalie Clifford Barney, 20 rue Jacob, Paris. Thus in a way, when Anna had her "Friday" at Natalie's famous salon, she was mak-

ing her Paris "debut" twenty years after she trained in the operatic repertoire with Jean de Reszke and others. She did it "singing" her own songs,
her startling rhythmic record of a woman who had lived her material and
shaped it to suit herself.

To sum it all up, if the asylum had knocked Anna off her feet only
to have her rise again as a woman with a will to have her own life, the
time spent in the presence of Natalie and her friends showed Anna a new
society spread out on the plains below, a camp where a woman could
refuge. Paradoxically, however, she found that her emotions could also be
held hostage there: misunderstood, mocked, celebrated, or avoided as the
will of what she called "the mob" proclaimed. A refuge but not a refuge,
and ruled by a leader, Natalie Barney, whose lust and love of conquest
vied with her political and artistic aim to make sure that women had a
place to be heard.

Anna had chosen for a husband a man who was brilliant in so many
ways and yet cold and bound-up emotionally. So she fell for Natalie, the
great seducer, the great salon leader whose charm was such that Anna
never completely lost her passion for her. What Patrick and Natalie had
in common was their desire to "instruct" Anna, treating her as an ine-
briate, correcting her table manners, trying to make her more conventional in dress, in volume, in impact. In short, trying to tone her down
to a neutral level.

But Anna was big physically, with a big voice and expansive gestures.
She had had big hopes for society and, when those were not fulfilled, a big
vision of poetry that would, as she said in 1922, function in "this interlude
between religions," to "generate spiritual energy by rapid impressions of
beauty, vigor, and truth."[134] She chose big projects for herself (the series of
letters and postcard poems written to Barney) and encouraged them in
others (Barney's 1929 anthology). But sometimes it is very uncomfortable
for others to be around someone big. Patrick felt it. Barney felt it. Both
tried to reduce her to a more manageable size. But she could not be shrunk.
She was, as she would call herself in the thirties, "a major woman." She
could not be shrunk unless it was at her peril, striking at the very core of
her identity, for she was, in the words of someone who knew her well:
"eccentric, erratic—many things, but not little."[135] In the years ahead, she
would free herself from limiting influences. Her most honest, her truly
confessional poetry, was still to come.

SEVENTEEN

Married Life (1928–1929)

Sometime in 1928 Anna and Patrick decided to live together again. Anna's living situation had never stabilized and Patrick had not always been doing well. In September 1926, during their separation, he overreached his strength in his walks over the mountains and passes of his beloved Lake district, suffered leg injuries, and "was found in an exhausted condition and taken to a neighboring inn."[1] Anna, who though moving from place to place during their separation often had the boys with her, sometime in 1927 sent the eldest two back to Parliament Hill.[2] Lonely with only a housekeeper, Patrick lived a less somber life when the boys were around. Some nights they would all plunge into one of the Hampstead ponds, sons trying to beat "the Old Man" in swimming to the opposite bank. One of Patrick's most interesting feats after they returned was going up in an airplane with a colleague and taking photographs and other observations of the great total eclipse of the sun.[3] He kept up his rigorous schedule of club and association meetings, but so neglected no. 68 that once Anna visited to find the roof leaking in three places. He remained a stickler for correctness, however, with his mixture of kindliness and condescension. Regarding the eclipse of the sun, he had written to the *Times* well ahead of the event, briskly correcting popular misconceptions and issuing instructions for the best viewing arrangements: "'Very nearly' will not do," he said, regarding one town out of the viewing zone, "not only is [the town] not an 'ideal place,' it is no place at all."[4]

Patrick's loneliness and unsettled feelings, Anna's own sometimes desperate situation, the lack of a home base for all three of the sons and finances that had become much tighter were probably the factors that led her, gradually, to return to no. 68.

"I found it necessary to attempt to be housewifely for this family," she told Natalie.[5] The wider Hepburn family appreciated her, inscribing on the flyleaf of a Hepburn family history: "with much admiration to a great Mother."[6] Though she despised the idea of mothering a husband, as she would later say in her autobiography, she was anxious to mother her sons. They, in turn, saw nothing too unusual about her return, since they knew Anna's dual feelings toward Patrick: fostering and loving the astronomer though often "at odds" with the lawyer.

Once again she was at the helm of her "fighting aristocracy."[7] The arguments and turbulence resumed, with shouting matches and Patrick's cursing and middle son John standing back amazed and troubled about it. Anna made up games in her head to convince herself she could function, clinging to her Paris connection by clutching a leather handbag Natalie had given her. She wrote to her, letters, poems such as "Poor Little Sadisms of Natly," and on March 8, 1929:

> Was it kind, was it kind
> To captivate my mind,
> To bind me to my husband
> And surrender me?
>
> What excuse
> For this abuse
> Of love's organizing use
> Can you tender me?[8]

Did Patrick know that Anna had fallen in love with Natalie? Hard to tell. Anna used The Poetry Bookshop to receive letters, a system subject to "breaking down."[9] Part of the difficulty of Anna's return may have been in having to keep that part of her life secret. For example, when Anna thought to come to Paris with Carmel Haden Guest, a friend who wrote articles, she became terrified at the thought that Carmel would interview someone there and "destroy me."[10] Anna also wrote to Natalie on April 1, 1929, after the worst of the return was over, saying that "the game I have been playing has hurt me enough to keep my powers awake. Otherwise in utter weariness my soul would have died."[11] What the game is Anna does not say.

Meanwhile, Anna's and Patrick's schedules meant that they would intersect only infrequently. Patrick would, on Saturday night "get into a train and go to Cumberland, walk about during Sunday, return by train on Sunday night, and go straight to the office. The journey to the Lakes was occasionally varied by a week-end trip to Paris, and during the week he would often sleep on a camp bed at his office, where he was frequently engaged at work until midnight."[12] Still, either relative peace or true faithfulness must have reigned between the two for Anna writes that she "kept his name dear / For that last awful year."[13] She even grew worried about him and convinced him to stop his daily swims in the Hampstead ponds until his health improved, which it did.

In 1927, Jim had joined a repertory theatre company and acted in several plays at the Century Theatrewell. Anna continued to give him formal singing lessons and tutor him in French songs, then was ecstatic when he auditioned at the Hippodrome and was admitted to the chorus for a rousing year's run of *Hit the Deck,* a musical comedy by Vincent Youmans of *No, No, Nanette* fame. Beginning in 1928 Jim toured North America in *This Year of Grace,* with Coward and Lillie, a nine-month run in cities from Cleveland to Canada. He spent his twenty-first birthday in a Baltimore speakeasy, played cards through the cigar smoke on a train out of Chicago and, when the show ran in New York for week after week, became the urbane Noel Coward's understudy. He attended Beatrice Lillie's hotel room parties where she used the bed as the hostess chair with a bottle and glass at her side. Jim also took tap lessons and began to develop the dance routines that would soon help to set him and his brother John apart from other English dancers.

There is no doubt that Patrick, who had hated his profession, did not want his sons to follow him into the law as he had followed his father and grandfather. On the other hand, having a son performing on the stage may have been as distasteful to him as having a wife who often wrote poetry from experience. If it was disturbing to Patrick, he had another shock in store as their second son, John, gave up an exhibition to Oxford and, surprising everyone, signed on with a first-rate touring company of the smash hit, *Journey's End.* For Anna, her sons' careers were extremely important.

Anna had worked hard for what she thought her own father wanted—success in the arts. "*Punch*, Anne, *Punch,*" he had said years before as his daughter's ship eased out of Sydney Harbor, and his shouted admonition had become a fulfilled prophecy when William Kean Seymour parodied two of Anna's most famous poems in his column "More Jackdaw in Georgia."[14] *Punch*, tweaking egos since 1841, was at the time targeting spoiled girls in flapper dresses, "lounge lizards," golfers, cricket players, bossy wives, bored children, clueless riders-to-the-hounds, earnest Ramsay MacDonald . . . and, of course, poets. By appearing in *Punch*, February 16, 1927, Anna not only had achieved success for her father while he could still appreciate it, but was in good company too: T. S. Eliot had been fried, Edward Shanks grilled, now Anna too was sautéed by Seymour with his irritated mimicry and silly imitation.[15]

Anna had never felt the same about her father since their trip to Ceylon together. He recognized that life was not "easy" for Anna, but felt mildly resentful that their correspondence had lapsed. Anna had written to him in 1924, and he had written back saying,

> I have not written you for a long time—I found it too difficult to write anything pleasant that was true, but now if this statement you finish your letter with is true "I don't suppose any daughter ever loved a father as much as I loved you" there is no difficulty in establishing the best possible relationship between us, and, if maintained with reasonable regularity it would be of the liveliest interest to me and could be made very very dear.[16]

That Geoffrey had spent much of his long letter talking about politics and had asked Anna to "help me write on current affairs . . . make yourself very informative . . . and get in the habit of tieing up a few of these [politics journals to send to him]." He also told her that she had hurt him by not understanding his divorce from Alice (March 1923), and that it was too late for him to make a writing success, just one of "the dun colored mob," he called himself, with time only for "earning my daily bread." In September, 1929, Anna received word that her father, William Geoffrey Harper, age sixty-nine, had died on September 18 at Melbourne Hospital due to respiratory failure following on several complaints.

From 1928 on, Anna made no. 68 her home base again. In the winter months she read philosophy: Kant and Spinoza. With her sons she traveled in the summer to Paris for the tennis championships. In the spring they all went into the French countryside around Dampierè at cherry blossom time. Home again, she posed for a "Bohemians" newspaper photograph with Nina Hamnett. She had a plaster cast made of her strong face. Her poems were requested for *The Sackbut*, for Harold Monro's new anthology of poetry and for *The London Aphrodite* ("in its little cotton nightie," said Anna, who thought its editors not as daring as they thought they were).[17] *The Encyclopedia Britannica*, in a "Modern Developments in British Poetry" entry by B.B.C. broadcaster and poetry advocate Humbert Wolfe, also mentioned Anna, to her great pleasure.[18] She attended P.E.N. dinners and sent its founder, Mrs. Dawson Scott, a poem at Christmas. She was kind to a young writer named Eliot Bliss (introducing her later to Dorothy Richardson).[19] For a time, in defiance of Natalie's hold on her imagination, Anna wrote poems to Una, Lady Troubridge. But John Middleton Murry and Harold Monro were described as no longer feeding her imagination, though Monro at least remained a friend.[20]

It may have been about this time that The Poetry Bookshop used her poem, "The Tired Man," in a rhyme sheet illustrated by Grace Golden.[21] But at some point in the past, Anna grew extremely irritated with Monro and wrote him a poem, "The Lesson according to Harold." Monro had been telling Anna to produce work despite any difficulties she might be having. In this poem she mocks both his concept of the businesslike artist ("Now why don't I attend and hark, / Act like a reputable clerk,") and the idea of art being able to make up for physical human attention ("Write rondolettes, when I am lonely / And type them clear on one side only").[22]

Ever fond of Natalie's imagination, Anna expended a lot of energy in 1929 trying to secure an English publisher for a novel Natalie had written, a dreamlike novel that deals with a hermaphroditic resurrected suicide.

Anna was not the only friend searching for a publisher for her, but she had begun as early as 1927. By April 13, 1929, Wickham was developing a new strategy, irritated that Boni and Liveright (with whose agent she had "a hell of a row") had turned down the chance to publish *The One Who Is Legion*.[23] Natalie wrote to her and Anna agreed then to "see the Misses Heath as you suggest—& I say we will not *touch* a publisher who will [print inferior authors]." The novel, with two illustrations by Romaine Brooks, was finally printed in 1930 in London by Eric Partridge (Scholartis Press). Anna also had ideas for publicizing the book.[24] Whether or not her marketing ideas were used is not known; there were only 560 copies and even today the book is usually "overlooked in discussions of Barney's work."[25]

EIGHTEEN

"How lovely you were / In your embrace of stars"[1]

Patrick Hepburn's "embrace of stars" was one of the things Anna never gave up admiring about her husband. His self-imposed testing of his own physical endurance was another.

Patrick had long been going to England's Lake District, a land of beauty and grandeur with "a stillness . . . not of this world," as poet William Wordsworth wrote, to climb the fells and walk the dales. Mere tourists might choose only familiar and gentle passes, but Patrick planned his routes by the compass and would not deviate though the climbing might be strenuous or dangerous. He sometimes even finished his walk in darkness, in 1926, for example, returning to his hotel "long after midnight," having injured his leg on Styhead Pass. Since the year of the marital separation Patrick had spent every Christmas in the Lake District. For Christmas 1929, he planned to walk from Grasmere to Borrowdale.

On Christmas Eve day, a Tuesday, he spent the afternoon with men from the Court of the Curriers' Company and seemed to them to be in the best of spirits.[2] He left his office at 5:00 p.m., first giving instructions to mail a package of clothing and a prescription, care of a Lake District hotel, then took an overnight train to Windermere. He hired a car from there to the Swan Hotel, Grasmere, arriving at 7:00 a.m. on Christmas morning for breakfast. But according to personnel at the hotel his mind "seemed perturbed." He spent the morning "walking restlessly about the hotel and doing mathematical problems for amusement," then ordered sandwiches for the journey and asked the desk clerk to mail another package (containing his city clothes) to London for him.[3]

Men at the hotel, locals, strongly advised against his going. The afternoon was misty and graying and the hour for starting was late. But Hepburn, known among his friends for night walks in the District, was not to be dissuaded. He said that he had been lost last Christmas on Black Sail Pass and did not worry. He set out carrying a rucksack and dressed in a knickerbocker suit, billed hiking cap and "shoes that were too light for the journey."

At 3:15 p.m., Boxing Day, December 26, a shepherd named Daniel Jophon found a man's body, with a cut at the top of the head, almost hidden behind big boulders and partially submerged in the flood-swollen Greenup Beck about a mile up the Langstrath Valley near Keswick. The shepherd had first thought an upraised hand a lamb. He rushed to the village and came back with a doctor and the police. By the light of lanterns and torches they wedged a short ladder between the rocks and lifted out the lifeless form. Over "rough and flooded ground the body was carried in relays to Stonethwaite, and then by car to the Keswick mortuary."

Headlines in one-half-inch type blared the death of MYSTERY MAN. The pathetic aspects of the story—unknown man climbing alone against local advice on Christmas Day defeated by the elements—prompted every paper from Belfast to London to report the news.

In the climber's pocket an old account bill led authorities to the Wastwater Hotel where Patrick had stayed on Christmas Day, 1928, and several times after that. The next day a man found a pack downstream in Greenup Ghyll. The rucksack contained £8 10s and papers with Patrick's name. Authorities traced these to Patrick's Grasmere hotel, and then through the package he had left to be mailed, traced him to 68 Parliament Hill.

George Hepburn was playing on the floor of the sitting room near the black Broadwood baby grand piano when the doorbell rang and a very large policeman filled the doorway. He remembers his mother speaking very seriously.

In answer to a *Manchester Evening Chronicle* reporter's questions, Anna responded formally at 8:00 a.m. the next morning, Saturday, December 28. "I have every reason to believe that my husband is dead," she said. "I have been unable to go to Keswick as yet, but from the descriptions I have received I have no doubt that the dead man is my husband."

When Anna had first received the news, she told reporters that Patrick must have gone for his usual daily swim and been overcome by the cold. On her advice he hadn't been swimming for the last month or two, she stated, and "his abstention may have laid him open to shock from the sudden immersion on a cold day." Secretly, however, Anna feared that Patrick had committed suicide. According to an early *Star* report the family had not even known he was headed for Cumberland but thought he intended to spend Christmas at Brighton. The *Penrith Observer* interviewer found that "one of the sons meant to have been with his father . . . but was unavoidably detained." If this were true, perhaps this was the reason Patrick delayed starting out on Christmas morning.

She arranged for George to stay with the neighbors and left with Jim and John for the Lake District. The family arrived on Sunday, December 29, and Anna identified the body. They were too late to attend the initial fact-finding, where it was determined that Patrick had not gone for a Christmas swim as Anna conjectured, but instead had fallen.

In that initial inquest opened in Keswick, Cumberland, on Saturday, December 28, the coroner found no foul play, the cut on Patrick's head coming from hitting the rocks when he fell. He called Patrick's attempt at crossing in the dark and in bad weather, not suicidal but sadly "foolish," and announced that "unless there is fresh evidence from the relatives" he would declare a verdict of accidental drowning. The inquest adjourned to Whitehaven until Monday the 30th. No new evidence was given at the inquest, Anna had requested not to be recalled, and the interim verdict quickly became the final one: Mr. Patrick Hepburn, aged fifty-six, "accidentally drowned."

At least one editorial faulted Patrick and climbers like him for giving the Lake District a bad name. "A little more common sense even at the expense of a little less science" [the newspaper accounts had stressed Patrick's scientific credentials] might have saved "a useful member of society," the correspondent wrote. Other headlines shouted "ASTRONOMER" and "POETESS" and gave lengthy accounts. The newspaper photos show a forty-seven-year-old Anna Wickham looking straight into the camera, straight out at the reader, her well-shaped eyebrows framing eyes with dark circles under them, her long mouth with lips closed almost serenely, as if through exhaustion all tension had slipped away. Most newspaper photographs are of Patrick in military uniform, the "keen" eyes on which so many had remarked looking out at some unknowable point.

The burial was on Tuesday, December 31, New Year's Eve day. Anna and her sons were, as the papers reported, the chief mourners, and "dalespeople," including the shepherd, and the inspector, were publicly thanked by Mrs. Hepburn for their support. Then, as the *Daily Chronicle* reported, "amid the fells he loved so much" he was "laid to rest today in Rosthwaite Churchyard, in the beautiful Borrowdale Valley."

Years earlier, in Anna's 1921 *The Little Old House*, a poem called "The Homecoming" seems to be describing one of her own fears. Or, according to R. D. Smith, it may have displayed the "clairvoyant powers" Anna's mother laid claim to.[4]

I waited ten years in the husk
That once had been our home
Waiting from dawn till dusk
To see if he would come.

And there he was beside me
Always at board and bed,
I looked and woe betide me
He whom I loved was dead.

He fell at night on the hill side,
They brought him home to his place;
I had not the solace of sorrow
Until I looked in his face.

Then I clutched the broken body
To see if he stirred or moved,
For there in the smile of his dying
Was the gallant man I had loved.

O wives come lend me your weeping
I have not enough of tears,
For he is dead who was sleeping
These ten accursed years.

NINETEEN

Reconfiguration: *La Tour Bourgeoise* (1930–1934)

All through early January, 1930, condolences poured in to Anna and the boys at 68 Parliament Hill. Tributes to Patrick appeared one after another. On January 1 the members of the Royal Astronomical Society stood at attention under "shadow of a great personal loss."[1] The next morning a letter to the editor of the *Times* by one of Patrick's friends from the Great Ormond Street days recounted Patrick's "lovable" ways and some of his more strenuous and memorable exploits, such as the time he, quite casually, rode his push-bicycle all the way to York, and the day the overturned observation balloon dumped its contents, but not its pilot, during tumultuous winds. Also in the *Times*, Professor H. H. Turner, F.R.S., noted that Hepburn had served during the war as a balloonist, "to keep the submarines under the sea" in postings ranging from the Irish Sea to German East Africa. In the *City Press* on January 3rd, he was called "a man highly respected by all who knew him." On January 11, *Nature*, the prestigious weekly journal of the natural sci-

ences since 1869, laid out Patrick's considerable accomplishments in photography, war service, and astronomy. *Shoe and Leather Record* devoted
articles to his work and also gave details of his three and one-half decades
of service to the Curriers' Company. The *Law Times* noted his death and
memorial service planned for mid-January at one of the city churches.
The larger world missed the calm adventurer, the scientist, the man of the
law, the friend.

So the decade of the 1920s began and ended, for Anna, in tragedy. She
and Patrick had lost their third son Richard as the decade opened. In mid-
September 1929, her father had died. Now she had lost her husband in the
decade's closing days. In the years between, they had fought often but
reunited when it seemed the way to health for the family. Patrick had been,
at various times—and sometimes simultaneously—her lover, her friend, and
her adversary. Now she was suddenly left without him. What a great weariness must have settled over her as the lean thirties loomed.

Gradually throughout the decade of the 1930s she began to understand and recover from that marriage and Patrick's sudden death. Time
did a lot of the work. But Anna actively worked at it too, later by writing
about her life, first by reconfiguring her living situation in La Tour
Bourgeoise.

To reinvent her living situation, Anna had to work with a well-known
myth of her life. This is not myth in the way of falsehood, but myth in the
way of an overarching tale of explanation.

To the crowd at Natalie Barney's salon in Paris Anna had been por-
trayed as a woman who had escaped from the castle tower of a tyrant. Her
1928 return to that tower must have occasioned more than a few raised
eyebrows. Now she herself would take possession of the "tower" and write
a new script: tall woman with resonant voice opens 68 Parliament Hill as
a haven for artistic freedom. This was later, of course. First, however, after
she and the boys returned home from the inquest and burial service, she
had to determine where the family stood.

For almost ten years Patrick had been without a partner in the office—
uninterested in acquiring new clients—and putting his energies elsewhere.
Anna faced up to the daunting task of closing up a neglected business. This
was a far cry from "going through the ledgers" as she and Patrick had play-
fully done in their courtship. "The less you have to do with your husband's
business, the better," former partner Cutcliffe had said before the marriage.
How she must now have cursed that advice and regretted both Patrick's

reluctance to go over the accounts with her and her own acquiescence. That Patrick had found it "necessary to his pride" to support the family and discourage "in every way" Anna's economic independence was one issue, but his tangled estate was now another.[2]

How many of Patrick's admiring colleagues knew what Anna knew: that Patrick Hepburn, who appeared to be so in control of his life and accomplishments, had been under a great strain in the previous few years. It is not even clear that his club friends, from the Savile Club to the Curriers Company, knew that he and Anna had been separated from 1926 to 1928. Patrick's older sons, with whom he swam, sailed, and climbed, knew that Patrick put on a front of good fellow well-met to cover the chasm of loneliness he faced during the separation. But not even they knew what Anna had seen gradually overtaking Patrick: some financial missteps, or perhaps market reversals in a year of market reversals, had put the estate in jeopardy.

In the will, made just after Anna had been released from the asylum in 1913 and altered by one minor codicil, Patrick left "my dear wife Edith" the sum of 100 pounds upon his death (150 pounds less than his own father had bequeathed his wife twenty-five years earlier) to cover initial expenses.[3] The household goods, jewelry, musical and scientific instruments, etc. were all left to Anna. After the funeral, testamentary expenses and debts were paid, the total value of the estate was £11,062 12s 4d. (one tenth the amount Patrick's father had left at his death).[4] The intent of the will was to put the money into a trust to be paid "to my wife so long as she shall continue my widow."

Anna, time and again, walked the narrow passage to "one of the oldest and quaintest" law offices in the city, turning, with the advice of her lawyer, and the occasional help of twenty-three-year-old Jim, to the accounts in a systematic attempt to wrap up a business that had spanned two generations. Jim kept his considerable tenderness wrapped in a veneer of stoicism and, at times, witty irony or heavy sarcasm: his father had insisted that Jim not enter the law. Now Jim had no choice but to help bring the tangled accounts in the bulging files into some sort of order. Eliot Bliss, a young novelist whom Anna and sons met in the twenties when staying at Hove, Brighton, had become Anna's friend. She often listened, sometimes sympathetically, sometimes not, as Anna bemoaned the seemingly endless complications of her tasks.

At first Anna was optimistic about the future. Though royalties from all her books were minuscule (and she had blithely or sadly once written that: ("The lyric poet must live like a beggar"), the Hepburn reputation for success in commerce must have overridden her earlier qualms about financial matters.[5] Her optimism is evident in letters to Natalie Barney written in the first months of 1930. Then suddenly something turned terribly wrong. Her optimism turned to a dark despair like those her mother suffered. Anna attempted to hang herself at the offices at 5 Bird-in-Hand Court. Only Jim's arrival saved her.[6]

Several explanations seem possible. Patrick's death finally hitting home. The bleak financial outlook taking away her desire to continue struggling. There is a also third possible explanation. One night Anna and Harold Monro had taken refuge in each others' arms. Thinking themselves secure from the party going on in the other rooms of the bookshop, Anna was horrified to see that Jim had entered the room. Before she could recover herself, Jim had bolted from the shop, stealing Harold Monro's wooden corkscrew in some sort of retribution for what he saw as their failure to control themselves, or disloyalty to the memory of Patrick.[7]

After the suicide attempt, bearing the rope burn that she often covered with a scarf, she stonily sat through a visit with Harper relatives: Geoffrey's younger sister (the faithful Auntie Gert) and Geoffrey's niece (twenty-six-year-old Miriam Herzog, by then a promising cellist in a women's trio).[8] They saw her scar. No one talked about it. But this act of Anna's caused some of the Harpers at least to get over their resentment of Anna's success in the arts and her upwardly mobile marriage. Some had resented her confidence ("such a lot of talk about it, and swank about it and *knew* it all, you know").[9] Some even thought that Patrick, whose "primness" they recognized, may have committed suicide to get away from Anna.[10] But this most recent evidence of personal anguish on Anna's part aroused some personal sympathy. Then too, their feelings over Geoffrey Harper's death in September, 1929 may have softened them into compassion. They may also have heard rumors that funds that Patrick controlled had been borrowed from, and that Anna, as heir, would inherit these debts.

Though during the marital separation Anna had had money troubles enough, they were nothing to those she now faced. By the time the will was proved on March 19, 1930, the "net personalty" had dropped to a mere £94. Anna must have doubted that there would be any money at all, for when the whole business was over she wrote to Natalie Barney with evident surprise, saying "Our estate is, after all, solvent *without accommodation.*" She added, gamely, "Our net—who need remember it?"[11] She told Natalie that an arrangement had been made for a lump sum payment "and the right to live in a house" while the income from the estate, funneled through Jim and John, was to provide a future education for George. By late April, 1930 she wrote to Natalie that she was "quarrelling with *everybody*." And money seems to have been a problem for the rest of her life.

As a temporary measure after Patrick's death Anna had sent her youngest son, George, to his aunt's house in Upper Tollington Park. Despite Gert's kindness, George felt lost. Away from his family, deposited in the school there, then demoted there by an entirely unsympathetic school master, George had refused one day to go back to classes. Anna had pleaded for his help and cooperation for the time being and he gave it. Later, flush with not-yet-dashed dreams for the future, she had started him in Kensington, a place run by Molly Grovenor and Poppy Vanda's aunt Molly Stamford, both friends of Anna's, where he began Latin and blossomed under careful tutelage and scholarly expectations. Now, however, realizing that expenses would have to be cut severely, she acted on Patrick's clerk's suggestion and applied to have ten-year-old George attend the Masonic School in Bushey free-of-charge since Patrick had been a Mason. This decision, made in haste and out of desperation, was probably the worst possible move for George.

Even cutting school tuition, however, did not alleviate the financial crunch. In the next few years Anna cast about for ways to bring in an income. She had amused herself writing (unsold) advertising jingles (she always said she would have been superb at writing lines for Christmas crackers). Now she tried prose. An agent, Horace Shipp, aiming at the publisher Sampson Low, urged her to write a novel or perhaps a book about her friendship with D. H. Lawrence who had just died recently. By September, 1931, Shipp wrote prodding her to complete something for him by the end of the year, although it is not clear if she even showed him "The Spirit of the Lawrence Women," an article that she did complete.

Anna, "gifted authoress" as Patrick's newspaper obituaries put it, also toyed with the idea of writing for magazines, which was a more lucrative market. She had written a few essays, probably in the 'teens.[12] She also wrote a few pieces of fiction, at times drawing the themes from her life. In "The Platonists" a beautiful young woman, "Cecilia," careless and almost boyish in her dress, captivates a Patrick-like character whose rooms are full of clutter. In "Our Lady of Bounties" (originally titled "The Killer"), she cobbles together traits of Patrick/Geoffrey and Anna/Alice. The last line of this is intriguing for its application in Anna's own life: "The man—who has tremendous unrealized potential—may still produce something outstanding if only 'the woman would cease to give.'"[13]

Again and again in her fiction (most pieces extant are unfinished) the real Anna makes a shadow appearance. Two characters named Lila and Lyon bring a sailboat into harbor; a Melissa is slowly killing her poet's genius by her overarching will and the unfettered expression of her own personality. In "Remembrance," "I" talks of the difficulty of communicating with a loved one. In a very different piece, "I," a seducer, is distracted from seduction by thoughts of another woman. And in still another fragment the reality of the world is altered by a character's own nervous troubles. Of course, the real story of a marriage like the Hepburns' would not have been commercial magazine material then, as it might be now, a real reason for Anna to try to fictionalize and dilute situations and truths in order to sell her work. But by watering down aspects of her own life, the stories became insipid, inoffensive hearts-and-flowers pieces. Anna did actually finish one story in the bland style of popular magazine fiction. In this "Sauce for the Gander," Dorothy Bonham, who intends to reveal an indiscretion to her attractive husband Kenneth, happily conceals it when her husband's lipsticked handkerchief signals his own indiscretion. Pretty tame stuff, no psychological complications.

The works are interesting for the way they play off Anna's own life and occasionally make some chiseled observation, life-related or otherwise, and if Anna had finished them we might have a better idea of her capabilities as a writer of fiction. Her inability or lack of desire to complete fiction works may just reinforce the fact that Anna Wickham's strong suits were skillful rhythms, trenchant commentary, epigrammatic assessments, and above all, the lyric impulse (or moment) when a single speaker in a short poem gives voice to his/her thoughts. Anna is still a few years away from the sustained voice that she will use in her long autobiographical writing in or shortly before 1935 nor has she adopted the brutally honest, bitter tone that comes with her longest and last poetical works done in those later years.

There is no evidence that Anna actually sent out any of these pieces to see if publishers wanted them. Had she done so, and been encouraged, she might have been a contender in the market, since magazines and even newspapers of the time published romantic pieces about men and women, but surely her poetic reputation would have been weakened by it, and maybe her art as well. Meanwhile, she kept her pen alert by writing poetry and corresponding with Natalie Barney.

Anna did at this time have a truly international reputation. And though she had been favorably mentioned in the *Encyclopaedia Britannica*'s article on modern poetry and was liberally represented in *The Home Book of Quotations Classical and Modern*, neither fiction, prose, nor poetry was even mildly lucrative for Anna. What she needed was ready money and a future income. What she had was a large house with large expenses on the edge of Parliament Hill, the financial obligations of raising her youngest son, and a desire to help her aspiring actor/dancers. Anna *liked* eccentricity. She had always cultivated it in her appearance, her behavior, and in her reputation. Now, in a move undoubtedly viewed as eccentric by those friends or business associates who saw her as an extension of Patrick, solicitor and serious astronomer, Anna decided to capitalize on her advantages. Thus, debonair and eccentric woman with a reputation for hospitality opens large house with park view. She planned it as an extension of the life that she wanted her and her sons to live. In a much freer and more comprehensive vein than Natalie Barney's scheduled "Fridays," she would keep an "open house," a place where the arts would flourish. And she would rent rooms.

It was a big, loose, inclusive plan. The core group consisted of John and Jim Hepburn, Anna, and their friends and acquaintances met in cafes, pubs, classes, or the theatre life. The renting of the rooms was accomplished with little fanfare and with Anna's characteristic aplomb.[14] But though her grandmother had for a time offered room and board on Henrietta Street, and Anna had spent whole seasons in Australia living in rented rooms, a practical grasp of such ventures had not sunk in. Anna not only made rents too cheap (two of the large rooms were let for £5 per month with no provision for increases), but provided free food and drink too often. Anna had a natural tendency to open her home to others, especially those with an interesting personal history, or those who were trying to make a go of it in the arts, or simply those who needed a place to live and who appealed to Anna in one way or another. This made life new and different every day but played havoc with any budget.

Household matters were addressed as they came up. Anna kept a suggestion book for entries designed to help keep order, for by this time "order" was of the self-help nature in England.[15] A scarcity of people willing to be household servants had put an end to large household staffs. Most people were getting by with occasional rather than regular, help. Anna still had a cleaner who came in twice a week (a job that must not have been for the faint-of-heart). She did most of the cooking herself, a "good plain cook" at basic dishes but was not usually interested in experimenting. Anna would often have food ready for the boys after the curtain came down on whatever matinee or evening show they were in; however, if a "creative mood" had struck her there was more likely to be chaos at home, dirty dishes piled on every available surface of the pantry, and definitely no delicious smell of roast meat or shepherd's pie coming from the kitchen. (This unpredictability was, her sons said, "a source of palpitations" for them.) By the same token, Anna might often stop whatever she was doing to offer an unexpected guest a cup of tea.

The mess could be appalling. George, on vacations home from school, would often make a thorough cleaning of the place a first priority. He liked things neat and wanted his mother to live in a clean place, but Anna had other priorities and even her best intentions toward order were usually knocked head over teakettle by a new dance routine, someone's emotional crisis, or the need to fix the "meals at all hours" that her signboard later so proudly proclaimed.

A free atmosphere encouraged the comings and goings of visitors at all hours. Dropping in was common. "Anna, I've come for a bath" an American friend named Harry would say, and slip up the steps to immerse himself.[16] People played games of table tennis on the large dining room table, wrote, along with Anna, their poetic thoughts on the kitchen wall until it was completely covered.[17] (Dylan Thomas would later add his too.) Tenant Hugo Ames's canaries sung from their large cage placed in the second floor bathroom. The large front room on the ground floor (previously the kitchen) became a dance studio with a barre. Glissandos from the Broadwood Grand piano accompanied the dancing. Over the years, Anna taught all the boys to sing. Though Anna did appreciate long and quiet discussions about literature, parties could be wild and noisy. Anna would sometimes have to ride herd, not always successfully. Some who knew the family, like one branch of her Harper relatives, were aghast at the free spirit of "Bohemian London" that had found a place at Anna's: "the boys all had different girlfriends there as far as we thought. . . . [we] rather left them to it."[18]

She was interested in everyone who wanted to create, and her warmth and vitality drew them in. It was the thirties, a time of worldwide economic depression. At Anna's house, a spirit of generosity prevailed. And this occurred at a time when Anna's own resources were strained. In the early 1930s, for example, the poet Beatrice Hastings, traveling to England, remarked that, except for Anna, Hannen Swaffer, and Ruth Pitter, "no one so much as invited us for lunch."[19] In Anna's hospitality perhaps there is an echo of the "looser, freer" sort of organization that had prevailed in Anna's bush days in Australia, where neighbors helped her parents and her parents helped them.[20]

Anna's expansiveness at this time was typical of her. "A giver" is even how she characterized herself.[21] And her sons noted the response this drew from people: who "would actually love her and they would look to her for sustenance" (something the sons were not always happy about).[22] Anna could finally fight the "villa dwellers" in their own backyard: take a house that had been built tall and imposing to imbue the residents with a well-to-do veneer of belonging to a certain "set," take that villa and fill it with the needy, the creative, the anti-bourgeois, and the outrageous. Anna had escaped from the "Croydon Class," which she'd satirized so fiercely in her poem "Nervous Prostration." Her life was changing so that she would have the "right to counsel beggars at my door" as she had written in her poem "Domestic Economy."

At 68 Parliament Hill, "swanking" was out, informality was in, once you walked through the heavy door of that brick villa. Anna had a critical streak, and she did not appreciate pretense and show. Especially if anyone outside Anna's growing group of dancers, writers, and artists attacked her friends "she could be extremely hard and (she actually had a great command of language), could be devastatingly rude."[23]

Rudeness, generosity, wit, and the type of mind that sparked creativity: because of these Anna became something of a legend. Her home overlooking Hampstead Heath became something of a legend too: pub, workspace, and socratic circle, "a large house through which a gale swept perpetually, tossing leaves and manuscripts in and out of the windows."[24] The house became lively again, much like 49 Downshire Hill, when Anna was first rediscovering both her gift for poetry and an independent life.

Malcolm Lowry hated "polite society" and felt eventually a "deep sense of alienation that took him well away from the mainstream of literary life."[25] With Anna and Malcolm, it was a "case of mutual adoption at first sight."[26] Lowry, who was the same age as John Hepburn, was one of those people whose creative fire burned brightly even in his teenage years. A student at Cambridge who, according to poet Kathleen Raine, was a "genius" though of "little use at examinations," Lowry had once signed on as deckhand for months at sea, though his comfortable middle-class background

made this type of service unnecessary.[27] The steamer had subsequently provided him with conversational fireworks and the material for a book,
Ultramarine, published in part in a magazine called *Experiment*, and as a
separate volume in 1933.

In the summer of 1932, Lowry, subject to violent literary admirations,
had just finished a stay at Rye with the writer Conrad Aiken and his wife
Clarrisa and come to London where both Cambridge friend John
Davenport and Lowry's unofficial tutor, Hugh Sykes Davies, were living.
Lowry had taken a succession of squalid rooms in Bloomsbury that were,
according to Davenport: "rooms that had no heat; rooms that had no light;
one room that could only be entered by squeezing through a broken panel
in the permanently locked door."[28] Though Lowry's father had made a
weekly £7 allowance for him, Lowry so disliked collecting it that he went
for weeks on end living in increasing poverty. When he picked up a check
he would blow it on drinks and other pleasures. It was probably in such a
post-spree state that Anna met the young man who "had a way of looking
up at you from under his eyes, foxy and twinkling. Mischief, the real thing,"
and from then on when Lowry was in London he often visited Anna.[29]
Anna and Lowry would talk deep into the night about writing and about
writers. He was full of admiration for her success both as a poet and as one
of the "leading lights" of the West End district.[30] "One of my best friends,"
he later called her.[31] She wrote proudly of him to Natalie Barney and felt
close enough to him ("For the next hours I am your nice little daughter of
five") to send him "The Widow," her poem about Patrick's death.[32]

When Lowry's agent broke the bad news that someone had stolen the
manuscript of *Ultramarine* from the agent's sports car, Lowry used retrieved
carbons and partial sheets from friend Martin Case to retype and do minor
reworking of the novel, a task he accomplished while at the Hepburn house.

Malcolm was fascinated by Tour Bourgeoise, by the Hepburn brothers, their dedication to rugger, cricket, cinema, pubs, and their stage
careers. Lowry himself played the ukelele and at age eighteen had aspired
to "Just the Latest Charleston Fox-Trot Ever" when he and singer/com-
poser Ronald Hill paid to have their composition, "Three Little Dog-Gone
Mice" printed.[33] This conjunction of interests between the Hepburns and
Lowry led to some improvisations at no. 68:

> He would play any of the "hot music" of the time. One of his other
> friends, Ralph Case . . . was an extraordinarily accomplished pianist

and at that time played "hot" piano in a way that was very beguiling
to us all, and he and Malcolm used to play duets together. . . . Then
my brother and I used to make a contribution by doing a bit of tap-
dancing during the "breaks" as it were.[34]

But though Anna and her family might fascinate Lowry, he could be
a trying guest, or as Anna told him in a poem: "I say / You have ability /
But no stability / That you will sink / Through drink."[35] Painting himself as a man doomed by fate, monopolizing conversations, Lowry, felt
Jim Hepburn, "ran the entire destiny thing rather hard at times."[36] He
tended to leave piles of papers in his wake and messes to clean up. One
pilgrimage to no. 68 ended in a loud and drunken quarrel with his wife-
to-be, Jan Gabrial. His worst offense at the Hepburns's was against a one-
month-old white rabbit that George kept in a box in the morning room.
Jim and John and Malcolm were sitting around the fire talking and having a drink when Malcolm, who had been stroking the rabbit, found to
his devastation that somehow he had broken its neck. He slipped it into
his briefcase and showed up at the Astoria Hotel in Greek Street for a literary lunch, dead rabbit still in his possession. Calder-Marshall, who
went with Lowry to his room to confer, suggested that if they ordered
beers from room service the waiter might be asked to take it away—they
did, and he did.[37]

Some critics have written that the Hepburn family was the model for
the Taskersons, a father and three sons in Lowry's later and more famous
novel, *Under the Volcano*.[38] Jim Hepburn himself did not think so. But
there were certainly elements of interests and behavior that might lead one
to believe this. Anna's sons were prodigious walkers, climbers too. Educated
and urbane, they were also capable of consuming, with gusto, quantities of
beer, and certainly never lacked for what Lowry describes as "erect manly
carriage" or for women in their lives.

Anna was shamelessly a stage mother, arranging introductions where
she could and taking immense pleasure in the acting and dancing of her
sons, whether they were on the bottom or the top of the bill, playing on
provincial stages or shaking up the West End. Eventually Jim and John
worked together. They became "The Two Madisons," and in 1932 publicity photos, "The Double Act." Agents seeking to find just the right publicity named them "The Worth Brothers," then "The Hepburn Brothers"
and, when in 1934 Serafina Astafieva's pupil and assistant, ballet dancer

Joan Lawson joined them, their suave act became "Hepburn, Stewart and Lawson" or "The Two Madisons and Sonia." They employed elements of ballet and, like Fred Astaire, performed with grace. Their jazz-age dancing, "snappy drumming with the feet . . . combine[d] with fast balletic routines" made their act a standout.[39] For their entrance number they often used Wagner, then Beethoven, but often they finished with "Some of These Days."[40] Brother John figured out the music; Jim the dance steps. They often wrote their own band parts for music-hall orchestras used to playing very different fare. In September of 1934 they took their act to variety show stages in England, for example, Darlington Hall, then on January 7, 1935, broke winter's grip with some hot dancing at the Hull Palace. Before long they were headed to the continent where they danced in many cities. But stage careers had lots of expenses also. By the time Anna wrote of them to Natalie, "Jim and John stars—but difficult" she was having to pawn or sell her gold watch to raise needed funds.[41]

Life was probably hardest during this time for George Hepburn, just ten years old when his father died. Royal Masonic Junior School terms were thirteen long weeks and rules were unbending. In the two dormitories, twenty-five boys slept in rows, personal effects to a minimum. The school was thirteen miles away but Anna visited George occasionally. These were high points of his time there despite his typical school-boy shyness around visiting parents. On Parents' Day all the families went to the same village cafe and, packed in painfully close to each other, had the stilted conversations one might expect in such a situation. In the evening, back in the dormitory rooms, the boys teased each other unmercifully about the more noticeable foibles of their elders. Though she had a handsome Harris tweed coat, Anna, and thus George, came up for a severe criticism from a boy named "Con," because she wore hand-knitted stockings of an uncompromising purple.[42] But another boy, obviously one who looked a little closer for signs of quality, rose to the defense and a counterattack by observing, "Well anyway, Con, Hepburn's mum speaks better than yourn!"

On one occasion Anna swept down on the school and, in outright defiance of the school rules that prohibited term-time visits home, spirited George out for a day at home in 68 Parliament Hill. His brothers were practicing their act in the large front room and George felt surrounded with the love and excitement that was his family. Coming back to the school was a more painful affair, since Anna's removing him without permission meant that he was subject to a public dressing-down in front of his classmates.

At Bushey, unlike at University College School, no one had heard of his mother and her poetic take on life. George had taken a book of his mother's poetry with him to the school in an effort to keep part of her with him, a sweet act on the part of a preadolescent boy. When he returned to his bed one night, fresh in his nightshirt from a bath, the man in charge confronted him with the volume, remarking that the book was about sex and "unsuitable" for a boy his age. The words choked in George's throat and he was unable to tell the man that the author was his mother, an explanation that would probably have earned him the right to keep the book that the headmaster confiscated.

When George came home on school vacations Anna and he would entertain themselves. George would read the popular "Sexton Blake" detective thrillers aloud, both he and his mother taking great pleasure in the process. It was George that Anna had years before comforted with the song about the thunder and the rain. And it was George that had to be dragged by his big brother John from out of the fountain at the Luxembourg Gardens when he fell in tightly clutching a coin. George was the brother who "led a band" on the Heath and, as Anna's youngest child, he evoked from her tender protective feelings. Added to the usual loneliness that some boys experience in the boarding school situation were the facts that he had recently lost his father and that his mother, with her charming ways and humor and love, was no longer available to him. The two corresponded with each other—in rhyming couplets, no less.

There are two other aspects of these first four years of the 1930s that should be mentioned. First was Anna's increasingly honest relationship with Natalie Barney, a subject that will be discussed more in the next chapter. The second was Anna's work along spiritualist dimensions.

Anna came into The Survival League through the indefatigable Catharine Amy (Mrs. Dawson) Scott, a founding member of P.E.N. with whom she had worked on various projects including the James Joyce dinner. Mrs. Dawson Scott wrote novels, children's books, poetry, travel books, and plays and was coeditor, with Ernest Rhys, of a short-story series. Her abundant energy was an attraction to Anna, who was always fascinated by people who *did* things. Her "Survival League," founded in London in October, 1929, was to "affirm the unity of all religions and spread the knowledge of the scientific demonstrability of *survival* after death."[43]

Mrs. Dawson Scott was just one of a number of people who were at that time interested in the occult, seances, and other communication with those who had died. For example, Hannen Swaffer, a journalist friend of Anna's, took the position that "Spiritualism and socialism were two halves of one great whole" and took over from Sir Arthur Conan Doyle as head of several spiritualist organizations when Doyle retired. Swaffer claimed to have strong evidence for the continued existence of Lord Northcliffe (the man who had listened to Anna's Russian spy scare and then shared a meat pie in her kitchen) who had died in 1922. Northcliffe had supposedly reached Swaffer through Mrs. Osborne (Gladys) Leonard, a famous medium used by Radclyffe Hall, among others.

Mrs. Dawson Scott, ever the effective recruiter, called on Anna to become a member of the council of the Survival League, which she did sometime around 1930.[44] Though Anna granted that executive meetings were conducted in business-like fashion, she complained that the leaders were "for the most part . . . not intellectually sensitive."

Certainly she was in sympathy with the belief that all religions had a common thread. Her Catholic education, Methodist Harper relatives and High Church Anglican Whelan relatives, Evangelical nanny, and agnostic/atheist father had given her an inquiring mind as far as religion was concerned. Did Anna ever try to contact Patrick? There is no evidence. But if she had, in a sense she would only have been coming back to her mother's way of thinking. Though her father had scoffed at what he saw as Alice's pseudo-science, Anna's mother had practiced a sort of intuitive psychology under the guise of phrenology and palm reading and healing by massage. Alice's fondness for ghosts and communication with the spirits of various houses had never alarmed Anna, in fact she had been proud of her mother's abilities. Nevertheless, all this seems to have played a rather minor part in Anna's adult life, with the exception of her curses, which were believed by some to have a malefic power. Natalie Barney, for example, finally came to fear that Anna's curse on Dolly Wilde had borne disaster.[45]

Emotionally, Anna moved on only gradually from Natalie Barney. Perhaps this was because she lost so many to death or distance in the five years from 1929 to 1935. Her father, her husband, early friends like D. H. Lawrence and her editor and friend Harold Monro all died within a few years of each other. She had seen others move on to new relationships. David Garnett had long since ceased to matter, though they retained a life-long fondness for each other. Griffin Barry had fallen deeply in love with Bertrand Russell's wife Dora Russell. (When Dora Russell, still married to the philosopher and mathematician, gave birth to Griffin Barry's child,

Anna visited at the end of July, 1930 with three hand-knit pair of socks and a poem for the new baby that prophesied that Harriet Ruth Barry, with "three good names" would be "three lovely things:" "A woman, an artist, a revolutionist.")[46] Yet she had excellent friends in Hampstead and beyond and above all the excitement of running what was in a sense her own art colony. She herself was one of her best students, embarking on a self-directed reading program that in addition to periodicals such as *Life and Letters*, included almost the whole of Shakespeare's plays. Seated at the kitchen table, she began her massive read on May 14, 1933 and finished in June. It must have been after a springtime of household and personal unrest, for lines marked include: "Too headstrong for their mother" (from *Troilus and Cressida*) and "he no more remembers his mother now, than an eight-year-old horse. The tartness of his face sours ripe grapes . . ." (from *Coriolanus*). Also marked was "yet the incessant weepings of my wife" (*The Comedy of Errors*) and "He that dies, pays all debts" (*The Tempest*).[47]

TWENTY

Writing Her Life (1934–1939)

A t age fifty-one, Anna was a lively mother, an excellent friend to the arts, a highly original poet whose lines ranged from sledgehammer-strong to ethereally delicate, and at times a woman in the grip of despair. The next years would be spent in writing her story, over and over again. But one of the first things she had to do was release herself from the hold that Natalie Barney had on her imagination.

"Song" and Natalie had not seen each other since around 1931, but letters and poems had continued. Anna hoped to see Natalie in a proposed visit to London around the end of 1933, promising dancing herons for Natalie and "all the taxi-men to adore you," but then Anna turned "ill and liable to die like Descartes of my lungs" and the meeting never took place.[1]

In April 1934 Natalie wrote fondly, "I'm always glad to see your writing because it has conveyed so much to me that is new and inspired."[2] One day in May of 1934 Anna retrieved her mail to find a letter inviting her to Paris. The paintings of Natalie's mother, Alice Pike Barney, were going to be displayed in Paris and Natalie wanted Anna to be present. Anna, busy with Tour Bourgeoise, did not go. But the letter that she wrote to Natalie on Sunday, May 27, though signed, "Your affec. Anna," has a cold clarity that sets it apart both from some of the raving letters she had written and certainly from the passionate ones.

> You will forgive me for speaking to you emotionally for the last time. Without your O.K. I shall not write to you again—& for this reason—When I met you eight years ago I had so much pleasure from contact with your mind, from your society & from the observation of your spirit—that I feared to drown of happiness. Fear tinged my behavior to you with protective eccentricity—In presenting to you who are so good a judge of truth something that was spurious, there was a shade of impertinence. I don't think this impertinence harmed you—for you are immune from it—But it hurt & lessened & strumpeted me—I had always been afraid of happiness. . . . Even in my silences there will be Truth—(a little arrogance perhaps in my speech!)—I no longer fear to drown. I will therefore write for you— if you tell me to [crossed out] ask me [penned in above].[3]

The last lines of another Wickham poem, "P. P. C.," also show her freeing herself artistically and emotionally from Barney: "Now my aspiration's new / I'll not dream again from you."[4]

Another letter, undated, shows part of the process of Anna coming to her senses in regard to Natalie. In this case a somber epiphany during an encounter in a café. She met there

> a fat blonde illiterate whore I have known by sight for years. She was amusing . . . & she began to be professionally inviting & brush her great breasts along my back & I liked her too much to repulse her—& I sat and cowered with repulsion & suddenly I thought of you! I remembered that I have been writing love-poetry to you for years—& that you have been nice about it / & I thought that your imagination— was to my imagination as was I to the large blonde whore—& I was sorry for you.[5]

Anna had closed that letter by saying that "as this part of my spirit dies" she asks for forgiveness, "& a beginning in good sense."

Natalie wrote again later in 1934, but this was to ask a favor. Dolly Wilde, Anna's irritant in the late 1920s, had been going through tough times and even tried to commit suicide in September. Natalie, who remained loyal to Dolly in her excesses, had written hoping that Anna would release Dolly from a curse made by Anna years before. Fearing that perhaps Anna's "malific [sic] light-hearted power . . . . may have brought about this unhappy chain of events," Natalie writes, "May I beg that you will exert your more serious power, in which I've unlimited faith, to bring about a change for the better?"[6] In gratitude (or bribery) Natalie bought Anna a much appreciated coat and skirt. Anna had an ornate certificate drawn up, taxing Natalie the sum of £9.4.6. (perhaps the cost of the clothing) "for mentioning a mistress to her true lover."[7]

Still, a bond survived. Natalie and Anna continue to send each other their newly published books, a few gifts, and tokens. During her various readings around the city Anna included poetry written to Barney. In November 1935 a "packet of poems" reached Natalie Barney then visiting in New York, and Anna still professes a desire "to beat Rémy [de Gourmont in] letters to you."[8] In 1936 there is a flurry of letters, a few undated letters discuss hopelessness in Anna's situation (Delarue-Mardrus unsympathetically said that no one could help Anna, while Anna, chillingly, responds that anyone who could send her a ladder could help her). Sometimes long-distance lust reappears, sometimes the love is likened to mother-love. But Anna never relinquishes her pleasure in Natalie's "exquisite" and "sustaining" appreciation.[9] And Barney continued to give that admiration to the verse of "Anna, dear and incorrigible Anna."[10]

The years from 1930 to 1934, in which Anna directed her attention outward, seem to give way to somewhat more of an inward focus in the years from 1935 to 1939, a woman trying to come to terms with herself, interpreting and reinterpreting her life over and over again in works that gradually become more and more truthful. And more bleak.

Anyone who wants to learn more about the poet behind Anna's poetry should read "Prelude to a Spring Clean," her partial autobiography in prose. A work funny, candid (but not too candid), emotional, she meant to explain the life of a "failure," but succeeded in telling a lively story. Never published until 1984, a British journalist and teacher, R. D. (Reggie) Smith, together with the Hepburn family, pored over stacks of material to bring out the largest-ever selection of Anna Wickham material. Included in that selection are portions of the autobiography covering her childhood, youth, marriage, and the first two years of their first son, James.[11] She wrote it beginning in March, 1935, as a survival technique during an extremely low and unstable point in her life, saying that "self-knowledge and self-expression are the only techniques of my continuance."[12] "For the whole twenty-nine years [since marriage] my resources have been decreasing," she writes.[13]

Her financial situation is as poor as ever. Her first publisher, Harold Monro, is dead, her new work has not been picked up by other book publishers (if she even offered it), her last volume was published in 1921, and most of the Americans who liked her work in Paris had gone home when the franc's hospitality diminished. She is older, getting shabby, and has no viable love interest. The gains of the last few years begin to seem inadequate and Tour Bourgeoise is proving to be a lot of work with little return. She loses a briefcase with a large notebook of poems.[14] New poets are taking over the field. She suffered toothaches and poor health in 1933. Then in June of 1934 her stepfather, William Henry Geake, committed suicide by drowning, leaving seventy-seven-year-old Alice a widow. By 1935 Alice was living in Russell, Bay of Islands, New Zealand, but she moved on from there, probably leaving New Zealand.[15]

Besides all the worries, Anna seems to be standing still while others are not: Natalie Barney is spending the winter in the U. S.; Anna's older sons, well-reviewed in *The Evening Standard*, are touring (with the famous "Crazy Gang" on the bill) and honing their act for the continent. John is soon to marry.[16] Within a year the Hampstead Scientific Society will build an observatory on the Heath "to the memory of Patrick Hepburn." With all this in mind, Anna begins to order the house.

Anna's house by this time was almost famously filthy, at least the kitchen. Disorder ruled. Now she cleaned and sorted, energy from those ongoing tasks providing energy for the task of writing. Her gruesome intent she depicts with a mordant twist—that one cannot commit suicide using a dirty oven:

> This year I shall conquer the sets of drawers; my self-discipline is complete enough. I shall have every pin, rag, tot and tittle in the villa in its place, and everything will be splendidly clean. But I am finished: I am utterly defeated: there is nothing before me but suicide. I order the villa for my death. When the stove is clean enough I shall turn on the gas.[17]

In many ways, Anna had been writing her life ever since she picked up pen and put it to paper. The poems often sprang out of incidents in her life, her speeches for the School for Mothers from the self-sufficiency she saw in her Whelan foremothers, her short stories by the raw material of her courtship and marriage to Patrick. Now for the first time Anna was ready, or forced herself to be ready, to write her life story in a more straightforward fashion. She began the work of revealing herself, perhaps the hardest, most original work an artist can do.

She wants to understand the roots of things: why she is antagonistic toward the more privileged, why she strives toward self-expression and self-knowledge, why she gave of herself to the extent that in trying "to serve three generations of men . . . I seem to have ruined them all," why she never felt completely at ease with her friends and was never really *sure* of another's affection.[18] It is a self-analysis to try to answer those and other questions.

About two-thirds of the autobiography, begun when she was fifty-two years old, is devoted to her ancestors and to her own youth and childhood. Much analysis of family dynamics is from a psychological point of view, not surprising since she had read Sigmund Freud (a Hampstead resident for a time) and probably Adler and Jung. She rejected Freud's conclusions about sons and mothers, but believed in the interpretation of dreams. She also conjectures about inferiority and superiority and analyzes the family romance with faint brush strokes. She uses a feminist interpretation of her mother's woes, ascribing much of the trouble to the limited stage available for her mother's talents (theatrical and in a larger sense), while her own troubles stemmed from, she thought, her father's and mother's own neuroses and displaced desires. She felt that in trying to please both parents she lost herself, while in choosing Patrick, another one she sought to please, she made both of them miserable and affected their sons as well.

This work is the first we have that shows Anna lengthening her stride, a writing style in a way cinematic, with strong visual appeal and a strong appeal to incident. In fact the story is so dramatic that the biographer tends to distrust it. Several extant versions of parts of the autobiography show that she did take a writer's license to exaggerate to create more drama when she felt it necessary, giving partial accounts of complicated matters and complicated accounts of simple matters.[19] But research reveals that though her style obfuscates at times (especially birth and marriage dates), events usually happened roughly how and when she says they did, though (distinct from editing cuts) there are tantalizing gaps.[20] Most of what initially makes the biographer uneasy turns out to be Anna Wickham's skillful crafting of the work, a selection of details, for example, which serves as a shorthand to character traits, or a picking and choosing of incidents, to give another example, for the way that they reinforce and comment on each other.

Anna, for example, gives us insight into each of the "characters" in the autobiography by their books. Alice Harper, the elocution specialist, teaches her children from "The Women of Mumbles Head." Her father's touchstone book is Darwin's *On the Origin of Species by Means of Natural Selection*. Patrick Hepburn reads aloud to Anna from Stevenson's "Wrecker." Anna the child reclines on a sofa with *Alice in Wonderland* and for her first grown-up novel reads Olive Schreiner's *Story of an African Farm*. When Anna's mother becomes extremely irritated at Geoffrey, what else does she throw at him but a book! Anna's selection of the titles, chosen from the many, many books that passed through the Harper household, lends humor to her autobiography *and* reveals the intellectual preoccupations of Victorian society moving toward modernism.

An example of the second aspect of Anna's craft in writing (how she connects events to each other) can be seen in her account of herself as an awkward, needy, and unbeautiful child. A Harper uncle offers a coin in return for eating what turned out to be a dreadful tasting pill; Anna is richer, but dismayed and betrayed. Her autobiography gives many instances of being dismayed by her own clumsiness, ineptness, and inaccuracy. The cumulative effect is to make plausible that Anna, too often feeling a failure, would be vulnerable to the rewards and the criticisms of the Alices and Patricks of the world.

Shifting judgments in the autobiography lend the work a kind of staggering gait that is hard to track at times. Sometimes she seems to be blaming one person, sometimes another, sometimes herself. This seems, however, the traditional progress of an analysis. As a person examines a memory or a dream, he or she begins to think deeper and differently about each person involved, and each person from the past may be seen in a new perspective.

Anna is trying to understand her adult character. Why am I disorderly? she is asking. Why am I lonely? Why do I write? Why did my parents act the way they did? Where did they come from? What effect did it all have on me? Why am I a failure? For in spite of Anna's past successes, this is how she felt:

> In spite of my long endurance and impotent courage, I have made some profound mistakes. I feel that I am myself a profound mistake and that I was doomed from my conception by being myself: I feel that women of my kind are a profound mistake. There have been few

women poets of distinction, and, if we count only the suicides of Sappho, Lawrence Hope [Violet Nicolson] and Charlotte Mew, their despair rate has been very high.[21]

But at the end of writing her autobiographical work in or around 1935, Anna did not try to commit suicide. There is no evidence that she finished cleaning the house either. Instead life had other things in store for her: new friends and new books.

Wickham, both according to her sons and judging from her letters, was a somewhat casual promoter of her own work. The coupling of her first efforts to publish with the volcanic scene with Patrick may have induced in her a detached attitude to publication efforts. At any rate, later books evidenced always the presence of such shepherds as Harold Monro, Anita Brackenbury, or Louis Untermeyer, who served as prod and guide through to print. This is not to say that Anna Wickham refused to deal with the publishing world directly. She had been tireless in trying to find an English publisher for Natalie Barney and could be very persistent in following up on a book's progress. It is also not to say that Wickham was one of those who wrote not caring if the poems would be read or heard, for as she wrote to Louis Untermeyer,

> I am sending you a few fragments that I have written during the last weeks—I am the vulgarian who must have a public.[22]

On February 2, 1935, Anna sent a young man frequently to be seen in the environs of Charlotte Street a postcard poem. "Little Shakespeare in a bonnet," the first line ran, for John Gawsworth claimed to be descended from Shakespeare's Dark Lady.[23] George Hepburn grew used to seeing this slightly fox-faced new visitor at the dining room table, which had a very pleasing view of the walled garden, as he quizzed Anna on her work while together they went through the hundreds of poems she had written in her lifetime so far. Time after time George found the pair laughing, for Gawsworth had a quick wit to match Anna's and a deep impulse to "resurrect" her poetic career.[24] "A rogue," Anna always said, "but a likeable rogue."[25] He collected her poems, a lock of her hair, and drew her likeness, all the while trying to convince Anna that the time was ripe for her poetry to be printed again. She was, as always, stimulated to write by the active interest of another person.

Born in 1912, Terence Ian Fytton Armstrong, or John Gawsworth, as he was known, was slightly younger than Anna's eldest sons. But there seems not to have been any sort of mother-figure yearning in Gawsworth's attentions. Friendship with Anna at Tour Bourgeoise would further his reputation as a Bohemian. And a connection with her works was part of his signature "warm-hearted concern" with those whose work he felt had met "unjustifiable neglect."[26]

Anna, writing to Natalie to request old poems be sent over to England for examination, describes him as a bibliographer who "likes to have all the verses."[27] He ingratiated himself as "This courtly boy who brings me books / Is agate in my childhood's brooks."[28] She calls him "very young & industrious" with a "very sincere & charming interest in poetry."

He was a writer himself, before age twenty publishing seven volumes of poetry, mostly with Twyn Barlwm Press of which he was director. His *A Study and Bibliography of P. Wyndham Lewis* came out in 1932, he wrote about Ernest Dowson and T. E. Lawrence, was a coauthor with the science fiction and detective novelist M. P. Shiel, and had also edited books of horror stories. His press connections included E. H. Samuel, Scholartis, and Richards (and by the late thirties included Secker and Oxford University Press).[29]

Gawsworth was entertaining. In October 1936 he and Shiel made a blood brother pact naming Gawsworth future "King of Redonda" (a real island in the Caribbean Sea, which was and still is a mythical and real international society). Anna chided him saying, "Proper kings / Wear better rings."[30] He enjoyed alcohol. On June 27, 1938, Audrey Beecham wrote to Lawrence Durrell, "Gawsworth is drinking himself into D.T.s. He'll be dead before he has time to sue you over your new novel [The Black Book]."[31] ("King Juan" Gawsworth lived until 1970.) He was a born mimic, a trader, and a scholar rolled into one. His friend Lawrence Durrell had known Gawsworth to purchase breakfast by buying low and selling high along the bookshops on the Charing Cross Road.[32]

A picture comes through of Anna being swept off her feet by Gawsworth's attentions and attentive reading and desire for collaborative efforts. Gawsworth becomes her editor and sometime amanuensis. From 1938 on he keeps a linen-bound book called "Poems by Anna Wickham" in which he records her poems. He seemed to take special pride in her bawdy ones such as the untitled quatrain, "I keep my cunt / In front / But you'll be kind / And see to me behind." He copies down some of her correspondence, jots down snippets of their conversations and, in a separate section called "Obiter Dicta," records Anna's conversational wit. "That's a nice kind of a bloke to meet on the underground" (upon seeing a photograph of the esteemed critic Walter Pater). Or "Beauty is truth in a net." Or on Henry Miller: "Miller represents the deep black hunger of America. He wanted publicity the way America wants bread. And it is a disgraceful thing that our men recognize him." Even years later in a bar around Notting Hill Gate he would repeat Anna's words to a young newcomer, Barry Humphries, now the illustrious Dame Edna Everage.[33]

As much as Anna liked Gawsworth, she was also deeply suspicious of her visitor. He had a habit of asking Anna to autograph her poems and then paying her a small sum for them. Anna was leery of Gawsworth's reputation as someone "making money out of my signatures."[34] He may have helped her to sell first editions when she needed money. He purchased "a great many" of her old broadsides for £10. He irritated her by proffering a pen with red ink for her to sign his second-hand "birthday book." When he criticized her phrasing Anna called it "savage" and battled until she convinced him of the rightness of her criticized punctuation. The two must have had many comma wars; Anna said he was too "economical" with them.

For his part, Gawsworth sometimes had to tiptoe around Anna's moods to avoid having any "injustice" he might do raise "obscenity" in Anna, arousing her "wicked" imagination.[35]

But Gawsworth seemed to have a special dispensation for avoiding Anna's real wrath. "Back to civilization," he would tell her, on leaving. He had figured out the right combination of flippancy and concern and, especially the ability to keep a certain distance when necessary. He adopted the attitude, according to Anna, that he was "wasting" his time in her house, and gave no encouragement to Anna when she talked of her "project to be a journalist."

She mused that she might find someone more "congenial" to work with, but ended up viewing him as "part of my destiny." But awful for Anna was the feeling that Gawsworth would prefer for her "a posthumous reputation" (made by him) and that she was a poet of the past.

There is little in Gawsworth's promotion of Anna to suggest this. He made sure her work was published: in her book, *Thirty-Six New Poems* and in two anthologies within a year and a half. Not coincidentally and not without effort, he thus gained another notch in his editor belt. Amanuensis, taskmaster, he also probably provided Anna with a notebook in which to record new work and then checked on her at intervals.[36] And the presence of the Anna Wickham collection at the University of Reading seems to bear out Gawsworth's good and honest intentions and support his notation: "The records of Richards Press & my cheque book will correct her 'impressions' if anyone is interested."[37]

Gawsworth had an acute awareness of the past and he relied on past successful models, hoping to be catapulted into like prominence. Edward Marsh, editor and force behind the *Georgian Poetry* anthologies issued before during and after World War I, was one of his models. Marsh's anthologies had provided some income for the poets lucky enough to be included (Anna and most other women were not). Gawsworth put together *Edwardian Poetry* hoping to imitate the success of Marsh's anthologies. His prefatory note quotes the earlier anthologies' disclaimer ("no pretension to cover the field") and also states a clear preference for formal, lyrical verse.

With *Edwardian Poetry,* issued sometime in the spring of 1936, Gawsworth expected to capitalize on the immense popularity of the attractive bachelor monarch, crowned Edward VIII in January of that year. The second poem of the volume was laureate material: "Prince, knight, pilot, king, guider / Captain, defender, adviser," an "Ode Royal Addressed to His Majesty King Edward VIII" by Herbert Palmer.[38]

This book was published by Richards, which had come down in the world. (Grant Richards, who had published Anna and was the founder of the company, had distanced himself from the firm as both bankruptcy and an uncongenial management team had soured him on involvement. Without Grant Richards's eye for quality the bulk of the business involved backlists and reprint rights.)[39] Forty-seven poems written by seventeen living poets, among them Ruth Pitter, Hugh MacDiarmid, and Roy Campbell, made up the anthology. It was attacked on several fronts. Following Marsh's example, Gawsworth had not identified himself as editor (though this may have been a politic move since he had included six poems of his own). Some reviewers were affronted that the editor was not named, others mulled over what they saw as the odd focus of the book. It purported to represent the new era, but excluded such famous names as W. H. Auden and Louis MacNeice. Other reviewers disputed the amount of talent displayed. Through this inky brouhaha Anna emerged almost shining, especially for her powerful "Mare Bred from Pegasus." She and Ruth Pitter were praised, even by reviewers who found the book otherwise lacking.[40]

Gawsworth almost immediately began a series (never completed) of inexpensive small books with yellow paper covers called, "Shilling Selections from Edwardian Poets." Three came out about the same time, one by E. H. Visiak, one by M. P. Shiel, and one by Anna Wickham (*Thirty-Six New Poems*, dedicated "to George Hepburn"). All three books were well reviewed, but mostly by obscure newspapers and journals. For Gawsworth's plan to capitalize on the new king's reign had backfired. The king decided to leave the throne for Wallis Simpson, the divorced woman he loved. He abdicated the throne in December 1936, giving a sad farewell broadcast to the nation. Just in time for the all-important Christmas market, the "Edwardian" poets had lost their reason for being collected together. As one reviewer stated, the series "will now presumably have to find another title."[41]

Not defeated, John Gawsworth charted a new course and adjusted his sails. His next anthology, issued in April, 1937, with Maurice Wollman's help "in selection and arrangement" carried a safe "Neo-Georgian" label; no kowtowing preface to the Royal Family, only a Latin quotation from Tacitus, a Roman historian. In this forty-two-page anthology (which could not seem to decide if it was a book or a periodical) issued in April of 1937, Anna had six poems. By this time Anna's opinion that poetry was not going to be her financial salvation was confirmed, and she could not, as she said, "pawn eloquence."[42] But she had made a friend for life, one of the most irrepressible and original drinkers of Fitzrovia and, as he would often say, a king.

As a result of John Gawsworth's hard work, Anna's name came up again before a new generation of poetry readers. A few new requests came in for use of her poems in anthologies.[43] Anna gave several readings and new faces came by Tour Bourgeoise.

By the time young Dylan Thomas met and married Caitlin Macnamara in July 1937, he had been a frequent visitor at Anna Wickham's house, usually arguing long and hard about something.

He had been introduced to Tour Bourgeoise by John Davenport and it fit his hopes to meet writers in London.[44] There he saw Malcolm Lowry and, later, Lawrence Durrell. Dylan Thomas's description of a bathroom in *Adventures in the Skin Trade* comes straight from no. 68, and perhaps the engaging title, too, from the Hepburn family's old commercial connection in the leather business.

Thomas hated Anna's method of producing a poem from the stimulus of reading. He felt this produced a bad poem and was unnecessary, since "with a little constriction of the muscles," [it] "could have been voided anyway."[45] Dylan himself had not, at that time, read widely, at least in the opinion of Lawrence Durrell.[46] But he was an extraordinary craftsman and this business of taking years to work over a poem as Thomas sometimes did must have seemed bewildering, if not downright obstructionist, to someone like Anna who said, "take time and think / and *then* spend ink."[47] Not that Anna didn't work over her poems—she did, and when she gave a reading she would often (at least in the later years) editorialize herself on the spot "with odd conversational asides and explanatory phrases," or write comments about her own work: "'Rubbish, but there it is,'" or "'Not much sense but some rhythm.'"[48] Thomas's agonizing method of revision would not have been something that Anna wanted to spend a lot of time doing.

Through Thomas, Anna met friends of his such as Rayner Heppenstall. Anna, Thomas, and Caitlin came together on the number twenty-four bus to visit Heppenstall, then living on Lisburne Road. Heppenstall, who had known of Anna because his friend George Orwell once lived across the road from no. 68, was quite intimidated by the poet. He found her "big" and "ferocious-looking" with a complexion "blackhead-pitted" and brown.[49] Her apparel too he found unusual: "rugger stockings" (undoubtedly hand-knit). Heppenstall was, by his own admission, frequently pugnacious and it might have been a sizing up of a potential adversary that made him so observant. She was, when drunk, Heppenstall said, "reputed to bite people's heads and try to pull other women's breasts off."

Twenty-five-year-old Lawrence Durrell, on the other hand, wrote back to Henry Miller in Paris saying Anna Wickham was "the most amazing woman I have yet met in England."[50] Durrell was impressed by Anna, "who in order to escape the brutality of men had to become first woman and then Lesbian," copying into his own notebook her comments about female artists and "submission" ("a leg that must be broken and re-set"). He, too, found her "rather formidable . . . of intimidating size and forthrightness" but relations between them were cordial and easy.[51] She probably respected his interest in psychology (he was there in late 1937 to talk with a London psychologist), and she responded to his personality, which Henry Miller called "always merry and bright . . . countenance a-gleam . . . youth incarnate. Plus brains. . . . Above all, he could laugh. . . ."[52] On returning to Paris, Durrell arranged to send Henry Miller's books to Anna via Anaïs Nin (who was "very keen" to meet Anna after hearing so much about her from

Durrell). And Henry Miller sent Durrell to London hoping to obtain from Anna "a large private diary for publication, parts of which might be regarded as actionable if produced in England itself."[53] But the juicy diary "was a myth," is what Durrell reported back to Miller.

Anna certainly knew enough people to fill one hundred diaries. If she recorded even half the trouble she saw, and sometimes participated in, the reading world would be a livelier place. Such a diary might explain just why she forbade the Thomases their bed on the dining room floor after a disagreement and threw them out "in a pantomime snow."[54] She might have related some of the dangerous antics of Napper Dean Paul, a friend she knew from the Kleinfeldts' tavern.[55] She might have explained why she lifted books from Anthony Thorne's orderly bookshelves and broke his china.[56] Or tormented poor Susan Miles.[57] Or scratched Wyn Henderson, another woman who had helped Dylan Thomas.[58] She might have explained her exchanges of wit with performer Bud Flanagan.[59] She might have recorded just what hymns she played when a wild party at Belsize Park was raided by police and Anna played church music to successfully give the appearance of decorum.[60] She might say just who were all those men in women's clothing at another Hampstead party or just what sort of conversations she and cape-wearing Count Potocki of Montalk enjoyed. And what she thought of friends like Nina Hamnett, who seemed ever less likely to work at their art and more and more likely to cadge drinks.

As the years went on she was much less likely to allow herself to be "muted." At the Green Curtain Club, a small Hampstead venue where one-act plays were staged during the hours the pubs were closed, she interrupted the drama to tell the actors to speak up.[61] She and son George once attended a West End performance, before World War II, at which Anna clapped so often in all the "wrong places" that the audience rose, turned, and said, "shut up!" to quiet her. At some parties she was the life and soul of the fun. At others she took over and raised havoc that was hard to put down. She bought a new hat and went with George to a party on Guy Fawkes Day where Hitler hung in effigy; Stephen Spender was there, and the master of Westminster school. Anna made such a continuous racket that people went from room to room saying, "Who is this dreadful woman?" Spender and the Westminster man stuck up for her and she stayed.[62] Probably there were champions for Anna even on the night of a Hampstead party when she was infuriated past endurance by some woman in a diamond necklace and proceeded to rip the necklace off the woman and toss it out the window. Anthony Thorne remembers, though, watching Anna being thrown out of one Hampstead party and, raging alone in the street, smash a storefront weighing machine with her fist. Once she knocked her son John to the floor with a blow that shot straight out and caught him before he knew what was happening. Oswell Blakeston, another writing and good pub friend, admitted that he was "petrified at the thought of her straight left."[63]

Of course, Anna was not the only person swinging her fists at that time; Malcolm Lowry, John Davenport, Roy Campbell, and many others were too. But she was one of the few women, and it gave her a reputation that she capitalized on. At an art show where she had criticized the works too loudly,

> the art dealer whispered to Oswell Blakeston to take her away: she stood up to her full height and muttered, "You'd better retract, my good man. I may be a minor poet, but I'm a major woman."[64]

She had her friends and enemies and a few in either camp might have actually sickened someone like Virginia Woolf who could not mix milieus the way Anna did.

In May, 1938, Anna suffered her second bout of pneumonia, at that time often fatal. She was hospitalized at New End hospital for over a week, visited by son Jim daily before he went on to sit for a portrait that Cedric Morris was doing of him. Perhaps, thought Jim later, Anna was "chatted up by some visiting clergy." Certainly she must have been upset by the sterile routine, and the disturbing visions it all conjured up for her, for she put her feelings into "Tribute to the Nursing Staff," a poem that like "The Homecoming" would foreshadow tragedy yet to come.[65]

Actually, it was Anna's illness and subsequent forced recovery time that gave her the opportunity "to be ambitious again."[66] When she got out of the hospital she concentrated her reading: "eight books on Marxism" and "four books on money." With the weak peace of the World War I agreements collapsing into murderous and land-grabbing chaos, Anna wanted to get to the root of the problem. Integrating the new information with her past reading and political thinking she devised a curious, poetic manifesto for an organization she titled "The League for the Protection of the Imagination of Women." Of course, her Manifesto had its roots in a very personal issue, a hatred of men correcting women's expression. When Eric

Partridge made changes to Natalie Barney's book Anna was extremely irritated by what she saw as his high-handedness. When her stepfather William Geake had "corrected" some of Alice's letters to her, she was aghast. And, of course, what she had suffered from Patrick's frequent "editing" of her speech and behavior, she said, "leaves my brain bleeding."[67] Now she married the issue of men editing women to the larger issue of tyrannical governments in Italy, Germany, and Russia:

> We do not like the way Mussolini has organised his colonial empire.
> We do not like the way Hitler has managed his Jews.
> And we don't like Stalin's effect on Russian poetry.[68]

Anna subscribed to what her eldest son has described as a "leadership principle." She had a belief that a strong leader "could . . . effect the development of, as it were, the nation's business. And she found such people attractive . . . . at one time she thought that, for instance, Mussolini, was effecting a necessary change in the arrangements that guided the forces of Italy." In fact, Anna had nicknamed her briefcase (presumably for organization reasons) Mussolini. But her admiration for Mussolini and an even shorter-lived interest in Hitler had given way quickly.[69]

Jim and John had come back from their dance engagement in Bucharest in 1938 with a clear understanding that the Nazis posed a great threat and that appeasement played right into their hands.[70] Her sons' firsthand knowledge, combined with Anna's old conversations with Israel Zangwill, who had called for safe haven for the persecuted Jews of Europe, convinced Anna to write the Manifesto.

The Manifesto, on first reading, is an incoherent, rambling connecting of all the big ideas of Anna's autodidactic programs, with a "slogan": "World's Management by Entertainment." Anna's aims for her league, however, are clearly stated in the last paragraph: "to stimulate original work from women in the fields of economics, psychology and political theory."

"Peace and Plenty," Anna explains in the first part of the Manifesto, is the modern problem for government and has been ever since society moved from matriarchy. "The machine," theorized and then materialized by man, actually liberates the spirit of woman who has all along been creative in the family, she continues. The stumbling block is the state of the world, and "we, the committee, have gathered ourselves together because the state of the world does not amuse us."

Anna's Manifesto, June 16, 1938, was signed by seven feminists, among them Charlotte Haldane, who had paid a lot of attention to Malcolm Lowry when he attended her Cambridge salon and who now went to the same Communist suppers that Anna did; Carmel Haden Guest, one of Anna's earliest friends in London; and Kate O'Brien. Anna's political thinking at this time brought her close to O'Brien, a writer, and to Pat Dooley, a fiery speaker on political issues. With O'Brien she fell in love. With Dooley she felt loved. Both of these people were important to Anna in the late 1930s.

Although Anna had lesbian affairs after Natalie Barney, there are no letters so far, with the exception of these to Kate O'Brien, that give hints to the nature of the relationships. In the case of O'Brien, Anna may have been the disappointed party in a love triangle. But before that happened she did write a few letters, parts of which show Anna at her most tender.

O'Brien started out her career in the 1920s as a playwright, but became best known for her novels. Born in Dublin and familiar with cultured middle-class Irish families, she plumbed this familiarity in her prize-winning 1931 first novel, *Without My Cloak*. O'Brien understood how Catholic puritanism could cripple the emotions and this must have struck a chord with Anna, who in Australia had seen the Catholicism of young women from inside the fort while remaining outside the practicing faith. By 1938 O'Brien had written three more novels, and *Farewell Spain*, a travel book.

She lived in Hampstead for a time and breezed in and out of no. 68 Parliament Hill. Then when O'Brien, and a friend who was recovering from pneumonia, stayed at an inn outside London, Anna was inspired to send several letters and poems.

"I feel very bitter and my soul in the corner like a sick bat," writes Anna on June 17, 1938, in mock agony, "because you are in the country with a routine breakfast, fresh air and friendly conversation . . . and no one supplies me with any routine whatever."[71] Anna mentions her own recent recovery from a severe case of pneumonia ("a fortnight" on the danger list as opposed to the friend's "not very poignant" two days), and describes her posthospitalization trials with a light touch. Her apt word choices, quotations, and helpless hands-in-the-air resignation at the loss of house "decorum" make high farce:

> . . . me tottering out of hospital to find daffodils in my room and . . .
> to retire with a book rest to read . . . the first week with everybody

watching me to see when I will become normal and take up my bag
of crosses. Then the charming young man on the top floor who sings
madly to start reforming a whore, and to sleep in the same bed with
her and his hag of a mistress. Innocently doubtless but so taking all
the validity out of my decorum. And him also letting the girl wash off
her whoreishness in the fine white bath upstairs, which is the delight
of old Mr. Ames whose brother was the tallest major in the Life
Guards, and the girl leaving her whoreishness visible in the Bath.
Never was there so dirty a bath. And after Mr. Ames with his Sultana
flouncing on me—For retribution and the cleaning of the Bath. And
from me—what a hero—"I will in person clean that Bath." And me
tottering to the scum refusing all rags but my own. Anointing all with
Vim, afterwards with eau de cologne thus restoring order.

After this crisis as landlady, another crisis (mother of dancing sons)
arises:

Whereat Jim "Can you bear a little worry." From me: "Let us try."
"Someone has stolen our stage clothes and on Monday we perform."
Then I must sell first editions and dress them in white face cloth.
Never any peace—never any love—never any easy conversation, no
organised sunshine.

After an Eeyore-like pause Anna adds the wry lament, "Never any
comrade but Almighty God who is not visibly a domestic executive" and
then calmly launches into an update of the league.

Anna sought to amuse O'Brien because, "I begin to want to have
phrases between us," which for Anna was a code for intimacy. "I love you
and no one may know—what we say." She wrote to O'Brien, whom she
called "the heart of Schubert's 'Young Nun,'" saying, "I put a kiss also on
the heart and inside the left hand and I summon five thousand holy bees
to wax up the ears—so that nothing at all boring is heard by my [brave]
baby for a fortnight." Anna paid O'Brien the same high compliment that
she gave Natalie and others who moved her only in the highest way: "For
I can imagine / From you."[72]

The second friend Anna saw a lot of around the time of the league and
after was Lawrence Dooley, who on Sundays during the 1930s and 1940s
would speak to the crowds who brought their chairs and sat down to listen

to his rousing speeches at the top of Parliament Hill only a short distance from Anna's house. Pat, as he was called, an antifascist who spoke movingly in favor of communism, was someone with whom Anna could feel completely at ease. In her poem to him, "Home for the Imagination," it is evident that she felt comfortable with the Dooley family in the same way that she had once felt with a few select others. Most likely it was partly Dooley's free and welcoming spirit, but not just that. Anna responded most fully to those who knew what she was getting at in her work and life, and Dooley did. A former miner himself, he became a skilled orator and debater by virtue of his passion for labor issues and his devotion to the intellectual life. According to his sister Kitty, he read a page of the dictionary each day while still a miner, and built up a wonderful library of books. For Anna, "in this frozen hour" he was "a tower," his wife was "a kind field," and their home a "summer landscape" and "refuge for starved birds, / Lamed rabbits, tortured kings, / And Words."[73]

For despite Anna's many interests, she had come to see herself as "at a frozen hour." And again she began to rewrite her life, this time in poetry. But where the 1935 autobiography's prose had considerable wit and charm, this new autobiographical writing is harsh. The types of images she was capable of in the past, those lines that poet Paul Dehn had described as "delicate as the wind on a saucer of milk" are missing.[74]

It was probably sometime in February or March, 1939, when Anna sat down to write this most bitter and probably most honest account she called, "Life Story."[75] For forty-nine pages she wrote, ending the poem

> With this narration I
>   could cloy myself/.
> But I've had fury to
>   destroy myself—
>
> I've suffered these
>   fool trials—
> Because of endless
>   self-denials/
> So much I'll yield
> I'm always some
>   [?] sadist field—

Anna the boxing fan pulls no punches here. She lays out the narrative of her life in such bald terms that the lines have a brute force. The rhyming couplets and the inexorable iambs double the strike value of the lines. In this work she doesn't hide behind pseudonyms—it is "Hepburn," "my father," "my mother," "my first son," etc. She is more honest than ever before about events that have happened, and is increasingly forthcoming about her own speculations, too, for example, saying Patrick committed suicide to "dodge gaol."[76]

The work answers unstated questions. Who was the first "sadist" in Anna's life? Who gave her "lust for sympathy?" Her beautiful mother. How did she feel about her father? Ashamed of his tuning forks and convinced that "he told Hepburn I was mad." Why, "revengefully," did she "whore" during the war years? To pay back Patrick for coming to her bed when she was still under threat of the asylum. Why did she sleep with Harold Monro? "I was maddened / by the tragedy." Why did she hang herself after Patrick's death? Her nerve broke. How did she feel about Jim's cutting her down from the rope? "Why did you cut me down I knew I'd had enough." How did she feel about some of her lovers? They were "bits and pieces . . . And later I'd burlesque—Love with fool women—how I was then / grotesque." Why was she writing "Life Story"? To "rage out my grief— / For my sick soul's relief / Then stutter to inanity." What is her life like at this point? Teeth knocked out by her last lover, poor, "snowing again and no coal," no prospects. Yet, and this is a pretty big yet, there could be possibility. "Life could be sweet," she writes, "Had I a conduit for my energy / And just one hand to succor me," for she still has her ability to converse.

> O I am brilliant—brilliant
> How splendidly I talk
> when I'm abroad—
> • • •
> . . . some public place
> Where there is interest & space
> And show my quality
> And earn its subsidy.

Anna's supreme frustration is with the state of her life at age fifty-five, a time when some people may be starting to enjoy rewards from their efforts, an age where the years left to achieve all the great things dreamed of may seem perilously few. She regrets her powerlessness, she crows over her powers and she lays them both out for inspection of the reader, or perhaps for herself, since this work was never published, or perhaps for John Gawsworth, who may have given her the notebook.

In this poem, as a confessional poet in a continuum from George Meredith's "Modern Love" to Robert Lowell's later works and beyond, she is concisely trying to lay out the impossible: a map of herself, with alliances broken and unbroken, hopes, anger, fears, and passions. She has too often been a burden or carried a burden, she writes: her husband "woke & found / himself an ass / That he had married far / beneath his class"; her third son, "has no start." She freely admits that she is struggling against the self-destructive urge. She doesn't *want* to commit suicide because it's "not new / with woman poets;" it would be almost the expected thing for a troubled woman poet and to Anna, doing the expected is anathema. She also remembers the "scant pity" that a suicide attempt elicits. Finally, Anna wants to live, simply because she has already survived so much. "I have come whole / from so much strife— / I have desire of life."

It is impossible not to be moved by her confession, and by her conclusion that in the important relationships with adults she'd too often been the "sadist field" for other people to work their pain upon.

How could a woman who positively terrorized some people paint herself as such a powerless figure? She answers this question toward the end of the poem: "I've suffered these / fool trials— / Because of endless / self-denials." Despite her constant criticism, found in other of her poems, of a sacrifice-based religion, in her life she kept throwing herself into the pit, onto the cross. This tendency for all-or-nothing led her affairs and her friendships into storms and difficulties, for many of the people she was attracted to were not the kind to reciprocate with her level of intensity. Patrick Hepburn wanted love, but would not or could not love back in a way that would satisfy her. Natalie Barney could easily shrug off any serious threats curtailing her freedom to love whomever and whenever she chose. Lately Kate O'Brien, John Gawsworth, her many pub friends, and theatre friends, were not interested in Anna's need to be devoted. Her devotion fell onto the one person who seems never to have disappointed her or quarreled with her, her son George. As youngest son, who still commanded her complete loyalty and returned it, she felt, correctly or not, that she owed him something that she could not deliver, especially protection, as war and conscription loomed ahead.

By the end of May, 1939, however, when Anna writes to Natalie Barney to thank her for a book, she's feeling good. Natalie has used one of Anna's poems in *Nouvelles Pensées de l'Amazone*.[77] Anna has been, independently of Natalie's interest, getting her manuscripts in order, "designing to devote the next seven years of my life almost exclusively to poetry."[78] Then too, a new venture has come her way: a swan song on television.

On at least a few occasions after he finished school at Bushey, George Hepburn had joined his brothers on the road, or helped out on the sets when John did some filming in London. Anna continued to be proud of her sons' interesting acting and dancing careers, but music hall performances, once so important to communities, had come into competition from radio and the cinema, making the Hepburn brothers rising stars in a falling universe. A new medium was about to change the world of entertainment, and Anna was getting in first.

The British Broadcasting Corporation had in 1936 purchased part of the North London Alexandra Palace complex for television studios, putting up the world's first television transmitter, making the first-ever transmission and by November 1936 broadcasting regularly.

Anna's longtime friend and neighbor, Poppy Vanda, had conceived the idea of a program on swans. The "presentation" was by Philip Bate. The music was "The Swan of Tuonela," which Finnish composer Jean Sibelius originally intended to be the overture for an opera. The BBC Orchestra, conducted by Hyam Greenbaum, was to play the score to "an original ballet for television."[79] Wendy Toye and Keith Lester were to appear and dancing the headliner on the program was Anna's friend from the 1920s and the Ballets Russes de Monte Carlo, Anton Dolin. Anna, famous for her voice, was to be the offstage narrator.

"The Swan," one of Sibelius's most striking and foreboding works, musically describes the dismal and melancholy setting along the banks of the River of Death (the river Tuonela) where a dwarf searches for the swan he must kill. Given that the dwarf had earlier been hacked into bits by a foe and then been pieced together (though resurrected by his mother's magical energy), the prognosis is naturally dim for the dwarf. The television program was, oddly enough, to be entitled "To the Praise of the Swan."[80] Anna must have enjoyed the prospect of narrating, for it brought out her sense of humor in some extra lines beginning, "Swan, I like thee not / nor any quality you've got."[81]

On August 25, 1939 she signed a contract with the BBC to be at the Alexandra Palace at 7:00 p.m. on September 8 to rehearse. At 10:05 p.m. the show would be broadcast, live, of course, and those people lucky enough to own televisions would see Dolin dance and hear Anna's voice reading extracts, off camera, for the half-hour show. And her eloquence would finally be earning funds—"five guineas, to include copyright in respect of this occasion of own original poem."[82] But the date was ill-fated; the broadcast never took place, though the guineas were paid in full. At Christmastime.

ONE

The Boys and the War
(1939–1942)

nna did, according to her son Jim, admire aspects of Rudyard
Kipling's work. But which aspects of Kipling, a many-faceted
writer, did she admire? A writer often accused of being "the
poet of Empire," he was also the man who wrote in "Epitaphs of the War
(1914–1918)":

> If any question why we died,
> Tell them, because our fathers lied.[1]

Anna had lived through the First World War, lost such friends as T. E.
Hulme, and her own brother-in-law, George Hepburn. She had seen the
maimed and the lame struggle to find a place in a society callous after that
war. She had read the searing poetry of Isaac Rosenberg, killed in action.
Anna's publisher and long-time advocate, Harold Monro, who had himself survived the war, wrote of the dead in "Carrion,"

> It is plain now what you are. Your head has dropped
> Into a furrow. And the lovely curve
> Of your strong leg has wasted and is propped
> Against a ridge of the ploughed land's watery swerve.[2]

Her friend Edgell Rickword, only twenty years old when he had finished fighting in World War I, masked a bayonet's stab in the seemingly mild iambs opening "The Soldier Addresses his Body," with the line, "I shall be mad if you get smashed about."[3] Now he and his wife Johnnie Bach often saw Anna at the Hampstead pubs they all frequented and it was clear they wanted no part of war.

This leads to the question of Anna's attitude toward war. Back in 1934 Anna had written to Natalie Barney mentioning that she had been requested to write songs for the English peace movement, a request she had largely ignored because "I am not sure whether I think peace practicable."[4] For though Anna wrote against injustice in her 1938 league statement, she also had feelings about the near-inevitability of wars. "As much peace as possible" was the slogan of the women's movement to which Anna belonged. Her attitude sprang from her belief that the premise of sacrifice for gain was built into the religion of the Western world:

> What hope for an escape
> from war
> Where agonies and crosses
> are
> Extolled and raised for
> veneration
> The hope of peace is
> vain
> War's increment is pain:
> Pain shown expedient
> in the cross
> Is an excuse for war's
> whole loss.
> Implied essential
> to creation[5]

On September 1, 1939, just as many of the intellectuals Anna admired had been predicting since appeasement, Germany invaded Poland. Then two days later England and France, following the terms of their earlier agreement, together declared war.

George, Anna's youngest son, says that she was not for World War II. Even though his two brothers signed up early to serve, she fought hard to keep him out of the deadly arms of war.

> In the First World War my mother was in a way quite patriotic . . .
> But in the Second World War she wasn't. And the point about it
> was, if we were called up in rotation I would have been the first one
> to be called up. Because I was the absolute right age. I was nineteen
> when the war started. . . . Now my mother had the feeling that I
> was the baby of the family, and I shouldn't be called up. I shouldn't
> go to war.[6]

All through the years George and his "Ma" had never argued the way she and her other sons did. George and Anna had a mutual regard for each other, a sort of understanding, a protectionist stance that extended to and included poetry. And Anna, his mother, might be a terrible housekeeper. Anna the woman might have explosive rows with her friends and try to capsize a party by surly displays of temper. But Anna the poet George had always understood and appreciated. From the time he left for boarding school he had read her work and could recite poems from memory. He saw that the writer of the lines, sometimes in contrast to the woman of flesh and blood, was measured, imaginative, and strong, even when admitting her weaknesses. He puzzled over how his mother could take her own poetry lightly, over what he saw as his mother's irritating and regrettable tendency not to take her own poetry seriously, pushing his brothers' dance act, he thought, when she would have been better advised to champion the merits of her own work. George had heard her magnificent voice carry out across a large hall, overheard the listeners praise his mother.[7] He was proud of his mother's abilities. Likewise, Anna, seeing her youngest son upon the stage in the late 1930s at the Mary Ward Center dancing in a Dick Whittington pantomime to "Hearts of Oak" and "Home Town," wanted nothing more than to encourage her son's talents.[8] War itself, in this case, was the enemy, a foe who would cut off her son's future.

Anna made arrangements to send him into the country. Nora Brawnshaw (Nora Back) was living with Gwyneth, her daughter by Augustus John, on a farm in Little Hautbois, north of Norwich. Anna hoped farm work, a reserve occupation, would keep George out of the service.[9]

When the war began Anna's eldest sons were still in the entertainment business. Then the Germans advanced across Europe and by June 22, 1940, Norway, Belgium, Holland, and finally, France, had fallen. The French defeat, especially, propelled British volunteers to enlist. Jim and John, like their father Patrick in the previous war, took to the skies. By July 19, 1940, Jim, age thirty-two, was in the Royal Air Force Volunteer Reserves. By August 10 he was an Acting Pilot Officer. He was sent to North Africa to do his training as a navigator with a bomber squadron and also trained as pilot and tail gunner.

John, 30, first joined the army, though like Jim, his six-foot-three-inch frame was soon wedged in the small cockpits of R.A.F. fighter aircraft. He enlisted without telling his wife Vicky, an impulsive act that did not help their already deteriorating relationship. She and their child Toni moved in with Anna temporarily.

In June 1940 Anna responded to Stanley Kunitz and Howard Haycraft, who were assembling their monumental *Twentieth Century Authors, A Biographical Dictionary of Modern Literature*:

> I am keeping this house, which adjoins Hampstead Heath, where it has been trenched against parachutists. I am standing behind my son James, who is commissioned to the air force; my son, John, who is an anti-aircraft gunner; and my son George, who is working on a farm.[10]

At the farm, however, George was chafing under his dual status: that of friend and equal who took meals with the family and that of milkman who had to do the chores and drive the slow horse on delivery rounds. It had only been a year or two since he and Gwyneth, his employer's daughter, had danced together in the Christmas pantomime. Now this social imbalance and his unfamiliarity with farm work were upsetting. Anna's plans for George fell through when, without warning, he quit his job and returned to London by train with Keith Lester, a sympathetic dancer friend of Anton Dolin's just ending a performance run at Norwich.

Undeterred, Anna next called on friends in Cambridge who arranged for her son to work in the Chivers Jam factory in nearby Histon. Within only a short time, however, with the need for recruits greater, and fewer and fewer occupations listed as reserve, the Cambridge Recruiting Officer was interviewing George. From factory labor, George found himself in the Royal Army Veterinary Corps caring for the horses, mules, and even camels, that a less-motorized war then required. Though Anna's plan for safe employment in England had not succeeded, it may have been George's brief experience in Little Hautbois that got him into the corps, rather than the front-line infantry.

When in September of 1939 war had been declared, Anna spent the first few months like the rest of London in the so-called Bore War. Every night residents of both the city and the countryside would black out their windows, dim their headlights to slits, and stop for traffic lights reduced to only delicate red crosses. People walked carrying gas masks, shelters went up in back gardens. Air Raid Wardens trained for disaster. Though the theatres were closed and enlisted men and women were training, no action was forthcoming. In "Fitzrovia," Anna's old haunt, pubs and clubs served the lonely, the exuberant, the idle, the frightened, and the gregarious, all those drawn out of their houses or on leave from their bases and looking for companionship and conversation.

Meanwhile, prices rose over 19 percent and wages only 11 percent. Refugees were often muttered against, pacifists and conscientious objectors barely tolerated. The citizenry listened to the radio news broadcasts expecting to hear at any moment news of combat. But nothing happened. This state of affairs went on so long that companies who had moved their personnel out of town brought them back, and many children who had been evacuated to the safety of the countryside successfully begged their parents for a return to London. Then on June 8, 1940, the first bombs fell on the London region. The Croydon airport was hit on August 15; later in August, the East End. On a clear Saturday, September 7, the big blitz began in earnest. The sky over London was a veritable grid for the inexorable movement of hundreds of fighter planes and bombers dropping destruction. That night the Germans returned again. The docks burned like hellfire, while over a hundred unexploded bombs blocked rescue efforts, and water supplies proved insufficient to fight the flames. More than 430 people died. Then night after night, day after day, the bombing, the casualties and the psychological toll continued. All around London fires burned. Bomb craters gave off a sickening stench. Though improvements in R.A.F. defense after a few weeks forced the Germans out of the daylight skies, the nights were given over to screaming sirens. The German raiders kept up this continuous attack until November 13, 1940. In that time

27,500 high explosive bombs, countless incendiaries and others explosives and mines had rained down on the streets and buildings of London. A change of German tactics for the next month and one-half meant that the blitz spread beyond London, and the capital slept again under mostly quiet skies. But on Sunday, December 29, 1940, an unprepared and resting city "endured its most severe test of the war so far, the great fire raid."[11] Fifteen hundred blazes lit the skyline, by far the most in the city of London since its trial by fire centuries before. On the "Last day of 1940" Anna wrote a puzzling poem of the same title. "When the command / Is traitor to the hand / And all goes ill / Since Subtlety is lost [?] / For an offence of Will."[12] This otherwise rather obscure poem is magnetized by its date of composition, coming as it does at the close of such a nightmarish stretch. If it was her will to be strong that failed, she had some company. For each story reported by Mass Observers of a Londoner laughing away the raids there seems another story of uncontrollable trembling or weeping against a ruined wall.

Six months before, at the conclusion of Anna's above-mentioned letter to editors Kunitz and Haycraft she had written, "As soon as I have time, I hope to put up a record in English poetry, equal to what will be the Allied victory in arms." In fact, however, although her will may have been to write a triumphant opus, a work that in tone would be quite at odds with the gut-wrenching bleakness of her last long work, "Life Story," it is possible that her hand was traitorous, and would not respond. This interpretation, of course, is almost purely speculation. But she did not produce much work during this time. Elizabeth Bowen, who most critics agree has best captured the tenor of wartime London, has a phrase in her novel *The Heat of the Day*: "Everyday the news hammered one more nail into a consciousness, which no longer resounded."[13] It is possible that this was also true for Anna: the subject of war was now too close to home and too difficult to bear.

The war went on with months of quiet interspersed with three nights of even deadlier raids. The screaming sounds of the JU88 dive-bombers on April 16 and 19 were followed by the most intense and lethal bombing of the war on May 10, 1940. 1,436 were killed.[14]

Psychiatric clinics had been set up to deal with neuroses arising from the bombing. They were, however, almost unused. During the blitz, "the number of patients attending hospital with neurotic illnesses declined . . . there were fewer suicides, drunkenness was halved."[15] Lack of sleep was evident on the faces of so many, and tempers easily frayed. But, as has so often been noted, the Londoners had been expected to hold firm, and for the most part, they did.[16] Morale might fluctuate, then and later, between an "active" and "passive" state, but Londoners had a will to prevail not only over their outward enemies but over their own fears.[17]

Anna did not keep herself a prisoner at home. Carrying a big shopping basket, since goods were no longer wrapped at the shops and almost all shop deliveries had been discontinued, she took to walking to market down the middle of the street rather than on the hazardous sidewalks.[18] In her dark, shapeless coat and hat, her tall frame now somewhat crow-like at the shoulders, she was a familiar figure, declaiming poetry at a time when not much poetry was to be heard.

Staying at Home (1943–1945)

Gradually the face of London changed for fifty-nine-year-old Anna as her circle of family and friends was dispersed by the war. Those fighting had to go where they were sent. Sons Jim, with a commission in the R.A.F., and George, now part of the Royal Army Veterinary Corp, were stationed out of the country, while John (in a Royal Artillery career with many surprising twists and turns), trained in Canada, wore R.A.F. wings on his tunic, and by 1942 would earn the Military Cross. Anna's grandchild Toni would soon board a train to York, the old walled city with the stumpy outlines and soaring remnants of a ruined abbey. Like many other children she was sent to the relative safety of the countryside to wait out the bombing.

Not only children decamped to the country. Eliot Bliss, the longtime friend Anna could usually count on, had gone to Essex with Patricia Allen-Burns where the two would remain even after the war.[1] Anna's aunt Norah Harper Anglin and her husband James, the man who'd cried when Anna sang Schubert so beautifully, both went to a cottage in Buckinghamshire where Norah died before the war was over. Some old friends, such as Griffin Barry, were caught in, or fled to, other countries. Barry had gone to the U. S. and couldn't return until after the war. Natalie Barney and

Romaine Brooks, who'd gone from France to Florence, Italy, in May, 1940, stayed there until May 1946. Anna lived out the war years in London. With no. 68 Parliament Hill only steps away from the open expanse of Hampstead Heath, trenched against the possibility of German attack, many people told her to go, that she didn't have to stay. Yet she did stay, for as her son Jim explained:

> But she was definitely here because this was the place she was going to be and the German Air Force was not going to move *her*. . . . Quite seriously, that was her contribution, you see. *They shall not be moved*, you know.[2]

She had lived through one war already; now the restrictions of a second war fell chillingly into place. Each person was issued an identity card to be presented upon demand of the authorities. Petrol and soap were rationed. Food rationing had begun on January 8, 1940.

After June 1941, clothing could be purchased only with ration coupons and coupon day meant people lining up outside the clothing shops waiting to get in. If you lost your coupons or needed extra because of causes outside your control, the red tape and waiting were enervating. One woman whose laundry lost her only nightgown went three times to stand in line and each time gave up after forty minutes when she had to return to work. The basic allowance was sixty-six coupons per year. A new dress would cost eleven coupons; a utility tweed suit and blouse twenty-three coupons. A short coat required fewer coupons than a long, lined coat. "Make do and mend" booklets and posters exhorted citizens to do their part. Anna, whose attention to appearance had gradually diminished after Patrick's death, became even shabbier in her person. Her coat went through season after season. (Even after the war was over this rationing continued; just before her death in 1947, Anna lost her clothing coupons. It was a loss that her family felt made her desperate.)

The whole consumer mentality of the country was re-gearing itself to scrimp, save, and extend precious stores. "Dig for Victory" campaign posters urged saving "Vital Shipping Space" by growing more food at home. Waste paper, metal, and textiles were salvaged. Bones were used to make fertilizer, scrap foodstuffs saved for pig and poultry feed. People were urged to switch off lights and save electricity, while black-out boards and curtains, and traffic lights covered to three crosses made the city dark and alien. People were urged to carry their gas masks. The sirens screamed and the night bombing continued. By the war's end, there would be 2,155 nights of blackout.[3]

Even the daylight was unsafe, for with the German development of a new rocket, quiet unmanned low-flying bombs sailed in to wreak their destruction, so that one of Anna's neighbors recalls standing at the crest of Parliament Hill and seeing one fly past, in front of and under her line of vision. From June 12, 1944 to the end of March, 1945, Britain was under heavy attack by the V1 (flying bombs known as doodlebugs or buzz-bombs) and the V2. In June and July of 1944 general morale was reported to be at its lowest. The first V2 rockets exploded in London on September 8, 1944. They arrived, each "unseen and unheard delivering nearly a ton of high explosive at a speed of 3,500 feet per second." A little over a month later, when Hitler ordered a V2 campaign to center on Britain and Belgium, London alone was hit with more than 500 of the rockets. There was no effective defense against these. By the end of the war 60,000 British civilians had been killed by German bombs.[4]

But ordinary life went on in the great city. People did go out to the cinema and theatres when they reopened, and worked and planned for a future whose boundaries and opportunities could only be guessed. And at least according to some who remember those days, it was a time of generosity and of compassion.

Anna knitted. From the making of the big square shawls she had knitted for the birth of each one of her sons, to the red socks she had made for the umpire at Wimbledon, this was one thing that she had done throughout her adult life. Now she would knit for the war. Not that she made a pious sacrifice of it. Her lines, "Picture me sitting, drunken with knitting," that she sent Natalie Barney in 1928 acknowledge the mix of pleasure and duty in the tedious work.[5] And for Anna, knitting, unlike writing poetry, was not a guilt-producing activity because the end product was practical. In a much earlier poem she had once mused,

> I always used to worry rather
> And think that for a girl it might be waste of time
> to spend her life and love in making rhyme;
> And I thought maybe
> I should be better, knitting for my baby.[6]

Knitting and darning now took center stage. Anna could talk and darn, and knit and walk, as observers testify; and in a time of severe shortage, her skills came in handy. Hester Henrietta Crouse, nicknamed Hetta, later remembered that Anna knitted her "a pair of multi-colored stockings— wonderful, so warm—stockings that went right up to my thighs."[7]

People were hungry for demonstrations of kindness and companionship. In what would later be dubbed "Fitzrovia," they gathered. During the war alcohol was hard to obtain and expensive; less entertaining was done at home. The Fitzroy Tavern (formerly Kleinfeldt's), and the so-called French pub (The York Minster) both received visits from Anna. The Wheatsheaf, a Younger's Scotch Ale house on Rathbone Place with Guinness as staple for the clientele had become a very popular place. "Red" Redvers, his unmarried sister Mona, and his tweed-clad wife Frances ran the cheerful well-lit bar, which boasted scarlet linoleum on the floor and Scottish tartans on the walls. There Anna also met up with her friends, though Julian Maclaren-Ross reports that at least one regular customer, a Mrs. Stewart, could not stand either "Dylan Thomas or the poetess Anna Wickham . . . at any price."[8] While Mrs. Stewart daily filled in her crossword puzzles beginning promptly at six, Maclaren-Ross does not record what Anna Wickham might have been doing that so provoked the elderly lady dressed in black silk.

Service members on leaves pending post, the BBC writers and broadcasters who worked through the war years, the older artists and writers who were regular customers, all met in the pubs of Fitzrovia, and as they became used to the raids, often awaited the all-clear in those same pubs instead of in the crowded shelters and tube stations. In the time of the blitz, at least, meeting under these feelings of shared danger and hardship had often forged a pleasing closeness. But as time went on in this "heart of Bohemian London," for certain individuals "meeting and talking and drinking" began to "take the place of achievement."[9]

Of course, the coming of war itself had already altered the larger poetic and artistic community. Some, like the poet W. H. Auden, had gone to the United States before the war. One old friend of Anna's, the painter Mark Gertler, had committed suicide on June 22, 1939. Virginia Woolf, in mental anguish, died in 1941 by walking into the River Ouse with her pockets laden with stones.

Yet even in the midst of war there was poetic activity in Fitzrovia, and Anna Wickham was there, even if her works were not often published.

Poetry London, the leading poetry magazine of the time, was edited by Tambimuttu, a wily and inspiring frequenter of Fitzrovia since his arrival from Ceylon in 1938. Tambimuttu published works by Anna's friend Lawrence Durrell as well as writers associated with or admired by The New Apocalypse who were then running up their flag of wild, often surrealistic images. On the opposite end of the spectrum was the Cambridge periodical *Scrutiny*, which had had a variety of editors since its beginnings but was dominated by F. R. Leavis. The radical Edgell Rickword, Anna's friend and an early model for Leavis, had edited *Scrutiny* from 1928 to 1932; his poems appeared in the magazine. And though paper was restricted, certain firms had access to supplies, and books were published during the war. Faber and Faber, for example, had large quantities of paper at their disposal. Walter de la Mare's 1943 Faber anthology, *Love*, used a fragment from Anna's "Song of Ophelia the Survivor," in the section "Grace and Beauty":

> One look from you taught me so much of love,
> I have all pleasure, just to watch you move.

If Anna was not writing much new poetry, her old works had not been forgotten. William Empson, who had altered the direction of literary criticism with his 1930s *Seven Types of Ambiguity*, "admired her poetry and he was very intolerant normally."[10] To him and to others Anna was a figure whose hard-hitting poetry and equally formidable presence had made her somewhat of a legend in artistic circles near and far.

In 1940, a Cunard liner pressed into war service took George Hepburn's unit swiftly and without escort to Durban. They changed ships and continued around the Cape of Good Hope. From then on, Anna's youngest son was stationed in the Middle East. There the Ninth Army, stationed in Palestine and Syria, awaited Hitler's pincer movement—which never came—while the Eighth Army fought in the desert. By August 1942, the Germans were checked in Egypt; in October and November Montgomery won over Rommel at El Alamein. The tide was turning in favor of the British.[11] When George's unit went to Egypt for about a year in 1943 or 1944 he found a veritable Fitzrovian reunion. Many of the men George had met when visiting the Charlotte Street pubs and clubs with Anna in the 1930s were now in Cairo. The Scots poet George S. Fraser, another of the New Apocalypse writers, was there, as were John Waller, Lawrence Durrell, and John Gawsworth, then of course in his

Air Force identity of Sergeant Terence Ian Fytton Armstrong.[12] They welcomed George, the poet's son who carried a manuscript of his mother's work with him, for most of them knew and admired Anna's work.[13]

Cairo was hot literary territory. No less than three little magazines were published there as well as an anthology of poetry written by those serving in the forces. Confounding his critics, who had told Durrell in 1938, "Gawsworth is drinking himself into D.T.'s. He'll be dead before he has time to sue you over your new novel," John Gawsworth was very much alive.[14] Anna had always called Gawsworth "a likeable rogue." In an even archer mood she had once said that if he were in prison he would undoubtedly publish a prison magazine. Gawsworth in fact had begun publishing *Salamander* in Cairo and later counted among his credits the post of "London President of the Cairene Salamander Society of Poets."

John, for his 1942 Military Cross, and Jim, who had earned the Distinguished Flying Cross in 1943, were to be decorated at a Buckingham Palace ceremony honoring war service. People close to Anna, those who knew her disdain of bathing and dressing up were worried. Never one to waste precious rationed soap or water, also in short supply since the six-months' drought, "I'll just go," she told her apprehensive friends, "the way I am." Actress Beatrice Lillie wanted to buy her a suit of clothes from Selfridge's, an elegant store on Oxford Street, for the ceremony. Anna's acrid response was her poem containing the line, "I'd rather death than be your pensioner. . . ." In the end, she did put in her ill-fitting and uncomfortable set of false teeth, take a bath, and wear some borrowed clothes. May Lawrence, a young woman who deeply admired her work and life, accompanied her to Buckingham Palace with granddaughter Toni, down from Heslington for the awarding of decorations. The event was filmed and shown soon the Everyman Theatre in Hampstead. A young Harper relative who went especially to see the film footage was so dismayed by Anna's appearance that he remembers feeling ashamed when he had hoped to be proud.[15]

Anna at this time seems to have produced one of two reactions in people. Some saw a generous, inquisitive, hospitable, and unique woman. Others saw a slightly menacing, physically intimidating, even distasteful, giantess.

Those in the first group remember not only Anna's kindnesses but the other major thing she did to keep things going during the war: she stayed at home. There might be little to eat there, the surroundings might be absolutely filthy (she had become "a dead loss" as a housekeeper, said son George), but she still had people in for cups of tea and conversation. She could keep up the old hectoring and curious and judgmental stance that some found so irresistible and some found so terrifying. And she could also be simply hospitable and stimulating to the intellect.

Hetta Crouse, the beautiful South African sculptor and an admirer of communism by then married to William Empson, broadcast over the BBC in her native Afrikaans language and also drove an ambulance during the London blitz.[16] She got to know Anna and then called on her. During the visit Hetta appreciated Anna's "little treasures . . . little stones or pebbles or glass beads in a bowl." Anna in turn wrote a poem for her and later, when fortune smiled in the shape of a pineapple in wartime, Anna took this splendid gift from her sons in Egypt and shared the hard-to-get fruit with Hetta at her BBC post. When the Empsons' son wanted to buy an expensive python, Anna made Hetta laugh by commenting, "Keep your money under the mattress and buy a goat." Hetta's free and easy spirit attracted Anna, and Hetta, for her part, admired Anna and disdained to notice what other people criticized: "Yes Anna looked kind of rough, but nobody cared!"

Oswell Blakeston, the writer afraid of her straight left punch, thought there was no one like Anna, whom he called "Olympian by nature." He knew she appreciated the irregular, the unusual, and the interesting. "So I saved things up to tell her, how I'd seen a drunk held at the edge of the table on the rim of his bowler hat, and how the editor of a socialist review had taken on holiday 'little things to eat, little things to read and little things to play with.'"[17] He allowed that it was "always a risk to introduce a friend to Anna," for you never knew if she would take to the person or be devastatingly, "crushingly," rude. Mary Butts had told Oswell of Anna's legendary beauty, but about this time Anna might appear with her shawl "skewered" together (in her practical fashion) by a knitting needle.

Anna's Harper cousin Peggy Chesters likewise remarked on Anna's dual nature and effect:

> I remember she would suddenly arrive at our house with a lobster and a bottle of wine and delight us with her company, or she would come and sit all day hunched up in a chair not removing her hat or coat and shed crumbs and ash all around, and talk, and give us an enlightened way of thinking. When she went we felt mentally nourished and physically like a piece of chewed string![18]

From time to time friends of Jim or John would appear at Anna's door. One, a gunner subaltern named Peter S. Edwards remembered Anna as "a woman of very wide interests indeed and of a very powerful and brilliant personality, but overshadowing this was her charm and kindness."[19] When Edwards and his friend dropped in they found Anna "building a wall, herself, in the garden and show[ing] a tremendous knowledge of the various brick bonds." Anna pulled on a pair of her hand-knit woolen stockings [khaki this time, and "with enormous holes in the heels"] and took the soldiers off to tea at Muriel Lilly's house, and from there to a pub. As they pushed open the door of the pub Anna topped off their conversation about what was "natural," by saying in a commanding voice that engaged even those at the bar, "Have you ever considered how unnatural it is to eat an egg?"

And of course there were always those eager for Anna's advice on their poetry and ready for a good conversation, as Raymond Marriott wrote in 1943 from his freezing rooms in Maida Vale, "Are you likely to be in the Swiss [a Soho pub] on, say, Saturday evening?" A warm pub and "a good talk with you" were things that a writer recently returned to London looked forward to.[20]

Granddaughter Toni also came to London occasionally, riding on trains with American servicemen kindly passing out sticks of gum to little girls traveling alone. At Anna's she was fascinated by the china cow on the fine Broadwood grand piano still in the "practice room" and by the huge barrage balloon floating above the Heath. But Anna (as Toni was told to call her) was an austere figure to the child. When Anna came to York to visit, Toni kept her eyes down as they walked, vaguely embarrassed by this grandmother clad in dark clothing who knitted as they walked through the stalls of the marketplace.[21] There seemed no question of Toni staying with Anna. At the country cottage there was a big vegetable plot. Percy the gardener taught her to say the alphabet backward and she made friends with Mucky Maggy, the resident duck. The country was better for a child, in terms of tenderness, stability, and safety.

By the war's end 80,000 buildings had been bombed. Tavistock Square, the first home for Anna and Patrick, was bombed and then razed. Patrick's old office at Bird-in-Hand Court, along with a good deal of the city of London, was destroyed by bombs and fire. Near the gates of Mecklenburgh Square, where she and Patrick had first kissed, an entire area was demolished. Brooke House, the asylum where she spent the summer of 1913, was bombed beyond repair. Hampstead had suffered bombing, but landmarks Anna knew were still intact. Her first Hampstead home at 49 Downshire Hill stood undamaged. The building at the top of Haverstock Hill that had once been her grandfather Harper's music shop escaped injury. Anna's house at 68 Parliament Hill, from its original proud standing as a "villa" with a far-reaching view, with a quite grand two-story entrance hall, a separate room for breakfast, a dining room with beautiful proportions, and a spacious bath that had once fired Dylan Thomas's imagination, had not only been portioned out into rented rooms but had slipped into disrepair. The vagaries of war appeared to have spared it but, with no money, time, or materials for repairs, like much of the housing in London it was much the worse for wear.

When George Hepburn walked up the hill, home from the war after five years away, he found a sad welcome. He entered no. 68 and was dismayed by what he saw. Dry rot had eaten away at the very supports of the house. The kitchen was filthy and the house's rooms, all once the province of Anna, Patrick, and the four boys, were many of them now parceled out to strangers who had found refuge when they discovered themselves displaced or bombed out. People were crowded together and making do, not always smoothly. Anna dubbed one of her tenants "Flatfoot," for obvious reasons, and found two other tenants manipulating for the continuation of a cheap roof overhead.

The stalwart red brick exterior of 68 Parliament Hill concealed common conditions: poverty, claustrophobic quarters, extended sacrifice, and continued belt-tightening. But the war was over. When Churchill stood down, a surprising socialist victory in July of 1945 promised to bring about the kinds of changes Anna and her father had so long ago hoped for: a dream of equality where England's social class system, weakened during the war, would perhaps become a thing of the past and the humiliations and inequities it fostered would be gone forever. And all of Anna's sons might soon be welcomed home.

"The astringency of wisdom" (1946–1947)¹

On the 30th of April, 1947, Wednesday, a spring day after the worst winter in recent memory, Anna told George to go out. She was in a good, possibly great mood, and George thought she might be in a writing frame of mind. He went out, later in the day continuing to the Polytechnic for a French class he was taking.²

When he let himself back in it was nearly night and he stopped in at her improvised bedroom, what in other days had been the breakfast room, basement level of 68 Parliament Hill. When he did not see her on the camp bed where she slept he thought with pleasure that she had gone to the Fitzroy—a good sign, since there she met friends and had a good time. But when he turned, he saw that his mother had hanged herself from the frame of the full-length French windows. He rushed upstairs to the phone, answered the kind policeman's questions, and went out into the street, moaning, others said howling, at the top of his voice.

An inquest was held, and a customary verdict ("while of unsound mind") delivered.[3] Son John Hepburn made the arrangements for a coffin of English oak. On May 6, the Vicar of St. John's, the Hampstead Parish church, Church Row, officiated at a funeral service attended by a few people. Anna's body was buried in the church's cemetery, one day before her sixty-fourth birthday.

A nna's physical health prior to her death was, for her, normal. She was always troubled by her lungs and had been again in 1947. She had unspecified "heart trouble" in 1946 but that was thought to be something that "will pass."[4] Her vision was still good; she had in the last year undertaken to read the entire twelve-volume, 6,000-page *Journal of John Wesley*; "pray for me," she wrote the irreligious Natalie.[5] She got out, would walk to join a few old friends for lunch (though sometimes she stopped on the curb to rest), or she would sit at the top of the Hill interrogating, as usual, those who interested her. She went to concerts, was still writing, and took tea or went to a pub with new young friends who liked her poetry and admired her inimitable brand of conversation. (One of those new friends was Margaret Telfer, nee Hope, who would meet and later marry Anna's son Jim; Margaret and her two-year-old daughter Alison found great pleasure in Anna's company.) In April, Anna met with John Gawsworth, a date he recorded in his book.

In cases of suicide, mood and personality disorders are often underlying factors. Opinion was, and is, divided about the state of Anna's mind.[6] A lodger at no. 68 said that Anna could sometimes be found "sitting on the pavement . . . in a kind of daze." A Hampstead neighbor, then a teenager, regarded Anna as "eccentric" when the war started but gradually veering toward madness. John Rodker came to the "very sympathetic" conclusion that she was suffering a "decline," after he witnessed a party where Anna dumped a bowl of soup over someone's head, possibly her own. John Hepburn had once years before accused her of being "paranoid" (for which Anna had knocked him flat on the floor). Sid Fig, a bartender at one of the Hampstead pubs, was still physically afraid of her, even in the 1940s when she was no longer young or powerful. Others had terminated their associations with her even years before for the same reason. Some people felt witchcraft was just one of Anna's "natural talents" and that one girl "tried to cut her throat as a result of a curse [uttered by Anna]."[7] Some of Anna's own journal entries from the late 1930s admit fear of another "break" like that which had precipitated her first suicide attempt. Some of her poems, especially after the mid-1920s, contained violent images. John Davenport, who had known Anna since the 1930s and called her "wickedly good," wrote the news of her death to Malcolm Lowry saying, "Deeps as well as danks & darks she had."[8]

Jim Hepburn, however, felt there was "no recognizable warning" in Anna's behavior. In April 1947, finished with his service on the Berlin Airlift, he had taken off with a crew on the second-ever east to west flight around the world. He returned a week after Anna's funeral, not knowing that she had died. Other friends saw in her only the willfully individualistic behavior she had always shown and they had always admired. Son John, who had once talked during the war of killing himself, seems to have felt uneasy. In the midst of an argument at one point in the past when she had threatened suicide, he told her he didn't give a damn if she did. She had said to him, "I have an assignation with my son George [still overseas] which I intend to keep." George Hepburn thought Anna's behavior had remained unchanged—that she was the same woman he had left on shipping out to the war. But that morning Anna's agreeable behavior may have been the standard ploy used by people intent on killing themselves, a deliberate plan of the kind that will, as Dr. Kay Redfield Jamison describes it, "secure the circumstances that will allow them to commit suicide."[9]

Most friends and neighbors were shocked. "Horrific," was one way the event was described. Many thought that Anna's allowing her twenty-seven-year-old son George to find her was the cruelest thing. She had even blocked the window with a screen so that no one else could see her from the outside and stop her, or find her.

When George came back to the house the morning after Anna's death he found a poem Anna had written. Eliot Bliss was asked, "Can you bear to read this," when she came to London as soon as she heard the news:

> I hung myself
> I was unconscious on the floor
> The rope slipped
> There'll be no hanging more.
> I've not strength to take my life
> By rope or bane or knife—
> I am iced in with terror
> At the sure doom
> Of my long pride and error.[10]

Eliot Bliss knew that Anna had already, on occasion, thought of taking her own life.[11] There were still people around who remembered her suicide attempt almost two decades before. Anyone who had read her "Life Story," would have known of her thoughts of suicidal death—but who had read it? The pub-goers who had heard her recite "Tribute to the Nursing Staff" when she once released herself prematurely from a hospital stay probably just thought, "That Anna!" But "Tribute to the Nursing Staff" gives a hint of the strong will that Anna brought to so much that she did:

> Let me die unafraid
> Beyond the reach of aid.
> Let me lie proudly dead
> Where no efficient smooths my bed—
> A lion in the wilderness
> In all my lovely loneliness,
> Unsoiled by science or the least
> Contamination of the priest.[12]

Just in the last year Anna had seen renewed interest in her work, not in most academic circles (a future professor had come to trade poetic knowledge and faintly praised her "vigor") but in the popular media. On April 27, 1946, the *Picture Post*, an illustrated weekly British equivalent of *Life* magazine with a huge circulation, devoted three pages to the "Great She," "a poet of a flavour which you won't find anywhere else."[13] She made great copy, with her history of "creative moods disrespected by the tyranny of the kitchen range, and the dictatorship of the darning needle." The house was "the battlefield," the "pots and pans still hang around, in gangs, at the scene of their crime." The main point of the article was that she was a free woman "abroad on the earth." "People stare? Of course, people stare."

The photographs, taken with Anna's gregarious, poetry-quoting friend May Lawrence and a new acquaintance, David Holbrook, show the poet center stage in a variety of settings.[14] Her kitchen was pictured just as many people who stopped for a visit found it: "*furry* with filth."[15] In a photograph lacking only the cough to show her years of allegiance to smoking, she sits pensively on a chair, a plume of white rising from her cigarette, her fingers not the cleanest. Pictured by the side of the road munching a bun, or looking delightedly around the trunk of a venerable cherry tree, "free" and "sovereign" do describe her. A joyful face, really, but also one, as the author of the article described it, "corrugated by the astringency of wisdom."

Fan mail came from people she had not seen for twenty years and from people she had never met, from Yorkshire to New Zealand. They seemed to take to heart the ending of the article, "I count Anna Wickham as a blessing, and . . . I would have you meet her." They sent books, poems, Samarkand figs, tinned meat, and requests for poetic opinions; Anna wrote back, at least to some. For one budding industrialist, Leslie Marr, reading about Anna and then meeting her son John (who was by then studying Mandarin Chinese at the School of Oriental Studies) convinced him to pursue his own artistic vision and become a painter. Only one person wrote the *Picture Post* in a dudgeon about the kitchen: "If this means 'poetry,' for heaven's sake," wrote the Rev. H. G. Wilks, "let's scrap it and go in for a tidy kitchen and consequently decent grub."[16]

Maybe all the fuss helped to convince her that she had not, as she wrote son Jim, "lost her beauty" and become "a grotesque."[17] She wrote Lionel Birch, the author of the piece, "Your article has done more for my lungs than Switzerland."[18] About once every decade people had been "discovering" her: Harold Monro in the 'teens, Louis Untermeyer and Natalie Barney in the 1920s, John Gawsworth in the 1930s; now she was back in the news, just about on schedule. The applause that met her in 1946 when she walked into a literary party attended by the likes of T. S. Eliot "amused" her, but better was the Empsons' guest who kissed her hand and called her "the most vital and interesting woman in the room."[19] It was even better than the attention she attracted walking into a pub in her Wellington boots, one pajama leg sticking out from under a greatcoat.[20]

Epilogue

In spending I have been most mad,
Giving of all good things I had.
Now that I have lost my treasure
I have great grief in fullest measure.
Yet if I spent, I had my spending;
And even grief must have an ending.[1]

A Selection of Poems

THE FIRED POT

In our town, people live in rows.
The only irregular thing in a street is the steeple;
And where that points to, God only knows,
And not the poor disciplined people!

And I have watched the women growing old,
Passionate about pins, and pence, and soap,
Till the heart within my wedded breast grew cold.
And I lost hope.

But a young soldier came to our town,
He spoke his mind most candidly.
He asked me quickly to lie down,
And that was very good for me.
For though I gave him no embrace—
Remembering my duty—
He altered the expression of my face,
And gave me back my beauty.

INSPIRATION

I tried to build perfection with my hands
  And failed.
Then with my will's most strict commands
  And naught availed.
What shall he gain but some poor miser's pelf,
Who thinks for ever of his silly self?
Then to the stars I flung my trust,
Scorning the menace of my coward dust;
Freed from my little will's control
To a good purpose marched my soul;
In nameless, shapeless God found I my rest,
Tho' for my solace I built God a breast.

NERVOUS PROSTRATION

I married a man of the Croydon class
When I was twenty-two.
And I vex him, and he bores me
Till we don't know what to do!
It isn't good form in the Croydon class
To say you love your wife,
So I spend my days with the tradesmen's books
And pray for the end of life.

In green fields are blossoming trees
And a golden wealth of gorse,
And young birds sing for joy of worms:
It's perfectly clear, of course,
That it wouldn't be taste in the Croydon class
To sing over dinner or tea:
But I sometimes wish the gentleman
Would turn and talk to me!

But every man of the Croydon class
Lives in terror of joy and speech.
"Words are betrayers," "Joys are brief"—
The maxims their wise ones teach—
And for all my labour of love and life
I shall be clothed and fed,
And they'll give me an orderly funeral
When I'm still enough to be dead.

I married a man of the Croydon class
When I was twenty-two.
And I vex him, and he bores me
Till we don't know what to do!
And as I sit in his ordered house,
I feel I must sob or shriek,
To force a man of the Croydon class
To live, or to love, or to speak!

ENVOI

God, thou great symmetry
Who put a biting lust in me
    From whence my sorrows spring,
For all the frittered days
That I have spent in shapeless ways,
    Give me one perfect thing.

THE SHOW

I am no man's love,
But a lonely devil
Tossing the balls of good and evil;
Slogging the air:
A mime at a fair!

I am no man's love,
But a bearded wench
Lolling in a booth on a scarlet bench,
Where yokels come to grin, and see
What I be!

I am no man's love,
But a five-legged calf;
And I am penned to raise a laugh;
And now and then I try to run—
And that's the fun.

Meditation at Kew

Alas! for all the pretty women who marry dull men,
Go into the suburbs and never come out again,
Who lose their pretty faces and dim their pretty eyes,
Because no one has skill or courage to organize.

What do these pretty women suffer when they marry?
They bear a boy who is like Uncle Harry,
A girl who is like Aunt Eliza, and not new,
These old dull races must breed true.

I would enclose a common in the sun,
And let the young wives out to laugh and run;
I would steal their dull clothes and go away,
And leave the pretty naked things to play.

Then I would make a contract with hard Fate
That they see all the men in the world and choose a mate,
And I would summon all the pipers in the town
That they dance with Love at a feast, and dance him down.

From the gay unions of choice
We'd have a race of splendid beauty and of thrilling voice.
The World whips frank, gay love with rods,
But frankly gaily shall we get the gods.

THE AVENUE

To the tired traveler in summer's heat,
The thought of airy trees is sweet.
Come, in my straight, stretched arms discover
A leafy road, thou weary Lover.

MARE BRED FROM PEGASUS

For God's sake, stand off from me:
There's a brood mare here going to kick like hell
With a mad up-rising energy;
And where the wreck will end who'll tell?
She'll splinter the stable and eat a groom.
For God's sake, give me room;
Give my will room.

"Make Beauty for me!"—that was what you said,
While I was cowering at your dying fire,
Laconic, blowing at your chill desire.
Then flame broke out in me to char you dead;
A fierce hope and a more fierce distrust
To char your bones to dust.

My pretty jockey, you've the weight
To be a rider, but not my mate;
And yet your spirit's bold to impregnate,
And I'm a lashing, butting hate.

Since my poor life began
I had desire to serve my man
With all my wit, all imagination,
And every subtle beauty of creation;
And you come late,
And mock me in my masterless hard state.

"Make Beauty for me!"—that was what you said,
Desire rose up in me to strike you dead,
With that mad mare my will
To lash and smash her fill.

Run, run, and hide you in some women's heart,
In a retreat I cannot kick apart!

Sung in a Grave-yard

O I'm a professional wife,
Tra la la
And I'm bound to the trade for my life,
Tra la la.
I hate to be slack
And I hope I'm not wrong,
But I find business hours most unbearably long,
As a thorough professional wife,
Tra la la.

I think in these organised days
They might run my poor job in relays;
I can work very well in the light,
But I'm tired of the business at night.
Although a professional wife,
Tra la la.

I'd carry a card-case and own a man's name,
I'd manage a house and take wage for the same;
But to bear a man's children and share a man's bed,
Should never be paid for in boots or in bread,
If a wench has the heart of a wife.
Tra la la!

Return of Pleasure

I thought there was no pleasure in the world
Because of my fears.
Then I remembered life and all the words in my language.
And I had courage even to despise form.
I thought, "I have skill to make words dance,
To clap hands and to shake feet,
But I will put myself, and everything I see, upon the page.
Why should I reject words because of their genealogy?
Or things, because of their association?
Why should I scorn a bus rather than a ship?

FEAR OF HUMOUR

When I mock beauty with burlesque,
With poor, impertinent grotesque,
I'm afraid.
But how else were desire allayed
And all my hunger stayed?
Love touched my backbone with his fist,
And laid her fingers on my wrist.
Yet all my body is unfed,
And I mock beauty, or lie dead.

A LOVE LETTER

You have given me some quality of the male,
While I have given you some qualities of myself.
You are the father of my action,
While I have begotten in you new courage.
Maybe we are completed by love,
So that we are beyond sex.
We have found the miraculous unity,
To which existence itself implies increase.

I do not grieve away my days
Because you are gone from me,
My mind is stimulated forever by the idea of you,
I do not ask that your love should be faithful to my body,
It is impossible that your soul should be faithless to my soul.

It is well I cannot eat with you all my days,
I would not take my soup from a consecrated cup.
I have before me a wealth of happy moments when I shall
    see you.
They are like holy wafers, which I will eat,
For stimulation, for absolution, and for my eternal hope.

I ask nothing of you, not even that you live,
If you die, I remember you
Till the blood in my wrists is cold.

DOMESTIC ECONOMY

I will have few cooking-pots,
They shall be bright,
They shall reflect to blinding
God's straight light.
I will have four garments,
They shall be clean,
My service shall be good,
Though my diet be mean.
Then I shall have excess to give the poor,
And right to counsel beggars at my door.

THE CHERRY-BLOSSOM WAND

(To be sung)

I will pluck from my tree a cherry-blossom wand,
And carry it in my merciless hand,
So I will drive you, so bewitch your eyes,
With a beautiful thing that can never grow wise.

Light are the petals that fall from the bough,
And lighter the love that I offer you now;
In a spring day shall the tale be told
Of the beautiful things that will never grow old.

The blossoms shall fall in the night wind,
And I will leave you so, to be kind:
Eternal in beauty are short-lived flowers,
Eternal in beauty, these exquisite hours.

I will pluck from my tree a cherry-blossom wand,
And carry it in my merciless hand,
So I will drive you, so bewitch your eyes,
With a beautiful thing that shall never grow wise.

Abbreviations

Addt'l   "Additional Manuscript" designation. BL.

AW   Anna Wickham.

BL   British Library and Manuscript Room, London, England.

UCLA   Special Collections of the University Research Library, University of California, Los Angeles.

HRHRC   The Harry Ransom Humanities Research Center, The University of Texas at Austin, Austin, Texas.

JD   Fonds Littéraire Jacques Doucet, Bibliothèque Ste. Geneviève, Paris.

LILLY   Manuscripts/Lilly Library, Indiana University, Bloomington, Indiana.

NCB   Natalie Clifford Barney.

Reading   The Library, University of Reading, Reading, England.

SUNY/B   Poetry/Rare Books Collections of University at Buffalo, State University of New York, Buffalo, New York.

SIU   Special Collections, Morris Library, Southern Illinois University, Carbondale, Illinois.

UCHGO   Special Collections, The Joseph Regenstein Library, The University of Chicago.

WAW   *The Writings of Anna Wickham, Free Woman and Poet.* Edited and Introduced by R. D. Smith. With a Preface by James Hepburn. (London: Virago, 1984).

Notes

NOTES CHAPTER ONE
(Wimbledon, and Then the Sea)

1. *The Writings of Anna Wickham, Free Woman and Poet.* Edited and Introduced by R. D. Smith. With a preface by James Hepburn. (London: Virago, 1984), p. 78. This includes 106 pages of autobiography which had never before been published. Subsequent quotation references will indicate the abbreviation WAW and the appropriate page number(s). References to Anna Wickham poems will give their WAW page number, even if they were first published in an earlier volume of poetry.

2. Christopher Wade's *Hampstead Past: A Visual History of Hampstead* (London: Historical Publications, Ltd., 1989) provides a vibrant portrait of the community in which Anna Wickham would live from 1909 until her death in 1947.

3. WAW, pp. 54–63. Anna Wickham used pseudonyms extensively in her journals and autobiographical writings. The autobiographical pieces in WAW had been carefully read by the Hepburn family and in most cases the pseudonyms were discovered, identified, and corrected. Still, important exceptions remain.

Proof of the fervent Harper strain appears in Geoffrey's grandfather William's unpublished reminiscences, "In March 1832 we had our first-born son Edwin, for whom from the day of his birth until now many an earnest prayer has ascended to heaven from both his Father, and now sainted Mother." Collection of Judith Swift.

4. One daughter, Norah Patti, was named after an Australian singer. Another child was named Edwina Haydn. Their last son, Edwin Athelstane, lived only twenty years but

while attending art school produced remarkable figure drawings, still owned by the family. Freda Anglin Mautner Letter to niece, Judith Swift. November 12, 1984. Collection of Judith Swift.

5. Miriam Herzog interview with the author, 12-10-1996. Beginning in 1992, the author conducted a series of interviews with family members and others. In subsequent endnotes, references to any interview not conducted by the author will be so identified.

6. Freda Anglin Mautner letter to Judith Swift 11-12-1984. Collection Judith Swift. This niece of Geoffrey's remembered him as "good-looking and charming," an opinion shared by her sister Miriam Herzog in a 12-10-1996 interview.

Even later in life he was impressive in both appearance and conversation according to New South Wales's Mitchell librarian Heather Sherrie. Heather Sherrie's letter to Jim Hepburn 3-1-1982 describes Geoffrey as "an extremely handsome man with a really beautiful brow and profile." Addt'l Manuscript 71894. BL. A photograph (taken of him around 1913, says Sherrie), reinforces the idea of his considerable charm. Hepburn Collection.

7. Alice's work at Hart and Weatherby's stationery factory—painting black borders on condolence notepaper—lasted only six weeks, but her repugnance at such painstaking repetitiveness lasted a lifetime. As a young woman, she worked for a time as secretary to Edward Aveling, a period which she remembered somewhat bitterly, as Aveling seemed to show preference to her sisters. When Christmas came, he bought elegant presents for the others, but gave Alice a utilitarian gift of notepaper, "which she afterwards used for his correspondence." WAW, p. 70.

Alice first auditioned for the stage without her mother's knowledge. Martha Whelan discouraged her but eventually she tried again. Then, with the help of Aveling, she obtained a job at the Royal Polytechnic on Regent Street and began to win an audience. All of these episodes from Alice's childhood and her experiments with making a living were recounted over and over again to her daughter Anna. They helped to create in Anna the mixture of pity and awe with which she long regarded her mother.

8. AW identifies her maternal grandfather as Michael Whelan, her maternal grandmother as Martha Whelan, and her maternal great grandmother as Jonanna Burnell. WAW, pp. 66–67. On their marriage certificate Anna's parents Alice Martha Whelan and William Geoffrey Crutchley Harper, both of "full" age, show their parents as William Whelan and Edwin Hazeldine Harper (records verify Edwin's full name). Since there is an Alice Martha Whelan, (father William Whelan) christened 6-14-1857 at Old Church, St. Pancras, London, it appears that Anna's mother Alice may have begun at some point to take two years off her age. Anna's father Geoffrey was born 12-15-1859.

9. WAW, p. 69. Also, the Tate Gallery's David Fraser Jenkins letter to the author 2-25-1897. Both works were exhibited 1887. Potter showed his paintings beginning in 1870.

And AW writes of Alice's mother, ". . . George Cruikshank gave her introductions to his friends. Middle-Victorian pictures seem full of her head and hands and feet. Often I see her or part of her in the Tate Gallery, and I am heartened as I think of the hours of patience and tedium that went to make the half-crowns to fill the little stomachs and cover the little bodies." WAW, p. 68.

10. Mary auditioned for the Royal Academy of Music in 1876, Beatrice studied composition and Gertrude, according to family history, attended art school at Heatherley's, where Frank Potter too had studied.

For the *Illustrated London News* comparison of Alice to Sarah Siddons (1755–1831), English tragedienne of legendary talent and celebrity status, see WAW, p. 70.

11. WAW, p. 70.

12. WAW, p. 71.

13. Peggy Chesters, unpublished memoir, n.d. Addt'l Manuscript 71896. BL.

14. WAW, p. 78.

15. Peggy Chesters, unpublished memoir, n.d. Addt'l Manuscript 71896. BL.

16. WAW, p. 78.

17. WAW, p. 79.

18. Heather Sherrie, librarian at Mitchell Library in Sydney, remembers her father telling her that "He [Geoff] came home one day and found she had vanished with the baby." Addt'l Manuscript 71894 p. 158–63, BL. (Sherrie's "Notes on the relationship between Mr. and Mrs. Harper.") Wickham's account of the matter is even stronger. She writes that Geoffrey did not know where they were for six months.

19. Helen R. Woolcock, *Rights of Passage: Emigration to Australia in the Nineteenth Century* (London: Tavistock Publications, 1986), xvi.

20. Woolcock, p. 20.

21. Woolcock, p. 4.

22. Even though most Australian colonies would, by the 1880s, have preferred rural settlers, the usual English immigrant during this time did come from an urban background. The English at this time were the majority group (except for native-born Australians) and the dominant group also. James Jupp, *Immigration* (Sydney: Sydney University Press in association with Oxford U P Australia, 1991), pp. 18–20, 127.

23. Woolcock, p. xviii.

24. By the year 1881. Don Charlwood, *The Long Farewell* (Ringwood, Victoria: Allen Lane, 1981), p. 1.

25. Woolcock, p. 76.

26. An average of eight passengers. Woolcock, p. 68.

27. WAW, p. 79.

28. This method of travel was soon to disappear almost completely and though Anna obviously valued the journey, it is the fast "iron ships" which she later uses as metaphor for the type of verse she sought to write.

29. Charlwood, p. 296.

30. Quoted in Charlwood, p. 307.

31. Woolcock, p. 80.

32. Woolcock, p. 80.

33. WAW, p. 80. All subsequent quotations in this chapter, unless otherwise identified by individual notes, are from WAW, pp. 80–92.

34. WAW, p. 90. Alice's parents, Emma Alice Whelan, nee Burnell and William Whelan, had her christened on June or July 14, 1857, Old Church, St. Pancras, London. No birth record has been found.

NOTES CHAPTER TWO
("I had traveled . . .")

1. WAW, p. 154.

2. Allen Keast, *Australia and the Pacific Islands: A Natural History*, with a foreword by Alan Moorehead (New York: Random House, 1966), p. 1. Also, William Henry Trait, *Historical Sketch of Queensland* (Sydney: Landsdowne Press), originally published in *Picturesque Atlas of Australasia*, Sydney: Picturesque Atlas Publishing Co., 1886. First published in this Format 1980, p. 80.

3. WAW, p. 97.

4. WAW, p. 92.

5. WAW, p. 92.

6. WAW, pp. 85, 92.

Wickham's use of the names of Australian flora in her autobiography and poetry is part of her general desire to incorporate exact terms—whether biological, geological, or legal—in her work. She also resurrects archaic words. This expanded and specific vocabulary lends a piquant quality to her work.

7. WAW, p. 94. In this they were certainly not alone. Joy Hooton notes in her study of 600 Australian autobiographies that a common theme heard in stories of settlers is the "nostalgic memories of the family at 'home'" and loneliness in the new land. Hooton notes, however, that "if the narrator is young" she might have only a "sympathetic awareness" of her parent's feelings. This was not true of Anna, who though aware of her parents' homesickness, was not sympathetic. Joy Hooton, *Stories of Herself When Young: Autobiographies of Childhood by Australian Women* (Melbourne: Oxford U P, 1990), pp. 15–16.

8. WAW, p. 92.

9. This may be the "North Street" location listed in an 1892–1893 Maryborough directory. In an 1894–1895 directory the residential listing is "Ernest Street, South Brisbane." A 1896–1897 residential listing is Gowrie House, Wickham Terrace, Brisbane.

10. WAW, p. 94.

11. *Sketch,* p. 81–82.

12. WAW, p. 94.

13. WAW, p. 95.

14. WAW, p. 95.

15. WAW, p. 95.

16. Joy Hooton, *Stories of Herself When Young: Autobiographies of Childhood by Australian Women* (Melbourne: Oxford U P, 1990).

17. WAW, p. 96.

18. WAW, p. 96.

19. WAW, p. 96.

20. WAW, p. 96.

21. WAW, p. 96.

22. Hector Holthouse, *Looking Back: The First 150 Years of Queensland Schools* (Queensland: Department of Education, 1975), p. 55.

23. Cannon, p. 206.

24. Henry Lawson, *Henry Lawson: Letters, 1890–1922,* edited and with an introduction by Colin Roderick (Sydney: Angus and Robertson Ltd., 1970), p. 53. The letter is from 1893.

25. *Annual Returns* of all teachers employed in state schools lists Alice's complete teaching record in the Queensland system and also gives details of her training in England. Supplied by Lex Brasher, Queensland historian.

The Education Act of 1875, establishing free primary public education in Australia, had created an initial demand for teachers which grew rapidly as Australia's population burgeoned. Normally the supply of women teachers usually outstripped the demand. However, Alice's position at Hughenden might have arisen because of the extraordinary overcrowding there or perhaps because fear of continued labor unrest in the area frightened prospective applicants.

26. "Provisional School—1880," *History of the Hughenden State School 1880–1980* (Hughenden, 1980), p. 8.

27. WAW, p. 98.

28. The striking shearers of the Queensland outback, often depicted as murderous enemies of the government, were the center of governmental overreaction to their desire to organize and the situation was tense. Palmer, Vance, *The Legend of the Nineties* (South Yarra, Victoria: Currey O'Neil Ross Pty, Ltd., 1954), pp. 127–33.

29. WAW, p. 98.

30. Olive Schreiner, *The Story of an African Farm* (1883) (London: Ernest Benn Limited [First published by T. Fisher Unwin Ltd., 1924], 1951), p. 29.

31. Queensland teacher records, *Annual Returns*, p. 97.

A female teacher just starting out would make £70 base but £110 was the standard salary for a Class II Division 3 female teacher. Men of the same class and division earned £130 base. But from February, 1893 to the end of 1895, government spending was cut severely and often "teacher's wages and allowances were cut, classifications suspended," and openings for classified teachers shrank. Hector Holthouse, *Looking Back: The First 150 years of Queensland Schools* (Queensland: Department of Education,

1975), p. 29, 57. There is no record of Alice having her salary cut; however, after 1-1-1893, Alice does not receive the "special" additional amount of £40 which she earned at Hughenden.

32. Anna's defense of her mother's conduct alternates with blame of her mother for instilling many feelings of inferiority (WAW, p. 100).

She generally appreciates her father's praise, yet in her autobiography she also depicts herself as sometimes suffering both from his intense attention to her, his only child, and from his concomitant disapproval of her as female, evidenced by his reportedly frequently saying to her "I hate women, old girl, thank God you're not a woman, darling" (WAW, p. 102). Anna later begins the poem "The Affinity" with the lines "I have to thank God I'm a woman, / For in these ordered days a woman only / Is free to be very hungry, very lonely" (WAW, p. 176). Anna deals with the man/woman question throughout her entire life and body of work.

33. Letter from G. A. in *Echoes From Our Nest By the Bend of the River*. A handwritten and illustrated notebook. All Hallows' archives, 1893.

34. Anna sometimes, but not always, disguised the names of the people she wrote about in her journals. However, in the Australian portion of the autobiographical writings, the names are often found to be correct, for example, names of people at Hughenden and at the Brisbane convent school. She is also usually accurate when giving dates and locations, as checks of postal directories, city directories, and ship's passenger lists show.

35. WAW, p. 99.

36. WAW, p. 99.

37. WAW, p. 102.

38. WAW, p. 100.

39. WAW, p. 103.

40. WAW, pp. 101–3 for these incidents.

41. The department, in July of 1893, began to require that students pay for their own books, pens, slate pencils, blotting paper, etc. Teachers were required to collect for the supplies—a practice that must have been abhorrent to Alice both as a teacher and a mother—since she realized the hardship this could be for students formerly given them free of charge (*Looking Back*, p. 57).

Also, J. G. Anderson, undersecretary of the department, even as a young inspector had shown "clear traces of that aloofness and love of sarcasm which he brought to perfection on his becoming Under Secretary" (*Looking Back*, p. 30). Alice would not have been one to brook this type of attitude.

42. Cannon, p. 226.

43. WAW, p. 105.

44. WAW, p. 105.

45. Lex Brasher, letter 6-25-1998, pinpoints this location "at the point where Wickham Terrace meets Turbot Street" [where] "it would be possible to hear the music from All Saints' Anglican and St. Andrew's Presbyterian Churches."

46. WAW, p. 102.

47. WAW, p. 101.

48. *The Story of All Hallows' School, Brisbane, 1861–1981* (Brisbane), p. 58 [p. 87 notes 107 day pupils].

49. *Story,* p. 64.

50. *Story,* p. 88, for school fees. All Hallows' Convent School official register for Alice's occupation.

51. WAW, p. 108.

52. WAW, p. 109. Tickie Curr's presence is indicated on Mother Patrick's handwritten school register. She's also mentioned in some of the student memoirs. What would make this lively, popular girl make friends with the younger Anna Wickham? Lex Brasher speculates that perhaps the death of Tickie's sister, Edith, in 1892, led her to appreciate Anna's devotion.

53. WAW, p. 107.

54. WAW, p. 109.

55. WAW, p. 110.

56. Lex Brasher. Letter, 6-25-1998. [All Hallows' register details.]

57. WAW, p. 102.

58. "Old Faith," John Gawsworth Notebook of Anna Wickham poetry. Reading.

NOTES CHAPTER THREE
(Life in Sydney)

1. Heather Sherrie letter to James Hepburn. 3-1-1982. Heather Sherrie, later librarian at the Mitchell Library in Sydney, first met Geoffrey Harper in 1906 when he was forty-seven and she was a young girl. He became a frequent and welcome visitor at the Sherrie home and profoundly influenced Sherrie in matters of art and literature. She found him to have "a wonderful sense of humor," "witty," "regarded in the town as the authority on anything to do with music and was asked to judge any competitions that were held." In addition to his finely tailored clothes and his handsome appearance, Ms. Sherrie adds that "His manners also endeared him to women, as he was always charming to them and took trouble to include them in conversation . . . a brilliant conversationalist. Father used to say that he should have had a Boswell."

2. *Australians: A Historical Atlas*, eds. J. C. R. Camm and John McQuilton (Broadway, New South Wales: Fairfax, Syme & Weldon Associates, 1987), p. 154.

3. *New South Wales Statistical Register for 1897 and Previous Years* (Sydney: William Applegate Gullick, Government Printer, 1898), p. 22.

4. This also took place in Melbourne, but only to a lesser extent in Brisbane. Michael Cannon, *Australia in the Victorian Age 3: Life in the Cities* (Melbourne: Thomas Nelson [Australia] Limited, 1975), p. 214.

5. I am indebted to Marsha Russell (her letter of 1-26-1994) who pointed out that Anna's "outrage at the rigid social strata of England must have been influenced by growing up surrounded by a 'first generation genteel' atmosphere."

6. Often young couples borrowed the money to obtain a typical single-story urban middle-class villa, commonly a 30–40-foot-wide rectangle, with a bay window in front, wide inner passage separating drawing room from dining room, venetian blinds or verandahs to keep out the sun, and a "typical Victorian demand for solidity and ornamentation" and decoration everywhere. Elaborate two-story villas required an even larger loan, hence a tendency for many young couples to look and act "respectable" and worthy of financing. Cannon, p. 233–36.

7. WAW, p. 102.

8. WAW, p. 98.

9. For information on 1890s Australian dating, mating, and household matters see Michael Cannon's above-mentioned *Australia in the Victorian Age* 3: *Life in the Cities*.

10. WAW, p. 98.

11. See Margaret Newlin's "Anna Wickham, 'The Sexless Part which is My Mind,'" *The Southern Review* 14.2 (April 1978), pp. 281–302.

12. D. H. Lawrence, *Kangaroo* (London: Heinemann, 1923), p. 73.

13. WAW, p. 112.

14. WAW, p. 112.

15. From Sydney Girls' High School, Shirley Hokin. Letter, 9-16-1998. Cites Admission Register No. 1588. Harpers' address listed as "Strathbogie," a boarding house in Wynyard Square, "which is nowadays a park in the oldest part of Sydney."

16. *New South Wales Statistical Register,* Part IX, p. 3.

17 Shirley Hokin. Letter, 10-9-2000.

18. WAW, p. 112.

19. WAW, p. 112.

20. David Walker, "Modern Nerves, Nervous Moderns: Notes on Male Neurasthenia," *Australian Cultural History*, eds. S. L. Goldberg and F. B. Smith (Cambridge: Cambridge University Press, 1988), p. 129.

21. Walker, p. 134.

22. At this time household help was high in demand and low in supply. This sometimes led to the "virtual enslavement of . . . middle class housewives and daughters" who were without help in households requiring constant attention. Cannon, p. 245.

23. Vera Brittain, *Testament of Youth: an autobiographical study of the years 1900–1925* (London: V. Gollancz, Ltd., 1933), pp. 69–74.

24. Quoted in Cannon: by 1898, well-off Sydney women were "'dressy, snobbish and idle.'" From 1860 to 1900 the "morning call" (done in the afternoon) was the major occupation of Australian middle-class women. The "At Home" day consisted of visitors staying fifteen or twenty minutes. There was a strict calling card etiquette. Newcomers could be snubbed. pp. 215–45.

25. WAW, p. 100.

26. Cannon, p. 203.

27. *New South Wales Statistical Register for 1897 and Previous Years: Part IV—Population and Vital Statistics,* by T. A. Goghlan, Government Statistician (Sydney: William Applegate Gullick, Government Printer, 1898), pp. 24, 26.

28. WAW, p. 114. Unless otherwise indicated, this and all following quotations in this chapter are from WAW, pp. 114–18.

29. Anna's interest in her family history may stem from this time. In later years she did genealogical research on both Harpers and Whelans and wrote about them in her unfinished autobiography.

30. Pseudonym or real name? I am not sure at this time.

31. WAW, p. 117.

32. Lilith Norman, *The Brown and Yellow, Sydney Girls' High School 1883–1983* (Melbourne: Oxford University Press, 1983), p. 248. According to an entry on Anna Wickham, her two plays were written for end-of-year school performances. Wickham makes no mention of this, however, and says that they were written for the children she and her mother were teaching.

33. Cannon, p. 200.

34. *Sands Directory* for 1903.

35. Heather Sherrie letter to James Hepburn. 8-31-1982. Heather Sherrie, librarian at Mitchell Library, Sydney, wrote personal reminiscences about Geoffrey and Alice Harper. She also passed on research notes she had made—such as on May Mückle's entry in the *Pratt Dictionary of Music and Musicians.* The entry shows Mückle born London 1880. Anna thought May was ten not just three years older than herself. I agree with Ms. Sherrie's opinion that this may have raised May's estimation in Anna's eyes.

36. Ships passenger lists shows twenty-year-old May arriving back in London on 8-30-1903. BT 26 215 record. Kew PRO.

37. WAW, p. 120.

38. "Cynthia on Deck" from Addt'l Manuscript 71887. BL.

NOTES CHAPTER FOUR
(Singing, London and Paris)

1. 150 passengers were on board, 39 cabin class, 111 steerage, most of them men, most born in England. The ratio of men to women was four to one. The boat stopped at Melbourne, Adelaide, Fremantle, Colombo, Port Said, Naples, and Gibraltar. Kew Public Records Office. Ships passengers list, Document BT 26 233.

2. Marina Warner, *The Crack in the Teacup: Britain in the 20th Century* (New York: Houghton Mifflin/Clarion Books, 1979).

3. WAW, p. 120. Anna Wickham's partial autobiography, "Prelude to a Spring Clean," is the basis for this chapter. Written when Anna was age 35, she constructed it using the premise "I am a woman artist, and the story of my failure should be known" (WAW, p. 52). Since an equally strong reading of the material can be justified which does not see her every past decision and every incident in her life as just more bricks in failure's wall, I have tried not to read all of Wickham's colorful and active life in terms of her later despair. The autobiography stands on its own as a moving document of studied bleakness and wry wit sparked to bright life by a wealth of unusual detail, description, and analysis. It was never published in her lifetime and can be found in the 1984 *The Writings of Anna Wickham, Free Woman and Poet*, pp. 51–157.

4. Edward (Teddy) Mautner, son-in-law of Norah Patti Harper Anglin. Interview, 11-20-1996. "Mrs. Anglin was this member of this women's orchestra that was run by the Countess of Warwick, who happened to be one of King Edward the Seventh's mistresses. . . . Mrs. Anglin would tell us that it often happened that in the course of playing, or whatever—in the West End (this was in hotels, Savoy Hotel or the Grand Hotel) . . . a message would come through from Buckingham Palace. . . ."

5. WAW, p. 121.

6. WAW, p. 122.

7. WAW, p. 122.

8. Miriam Herzog (daughter of Norah Patti Harper and James Anglin). Interview, 12-10-1996.

9. WAW, p. 123.

10. WAW, p. 123.

11. Footnote 13 28. WAW, p. 387.

12. Anna called him William Ray in her autobiography. Miriam Herzog (Interview, 12-10-1996) knew him as "Ray." Given Anna's penchant for using pseudonyms in the autobiography, and the fact that this name doesn't turn up in dictionaries of London journalists, his true name may not yet be known.

13. Notes from a planned "appreciation" of the poet Anna Wickham by John Kershaw, n.d. Courtesy of the John Kershaw family.

14. WAW, p. 126.

15. Gavin Lambert, *Nazimova: A Biography* (New York: Albert A. Knopf, 1997), p. 109.

16. Lambert, pp. 110–15.

17. AW to NCB. Letter, "Monday," n.d. NCB C2 2908 284. JD. Anna identifies the women as Carmel Haden Guest (for years her close friend) and Betty Kallisch.

18. WAW, p. 52.

19. Master W. Valentine Ball. Letter to the *Times*, 1-2-1930. Lines written in memory "of a most lovable character." Ball admired Patrick's intellect, physical prowess, and imperturbability, for the latter citing an instance in which he witnessed Patrick take a

river dunking and come up "with his pipe still in his mouth" to swim calmly after his hat floating downstream.

20. Anna's meeting and subsequent friendship with Patrick are found in WAW, pp. 126–37. Unless otherwise indicated, subsequent unidentified quotations are from this section.

21. Marina Warner, p. 24. Hepburn would have been considered well-off, but not wealthy in the way that some were wealthy. Warner notes that around this time 13 percent of the people owned 92 percent of the wealth and that "the gap between rich and poor was wider than it had been since the days of serfs." Anna was not serf-poor; Patrick was not among the tremendously wealthy.

22. WAW, p. 125.

23. Charterhouse Archivist S. Cole. Letter, 4-15-1998 (for London University reference). Bookplate in *History of England* prize books (for "Clifford's Inn" Prize awarded November 1894). Hepburn collection. *The Solicitor's Journal*, Vol. 39, p. 84 (for Patrick's final examination success).

24. Obituary of P. H. Hepburn in *Nature*, 1-11-1930.

25. Miriam Herzog. Interview, 12-10-1996.

26. WAW, p. 131.

27. John Galsworthy, *The Forsyte Saga* (London: The Reprint Society by Arrangement with Wm. Heinemann Ltd. First published May 1922. This edition published 1949), p. 719. Note: the book is dedicated to Edward Garnett, whose spouse, the noted translator Constance Garnett, tried to help Anna during 1913.

28. Addt'l Manuscript 71892. BL.

29. Unless otherwise indicated the rest of the quotations in this chapter are from WAW, pp. 133–42.

30. Sisley Huddleston, *Bohemian Literary and Social Life in Paris: Salons, Cafés Studios* (London: George G. Harrap & Co., Ltd., 1928), p. 18.

31. *The London Encyclopedia,* 1983, eds. Ben Weinreb and Christopher Hibbert (London: Macmillan, 1995), pp. 300–301.

32. Thanks to Margaret Hepburn, who says that this refers to the folk wisdom that you should "turn your money in your pocket whenever you see a new moon."

33. Hepburn family collection.

34. The autobiography, however, states, "We were married in the autumn."

NOTES CHAPTER FIVE
("Not a Single Crumpled Rose Leaf")

1. WAW, p. 144.
2. WAW, pp. 256–57.
3. Hepburn Collection.

4. WAW, p. 143.

5. WAW, p. 143.

6. Addt'l Manuscript 71892. BL.

7. WAW, p. 135.

8. "Mr. P. H. Hepburn: Remarkable City Personality," *City Press*, 1-3-1930.

9. WAW, p. 143.

10. WAW, p. 186.

11. WAW, p. 150.

12. WAW, p. 144.

13. Barry Humphries, the body for his creation, Dame Edna Everage (11-3-1999 interview with the author), states that his conversations with Heather Sherrie, who knew Geoffrey Harper as a friend of her parents, made discreetly clear that Geoffrey was "a bender drinker."

14. WAW, p. 125, and Heather Sherrie quotes Anna Wickham's son John as saying that whenever Edith got a letter from her mother, "she took to her bed for a few days." Heather Sherrie. Letter to Jim Hepburn, 8-31-1982. Addt'l Manuscript 71894. BL.

15. WAW, p. 145.

16. WAW, p. 145.

17. WAW, p. 146.

18. Addt'l Manuscript 71892. BL. This is an uncut version of the autobiographical writings which appear in WAW.

19. Addt'l Manuscript 71892. BL.

NOTES CHAPTER SIX
("An Admirable Mother")

1. From David Garnett's Introduction to Anna Wickham's "The Spirit of the Lawrence Women, A Posthumous Memoir," *The Texas Quarterly* IX, No. 3 (Autumn 1966), pp. 31–32.

2. "The Foundling," WAW, pp. 242–43.

3. "The Deficit," WAW, pp. 379–81, in which Anna assessed a well-to-do but dull Bloomsbury family.

4. I am indebted to Anna Davin for her "Imperialism and Motherhood," *History Workshop* 5 (Spring 1978), pp. 9–65.

5. Quoted in Davin, "Imperialism and Motherhood," which relied on Dora Bunting, "School for Mothers," in ed. Kelynack, *Infancy*, and McCleary, *Infant Welfare Movement*, pp.123–30, for the St. Pancras discussion. Dora Bunting was the school's Medical Officer.

6. Bunting, quoted in Davin, "Imperialism and Motherhood," p. 40.

7. Somerset Maugham, *Of Human Bondage* (1915), p. 560, quoted in Endnote 110 to Davin, *"Imperialism and Motherhood,"* p. 63.

8. Davin, pp. 30–31.

9. Davin, p. 31.

10. WAW, p. 148.

11. "Lecture: School for Mothers," WAW, pp. 372–73.

12. WAW, p. 374.

13. James Hepburn. Interview, 5-25-92.

14. Reprinted 1916 by the National Food Reform League.

15. WAW, p. 154.

16. WAW, pp. 152–55, for these quotes and the following information on AW diet.

17. WAW, p. 153.

18. WAW, p. 149.

19. "Suppression," Addt'l Manuscript 71892. BL.; "wife," WAW, p. 155.

20. Addt'l Manuscript 71879. BL. "Life Story," unpublished AW poem. "My Mother should have losed her rage / On the Shakespearean stage. / My birth would not have doomed / me to a life long death / Had she been partnered by the right Macbeth."

21. Addt'l Manuscript 71892. BL.

22. The quotations in this paragraph come from WAW, pp. 150–55.

23. WAW, p. 149. The Margaret Sanger information, from her *What Every Girl Should Know* (1912) was quoted in "When Nice Girls Didn't" (a sidebar to Natalie Angier's "A Sex Guide for Girls, Minus Homilies") *The New York Times,* November 16, 1999, Nat'l Edition, D7. Sanger wrote: "Every girl should know that to hold in check the sexual impulse, to absorb this power into the system until there is a freely conscious sympathy, a confidence and respect between her and her ideal, that this will go toward building up the sexual impulse and will make the purest, strongest and most sacred passion of adult life, compared to which all other passions pale into insignificance."

24. WAW, p. 156.

25. "Words," WAW, p. 208.

26. WAW, p. 157.

27. WAW, p. 157.

NOTES CHAPTER SEVEN
("I tried to build perfection with my hands")

1. From "Inspiration," in *Songs*, the first book of poetry Anna Wickham wrote. It was published under the name John Oland.

2. Christopher Wade, *Hampstead Past: A Visual History of Hampstead* (New Barnet, Herts.: Historical Publications, 1989), p. 8. This is a marvelous collection of photographs, paintings, illustrations, and maps of Hampstead with a beautifully written and researched text.

3. I am grateful to Mrs. H. Stadlen, owner of the house since 1972, who graciously gave a tour of the home and provided me with the extensive and useful materials she has been collecting on its history.

4. "A House in Hampstead," WAW, p. 225.

5. WAW, p. 151.

6. Peter D. Hingley, librarian, Royal Astronomical Society, London. Letter to the author, 2-17-1998, with *Report of the Council to the Hundred and Tenth Annual General Meeting*, Royal Astronomical Society, XC. 4, 2-4-1930, pp. 366–69.

7. Obituary in *Journal of the British Astronomical Association* 40, No. 5 (March 1930), p. 166–67.

8. WAW, p. 148.

9. The Hepburn family history appears in *Some Family Leaves*, eds. James Alexander Duncan and Robert Duncan (Edinburgh: privately printed T. N. Foulis, 1911) and *The Descent of the Hepburns of Monkrig*, James Alexander Duncan (T. N. Foulis, privately printed, 1911). The writers include a quotation from Dr. Taylor's *Great Historic Families of Scotland*, who said that the Hepburns were: "an old and powerful family located on the Eastern Marches, and noted throughout the whole History of Scotland for their turbulence, and, not unfrequently, for their disloyalty." *The Descent of the Hepburns of Monkrig*, p. 3.

10. For Frances, (b. 1886) WAW, p. 141. For Jonathan, the Last Will and Testament of James Smith Hepburn, dated 12-23-1904.

11. This is another instance of the Hepburn's long family history. Then in its building at Cripplegate, The Curriers' Company held dinners, gave money to support technical colleges and the needy and, then as now, are one of the City Livery Companies which make up the electorate for choosing the Lord Mayor and the sheriffs every year. (So that when Patrick who was Curriers' Clerk in the late twenties took his youngest son George to the Lord Mayor's Show he would have had more than a mere spectator's interest.) Though the Curriers', with a livery of 93, is one of the smaller companies, its origins as far back as 1300 make it venerable—being number 29 of 97 in the "order of precedence." Curriers traditionally were those who "dressed, leveled and greased" leather already tanned. "City Livery Companies," *The London Encyclopaedia*, eds. Ben Weinreb and Christopher Hibbert (London: Macmillan, 1983), pp. 166–69.

12. WAW, p. 157.

13. WAW, p. 153.

14. Anna Wickham, "I & My Genius," *Women's Review* (March 1986), pp. 16–20.

15. "Song to the Young John," WAW, p. 169.

16. "Work of James and the Nation Builders," WAW, p. 250. The characterization of John as an artist is found within "The Impressionist":

"With gold hair ruffled like fire at a shrine, he called

'Brother come and see,

I have made this very beautiful picture of the black night.'" WAW, p. 36.

"Song to a Young John" was later published in *Vanity Fair*, July 1921.

17. For the list of servants, see James Hepburn. Interview, 1-14-1995.

18. "Forty-six per cent. . ." Marina Warner, *The Crack in the Teacup: Britain in the 20th Century* (New York: Houghton Mifflin, 1979), p. 27.

19. Unpublished AW Manuscript. Hepburn Collection.

20. "An ugly noxious race," WAW, p. 40.

21. WAW, p. 153.

22. WAW, p. 155.

23. Addt'l Manuscript 71892. BL.

24. "The Town Dirge," WAW, p. 168.

25. WAW, p. 393.

26. From "Song," WAW, p. 189.

27. WAW, p. 47.

28. "I & My Genius," *Women's Review*, p. 19.

29. "How we came to have a Stuffed Pike in the attic," unpublished manuscript by James Hepburn. Hepburn Collection.

30. Addt'l Manuscript 71894. BL. Heather Sherrie to James Hepburn. Letter, 3-1-1982. Her account says, "He [Geoffrey] arranged another trip to Ceylon and Edith was to meet him there, and they were to explore it together. When Edith arrived, he found she was ill and had a nurse with her. He was very striken [sic] about this. . . ." As far as I know, Anna had a "nurse" only after the coming asylum incident beginning May, 1913. Yet Geoffrey was in England in February 1913 and Patrick did write to Anna in Colombo before May 1913. Either Heather Sherrie is conflating two experiences—the trip to Ceylon and the repercussions of the asylum—or Geoffrey traveled a lot in 1913. At this point I go for the former explanation.

31. An unpublished poem of Anna's, written decades later, states that she would have had a "nobler art / Had I not left my fathers heart— / But I was capable of such foul work / In time I scorned his tuning fork." Addt'l Manuscript 71879. BL.

32. Addt'l Manuscript 71879. BL.

33. First published in *Songs of John Oland*. Also in WAW, p. 169.

34. WAW, p. 154.

35. "The Call for Faith," WAW, p. 163.

36. WAW, pp. 166–67.

37. Formed in 1876 to provide jobs for "wage-earning" middle-class women and thus combat the specter of impoverished "spinsterhood" for those who did not marry, it had its own new three-story building in Brick Street, Picadilly. "A Women's Printing Society," *The British Printer* 21, No. 125 (October–November 1908), p. 230–31. I have been unable to find this organization's archives, which might provide a month and year of printing Wickham's work. The British Library catalogue shows a date of 1912 (shelf-mark X900/11088) of *Songs*, actually recorded received 3-15-1969 from Alida (Mrs. Harold) Monro.

38. "Ladies at Case: A Few Words About the W.P.S." 1, No. 3 (July 1896), 1.

39. *The World of Today: The Marvels of Nature and the Creations of Man*, eds. Sir Harry Johnston and Dr. Haden Guest (New York: William Wise & Co., 1937, copyright 1924, G. P. Putnam's Sons), p. 553.

40. Certainly this is the earliest it would have been printed, though other sources put it at 1912 (the British Library copy) or 1913 (the date used in certain biographical sketches).

41. WAW, pp. 226–27.

NOTES CHAPTER EIGHT
(May, 1913)

1. Copy of unpublished manuscript. Collection of the author. Anna calls the man Mr. Carrington, identified as heir to a cocoa fortune. Given that Patrick is identified as "Horatio," neither the man's name nor the origins of the fortune should be taken as fact. However, support for the truth of the incidents is found in "Life Story," a late, unpublished poem where Anna seems to have told a fuller truth than any time previously. "Life Story" will be discussed in later chapters.

2. Ibid.

3. WAW, p. 133.

4. Marina Warner, *The Crack in the Teacup: Britain in the 20th Century* (New York: Houghton Mifflin, 1979), p. 39.

5. Ibid.

6. Anna Wickham, "I & My Genius," *Women's Review* (March 1986), p. 16.

7. Quoted in "I & My Genius," *Women's Review*, p. 17.

8. WAW, p. 138.

9. David Garnett's introduction to Anna Wickham's "The Spirit of the Lawrence Women, A Posthumous Memoir," *The Texas Quarterly* IX, No. 3 (Autumn 1966), 31–32.

NOTES CHAPTER NINE
("I Got My Courage")

1. Anna Wickham's "I & My Genius," *Women's Review* 5 (March 1986), 16–20, is the main source for this chapter. The essay was never published in Anna's lifetime.

2. WAW, p. 227.

3. *Private Admissions 1909–1916.* MH 94 109 Kew Public Records Office. Patient #53827. Admitted 5-28-1913, discharged 9-17-1913, recovered.

4. Commitment at the time was either on the basis of a "reception order" signed by a magistrate, judge or specially appointed justice—or was by an "urgency certificate," which found "for the welfare" of either the patient or the public safety." "Principal Laws Affecting the Medical Profession," *The Medical Directory 1913* (London: J. & A. Churchill), pp. 20–33. For Brooke House, see pp. 1917 and 2068.

5. *Review*, p. 18.

6. Martin Taylor, Hackney Archives Dept., London. Letter, 6-16-1998.

7. *The Medical Directory* 1913, p. 2068.

8. MH 94 109 record of *Private Admissions 1909–1916*. Kew PRO.

9. "Genuflection," WAW, p. 185.

10. Gwendoline Hepburn may be this woman. Between 1909 and 1915 she was admitted to three different facilities. Per *Private Admissions 1909–1916*, MH 94 109, Kew Public Records Office. For "long shut away," see Addt'l Manuscript 71879. BL.

11. WAW, p. 210. The poem, which has four stanzas, often appears in anthologies.

12. The poem contains "solemn will" as a variation. Addt'l Manuscript 71879. BL.

13. Addt'l Manuscript 71879. BL.

14. *Private Admissions 1909–1916*, MH 94 109. Kew Public Records Office.

15. WAW, pp. 128–29. To "respect pride . . . prerogative" is also a quote, though I am unable to find the source.

16. Wickham MS 523. Reading.

NOTES CHAPTER TEN
(A Changed Anna)

1. WAW, p. 186. Title, "Weak Will," added by editor R. D. Smith.

2. Unless otherwise noted, quotes in this chapter are from "I & My Genius," *Women's Review* (March 1986), pp. 16–20.

3. Marina Warner, *The Crack in the Teacup: Britain in the 20th Century* (New York: Houghton Mifflin/Clarion Books, 1979), p. 38.

4. "Betwixt the baked and boiled," from "Dedication of the Cook," most recently published in *The Norton Anthology, Literature by Women: The Traditions in English*, 2nd. edition, eds. Sandra M. Gilbert and Susan Gubar (New York: W. W. Norton & Company, 1996), p. 1382. Contains an introduction. For a fuller introduction, see Celeste Schenck's Anna Wickham entry in *The Gender of Modernism*, ed. Bonnie Kime Scott (Bloomington: Indiana University Press, 1990), pp. 613–21.

5. From "Life Story," unpublished manuscript. Addt'l Manuscript 71879. BL.

6. James Hepburn. Interview, 5-30-92.

7. James Hepburn. Interview, 5-25-92.

8. WAW, p. 189.

9. The wording is ambiguous: "filling its rooms with cubists"—does she mean the painters or the paintings? Given her collection of works by Hamnett, John Flanagan, and later artists, and her growing tendency to invite people in, I assume she means both painters and paintings.

10. "I & My Genius," p. 20.

11. Dated "the twenty fourth day of October" 1913. His brother George and partner George Cutcliffe were appointed executors and trustees, directed to pay out money to Anna unless "any part thereof would . . . become vested in or charged in favour of some other person or persons or a corporation." In that case it would be "as if she were then dead."

12. I have not been able to determine Corky's real name.

13. Oswell Blakeston. Addt'l Manuscript 71896. BL.

14. We know of too many instances—for example in the poem, "Imperatrix," which she developed from an incident in Frieda Lawrence's life, to simplify the matter into purely autobiographical readings.

15. WAW, p. 189.

16. *Poetry and Drama* 2, No. 6 (June 1914).

17. Whistler's enthusiasm for Japanese art, for example, as well as Monet's Giverny collection of Japanese woodblock prints (ukiyo-e), illustrate the importance of such art in the development of new directions in painting and printmaking. Anna Wickham's eye was similarly thus influenced.

18. WAW, p. 59.

19. Denise Hooker, p. 38. Also, *London Encyclopaedia* notes café instructions for Edward VIII: "Always plain food. No fuss. Call head waiter at once and notify manager," p. 116.

20. Denise Hooker, *Nina Hamnett, Queen of Bohemia* (London: Constable, 1986), pp. 46–47. For discussion of Nina Hamnett I have relied on this biography, with additional material from Hamnett's own writings. Hamnett dates her stay at Anna's 1913. If this is true, then Anna knew the Lawrences earlier than 1915.

21. WAW, p. 124.

22. Nina Hamnett, *Laughing Torso: Reminiscences of Nina Hamnett* (London: Constable & Co., 1932), pp. 87–88. The book is dedicated to Harold Nicolson and Douglas Goldring. The latter called Anna Wickham, whom he knew, "One of the outstanding literary personalities of the twenties." *The Nineteen Twenties: A General Survey and Some Personal Memories* (London: Nicholson & Watson, 1945), p. 99.

23. David Garnett, *The Flowers of the Forest* (London: Chatto & Windus, 1955), p. 54.

24. David Garnett manuscript, n.d. Courtesy Richard Garnett.

25. David Garnett manuscript. Courtesy Richard Garnett.

26. "I & My Genius," *Women's Review* 5 (March 1986), pp. 16–20. In other sources David Garnett said that both he and Constance called at 49 Downshire Hill.

27. Richard Garnett, *Constance Garnett: A Heroic Life* (London: Sinclair-Stevenson Limited, 1991) for material about the Garnett family.

28. Richard Garnett, p. 133.

29. David Garnett, *The Golden Echo* (London: Chatto & Windus, 1953).

30. Both the Hawthornden Prize and the James Tait Black Memorial Prize for 1923. Garnett later owned a bookstore in Soho, helped to found Nonesuch Press, produced

three volumes of memoirs, edited *The Letters of T. E. Lawrence,* and wrote and trans-lated many other books in his long career. His 1955 *Aspects of Love* later was adapted for the London stage.

31. David Garnett manuscript. Courtesy Richard Garnett.

32. David Garnett manuscript. Courtesy Richard Garnett.

33. *Mark Gertler: Selected Letters,* ed. Noel Carrington, with an introduction on his work as an artist by Quentin Bell (London: Rupert Hart-Davis, 1965), p. 66.

34. WAW, p. 44.

35. David Garnett diary. Courtesy Richard Garnett.

36. David Garnett diary entry for March 10, 1915. Courtesy Richard Garnett.

37. Roger Fry was largely responsible for the large Post-Impressionist Grafton Gallery shows in 1910 and 1912. These predate the radical New York Armory show of 1913.

38. For Lawrence's attraction to Garnett, see Earl G. Ingersoll, "Lawrence and 'Bloomsbury': The Friendship with David Garnett," *D. H. Lawrence Review* 26, Nos. 1–3, pp. 5–34.

39. David Garnett manuscript. Courtesy Richard Garnett.

40. *The Dictionary of Art,* ed. Jane Turner. (London: Macmillan Publishers Limited, distributed by New York: Grove's Dictionaries Inc., 1996). For Bell, Vol. 3, pp. 630–31; for Bloomsbury Group, Vol. 4, pp. 168–69; for Grant (including date of Garnett's move), Vol. 13, pp. 313–14.

41. Anna Wickham, *Selected Poems,* with an Introduction by David Garnett (London: Chatto & Windus, 1971), p. 11.

NOTES CHAPTER ELEVEN
(Anna Wickham and Harold Monro)

1. Rose Macaulay's term "poetry intoxication," referring to years preceding the First World War, is quoted by Penelope Fitzgerald on p. xxv of her intro. to J. Howard Woolmer's *The Poetry Bookshop 1912–1935* (Revere, Pennsylvania, 1988).

2. Anne Born, "Harold Monro & The Poetry Bookshop," *Antiquarian Book Monthly Review* VII, No. 4 (April 1980), pp. 184–95. The others were poet F. S. Flint, chronicler of French imagism, and Charlotte Mew, poet and short-story writer. Monro published two collections each of the work of Wickham, Flint, and Mew.

3. Arundell Del Re, "Georgian Reminiscences," Eibungaku kenky-u (Studies in English Literature) XII (April 1932), pp. 322–31.

4. Anna Wickham to Harold Monro. Special Collections, University Research Library, University of California, Los Angeles.

5. Joy Grant, *Harold Monro and the Poetry Bookshop* (Berkeley: University of California Press, 1967), p. 24. Grant is somewhat suspicious about the neatness of the "do something" exhortation supposedly made by Maurice Hewlett, already a famous

author, to Monro, but the words do capture the zeal and spirit with which Monro began his work in England.

6. *Poetry and Drama* was first issued in March, 1913. Anna Wickham's first appearance in any little magazine was in vol. 2, no. 6, an issue containing criticism and reviews by Ford Madox Hueffer (later, Ford), Edward Thomas, T. E. Hulme, and F. S. Flint, as well as poetry by Maurice Hewlett and John Gould Fletcher.

7. The June, 1914 issue of Monro's *Poetry and Drama* contained Wickham's "Bad Little Song," "The Cherry-Blossom Wand," "The Comment," "Gift to a Jade," "Sehnsucht," "Self-Analysis," "The Singer," "The Slighted Lady," "Song" ("I was so chill . . ."), "A Song of Morning," "Susannah in the Morning," "The Tired Man," "To D.M.," "To a Young Boy," and "The Woman of the Hill."

8. Harold Monro, *Collected Poems*, ed. Alida Monro with a preface by Ruth Tomalin (London: Duckworth, 1970, first published 1933), p. xxv.

9. "Envoi," WAW, p. 46.

10. Ruth Tomalin, preface to Harold Monro's *Collected Poems*, pp. xxv.

11. Tomalin, p. vii.

12. *Songs*, p. 18.

13. For Monro, "Unto Her," *Collected Poems*, p. 6. For Wickham's "The Wife's Song," *Songs*, p. 13.

14. Alida Klemantaski to Harold Monro. Letter, 2-8-1916. Addt'l Manuscript 57748. BL.

15. Alida Klemantaski to Harold Monro. Letter, 8-28-1916. Addt'l Manuscript 57748. BL.

16. Harold Monro, *Some Contemporary Poets* (London: Leonard Parsons, 1920), pp. 196–99.

17. James Hepburn. Interview, 5-30-92.

18. Penelope Fitzgerald, *Charlotte Mew and Her Friends: With a Selection of Her Poems,* foreword by Brad Leithauser (Reading, Massachusetts: Addison-Wesley Publishing Company, Inc. [Radcliffe Biography Series, 1988; first published 1984, London: William Collins Sons & Co. Ltd.]), p. 156.

19. Dominic Hibberd, *Harold Monro, Poet of the New Age* (Houndmills, Basingstoke, England, and New York: Palgrave, 2001), p. 206.

20. Inscription to "G. 3" and "my beloved Uncle," in the frontispiece of *The Chapbook* No. 39 (1924), Hepburn Collection.

21. "To Harold Monro," WAW, p. 332. Not published in Anna's (or Harold Monro's) lifetime.

22. AW to NCB. Letter, 1-24-1927. JD.

23. Fitzgerald, p. 43.

24. Grant, p. 6; Tomalin, p. xviii.

25. Hibberd, pp. 177, 240.

26. *The Medical Directory* 1913 (London: J. & A. Churchill), pp. 1917, 2068.

27. Brooke House was damaged by bombing in 1940, demolished in 1955.

28. Anna's granddaughter Antonia Patricia Hepburn (Toni) had never been told this by her father, John Hepburn. Toni Price. Interview, 1-22-2000.

29. In both cases, Monro came to regret his decision and later publicly praised the work of both Eliot and Thomas. "Harold Monro & The Poetry Bookshop," *Antiquarian Book Monthly Review* VII, No. 4 (April, 1980), pp. 184–95.

30. John Drinkwater, *Discovery: Being the Second Book of an Autobiography, 1897–1913* (Boston: Houghton, 1933), p. 224.

31. Marvin Magalaner's "Harold Monro—Literary Midwife," *Arizona Quarterly* (Winter 1949), pp. 328–38. Magalaner explains this attitude, though he disagrees with it.

32. Roberta Smith, "Where Insanity and Modernism Intersect," *The New York Times*, 4-21-2000, p. B34.

33. George Hepburn. Interview, 11-25-96.

34. Anna Wickham, "I & My Genius," *Women's Review* (March 1986), pp. 16–20.

NOTES CHAPTER TWELVE
(Anna Wickham and D. H. Lawrence)

1. The agreement between Harold Monro and "Anna Wickham, Authoress," dated March 29, 1915, specified one half-penny royalty be paid to Anna for each copy sold.

2. Anna Wickham, "The Spirit of the Lawrence Women," Introduction by David Garnett, *The Texas Quarterly* IX, No. 3 (Autumn 1966), pp. 31–50. Shortened version, WAW, pp. 355–72. Unless otherwise specified, quotations in this chapter are from the *Texas Quarterly*.

3. p. 37.

4. D. H. Lawrence, *The First "Women in Love,"* eds. John Worthen and Lindeth Vasey, The Cambridge Edition of the Letters and Works of D. H. Lawrence (Cambridge: Cambridge University Press, 1998).

5. *D. H. Lawrence and his Hampstead Circle*, compiled by Christopher Wade (London: Hampstead Museum, Burgh House, New End Square, 1985).

6. Quoted in *D. H. Lawrence and His Hampstead Circle*, p. 2.

7. p. 36.

8. James Hepburn. Interview, 5-25-1992.

9. For Lawrence's attraction to Garnett, see Earl G. Ingersoll, "Lawrence and 'Bloomsbury': The Friendship with David Garnett," *D. H. Lawrence Review* 26, Nos. 1–3, pp. 5–34.

10. p. 37.

11. p. 36.

12. D. H. Lawrence, *The Ladybird, The Fox, The Captain's Doll* (London: Martin Secker, 1923), p. 164.

13. *The Captain's Doll*, p. 208.

14. See *The Fox, The Captain's Doll, The Ladybird*, The Cambridge Edition of The Letters and Works of D. H. Lawrence, ed. Dieter Mehl (Cambridge: Cambridge University Press, 1992). I take a stronger position on the importance of Patrick Hepburn to Lawrence's work, feeling that the Captain's character was borrowed to quite an extent. As to Anna's feelings about this, we will see in a 1920s letter to Natalie Barney that Anna could be quite emphatic in requesting others to refrain from criticizing her husband.

15. p. 37.

16. p. 33.

17. p. 33, p. 44.

18. p. 38.

19. p. 38.

20. Robert Graves, *Goodbye to All That*, new edition, revised, with a prologue and epilogue (1929; reprint London: Cassell, 1966), p. 71.

21. *The Letters of D. H. Lawrence Volume II, 1913–1916*, eds. George J. Zytaruk and James T. Boulton (Cambridge: Cambridge University Press, 1981), p. 392.

22. *Signature* ran for three numbers between October 4 and November 1, 1915.

23. See *The Hand of the Poet: Poems and Papers in Manuscript*, ed. Rodney Phillips (New York: New York Public Library, 1997).

24. Christopher Hassall, *Edward Marsh, Patron of the Arts: A Biography* (London: Longmans, Green and Co., Ltd., 1959).

25. *Letters Vol. II*, p. 400–401.

26. Robert Nichols, who says that he was so happy to be included in the 1918 anthology that "I walked as Anna Wickham so naively remarks 'with a new rhythm from the hips.'" Quoted in Hassall, p. 447.

27. Harriet Monroe, *A Poet's Life: Seventy Years in a Changing World* (New York: Macmillan Company, 1938), pp. 241–47.

28. Monroe, p. 249.

29. p. 35.

30. p. 34.

31. WAW, p. 41.

32. Wickham collection, University of Reading Library, Reading.

33. Harry T. Moore, *The Priest of Love: A Life of D. H. Lawrence*, revised edition (New York: Farrar, Straus and Giroux, 1974), p. 234.

NOTES CHAPTER THIRTEEN
(The Hepburn Family during the War)

1. Anna Wickham, "London Scenes: The Night March," WAW, p. 381.

2. WAW, p. 381.

3. WAW, p. 67.

4. Lady Cynthia Asquith, *Diaries 1915–1918*, with a foreword by L. P. Hartley, ed. E. M. Horsley (New York: Alfred A. Knopf, 1969), p. 109.

5. This opinion based on a letter to Anna from her mother, Alice Harper, 2-12-1917. Hepburn Collection.

6. Annis Meo. Letter, 6-22-1998.

7. "Hommage Eternel."

8. James Hepburn. Interview, 6-14-1992.

9. "To Anita the Gardener," WAW, p. 229. In still another poem, this one not published until 1937, Anna praises the garden in winter and the "kind care" with which Anita has dug out each root for the winter and has thriftily brought out "ashes, from the kind house fire" to replenish the soil for the "rich" and "genial Spring."

10. Richards to Mrs. Hepburn. Letter, 10-4-1915; Richards to Mrs. Brackenbury. Letter, 9-23-1915. Grant Richards, *Letters and Papers in Publishers Archives, Grant Richards 1897–1948* (Cambridge: Chadwyck-Healey Ltd., 1979).

11. Richards to Mrs. Brackenbury. Letter, 11-6-1914. Richards said, of another poet's work, "I fear that the sale at a time like this would not pay the cost of production."

12. Richards to Mrs. Hepburn. Letter, 1-14-1916.

13. Richards is also credited with being one of the first to radically change the style of publishers' advertising, a change which may have resulted from his bleak experiences as a novice publisher viewed, he felt, as the "foreordained enemy" by booksellers whose attitude toward him seemed to be, "Here's a new publisher; let's heave half a brick at him!" Grant Richards, *Author Hunting By an Old Literary Sports Man: Memories of Years Spent Mainly in Publishing* (London: Hamilton, 1934; New York: Coward-McCann, Inc., 1934), p. 58.

14. Theodore Dreiser. *New York Times*, interview, 11-30-1913, quoted in Grant Richards, *Author Hunting*, p. 182.

15. William S. Brockman, "Grant Richards," *British Literary Publishing Houses, 1881–1965*, Dictionary of Literary Biography, Vol. 112 (Detroit: Gale Research, 1991), pp. 272–79.

16. Grant Richards to Mrs. Brackenbury. Letter, 10-14-1915.

17. Grant Richards Limited to Messrs Harcourt Brace and Howe (who would publish Anna in the United States). Letter, 4-7-1921.

18. "Grant Richards Ltd. Spring Books" advertisement printed in the *Saturday Review*, February 12, 1916.

19. Title "Need to Rest," added by WAW editor R. D. Smith. WAW, p. 174.

20. Asquith, p. 266.

21. Alice Harper to Anna Wickham. Letter, 2-12-1917.

22. The British public who had earlier seen the Belgian refugees detraining in London looking dazed, bedraggled, plucky, or upbeat had felt "guilty and miserable" at their neutral status. Vera Brittain, *Testament of Youth: An Autobiographical Study of*

the Years 1900–1925 (London: V. Gollancz, Ltd., 1933), p. 99. "Women, particularly from the upper and middle classes were active in collecting comforts for the troops or in fund-raising." On August 6, 1914, the Prince of Wales had launched the National Relief Fund and on August 24, 1914, the War Refugees Committee began working for accommodation for Belgians. World Wars Exhibit, Imperial War Museum, 1996.

23. Anna Wickham to Patrick Hepburn. Letter, September 5, n.d. Hepburn Collection.

24. Margaret Hepburn. Interview, 10-16-1998.

25. James Hepburn, n.d. "How We Came to Have a Stuffed Pike in the Attic," unpublished manuscript. Hepburn Collection.

26. Arthur Marwick, *Britain in Our Century: Images and Controversies* (London: Thames and Hudson, 1984).

27. This chapter indebted to 1996 exhibits at the Imperial War Museum, London.

28. Peggy Chesters, unpublished memoir, n.d. Addt'l Manuscript 71896. BL.

29. WAW, p. 40.

30. James Hepburn. Interview, 5-30-1992.

31. James Hepburn. Interview, 5-30-1992.

32. James Hepburn. Interview, 5-30-1992.

33. James Hepburn. Interview, 5-30-1992.

34. Miriam Herzog. Interview, 12-10-1996.

35. Peggy Chesters, unpublished memoir, n.d. Addt'l Manuscript 71896. BL.

36. WAW, pp. 20, 389.

37. WAW, p. 197 for "workman's shirt." Anna's sons have said she also wrote in bed, in the bath, and in the kitchen on the wall, and others also attest to her ability to write practically anywhere.

38. R. D. Smith, quoting AW, WAW, p. 3.

39. Alice Harper to Anna Wickham. Letter, 2-12-1917. Hepburn Collection.

40. Royal Naval Air Service Register of Officers Service. ADM 273. Kew Public Records Office.

41. Wing Commander A. W. H. James, quoted in Lee Kennett's *The First Air War 1914–1918* (New York: The Free Press, A Division of Macmillan, Inc., 1991), p. 116.

42. WAW, p. 129.

43. The balloons had to go even higher in the mountainous Italian terrain.

44. This account is from Patrick Hepburn's obituary in *Nature*, 1-11-1930. A similar account comes from a *Times* "Letter to the Editor," 1-2-1930, written by Patrick's friend Master W. Valentine Ball. The *City Press*, 1-3-1930, however, says the incident was at Gibraltar with the winds coming from the Algeciras Bay.

45. Miriam Herzog. Interview, 12-10-1996.

46. Lee Kennett, quoting from Charles D. Bright, "Air Power in World War I: Sideshow or Decisive Factor?" *Aerospace Historian* (Summer 1971), p. 58.

47. Anna Wickham to Patrick Hepburn. Letter, September 5, n.d. Hepburn Collection.

48. His rank of Acting Major lasted until January 21, 1919, when that rank was relinquished and he received the rank of Captain, Kite Balloon Section. On March 6 he was given the customary transfer to "Unemployed List," though of course he had, unlike many others, a ready-made position to return to.

NOTES CHAPTER FOURTEEN
("O Give Me Back . . .")

1. First line of "The Fresh Start" (WAW, p. 240), first published in *The Man With a Hammer.*

2. Robert Graves and Alan Hodge, *The Long Week-end: A Social History of Great Britain, 1918–1939* (New York: W. W. Norton & Company, 1940).

3. James Hepburn. Interview, 1-16-1995.

4. Anna Wickham, "The Comfortable Palace," n.d., unpublished. Addt'l Manuscript 71891. BL. The marked differences in tone and concerns in early dated poems compared to late dated poems and the similarity in tone and concern between this piece and *The Little Old House* lead me to date this sometime between 1917 and late 1921.

5. Anna discussed with her children the importance of being a mother (George Hepburn. Interview, 11-25-1996). On raising "artists," refer to various letters AW to NCB. JD.

6. Miriam Herzog. Interview, 12-10-1996.

7. George Hepburn. Interview, 11-25-1996.

8. From "Conflicting Occupation," WAW, pp. 39–40. (Manuscript version here.)

9. Grant Richards to Harold Monro, 12-30-1920. Grant Richards, *Letters and Papers in Publishers Archives, Grant Richards 1897–1948* (Cambridge: Chadwyck-Healey Ltd., 1979).

10. Penelope Fitzgerald, *Charlotte Mew and Her Friends, with a Selection of Her Poems,* Foreword by Brad Leithauser (Reading, Massachusetts: Addison-Wesley Publishing Company, Inc./Radcliffe Biography Series, 1988; First published London: William Collins Sons & Co. Ltd., 1984), p. 150.

11. Charlotte Mew and Eliot Bliss are referred to in an unpublished AW poem, "Pyramus & Thisbe." Notebook "Book III," 91 pages of poems in AW's hand. Addt'l Manuscript 71877A. BL.

12. "Anna Wickham and The Poetry Bookshop Readings," in Anna Wickham, chapter 1 of *The Poetry and Place of Anna Wickham, 1910–1930* (Ph.D. diss., University of Wisconsin-Madison) 1994, pp. 43–57.

13. Their records, though detailed, are not complete. For example, in the 1916 reader index (the year Monro divorced and was called up to serve in an antiaircraft

battery), Wickham is not shown though later records substantiate the reading and the number of people attending. Addt'l Manuscript 57756A. BL.

14. Hibberd, p. 120.

15. Graves and Hodge, p. 26.

16. Grant Richards to Harold Monro. Letter, 12-30-1920. Addt'l Manuscript 57740. BL.

17. Printed on laid paper watermarked "Pioneer," stiff green paper wrappers with black lettering and black-checked borders similar to the design of the 1915 volume. Price was 2s. 6d. or 3s. net. She earned 10% on the first 500, 15% on copies over 500, an increase over previous arrangement. Addt'l Manuscript 57757. BL.

18. N.d., n.p., review of LOH. Addt'l Manuscript 71895. BL.

19. Of these the only review signed was by Gerald Bullett, "Six Hardly Necessary Books," n.d., n.p. Addt'l Manuscript 71895. BL.

20. AW to Harold Monro. Letter, 6-8-1925. Addt'l Manuscript 57741. BL. AW to Louis Untermeyer. Letter, 9-21-1921. LILLY.

21. Padraic Colum, "Chap Books and Broadsheets," rev. of CQ, *Poetry: A Magazine of Verse* (August 1915), p. 255.

22. Louis Untermeyer, *From Another World: The Autobiography of Louis Untermeyer* (New York: Harcourt, Brace and Company, 1939), p. 340.

23. *Modern British Poetry*, ed. Louis Untermeyer (New York: Harcourt, Brace & Company, 1920), p. 186.

24. AW to Louis Untermeyer. Letter, 6-10-1920. LILLY.

25. See *Vanity Fair*, where Louis Untermeyer, along with actor Henry Ainley, writer Sherwood Anderson, and physicist Marie Curie, are pictured in the "We Nominate for the Hall of Fame" (July 1921), p. 48.

26 . Untermeyer's Revised and Enlarged 2nd edition of *Modern British Poetry*, 1925, with an enlarged introduction to Anna Wickham's poems. The other "unaffiliated" poets were Walter De la Mare, Ralph Hodgson, Charlotte Mew, James Stephens, and D. H. Lawrence, see p. 18.

27. J. Howard Woolmer, *The Poetry Bookshop, 1912–1935, A Bibliography*, with an introduction by Penelope Fitzgerald (Revere, PA: Woolmer/Brotherson Ltd., 1988), p. xxviii.

28. Grant Richards to Harold Monro. Letter, 12-7-1920. Grant Richards, *Letters and Papers . . .* Reel 30.

29. Addt'l Manuscript 57757. BL.

30. Anna Wickham, *The Contemplative Quarry and The Man With a Hammer*, with an introduction by Louis Untermeyer (New York: Harcourt, Brace and Company, 1921).

31. "Womans Art," rev. of CQ and MWH. *Evening Post WYC* 9-3-1921.

32. "Four Phases of Modern Poetry," 9-4-1921, sec. 3:14.

33. WAW, p. 328.

34. Mark Van Doren, "Women of Wit," *The Nation*, October 26, 1921, pp. 481–82.

35. *Current Opinion*, 71:239 (August 1921) and 71:515 (October 1921).

36. Richard Aldington, *Life for Life's Sake: A Book of Reminiscences* (New York: The Viking Press, 1941), p. 272.

37. Anna Wickham, "Nurse Song." Addt'l Manuscript 71889C. BL.

NOTES CHAPTER FIFTEEN
(Paris, and Return)

1. Anna Wickham, quoted by R. D. Smith in WAW, p. 21.

2. James Hepburn, preface to WAW, p. xxi.

3. WAW, pp. 77–78.

4. Douglas Goldring, *The Nineteen Twenties: A General Survey and Some Personal Memories* (London: Nicholson & Watson, 1945), p. 130.

5. George Slocombe, *The Tumult and the Shouting: The Memoirs of George Slocombe* (New York: Macmillan Company, 1936), p. 234.

6. Richard Aldington, *Life for Life's Sake: A Book of Reminiscences* (New York: The Viking Press, 1941), p. 312.

7. Aldington, p. 312.

8. Goldring, p. 103.

9. Unsigned review, *Dial* (December 1921), p. 716.

10. Addt'l Manuscript 71878. BL. Not all the poems appear in WAW.

11. Edna St. Vincent Millay, *Letters of Edna St. Vincent Millay* (New York: Harper, 1952), p. 154.

12. "Song to Amidon," WAW, p. 280.

13. *The Chapbook (A Monthly Miscellany)*, ed. Harold Monro (July 1922), p. 23.

14. James Hepburn, p. xxi.

15. Hepburn Collection.

16. Denise Hooker, p. 131.

17. James Hepburn, p. xxii.

18. James Hepburn, p. xxii.

19. In "The Poems of the Month," *The Bookman* 55 (April 1922), pp. 188–89. Wylie admired "The Winds" for its clear "quality of courage" as well as its "defiance."

20. Frederick J. Hoffman, Charles Allen, and Carolyn F. Ulrich, *The Little Magazine: A History and a Bibliography* (Princeton: Princeton University Press, 1946), p. 263.

21. *Directory of C. R. B. Members* (New York: Commission for Relief in Belgium, 1925), p. 1. Hoover Institution on War, Revolution and Peace, Stanford, CA.

22. "Toasts" (information on contributors), *The Forum* (May 1924).

23. Slocombe, p. 231.

24. Nancy Winston Milford, *Savage Beauty: The Life of Edna St. Vincent Millay* (New York: Random House, 2001), p. 225.

25. Dora Russell, *The Tamarisk Tree* (London: Elek/Pemberton, 1975), p. 205.

26. Slocombe, pp. 226–27.

27. Millay, p. 154.

28. Anna Wickham, "The Disorderly Shepherdess (an Interlude written for two children and a grown-up)," which got as far as corrected page proofs (London: The Salamander Press; proofs dated 7-31-1919 stamped "Women's Printing Society, Brick Street, Mayfair"). [Since this printer was the same Anna had used for her first volume, *Songs*, perhaps she had originally intended to self-publish "Shepherdess."] SUNY/B.

29. Anna Wickham letter to Natalie Clifford Barney, 10-21-1936. JD.

30. Slocombe, p. 227.

31. Slocombe, p. 226. He gives examples of this misplaced admiration: "Lord Northcliffe, the Russian Diaghilev, my friend Hannen Swaffer, and Mussolini."

32. Millay, p. 154.

33. Hearsay. Where is documentation when you need it?

34. Anna Wickham, (*Spirit*), p. 41. (Note: this version is more complete than the WAW version.)

35. Wickham, (*Spirit*), pp. 41, 47.

36. Jim Hepburn's unpublished notes on family history, n.d. Hepburn Collection.

37. WAW, p. 149.

38. Smith, p. 22.

39. Smith, p. 22.

40. James Hepburn, "Anna Wickham," *Women's Review* (May 1986), p. 41.

41. The archives of Grant Richards, University of Illinois at Urbana-Champaign (Cambridge: Chadwyck-Healey). Microfilm reproduction reel 34.

42. This manuscript may be "The Disorderly Shepherdess." She had sent "The Noiseless Propeller" to Louis Untermeyer in 1921. He found it less "even" than the rest of her work and it was not published. Addt'l Manuscript 71894. BL.

43. Three poems in *The Little Book of Modern British Verse: One Hundred Poets Since Henley*, ed. Jessie B. Rittenhouse (Boston: Houghton Mifflin Company, 1924), pp. 180–81. [In her introduction Rittenhouse independently positions W. E. Henley (1849–1903) as the best starting point for modern poetry because of his decisive "departure from the Victorian tradition" and his "virile" challenge to the Decadents.] Anna also appeared in *The Poetry Cure: A Pocket Medicine Chest of Verse*, wonderfully compiled by Robert Haven Schauffler (New York: Dodd, Mead, 1925).

44. December 21, 1923.

45. Harriet Monroe, *A Poet's Life: Seventy Years in a Changing World* (New York: The MacMillan Company, 1938), p. 432.

46. Unsigned, 2-15-1924. n.p. Addt'l Manuscript 71895. BL.

47. James Hepburn, unpublished memoir, "How I came to spend midnight of my 21st birthday in a speakeasy in Baltimore." Hepburn collection.

48. Margaret Hepburn. Interview, 11-14-1996.

49. Griffin Barry, "The British Soviet," *The Forum* (May 1924), p. 581, and Slocombe, p. 227.

50. Anton Dolin, *Last Words: A Final Autobiography*, ed. Kay Hunter, foreword by John Gilpin (London: Century Publishing, 1985), p. 29.

51. Anna Wickham, "Life Story." Addt'l Manuscript 71879. BL.

52. Margaret Hepburn. Interview, 4-21-1998.

53. Addt'l Manuscript 71879. BL.

54. James Hepburn. Letter, 8-31-93.

NOTES CHAPTER SIXTEEN
("I have a skin for what is false in you")

1. "Saturday," Anna Wickham to Natalie Barney. Letter, 12-15-1928. Document # NCB C2 2908 139-143. JD. All letters from Anna Wickham to Natalie Clifford Barney cited in the following notes are archived in the Natalie Barney Collection of the Fonds Littéraire Jacques Doucet, Bibliothèque Ste. Geneviève, Paris, where they are filed under NCB C2 2908 (document numbers 1 through 323). In the following references either correspondence date or the date of the postmark will be given. If those dates are not known the Jacques Doucet (JD) reference numbers (beginning with file number 2908 and followed by document number) will be given.

The Hepburn family was able to date some previously undated letters. When the Hepburn family dates are used they will be given in brackets. Estimated dates will be indicated by a question mark.

Most letters from Natalie Barney to Anna Wickham are held in the British Library and the collection name and appropriate locating numbers will be given.

2. A variation on George Wickes's comment that for Natalie Barney, "Passion was brief but friendship endured." George Wickes, *The Amazon of Letters* (London: W. H. Allen, 1977), p. 87.

3. Janet Flanner interview, quoted in Wickes, p. 268.

4. Sylvia Beach, *Shakespeare and Company* (New York: Harcourt, Brace and Company, 1956), p. 114.

5. Lucie Delarue-Mardrus, quoted in Natalie Clifford Barney, *Adventures of the Mind* series, intro. by Karla Jay, trans. with annotations by John Spalding Gatton, The Cutting Edge: Lesbian Life and Literature (New York: New York University Press, 1992), p. 140.

6. Djuna Barnes, *Ladies Almanack* (1928; Elmwood Park, IL: Dalkey Archive Press, 1992), p. 9.

7. Wickes, p. 108

8. 5-27-1934 letter. JD. For additional discussion of NCB and AW, see the author's unpublished doctoral dissertation, "The Poetry and Place of Anna Wickham: 1910–1930."

9. Karla Jay notes that for Barney lesbianism was "less a sexual preference than a total commitment to women and the values they represented." *The Amazon and the Page: Natalie Clifford Barney and Renée Vivien* (Bloomington: Indiana University Press, 1988), p. 113.

10. Shari Benstock, *Women of the Left Bank: Paris, 1900–1940* (Austin: University of Texas Press, 1986), p. 95.

11. The portrait, measuring 157 x 115, is #P2302 in the collection. There is also a photograph of the portrait (reference ING 650) in the JD.

12. Salomon Reinach, quoted in Wickes, p. 8.

13. Quoted in Wickes, 252.

14. Benstock, pp. 12–15.

15. Natalie Clifford Barney, ed., *In Memory of Dorothy Ierne Wilde: Oscaria* (Dijon: Darentiere, 1951), p. 50.

16. Jay, intro. to *Adventures,* pp. 3–6.

17. Barney "undertook the mission of bringing Gourmont back to life" after his long, self-imposed near seclusion. Wickes, p. 121. De Gourmont's "*Lettres à l'Amazone*" gave Natalie her nickname and the reputation, which she was to bear throughout life, of having inspired one of the finest intellects of her time." Wickes, p. 119. Wickes also points out de Gourmont's importance to writers such as T. S. Eliot and Ezra Pound who both "drew heavily on Gourmont's ideas," p. 119.

18. Patience Ross, a London editor, was one so described. 4-19-1929 letter to NCB. JD.

19. Natalie Clifford Barney, *A Perilous Advantage: The Best of Natalie Clifford Barney,* ed. and trans. by Anna Livia, with an introduction by Karla Jay (Norwich, Vermont: New Victoria Publishers Inc., 1992), p. 92.

20. Benstock, p. 289.

21. Barney quoted in Joan Schenkar, *Truly Wilde: The Unsettling Story of Dolly Wilde, Oscar's Unusual Niece* (New York: Basic Books, 2000), p. 163.

22. Wickes, pp. 165–67.

23. Sisley Huddleston, *Bohemian Literary and Social Life in Paris, Salons, Cafés, Studios* (London: George G. Harrap and Co., Ltd., 1928), p. 70.

24. John Spalding Gatton, in Barney *Adventures,* p. 242n.

25. Barney, *Adventures,* p. 142. Also see Tama Lea. Engelking, "The Literary Friendships of Natalie Clifford Barney: The Case of Lucie Delarue-Mardrus," *Women in French Studies* 7 (1999), pp. 101–16. Delarue-Mardrus, who died in 1945, would show the same depth of gratitude to Barney that AW often expressed.

26. 11-23-1927 letter. JD.

27. Benstock, p. 80.

28. "Sunday," 11-27-1934. 2908 301? JD.

29. Lucie Delarue-Mardrus, "Une poétesse anglaise: Anna Wickham," *La Grande Revue* 123 (April 1927), pp. 175–80. The author's translation by Francine H. Conley.

30. Delarue-Mardrus, p. 12. She eventually wrote "some fifty novels." Clarissa Burnham Cooper, *Women Poets of the Twentieth Century in France* (New York: King's Crown Press, 1943), pp. 120–26.

31. NCB to James Hepburn. Letter, 6-23-1964. Addt'l Manuscript 7894. BL.

32. Delarue-Mardrus, p. 12.

33. 4-29-1927 letter. JD.

34. Griffin Barry, "Tuesday" letter to AW. Collection of the author.

35. Poem written by AW to NCB in March, 1927. WAW, p. 324.

36. "Tuesday" letter. 2908 302. JD.

37. "Tuesday" letter. 2908 302. JD.

38. [October? 1928] letter. 2908 133-36. JD.

39. "Tuesday" [1927?] letter. 2908 306. JD.

40. "Sunday," 11-3[13?]-1927. 2908 52. JD.

41. Dominic Hibberd, *Harold Monro, Poet of the New Age* (New York: Palgrave, 2001), p. 233. Also James Hepburn and Margaret Hepburn. Interview, 6-8-1993.

42. "Monday" 3-14-1927 letter. JD.

43. 11-25-1926 letter. JD.

44. From Hampstead she sent a postcard postmarked August 6, 1927, to Natalie in Italy, which berates Natalie for silence and ignoring her, signed "A. 'Anniversary of Vasco da Gambal.'" This playful use of Vasco da Gama, the Portuguese explorer who reached India by sailing around Africa, may indicate Anna's feeling of "discovery" of Natalie as a lover, on August 6, 1926. JD.

45. 8-6-1927 postcard. JD.

46. The move in June 6, 1927. Letter. JD.

47. For a few weeks the bookshop was open at both 35 Devonshire Street and 38 Great Russell Street locations. Hibberd, p. 234.

48. 11-25-1926 letter. JD.

49. "Wednesday" 10-29-1936 letter. JD.

50. Nina Hamnett, *Is She a Lady? A Problem in Autobiography* (London: Allen Wingate, 1955), p. 77.

51. 12-1-1926 postcard (signed "A, November"). JD.

52. Benstock points out that "[Barney's] distaste for sentimentality and a hatred of hypocrisy [was] often read by her friends as a form of callousness," p. 292.

Wickes notes that Barney's "view of love is unsentimental, not to say disillusioned: infidelity makes the heart grow fonder; habit dulls the lover's charm . . ." and feels that her aphorisms might be taken as expressions only of a certain "mood" in a general fascination with the subject of love (p. 115).

53. "Saturday" [March 1927 or earlier] letter. 2908 17. JD.

54. March 1927. JD.

55. Barney helped Robert McAlmon in paying for the publication of the work. Per Steven Moore, "Afterword," in *Ladies Almanack*, p. 88.

56. "Tuesday" [probably early April, 1927] letter. 2908 278. JD.

57. *The Letters of James Joyce, Vol III*, ed. Richard Ellmann (New York, The Viking Press, 1966), pp. 152–53.

58. Delarue-Mardrus, p. 178.

59. Harold Acton, *Memoirs of an Aesthete* (London: Methuen, 1948), pp. 183–84.

60. Barney, *Adventures*, trans. Gatton, p. 145.

61. Gatton, p. 245, notes both Christian representation of the pelican to symbolize Christ and Greek myth which tells of Philomela transformed to a nightingale.

62. Barney, *Adventures*, p. 148.

63. Acton, pp. 183–84.

64. This illustration can be found, most recently, inside the front and back covers of Joan Schenkar's *Truly Wilde*. "Song" is to the left of the tea table, immediately above the name of Romaine Brooks.

65. Mardrus knew a lot about religion. In March 1927, *Collier's* magazine reports that Portugal had recently conferred "The Order of Christ" upon Mme. Delarue-Mardrus, giving her the right to ride a horse into church. "She threatens to make good," they added, next to a photograph of the scowling kohl-eyed writer.

66. "Tuesday" letter. 2908 302. JD.

67. "Saturday," 5-4-1929, letter. JD.

68. Schenkar, p. 340.

69. NCB to AW. Letter, 10-11-1934. Addt'l Manuscript 71894. BL.

70. "July 4th" or 6th? n.y. letter. 2908 290-291. JD.

71. "Monday," 6-25-1928, letter. JD.

72. Dated "towards the end of 1934." 2908 223. JD.

73. "Monday," 4-29-1929, letter. JD.

74. Meryle Secrest, *Between Me and Life: A Biography of Romaine Brooks* (London: MacDonald and Jane's, 1976), p. C1-2. The AW reference is from AW to NCB. Letter, 9-23-1926. JD.

75. Recounted in a 4-29-1929 letter. JD.

76. Delarue-Mardrus, p. 178.

77. Victor Seroff, *The Real Isadora* (New York: Dial Press, 1971), pp. 401-402.

78. 6-6-1927 letter. JD.

79. "Tuesday" [1927?] letter. 2908 304. JD.

80. "Tuesday" letter. 2908 303. JD.

81. Delarue-Mardrus, quoted in Barney, *Adventures*, p. 140.

82. [1928?] letter. 2908 321–23. JD.

83. "Sunday," 11-3?-1927, letter. JD.

84. "Friday" [1928? 1932?] letter. 2908 308–15. JD.

85. 1-28-1928 letter. JD.

86. "Friday" [1928?] letter. 2908 308–15. JD.

87. 5-4-1929 letter. JD.

88. Delarue-Mardrus, quoted in Barney, *Adventures*, p. 139.

89. AW to NCB. Letter, "Friday," 2908 308 to 315. JD. The Hepburns have tentatively dated this 1928. In the JD, a date of 1932 is written in red ink on this letter's flyleaf but the Hepburns' date seems right.

90. "Saturday," 5-4-1929, letter. JD.

91. "Saturday," 5-4-1929, letter. JD.

92. "Friday" [1928?] letter. 2908 308–15. JD.

93. Djuna Barnes, "Farewell Paris," Papers of Djuna Barnes, Special Collections, University of Maryland Libraries.

94. "Saturday," 12-15-1928, letter. 2908 278–79. JD.

95. "Tuesday" [Mar./April 1927?] letter. 2908 278. JD.

96. 6-11-1928 letter. JD.

97. "Friday," 11-25-1927, 2908, between 44 and 50. JD.

98. "Monday" [Dec. 1928 or Jan. 1929] letter. 2908 284. JD.

99. April 1 [1929] letter. JD.

100. April 1 [1928 or 1929?] letter. 2908 145. JD.

101. 5-4-1929 letter. JD.

102. By mid-1928 she and George lived at 55 High Street, a school called "St. Edward's" where Anna was so fed up that she was threatening to stick "plasticine noses" on the annoying plaster saints. Anna and George lived here with tall, thin Miss Cox.

103. "Wednesday," "By Hand" [May 1928?] letter. 2908 112–13. JD.

104. The sentence is difficult to read but this is what it appears to say. 5-16?-1928 letter. JD.

105. Thanks to the Hepburns for this clarification. Never having eaten the dessert called a "syllabubs" I had misread the cursive script and thought Wickham was being academic and working up the world into a "syllabus." Researcher pitfalls.

106. "I ask:" April 1 [1928 or 1929?] letter. 2908 145. JD. "dope of inventing:" "Monday," 2-13-1928, letter. JD.

107. Jean Chalon, *Portrait of a Seductress: The World of Natalie Barney*, trans. from the French by Carol Burko (New York: Crown, 1979), p. 147. Chalon says Berthe was twenty-three.

108. According to Joan Schenkar, Wilde tried to take her own life on four separate occasions: 1931, 1933, 1934 (March or April and September), p. 249.

109. Berthe Cleyrergue, *Berthe ou un demi-siècle auprès de l'Amazone: Souvenirs de Berthe Cleyrergue recueillis et précédés d'une étude sur Natalie C. Barney par Michèle Causse* (Paris: Editions Tierce, 1980), p. 110–15.

110. Sally Cline, *Radclyffe Hall, A Woman Called John* (Woodstock: The Overlook Press, 1997), p. 213.

111. Wickes, p. 123.

112. "Friday" letter. 2908 01. JD.

113. [1928? or 1932-36 noted on JD flyleaf] letter on La Coupole stationery. 2908 321–23. JD.

114. "Monday," 3-14-1927, letter. JD.

115. Barney, *Adventures*, p. 133.

116. Barney, *Adventures*, pp. 144–50.

117. Addt'l Manuscript 71879. BL. For Barney, *Perilous,* pp. ix, 114.

118. Natalie had a few years before, according to biographer Jean Chalon, paid the famous couturier, Paul Poiret, 3,626 francs and 50 centimes for a wardrobe. See p. 139.

119. Thomson quoted in Wickes, p. 250.

120. "Tuesday" [1927? or Dec., 1929 on JD flyleaf] letter. 2908 301–7. JD.

121. Natalie, in a plan put forth by Pound, sought to benefit T. S. Eliot and Paul Valéry by "shares in an artist plan." Too many thought the plan, *Bel Esprit*, which would have allowed 15,000 francs per year—to be divided between as many as five authors—was demeaning. Help for the men came about through other means. The *Esprit* proposal was in 1922, too early to have helped Anna during her 1926 marital separation.

122. AW to NCB. Letter. 2908 302. JD. The Hepburns tentatively dated this 1929, but it may be before 1928.

123. Hepburn document # 60 1/2 A-H.

124. Nothing indicates, however, that Wickham ever read Barney's poetry at a reading at the Poetry Bookshop as she had once done with the poetry of Edna St. Vincent Millay.

125. AW to NCB. Letter. 2908 302. JD. The Hepburns tentatively dated this 1929, but it may be before 1928.

126. R. D. Smith, WAW, p. 25.

127. I have still to see if Anna's name appears in the list of liaisons or demi-liaisons that Natalie compiled. See Wickes, p. 98.

128. 2908 43. JD.

129. Poem signed "A.W., Feb. 1928." JD.

130. "Thursday," October 1936, letter. JD.

131. She remembered Anna's work long after Anna's death, as a 1-20-1951 letter to James Hepburn shows, when she wrote asking if the family had the so-called butcher's book of poems (Anna nicknamed this large account book, "Mussolini") in which Wickham had recorded her poems to Natalie. She may have been thinking of publishing Anna's work elsewhere; she certainly helped to put four of Anna's poems in French translation in *Les amis de Lucie Delarue Mardrus.* In the early 1960s Miron Grindea brought out an issue of *Adam International Review* titled "The Amazon of Letters: A World Tribute to Natalie Clifford Barney" for which Barney provided Anna's poem titled "Technician." So Natalie did remain sympathetic to Anna and true to what she wrote James Hepburn in 1951, "my friendships do not cease with death."

132. In the last stages of my research for this biography I obtained Nelljean McConeghey Rice's unpublished doctoral dissertation "A New Matrix for Modernism: A Study of the Lives and Poetry of Charlotte Mew and Anna Wickham" (University of

South Carolina, 1997). Rice asks the pertinent question about Anna: given "the alterations, the renovations, she made for her parents, her husband, her sons, and her literary friends and protegees," was Anna Wickham in the position of someone who had 'rented out' her creative space?" The Hepburn sons asked themselves the same question. James Hepburn thought that she gave "an immense amount of energy" to those she liked. George Hepburn thought that she aided other people's interests even to the neglect of her own.

133. Tama Lea Engelking, "The Literary Friendships of Natalie Clifford Barney: The Case of Lucie Delarue-Mardrus," *Women in French Studies* 7 (1999), pp. 101–16.

134. AW's answers to Harold Monro's "Three Questions Regarding the Necessity, the Function, and the Form of Poetry," in *The Chapbook: A Monthly Miscellany*, ed. Harold Monro, No. 27 (July 1922), p. 23.

135. Peggy Chesters, "Anna Wickham," Unpublished memoir. Addt'l Manuscript 71896. BL.

NOTES CHAPTER SEVENTEEN
(Married Life)

1. *Nature*, Jan. 11, 1930.

2. Family information in this chapter, unless otherwise indicated, from James Hepburn. Interviews, 6-8-1993 and other occasions.

3. *Nature*, Jan. 11, 1930.

4. Patrick Hepburn, "Letter to the Editor: The Solar Eclipse," *Times*, April 21, 1927, p. 13.

5. AW to NCB. Letter, 1-13-1935. JD.

6. *Some Family Leaves*, ed. James Alexander Duncan and Robert Duncan (Edinburgh: Privately Printed T. N. Foulis, 1911). Inscription from Mildred Hepburn.

7. AW to NCB. Letter, "Friday" [1928? 1932?]. NCB C2 2908 308. JD.

8. The first eight lines of "Sweat of the Slave." In typescript of Post-card Poems prepared by Hepburn family. Addt'l Manuscript 71878. BL.

9. AW to NCB. Letter, "Monday" 4-29-1929. JD.

10. AW to NCB. Letter, "Monday" [Dec. 1928 or Jan. 1929]. NCB C2 2908 284. JD.

11. AW to NCB. Letter, 4-1-1929. JD.

12. "Mr. P. H. Hepburn, Remarkable City Personality," *City Press*, 1-3-1930.

13. "Life Story." Addt'l Manuscript 71879. BL.

14. WAW, p. 120.

15. Parodying "Cherry-Blossom Wand." Seymour subtitles his piece, "The Man with a Trowel," and has the speaker trying to bewitch a loved one with "an onion in its pride." *Punch, or the London Charivari* CLXXII, p. 192.

16. Geoffrey Harper to AW. Letter, "August 6th, '24." Hepburn Collection.

17. "Poems by Anna Wickham," John Gawsworth notebook. Reading.

18. 14th Edition, 1929, Vol. 18, pp. 110–13.

19. Joan Maizels, "Eliot Bliss, 1903–1990: An Appraisal of Her Novels" (M.A. diss.), University of Warwick, Sept. 1994.

20. AW to NCB. Letter, 3-14-1927. JD.

21. Howard Woolmer, *Bibliography*, identifies this rhyme sheet, illustrated by Grace Golden, printed by W. H. Smith & Son, as series B3:21.

22. Addt'l Manuscript 71883. BL.

23. AW to NCB. Letter, 4-13-1929. JD.

24. AW to NCB. Letter, 1930, n.d. NCB C2 2908 301. JD.

25. Shari Benstock, *Women of the Left Bank, Paris, 1900–1940* (Austin: University of Texas Press, 1986), p. 298.

NOTES CHAPTER EIGHTEEN
("How lovely you were . . .")

1. Anna Wickham, "Of Patrick Henry Hepburn." Addt'l Manuscript 71877. BL.

2. "Mr. P. H. Hepburn, Remarkable City Personality," *City Press*, 1-3-1929.

3. This chapter relies on dozens of articles dated on and after 12-28-1929, from newspapers in London, Carlisle, Hampstead, Liverpool, Westmorland, Islington, Edinburgh, Northhampton, Brighton, and elsewhere. *The Evening Standard* quotes extensively both from Anna and from Patrick's friend and associate W. H. Stevenson, past president of the British Astronomical Association. *The Cumberland Herald*, Jan. 4, 1930, published a detailed account of the inquest and an editorial.

4. R. D. Smith, WAW, p. 23. Anna Wickham's "The Homecoming," WAW, p. 256.

NOTES CHAPTER NINETEEN
(Reconfiguration: *La Tour Bourgeoise*)

1. "The Report of the Meeting of the Association," *The Journal of the British Astronomical Association* 40, No. 3.

2. Anna Wickham. Addt'l Manuscript 71892. BL.

3. The will had been written almost seventeen years before, on 10-24-1913, three weeks after Anna had been released "recovered" from Brooke House; revoking all previous wills, it made careful provision for cessation of the trust life interest in the event Anna became incapacitated and "some other person or persons or a corporation" would come in line for the trust income.

4. As one account of his death pointed out, Patrick had "devoted much time and money" to his pursuit of the planets in their orbits. How much money? In the course of thirty plus years of following the stars, probably quite a bit. Anna never complained about this, and in fact son Jim may have taken his sympathetic cue from her attitude. Jim knew that his father's real interest was astronomy and recalled in an unpublished autobiographical essay ("How I came to spend midnight of my 21st birthday in a speakeasy in Baltimore") how his father "As a boy at Charterhouse . . . stole out of his dormitory on fine summer nights and lay on his back on the lawn to identify the stars and place them in their constellations."

Jim had sympathy toward his father (always interested in science but often denied help to pursue it).

5. Anna Wickham. Addt'l Manuscript 71889. BL.

6. James Hepburn, notebook entry. Collection of the author.

7. Margaret Hepburn. Interview, 11-14-1996. Dominic Hibberd, in *Harold Monro, Poet of the New Age* (Houndmills: Palgrave, 2001), notes that an October 27, 1930 letter from Alida Klemantaski to Harold Monro implies that Monro and Wickham spent a night together. Note 7, p. 282.

8. Miriam Herzog. Interview, 12-10-1996.

9. Herzog. Interview.

10. Herzog. Interview.

11. AW to NCB. Letter, 4-12-1930. JD. In this letter AW puts the gross estate at £22,000. "I alone," she says, "have remembered the 'probable asset' which is this wall [office wall dating from before the Great Fire of London]." This wall may account for why Anna's valuation is double the official records, although it may be that Anna was exaggerating for Barney's benefit.

12. "Studies in Two Dimensions: The Admirable Housekeeper" and "The Deficit." WAW, pp. 379–84.

13. Addt'l Manuscript 71891. BL.

14. Hugo Ames, Hazel Hendon, Margot Miller, and Mrs. Dunlop were early tenants. Mrs. Dunlop stayed through World War II. Hazel Hendon lived decades longer than AW and died at "La Tour Bourgeoise" in 1970.

15. WAW, p. 389.

16. James Hepburn. Interview, 1992.

17. Jim Hepburn returned home one night from the theatre to find a new poem on the kitchen wall

> I'll take my time
> I'll take a lot
> Not hoity-toity from a London Scot.

Thinking that Anna was criticizing him, he penned a sarcastic, "You'll take your time / You'll make your wine / You'll posture long in static mime." He was surprised to find out later that Anna had written her irritated lines to a magazine editor hounding her for a poem.

18. Miriam Herzog. Interview, 12-10-1996.

19. Elaine Bazard letter to James Hepburn. October 1984. Hepburn Collection.

20. Margaret Hepburn. Interview, 5-25-1992.

21. AW to NCB. Letter, 6-27-1937. JD.

22. James Hepburn. Interview, 5-25-1992.

23. James Hepburn. Interview.

24. John Davenport, "The Doomed Sailor of Genius," *Malcolm Lowry Remembered*, ed. Gordon Bowker (London: Ariel Books, BBC, 1975), p. 66.

25. Gordon Bowker, *Pursued by Furies: A Life of Malcolm Lowry* (London: HarperCollins Publishers, 1993), p. xx.

26. Conrad Knickerbocker, "Swinging the Paradise Street Blues," *The Paris Review* 38 (Summer, 1966), 32.

27. Kathleen Raine, "'The Word Genius Can Be Truly Applied," *Malcolm Lowry Remembered* (London: BBC [Ariel Books], 1985), pp. 52–55.

28. John Davenport, "'The Doomed Sailor of Genius,'" *Malcolm Lowry Remembered* (London: BBC [Ariel Books], 1985), pp. 66–67.

29. James Hepburn, quoted in Knickerbocker, p. 33.

30. Edward Mautner. Interview, 11-20-1996.

31. Malcolm Lowry, *Sursum Corda! The Collected Letters of Malcolm Lowry, Volume II: 1947–1957*, ed. with Introductions and Annotations by Sherrill E. Grace, Assistant Editor Kathy K. Y. Chung (London: Jonathan Cape, 1996), p. 53.

32. AW, "October 21st" letter to Malcolm Lowry. Henry E. Huntington Library and Art Gallery.

33. Knickerbocker, p. 21.

34. James Hepburn, *Malcolm Lowry Remembered*, p. 60.

35. Anna Wickham, "Words" (Huntington).

36. Knickerbocker, p. 32.

37. Gordon Bowker, *Pursued by Furies: A Life of Malcolm Lowry* (London: HarperCollins, 1993), p. 147.

38. Knickerbocker, for example, holds this opinion. Day says Knickerbocker "erred greatly in equating" Hepburns and Taskersons. Knickerbocker, p. 32. Day, p. 156.

39. Tim Hilton, "Tapping Talents," *Guardian*, December 18, 1995. James Hepburn died December 15, 1995.

40. Jim and Margaret Hepburn. Interview, 1-17-1995.

41. AW to NCB. "Saturday," 1933, letter. NCB C2 2908 190–94. JD.

42. George Hepburn. Interview, 1-14-1995.

43. *Encyclopedia of Occultism and Parapsychology*, 2d Edition, p. 1307.

44. AW to NCB. [1930] letter. NCB C2 2908 301. JD.

45. NCB to AW. Letter, 10-11-1934. Addt'l Manuscript 71894. BL.

46. The socks were: white for the woman, red for the revolutionary, colorful stripes for the artist. Poem in Harriet Ward Collection.

47. Shakespeare volume. Hepburn collection.

NOTES CHAPTER TWENTY
(Writing Her Life)

1. AW to NCB. Letter, 11-16-1933. JD.

2. NCB to AW. Letter, 4-24-1934. Addt'l Manuscript 78194. BL.

3. AW to NCB. Letter, 5-27-1994. JD.

4. Dated 6-24-1930. Hepburn Collection.

5. AW to NCB. Letter, "Monday." NCB C2 2908 276. JD.

6. NCB to AW. Letter, "November 4, 1934." Addt'l Manuscript 71894. BL.

7. "Item" dated "towards the end of 1934." NCB C2 2908 223. JD.

8. AW to NCB. Letter, 10-26-1935, copied into John Gawsworth's "Poems by Anna Wickham. Taken Down from the Author by John Gawsworth, 1938–1947." References in this chapter not otherwise described have come from this notebook. Wickham MS 523. Reading University Library archives, Reading, England.

9. AW to NCB. Letter, 5-22-1939. JD. Barney has sent Wickham her book, to which Anna responds: "so much pleasure to read & so much pride to have a poem in it."

10. Typed copy of letter in Hepburn collection. Dated "November," n.d.

11. Additional autobiographical material now under a twenty-five year seal of privacy will be available after the year 2020. Perhaps Eliot Bliss's papers or other material in the Natalie Clifford Barney Collection in JD will also provide material not researched for this biography. BL.

12. WAW, p. 53.

13. WAW, p. 53.

14. In 1933. James Hepburn. Letter, 8-2-1993.

15. Delyth Sunley, Dunedin (NZ) Public Library. Letter 6-21-2000.

16. On 1-7-1936, John, aged twenty-six, married Victorine (Vicky) Buesst, age twenty-five, daughter of Vanda and London music conductor Aylmer Buesst. Despite Buesst's caring family and her good education, capped by Swiss finishing school, Anna felt that her son had chosen wrongly. John planned a secret wedding but reporters called Anna for a statement. She did then attend the wedding, and when baby Antonia Patricia Hepburn arrived later that year Anna is said to have welcomed the child and never lost the feeling of pride in her granddaughter.

17. WAW, p. 52.

18. WAW, p. 52.

19. For WAW the Hepburn family and R. D. Smith identified most of the real names behind the pseudonyms. BL AW manuscripts will of course show the pseudonyms.

20. Nelljean McConeghey Rice, "A New Matrix for Modernism: A Study of the Lives and Poetry of Charlotte Mew and Anna Wickham," an unpublished 1997 dissertation, uses the WAW version of the autobiography to make several speculations on "the pattern of freedom in . . . dealings with men" among Whelan women. According to McConeghey's speculations, Alice Whelan was probably the child of the artist George Cruikshank, a family friend and sometimes her mother's employer (WAW, p. 74). Rice surmises that Alice's son (William Harper, lived only eighteen hours) was probably the son of Edward Aveling. In her writings Anna does often make allusions to "premature" births and uncertain parentage. For example, a letter to Natalie Clifford Barney dated 5-27-1934, [JD] references "the royal bastard blood of my mother" [a reference to a connection between Emma Alice Whelan nee Burnell and the Belgian Court]. Anna deliberately makes the chronology of her relationship to Patrick misleading—she intimates a long courtship when actually it was short, and states "we were married in the autumn" [WAW, p. 140] when they were actually married in February, probably only a little over a month after Geoffrey proposed. As far as her mother is concerned, however, Anna has written that Aveling seemed to have preferred Alice's elder sister.

Rice goes on to make a strong case for Anna as a leading Modernist poet in a vein different from male modernist poets such as Ezra Pound and T. S. Eliot.

21. WAW, p. 53.

22. 9-21-1921. Untermeyer mss., Manuscripts Department. Courtesy Lilly Library. Indiana University, Bloomington, Indiana.

23. Anna Wickham, "Apostrophe X." Reading.

24. George Hepburn. Interview, 4-14-2000.

25. George Hepburn. Interview, 1-17-1995.

26. Hugh MacDiarmid, *When the Rat-Race is Over: An Essay in Honour of the Fiftieth Birthday of John Gawsworth* (London: n.p., 1962).

27. AW to NCB. Letter, "Tuesday." [1936] n.d. NCB C2 2908 272–3. JD.

28. Addt'l Manuscript 71879. BL.

29. *Contemporary Authors*. Entry for Armstrong, Terence Ian Fytton. Gale Research, 1997. Available from http:galenet.gale.com/m/mcp/neta.

30. 2-9-1935. Reading.

31. Poetry Notebook, 1938. SIU.

32. Lawrence Durrell, "My Friend John Gawsworth," *The Kingdom of Redonda 1865–1990*, ed. Paul de Fortis (Wirral: Aylesford Press, 1991), p. 56.

33. Barry Humphries. Telephone conversation, 11-3-1999.

34. "August 22, From Book Ten." Reading.

35. This is how she characterized herself to Natalie Barney. AW to NCB. "Saturday," 5-4-1929. JD.

36. "Life Story." Addt'l Manuscript 71879. BL.

37. "Aug 24, From Book Ten." Reading.

38. *Edwardian Poetry Book One* (London: Richards, 1936).

39. William S. Brockman, "Grant Richards," *British Literary Publishing Houses, 1881–1965*, Dictionary of Literary Biography, Vol. 112 (Detroit: Gale Research Inc., 1991), pp. 272–79.

40. Publishers Archives, Grant Richards, 1897–1948, Reel 49 Review Scrapbooks, Vol. 2, 1929–1937.

41. *Cornish Guardian*, January 28, 1937.

42. "Life Story." Addt'l Manuscript 71879. BL.

43. A. S. Cairncross, scholar of Thomas Kyd and Shakespeare, requested "The Fresh Start" for his *More Poems Old and New*, of the "Scholar's Library Series." The publisher J. M. Dent requested "The Mummer" and "Sehnsucht" for *Selection of English Poetry* planned for 1938.

44. Gordon Bowker, *Pursued by Furies: A Life of Malcolm Lowry* (London: HarperCollins Publishers, 1993), p. 163.

45. Dylan Thomas, *The Collected Letters of Dylan Thomas,* ed. Paul Ferris (London: JM Dent & Sons, Ltd., 1985), p. 266.

46. Lawrence Durrell, "The Shades of Dylan Thomas," *Encounter*, IX (December, 1957), p. 57.

47. In Gawsworth's "Poems by Anna Wickham," notebook. Reading.

48. WAW, p. 3.

49. Rayner Heppenstall, *Four Absentees* (London: Barrie and Rockliff, 1960), pp. 142–43.

50. Durrell, "The Shades of Dylan Thomas," pp. 56–59.

51. Ibid.

52. Henry Miller, "The Durrell of the Black Book Days," *The World of Lawrence Durrell*, ed. Harry T. Moore (Carbondale: Southern Illinois University Press, 1962), p. 95.

53. Ibid.

54. Dylan Thomas to Lawrence Durrell. Letter [?Dec. 1937]. "Morals are her cup of tea," said Thomas. *The Collected Letters*, pp. 265–66.

55. His unpublished autobiography mentions AW. Huntington.

56. Anthony Thorne, "Anna Wickham," unpublished memoir, n.d. [March 1955]. Courtesy Kershaw family. Thorne found Anna "alarming" and "intensely feminine" and was present once when she and Dylan Thomas were arguing at 68 Parliament Hill.

57. Susan Miles to James Hepburn. Letter, 10-28-1972. Addt'l Manuscript 71894. BL.

58. Susan Watson (Wyn Henderson's daughter). Interview, 1-17-1995. Susan Watson was cheerful when she talked about Anna: "I liked her bizarre behavior."

59. Flanagan told the crowd, "You know who's in the audience tonight." James Hepburn notebook, n.d. Collection of the author. Peggy Chesters' unpublished manuscript retells the same anecdote but with impresario C. B. Cochrane recognizing Anna. Addt'l Manuscript 71896. BL.

60. George Hepburn. Interview, 10-16-1998.

61. John Rowland to John Kershaw. Letter, 3-4-1955. Courtesy Kershaw family.

62. George Hepburn. Interview, 1-17-1995.

63. Oswell Blakeston, "Anna Wickham," unpublished memoir, 1972. Addt'l Manuscript 71896. BL.

64. WAW, p. 27.

65. WAW, p. 47.

66. AW to Kate O'Brien. Letter, "Friday, 17 June [1938]." Reading.

67. AW to NCB. Letter, n.d. [1930] headed "Tour Bourgeoise." NCB C2 2908 301. JD.

68. WAW, pp. 390–91.

69. George Hepburn. Interview, 6-14-1992.

70. WAW, p. 27.

71. All AW to O'Brien. Letters are at Reading.

72. AW poem "Curve on the Category." Sent to Kate O'Brien on 5-23-19[38?]. Reading.

73. Kathleen Gibbons. Interview 12-10-1996. The poem is also in Addt'l Manuscript 71889.

74. Paul Dehn, "Mustard and Cress," *Sunday Referee*, June 12, 1938.

75. Addt'l Manuscript 71879. BL.

76. James Hepburn, who knew his father well, rejected this opinion completely. John, who presumably knew him just as well, thought he did commit suicide by jumping deliberately.

77. "For now I am a clear passivity. . . ." The other poets Natalie Barney used on the same page are Renée Vivien and W. B. Yeats. (Paris: Mercure de France, 1939), p. 14.

78. AW to NCB. Letter, 5-22-1939. JD. The poem is a shortened version of "Technician." The beginning lines are omitted in WAW, p. 323.

79. George Hepburn. Interview, 1-17-1995. George had a copy of p. 19 of a BBC magazine giving the details.

80. George Hepburn. Interview, 5-23-1992.

81. George Hepburn. Interview, 5-23-1994.

82. BBC Contract. Addt'l Manuscript 71894. BL.

NOTES CHAPTER TWENTY-ONE
(The Boys and the War)

1. "Common Form," from "Epitaphs . . . ," *The Penguin Book of First World War Poetry*, 2d ed., ed. and with an introduction by John Silkin (London: Penguin Books, 1981), p. 175.

2. "Carrion," from *Youth in Arms*, in *The Penguin Book of First World War Poetry*.

3. *The Penguin Book of First World War Poetry*, p. 138.

4. AW to NCB. Letter, "Sunday" [May 27, 1934]. JD.

5. Unpublished, untitled poem. Manuscript 9. Hepburn Collection. Now in BL.

6. George Hepburn. Interview, 11-25-1996.

7. George Hepburn. Interview, 5-23-1994.

8. George Hepburn. Interview, 11-25-1996.

9. George Hepburn. Interview, 11-25-1996.

10. *Twentieth Century Authors: A Biographical Dictionary of Modern Literature*, eds. Stanley J. Kunitz and Howard Haycraft (New York: H. W. Wilson Company, 1942), pp. 1515–16.

11. Philip Ziegler, *London at War, 1939–1945* (New York: Knopf, 1995), p. 144.

12. Book One. Addt'l Manuscript 71877. BL.

13. Elizabeth Bowen, *The Heat of the Day* (London: Penguin Books, 1962, published USA Alfred A. Knopf, 1948), p. 92.

14. Ziegler, pp. 151–61.

15. Ziegler, p. 170.

16. Ziegler's chapter, "Is There a Myth of the Blitz?" giving evidence from his base of first-person accounts as well as newspaper and other records, agrees with Angus Calder, author of *The Myth of the Blitz*, on this. Ziegler states that "the population of London as a whole endured the blitz with dignity, courage, resolution and astonishing good humour" and restates Calder's emphasis on myth not as "untruth" but as accepted and verifiable legend of the London citizenry.

17. Ziegler draws this distinction from Arthur Marwick, *The Home Front*. "Active" morale is exuberant, gallant and defiant, with "laughter in the face of adversity." "Passive" is "'a grim if often baffled willingness to carry on,'" p. 177.

18. For shops, Ziegler, p. 205.

NOTES CHAPTER TWENTY-TWO
(Staying at Home)

1. *Windows on Modernism: Selected Letters of Dorothy Richardson*, ed. Gloria G. Fromm (Athens: The University of Georgia Press, 1995), p. 410.

2. James Hepburn. Interview, 5-1992.

3. Christopher Wade, *Hampstead Past, A Visual History of Hampstead* (London: Historical Publications Ltd., 1989), p. 136.

4. London's Imperial War Museum made graphic the war's effect on children (special exhibit "Evacuees," 3-14-1996, 11-27-1996). The museum's permanent exhibit includes the war's chronology and "The Blitz Experience."

5. "For Pity," 11-16-1928 poem copied into a notebook titled "Postcard Poems." Addt'l Manuscript 71878. BL.

6. From "Letter to a Boy at School," WAW, p. 37. A slightly different manuscript version is at the HRHRC.

7. Hetta Empson. Interview, 12-3-1996.

8. J. Maclaren-Ross, *Memoirs of the Forties* (London: Alan Ross Ltd., 1965), pp. 153–57.

9. Andrew Sinclair, *War Like a Wasp* (London: Hamish Hamilton, 1989), p. 201.

10. Hetta Empson. Interview.

11. Ziegler, p. 212.

12. R. D. Smith, who would eventually edit *The Writings of Anna Wickham,* was also in Cairo with the British Council.

13. Barry Humphries, *Dame Edna Everage* on stage, became interested in Anna Wickham's poetry through John Gawsworth, who used to spontaneously recite her lyrics (especially the ribald ones) in London pubs when Humphries first came to London from Australia. Barry Humphries. Telephone conversation, 11-3-1999.

14. 6-27-1938 letter from Audrey [Beecham] to Durrell. SIU.

15. Miriam Herzog. Interview, 12-10-1996.

16. "Unambiguously Magnificent," obit. in *Guardian*, Jan. 10, 1997.

17. Oswell Blakeston, unpublished memoir, 1972. Addt'l Manuscript 71896. BL.

18. Peggy Chesters, unpublished memoir, n.d. Addt'l Manuscript 71896. BL.

19. Peter S. Edwards to John Kershaw. Letter, 3-4-1955. Courtesy Kershaw Family.

20. Addt'l Manuscript 71894. BL.

21. Toni Hepburn Price. Interview, 1-22-2000. Her trip to York was not part of the great evacuation of children but was personally arranged by her father. John Hepburn's original plan for her to stay with a certain family fell through when conditions there aggravated Toni's serious asthma. It was Mrs. Jenny Leeves and Miss Mary Coutts, two sisters who lived in Heslington, one-half mile from York, who cared for Anna Wickham's granddaughter, Toni, from 1942–1948.

NOTES CHAPTER TWENTY-THREE
("The astringency of wisdom")

1. From Lionel Birch's description of Anna's face in "Anna Wickham: A Poetess Landlady," *Picture Post*, April 27, 1947.

2. Information for this chapter comes from official records and, unless otherwise indicated, from George Hepburn. Interview, 11-25-1996.

3. Asphyxsis due to strangulation by hanging—self-inflicted suicide. Inquest May 2, death registered May 3.

"Non compos mentis" was the general verdict in suicides in England. Suicide was still a crime there until 1961. Kay Redfield Jamison, *Night Falls Fast: Understanding Suicide* (New York: Knopf, 1999), p. 18.

4. AW to "Jim darling" [James Hepburn]. Letter, 3-26-1947. Addt'l Manuscript 71894. BL.

5. AW to NCB. Letter, 11-20-1946. JD.

6. Based on interviews or information from Hampstead residents, family members, and Susan Watson, Leslie Marr, Hetta Empson, John Heath-Stubbs, and Joan Maizels as well as a memoir by Anthony Thorne (courtesy Kershaw family).

7. John Heath-Stubbs, *Hindsights: An Autobiography* (London: Hodder & Stoughton, 1993), p. 157.

8. John Davenport to Malcolm Lowry. Letter, 5-1-1947. Quoted in Gordon Bowker, *Pursued by Furies, A Life of Malcolm Lowry* (London: HarperCollins Publishers, 1993), p. 413.

9. *Night Falls Fast*, p. 115. Studies have shown that for England, April and May are the months of highest numbers of suicides. See p. 207. Anna's suicide fit this seasonal pattern.

10. Copyright James Hepburn, 1986. First appeared in *Women's Review* 7 (May 1986), 41.

11. Joan Maizels. Letter, 3-26-1996.

12. WAW, p. 47. R. D. Smith (editor of WAW and author of that book's biographical memoir), who worked extensively on Anna Wickham and her poetry before his death in 1984, saw this poem as "a summing up of her character, and of her personal style."

13. Lionel Birch, "Anna Wickham: A Poetess Landlady," in *Picture Post*, p. 23–25. Photographs by K. Hutton.

14. David Holbrook. Letter, 4-18-2000.

15. David Holbrook. Letter, 5-15-2001.

16. "Readers' Letters," *Picture Post*, May 18, 1946, p. 4.

17. AW to James Hepburn. Letter 3-26-1946. Addt'l Manuscript 71894. BL.

18. "Singer on the Heath," *Sunday Telegraph*, Dec. 5, 1971.

19. AW to James Hepburn. Letter, 3-26-1946. "Cheers for Anna" also mentioned by John Heath-Stubbs (Interview, 1-17-1995), who said that someone rushed to get Anna a chair (everyone else was sitting on the floor) and that she gave an audible running commentary on the reading that followed.

20. From John Kershaw, a lodger at no. 68 Parliament Hill after Anna's death. He began notes for "an appreciation of Anna Wickham" in 1955 and collected much original material. Courtesy Kershaw family.

NOTE EPILOGUE

1. Anna Wickham, untitled. In Dame Mary Gilmore manuscripts. University at Buffalo, State University of New York. Poetry/Rare Books Collection.

Selected Bibliography on Anna Wickham (1883–1947)

PRIMARY SOURCE BIBLIOGRAPHY

Chronological Listing of Anna Wickham's Publications in Book Form

1902 *The Seasons: A Speaking Tableau for Girls*. (Edith Harper) Sydney: W. A. Pepperday and Co., Printers.

1903 *Wonder Eyes: A Journey to Slumbertown*. (Edith Harper) Sydney: W. A. Pepperday and Co., Printers.

1911 [?] *Songs*. (pseudonym: John Oland.) Privately printed London: Women's Printing Society.

1915 *The Contemplative Quarry*. London: The Poetry Bookshop.

1916 *The Man with a Hammer*. London: G. Richards. [Known as "The Revolving Light" in the Richards's contract.]

1919 *The Disorderly Shepherdess (an Interlude written for two children and a grown-up)*. Rough proof only, dated July 19, 1919. London: The Salamander Press.

1921 *The Contemplative Quarry, and The Man with a Hammer*. With an introduction by Louis Untermeyer. New York: Harcourt, Brace.

1921 *The Little Old House*. London: Poetry Bookshop.

1936 *Thirty-Six New Poems*. Shilling Selections from Edwardian Poets. London: Richards Press.

1971 *Selected Poems*. With an introduction by David Garnett. London: Chatto & Windus.

1984 *The Writings of Anna Wickham, Free Woman and Poet*. Ed. and with an introduction by R. D. Smith. Preface by James Hepburn. London: Virago.

n.d. *The Boy and the Daffodil, Play for Two Children*. [probably] Twyn Barlwm Press.

1991 *Prélude à un Nettoyage de Printemps: Fragments d'une autobiographie*. Trans. by Jean-Louis Chevalier with a preface by James Hepburn. Paris: Editions des Cendres, 1991. A version published in English in *The Writings of Anna Wickham*, ed. by R. D. Smith. London: Virago, 1984.

Published Articles by Anna Wickham

"The Spirit of the Lawrence Women: A Posthumous Memoir." *The Texas Quarterly* 9.3 (Autumn 1966): 33–50.

"I and My Genius." *Women's Review* (March 1986): 16–20.

Translations of Anna Wickham's Poetry

Delarue-Mardrus, Lucie. "Poèmes" in "Une poétess anglaise: Anna Wickham." *La Grande Revue* (April 1927): 181–86.

Delarue-Mardrus, Lucie. *Choix de Poemes: Derniers Vers inedits, Traductions.* Paris: A Lemerre, 1951.

Note: for translation of Anna Wickham autobiography see Primary Sources listed above.

Poetry of Anna Wickham in "Little Magazines" and Periodicals

Bookman. 55 (April, 1922): 189.
The Chapbook: A Monthly Miscellany. (January 1920): 30–32.
The Chapbook: A Monthly Miscellany. (March 1923): 6–7.
The Chapbook: A Miscellany. (1924): 32.
Current Opinion. 71 (August 1921): 239.
Current Opinion. 71 (October 1921): 515.
Egoist (June 1915): 96.
The Lantern (September 1917): 194.
The Liberator (January 1922): 20.
The Liberator (April 1923): 26.
The Liberator (July 1923): 6.
The London Aphrodite (October 1928): 92.
The Measure (August 1922): 9–10.
New Republic (January 4, 1922): 156.
New Republic (January 18, 1922): 203.
New Republic (January 25, 1922): 242.
Poetry: A Magazine of Verse (January 1917): 182–83.
Poetry: A Magazine of Verse (July 1922): 198–99.
Poetry and Drama (June 1914): 129–36.
The Sackbut (November 1928): 128.
The Sackbut (November 1929): 102.
Vanity Fair (July 1921): 53.
Women's Review (March 1986): 41.

Newspapers Carrying the Poetry of Anna Wickham

"Courage," *Daily Citizen,* n.d. 1914.
"Envoi," *The Daily Mail,* August 13, 1937.
"Laura Grey," *Daily Herald,* June 16, 1914.
"The Little Language," *Daily Citizen,* June 27, 1914.
"A Question," *Daily Citizen,* n.d.
"A Song of Pride," *Daily Citizen,* n.d. 1914.
"Unhappy Lovers," *Daily Citizen,* June 26, 1914.

Selected Anthologies Carrying the Poetry of Anna Wickham

Adcock, Fleur, ed. *The Faber Book of 20th Century Women's Poetry.* London: Faber, 1987.

Aldington, Richard, comp. and ed. *Poetry of the English-Speaking World.* London: Heinemann, 1947.

Aldington, Richard, comp. and ed. *The Viking Book of Poetry of the English-Speaking World.* New York: Viking, 1946.

Bernikow, Louise, ed. and with an introduction by. *The World Split Open: Four Centuries of Women Poets in England and America 1552–1950.* Preface by Muriel Rukeyser. New York: Vintage, 1974.

Dawson, Jill. *The Virago Book of Wicked Verse.* London: Virago, A Division of Little, Brown and Company, 1992, reprinted 2001.

Dowson, Jane. *Women's Poetry of the 1930s: A Critical Anthology.* London: Routledge, 1996.

Eastman, Max, ed. *Enjoyment of Poetry with Anthology for Enjoyment of Poetry.* One-volume ed. New York: Scribner's, 1951.

Edwardian Poetry Book One, 1936. London: Richards Press, 1936.

Gawsworth, John, ed. *Fifty Modern Poems by Forty Famous Poets.* Calcutta: Susil Gupta, 1945.

Gawsworth, John, ed. *Fifty Years of Modern Verse: An Anthology.* London: Martin Secker, as publisher to the Richards Press, 1938.

Gawsworth, John, ed. *Neo-Georgian Poetry 1936–1937.* London: Richards Press: 1937.

Gilbert, Sandra M. and Susan Gubar, eds. *The Norton Anthology of Literature by Women: The Traditions in English.* 2d Edition. New York: W. W. Norton & Co., 1996.

Guest, Carmel Haden, ed. *Princess Marie-Jose's Children's Book.* London: Cassell, 1916.

Hampton, Susan and Kate Llewellyn, eds. *The Penguin Book of Australian Woman Poets.* Ringwood, Australia: Penguin, 1986.

Keegan, Paul, ed. *The New Penguin Book of English Verse.* London: Penguin, 2000.

Larkin, Philip, ed. *The Oxford Book of Twentieth-Century English Verse.* Oxford: Clarendon Press, 1973.

Linthwaite, Illona, ed. *Ain't I a Woman! A Book of Women's Poetry From Around the World.* 1987. Reprint, New York: Peter Bedrick Books, 1990.

Markham, Edwin, ed. *The Book of Modern English Poetry: 1830–1934.* New York: Wm. H. Wise, 1934.

Michie, James. Chosen and introduction by. *The Folio Golden Treasury: The Best Songs and Lyrical Poems in the English Language.* London: Folio Society, 1997.

Monro, Harold, ed. *Twentieth Century Poetry: An Anthology.* Phoenix Series 48. London: Chatto and Windus, 1929.

Monroe, Harriet and Alice Corbin Henderson, eds. *The New Poetry: An Anthology of Twentieth-Century Verse in English.* New York: Macmillan, 1923.

Morton, David, comp. *Shorter Modern Poems: 1900–1931.* New York: Harper and Brothers, 1932.

O'Connor, Mark, ed. *Two Centuries of Australian Poetry*. Melbourne: Oxford, 1988.

Rae, Simon. *News that Stays News: The Twentieth Century in Poems*. London: Faber and Faber, 1999.

Rittenhouse, Jessie B., ed. *The Little Book of Modern British Verse: One Hundred Poets Since Henley*. Boston: Houghton Mifflin Company, 1924.

Rodney Phillips, ed. *The Hand of the Poet: Poems and Papers in Manuscript*. New York: New York Public Library, 1997.

Schauffler, Robert Haven, comp. *The Poetry Cure: A Pocket Medicine Chest of Verse*. New York: Dodd, Mead, 1925.

Stevenson, Burton, selected and arranged by. *The Home Book of Quotations, Classical and Modern*. 8th Ed. New York: Dodd, Mead & Company, 1956.

Untermeyer, Louis, ed. *The Albatross Book of Living Verse: English and American Poetry From the Thirteenth Century to the Present Day*. London: William Collins Son & Co., Ltd., 1933.

Untermeyer, Louis, ed. *Modern British Poetry: A Critical Anthology*. New York: Harcourt, Brace and Company, 1920.

Untermeyer, Louis, ed. *Modern British Poetry, New and Enlarged Edition*. 1962. New York: Harcourt, Brace and World, 1969.

SECONDARY SOURCE BIBLIOGRAPHY

I. Books, Periodicals, and Manuscripts

Birch, Lionel. "The Poet Landlady." *Picture Post* 27 (April 1946): 23–25.

Barney, Natalie Clifford. *Adventures of the Mind*. Intro. by Karla Jay, trans. with annotations by John Spalding Gatton. Series The Cutting Edge: Lesbian Life and Literature. New York: New York University Press, 1992.

Delarue-Mardrus, Lucie. "Une poétesse anglaise: Anna Wickham." *La Grande Revue*, (April 1927): 177–86.

Dowson, Jane. *Women, Modernism and British Poetry, 1910–1939: Resisting Femininity*. Aldershot, Hants, England: Ashgate Publishing Limited, 2002.

Garnett, David. "Introduction" to *Selected Poems*, by Anna Wickham. London: Chatto & Windus, 1971.

Garnett, David. "Introduction" to "The Spirit of the Lawrence Women," by Anna Wickham. *The Texas Quarterly* (Autumn 1966): 31–33.

Hepburn, James. "Anna Wickham." *Women's Review*. (May 1986): 41.

Hepburn, James. Preface, *The Writings of Anna Wickham, Free Woman and Poet*, by Anna Wickham. London: Virago, 1984.

Jones, Jennifer Vaughan. *The Poetry and Place of Anna Wickham, 1910–1930*. Ph.D. diss., University of Wisconsin-Madison, 1994.

Newlin, Margaret. "Anna Wickham, 'The Sexless Part which is My Mind.'" *The Southern Review* 14.2 (April 1978): 281–302.

Rice, Nelljean McConeghey. *A New Matrix for Modernism: A Study of the Lives and Poetry of Charlotte Mew and Anna Wickham.* Ph.D. diss., University of South Carolina, 1997.

Schenck, Celeste. "Anna Wickham (1884–1947)." *The Gender of Modernism: A Critical Anthology.* Bloomington: Indiana U P, 1990.

Smith, R. D. "Anna Wickham: A Memoir by R. D. Smith." *The Writings of Anna Wickham, Free Woman and Poet.* By Anna Wickham. London: Virago, 1984.

Stark, Myra. "Feminist Themes in Anna Wickham's *The Contemplative Quarry* and *The Man with a Hammer.*" *Four Decades of Poetry 1890–1930* 3 (1978): 101–6.

II. Reviews

Aldington, Richard. "New Poetry." Rev. of *The Contemplative Quarry,* by Anna Wickham. *The Egoist* 1 (June 1915): 89–90.

Blakeston, Oswell. Rev. of *Selected Poems,* by Anna Wickham. *Books and Bookmen* Mar. 1972: 34.

Bracy, Leila E. "Dreams and Domesticity." Rev. of *The Contemplative Quarry and The Man with a Hammer,* by Anna Wickham. n.o. n.d. n.p.

Bullett, Gerald. "Grain and Chaff—A study of Some New Books of Verse." Rev. of *The Little Old House,* n.d. n.p.

Colum, Padraic. "Chap Books and Broadsheets." Rev. of *The Contemplative Quarry,* by Anna Wickham. *Poetry: A Magazine of Verse* (August 1915): 252–56.

Rev. of *The Contemplative Quarry and The Man with a Hammer,* by Anna Wickham. *The Brooklyn Daily Eagle* 1 (October 1921).

Rev. of *The Contemplative Quarry and The Man with the [sic] Hammer,* by Anna Wickham. *The Dial* (December 1921): 716.

Rev. of *The Contemplative Quarry and The Man with a Hammer,* by Anna Wickham. *Journal Providence* (October 1921): n.p.

Rev. of *The Contemplative Quarry and The Man with a Hammer,* by Anna Wickham. *Prescott Journal Times,* n.d.

Davis, Dick. "All Too Immediate." Rev. of *The Writings of Anna Wickham, Free Woman and Poet,* by Anna Wickham. *Times Literary Supplement* (August 10, 1984).

Enright, D. J. "Pride of Ink." Rev. of *The Writings of Anna Wickham, Free Woman and Poet,* by Anna Wickham. *The Listener* (May 17, 1984): 24.

"An Eye for the Country." Rev. of *Selected Poems,* by Anna Wickham. *Times Literary Supplement* (January 28, 1972): 94.

Gorman, Herbert S. "Four Phases of Modern Poetry." Rev. of *The Contemplative Quarry and The Man with a Hammer,* by Anna Wickham. *New York Times Book Review and Magazine* (September 4, 1921), section 3:14.

Holland, Matt. "Anna Wickham: Fettered Woman, Free Spirit." Rev. of *The Writings of Anna Wickham, Free Woman and Poet*, by Anna Wickham. *Poetry Review* 78 (2)(Summer 1988): 44–45.

Jordis, Christine. "Anna Wickham vaincue." Rev. of *Prélude à un Nettoyage de Printemps*, trans. Jean-Louis Chevalier. *Le Monde* (March 27, 1992): 34.

Krutch, Joseph Wood. "Womans Art." Rev. of *The Contemplative Quarry and The Man with a Hammer*, by Anna Wickham. *Evening Post* WYC (September 3, 1921): n.p.

Rev. of *The Little Old House*, by Anna Wickham, n.o. n.d.

Rev. of *The Little Old House*, by Anna Wickham. *Daily News* (August, 17), n.d.

Rev. of *The Little Old House*, by Anna Wickham. *Country Life*. n.d.

Rev. of *The Little Old House*, by Anna Wickham. *The New Republic* (May 4, 1921): 304.

Rev. of *The Little Old House*, by Anna Wickham, *Times* n.d.

"The Poetry Bookshop's Booklets of Verse." Rev. of *The Contemplative Quarry*, by Anna Wickham, n.o. n.d.

"Personalities and Powers: Anna Wickham," n.o. Feb. 15 1924.

Saunders, John. "Two Earlier Poets." Rev. of *Selected Poems*, by Anna Wickham. *Stand* 13.4 (1974): 74–77.

Taylor, Doreen. "There is the sexless part of me that is my mind." Rev. of *The Writings of Anna Wickham, Free Woman and Poet*, by Anna Wickham. *Manchester Guardian* (May 11, 1984): 12.

Untermeyer, Louis. Rev. of *The Contemplative Quarry and The Man with a Hammer*, by Anna Wickham. *New Republic* (April 27, 1921): 269–72.

Van Doren, Mark. "Women of Wit." Rev. of *The Contemplative Quarry and The Man with a Hammer*, by Anna Wickham. *The Nation* 26 (October 1921): 481–82.

"Voices of Living Poets." Rev. of *The Contemplative Quarry and The Man with a Hammer*. n.o. n.d.

Wilkinson, Marguerite. "Here are the Ladies." Rev. of *The Contemplative Quarry and The Man with a Hammer*, by Anna Wickham. *The Bookman* 21 Dec. 1923.

Winters, Yvor. "A Woman with a Hammer." Rev. of *The Contemplative Quarry and The Man with a Hammer*, by Anna Wickham. *Poetry: A Magazine of Verse* (May 1922): 93–95.

"A Woman's Song." Rev. of *The Contemplative Quarry and The Man with a Hammer*, by Anna Wickham, n.o. n.d.

III. Other

Blakeston, Oswell. "Anna Wickham." Unpublished memoir, 1970s. BL.

Bliss, Eliot. "A First Meeting with God." Unpublished memoir, 1965. BL.

Chesters, Peggy. "Recollections of Anna Wickham by Peggy Chesters, her first cousin on her father's side." Unpublished memoir, 1960s. BL.

Dollarhide, Theodore. "A Love Letter," score for mezzo-soprano, flute, clarinet, bassoon, percussion, piano, violin, and violoncello, 1985. Words by Anna Wickham. PerfArts-Music, The New York Public Library.

Mitchell, Adrian. *Anna on Anna*. Unpublished play based on *The Writings of Anna Wickham, Free Woman and Poet*. Copyright Adrian Mitchell and James Hepburn. First performed August, 1988, Edinburgh Festival.

Smith, R. D. and Judi Dench. *Anna Wickham, Free Woman and Poet*. Radio 3, BBC Radio (London, 1976 and July 31, 1977).

Wickham, Anna. "Interview." With Paul Dehn. *Sunday Referee* (June 12, 1935).

IV. Sound Recordings of Anna Wickham's Poetry

"Cherry-Blossom Wand." Words and music by Anna Wickham."Proud." Words by Anna Wickham; music by James Hepburn. "Song of the Old Mother." Words by Anna Wickham; music by James Hepburn. Arranged and recorded by Peter Salem; José Benson, Mezzo-soprano; Judy Ososki, piano. Audiocassette recording, Hampstead (London), Summer 1991.

The Cloths of Heaven [recording]: songs and chamber works. Music by Rebecca Clarke. Includes "The Cherry-Blossom Wand" by Anna Wickham. Patricia Wright, soprano; Jonathan Rees, violin; Kathron Sturrock, piano. May, 1992. Previously issued on Gamut GAM CD 534; St. Helier, Jersey UK: Guild GM CD 7208.

Anna on Anna. Adrian Mitchell play, copyright Adrian Mitchell and James Hepburn; performed by Illona Linthwaite. Recorded December 1996 for BBC World Service broadcast.

Index

About the Author

D r. Jennifer Vaughan Jones teaches composition and literature at Viterbo University in La Crosse, Wisconsin. She lives in Madison, Wisconsin.